Landscape, Process and Power

Studies in Environmental Anthropology and Ethnobiology

General Editor: **Roy Ellen**, FBA
Professor of Anthropology, University of Kent at Canterbury

Interest in environmental anthropology has grown steadily in recent years, reflecting national and international concern about the environment and developing research priorities. This major new international series, which continues a series first published by Harwood and Routledge, is a vehicle for publishing up-to-date monographs and edited works on particular issues, themes, places or peoples which focus on the interrelationship between society, culture and environment. Relevant areas include human ecology, the perception and representation of the environment, ethno-ecological knowledge, the human dimension of biodiversity conservation and the ethnography of environmental problems. While the underlying ethos of the series will be anthropological, the approach is interdisciplinary.

Landscape, Process and Power

Re-evaluating Traditional Environmental Knowledge

Edited by

Serena Heckler

Berghahn Books
New York • Oxford

Published in 2009 by
Berghahn Books

www.berghahnbooks.com

©2009 Serena Heckler

Library of Congress Cataloging-in-Publication Data

Landscape, process and power : a new environmental knowledge synthesis / edited by Serena
Heckler.
     p. cm. -- (Studies in environmental anthropology ; v. 10)
  Includes bibliographical references and index.
  ISBN 978-1-84545-549-1 (hardback : alk. paper)
  1. Indigenous peoples--Ecology. 2. Conservation of natural resources. 3. Sustainable
development. 4. Environmental education. I. Heckler, Serena.

  GF50.L35 2009
  333.72--dc22

                            2008033907

British Library Cataloguing in Publication Data

A catalogue record for this book is available from the British Library

Printed in the United States on acid-free paper

ISBN: 978-1-84545-549-1 (hardback)

Contents

List of Figures and Tables

Figures

Tables

List of Contributors

Miguel N. Alexiades has conducted extensive ethnobotanical and ethnoecological fieldwork among the indigenous Ese Eja in the border areas of Amazonian Peru and Bolivia on a broad number of issues relating to human-environment relations. His current research focuses on the historical and political ecology of cultural landscapes and ancestrally-occupied lands. He has published extensively on various methodological, ethical and political aspects of ethnobotanical fieldwork. He has recently finished editing a volume on indigenous mobility and migration and human-environment interactions, *Mobility and Migration in Indigenous Amazonia: Contemporary Ethnoecological Perspectives* (Berghahn Books, forthcoming).

Sandra Bell is Senior Lecturer in the Department of Anthropology at Durham University, UK. She is an environmental anthropologist with an interest in interdisciplinary research. From 2001–2004 she led an EU funded project on European wetlands and recently completed a project on the participation of amateur naturalists in the scientific monitoring of biodiversity.

Manuel Boissière is an ethnobotanist, working at the French Agricultural Research Centre for International Development (CIRAD). Since 2003, he has been seconded to the Centre for International Forestry Research (CIFOR) in Indonesia, studying the relationships between local forest dependent communities and protected areas in West Papua, and working on the local uses of biodiversity in the Mekong Region (Laos and Cambodia). This chapter is based on the work that he undertook for his PhD in West Papua, where he was analyzing a rural, highland society's relationship with the environment.

David N. Carss is a vertebrate ecologist specialising in predator-prey relationships, particularly those involving fish-eating predators. His research at the Centre for Ecology Edinburgh (and formerly Banchory) has included work on amphibians, fishes, mammals and birds. He has also developed a number of collaborative interdisciplinary research projects with social scientists and has begun exploring the links between science, society and policy-making.

Takeshi Fujimoto received his Ph.D. from Kyoto University in 2002 and currently works at the University of Human Environments, Okazaki, Japan. Since 1993, he has undertaken anthropological fieldwork among the Malo and neighbouring peoples in southwestern Ethiopia. His major interest is in sustainable environmental use and livelihood systems in mountainous societies. His publications include those on cultivation and folk classification systems of cereals (tef and barley/wheat) and root crops (enset and taro), dynamics of local crop diversity, ethnogenesis and ethnohistory, social stratification and marginalisation of artisan groups, and herder–farmer conflicts. Recently, he extended his fieldwork into South India and rural Japan.

Francis Chachu Ganya undertook his graduate and post-graduate studies in the USA. After obtaining his M.A. in Public Management in 1999, he became executive director of the Pastoralist Integrated Support Programme based in Marsabit, N. Kenya. Since late 2007, he has served as the president of the World Alliance of Mobile Indigenous Peoples. In early 2008, he was elected to the Kenya National Assembly as the Member of Parliament for North Horr, his home constituency. He has shared his experiences of living and working in N. Kenya in a number of published papers and at international fora.

Emma Gilberthorpe is a Lecturer in social anthropology at Durham University, UK. She has worked extensively with the Fasu language group in Kutubu, Papua New Guinea and the Min people of Ok Tedi, Papua New Guinea. Her research objective is to analyse the impact extractive industries and resource rents have on indigenous livelihoods.

Serena Heckler received her Ph.D. in ethnobotany, environmental anthropology and sustainable development from Cornell University and is a research fellow at Durham University, UK. She has lived and worked with the Wōthihā of the Venezuelan Amazon, studying the ways in which the market economy and demographic change have affected their environmental knowledge. She is currently undertaking participatory research on similar themes with the Shuar of Ecuador, in collaboration with the Intercultural University of Indigenous Peoples and Nations-Amawtay Wasi based in Quito, Ecuador.

Aneesa Kassam did her doctoral research on the oral traditions of the Gabra Oromo in Northern Kenya in the early 1980s and has continued to work amongst the Gabra and other sub-groups of the Oromo both in Kenya and in Ethiopia. She has published widely on different aspects of the culture. Her main focus of interest has been on the indigenous knowledge system and the key cultural concepts of the Oromo. She is currently working with Gemetchu Meyersaa colleague on a book provisionally entitled, *Knowledge Identity and the Colonising Structure: Problematising the Oromo Situation in Ethiopia.*

Mariella Marzano has researched rural development and natural resource management issues in Sri Lanka and volunteer biodiversity monitoring networks. She has co-managed a pan-European COST Action (INTERCAFE) aimed at developing interdisciplinary networks for the management of human-wildlife conflicts, specifically cormorant-fisheries. Recently she joined Forest Research and is working on social forestry and sustainable forest management issues.

Paul Sillitoe's research interests focus on local farming systems and indigenous natural resource management strategies. A champion of indigenous knowledge in development, he specialises in international development and social change, livelihood and technology, human ecology and ethno-science. He has conducted extensive fieldwork in the Pacific region and has been involved in projects in South Asia, researching local agricultural knowledge and development programmes.

William Thomas is Director of the New Jersey School of Conservation. He has a Ph.D. in Anthropology from Arizona State University. His research interests include conservation/sustainable use and traditional ecological wisdom of indigenous people. Since 1988, he has conducted ethno-ecological research in Papua New Guinea. Dr. Thomas has been recognized by UNESCO's Management of Social Transformations Program (MOST) for his development of a "Best Practices Using Indigenous Knowledge." He is currently working with the communities of the upper Strickland River catchment to conserve their heritage.

Daniel Vermonden received his Ph.D. in Anthropology from Brussels University (Université Libre de Bruxelles, ULB) in 2008. He has conducted extensive ethnographic fieldwork among coastal communities of Buton Island, Sulawesi, focusing his research on maritime activities: fishing, boat building and navigation. In his thesis, he combines a phenomenological analysis of the ethnographic experience with a comparative perspective in order to set up a dialogue between the local Butonese case study and its larger historical context, the Austronesian world. As a result, he is interested in the following thematics: learning and transmission, the structuring of perception, expertise and activity development, ethnosciences, and the relations between practice and knowledge.

Stanford Zent was trained as an ecological anthropologist at Tulane University and Columbia University, and he is presently employed as a tenured researcher in the Anthropology Center of the Venezuelan Institute for Scientific Research (IVIC), located in Caracas, Venezuela. He has carried out fieldwork among the Piaroa, Jotï and Eñepa indigenous groups of the Venezuelan Amazon region since 1984. His work has dealt mainly with the historical ecology, medical ecology, traditional environmental knowledge and practices, and ethnocartography of these groups and has published approximately 40 journal articles or book chapters.

# Foreword

Roy Ellen

As Serena Heckler explains in her introduction, the present volume arose from a panel organized for the Ninth International Congress of Ethnobiology in 2004. It is one of several volumes originating from that Congress and published (or to be published) in *Studies in Environmental Anthropology and Ethnobiology*. The Congress sought to address, in particular, the reality of traditional environmental knowledge in situations of social and ecological change. Such knowledge was not to be understood as merely an inventory of arcane trivia, destined - under conditions of modernity - for oblivion; but was asserted to be necessarily part of a dynamic cultural process, entailing erosion certainly, but also reproducing itself where adaptive, constantly innovating and changing; simultaneously an accumulation of local observations about the empirical world, combined with theories of how to interpret them. Each Congress volume speaks of the vitality of studies of local knowledge, while taking the debate in new and different directions: for example, in relation to migration and displacement (Alexiades, Pieroni and Vandebroek), or socio-environmental crisis (Ellen). Indeed, the increase in publishing activity related to these and similar subjects continues seemingly unabated, as various academic disciplines, professional bodies, governments, agencies and other organizations promote the virtues of maintaining knowledge diversity embedded at a local level in a world where corporate and global economic forces appear to be ever-reducing that diversity.

So, what does this volume offer that we do not find elsewhere? For one thing, especially given the rapidity of developments in the field, we need to take stock periodically: to re-appraise the core issues, recalibrate our analytic tools, and adjust our research, applied and moral agendas. If we agree with Stanford Zent that confusion is an indication of vigour, then there is all the more reason to insist - as he does - that we continuously seek to bring order to that confusion. Even - or we might say especially - in the cybersphere (where it is so easy to peruse information but less easy to evaluate its worth) there remains an important place for collections of this kind. Well done, they provide us with clear benchmarks: reviewing points of growth, trends, and distinguishing what is significant from what is merely ordinary or gratuitous. This book accomplishes this task most effectively, engaging, in both its review chapters and various case studies, with the range of current approaches and methodologies, particularly with respect to the notions of landscape, power and process. Heckler's approach is nuanced, theoretically astute and critical, and we need only compare this volume with writings on TEK (Traditional Environmental Knowledge) or its conceptual cognates up to the transformative phase of the 1990s to realize just how far we have travelled in a short time.

The modern debate concerning traditional environmental knowledge and its applications is now more than 30 years old. During that period a not insignificant amount of time has been spent on what words we should use to properly describe it. Given its manifest ideological ramifications, Heckler rightly rejects dismissing the 'terminological issue' (whether we should speak of 'traditional', 'indigenous', 'folk' or 'local', or indeed of something else entirely) as a mere irrelevant sideshow, but she is not prepared to let it stand in the way of grappling with the substantive issues that it occasionally obscures. And the same is true of the debate concerning its constituent features, where she resists the temptation to characterize it as a single cognitive entity. For Heckler, then, environmental knowledge is not just in the head, it is devolved in material practices, and by extension in the landscape too, retrievable only through an understanding of individual and collective interaction. From a phase in which it sometimes seemed sufficient to document knowledge in restricted domains, we now accept the danger of treating knowledge as disembodied information, and the importance of reinserting it back into living contexts. We cannot expect knowledge to be conveniently encoded in abstract non-overlapping domains, even less neatly lexicalized and arranged in formal taxonomies. This is not to say that such representations are not useful, but they are generally insufficient to capture the fluid character of applied knowledge organization.

Although the advantages of incorporating local and traditional knowledge into development projects and scenarios have been demonstrated, both qualitatively and quantitatively, we are still in danger of forgetting the lessons that have been hard won, either as new technologies dazzle us, or when the problems of hunger, global warming, poverty, or biodiversity depletion just seem to overwhelm us, or when the application of 'TEK-shaped instruments' fail, as they often do when packaged and applied simplistically, when the context in which they are appropriate has itself altered, when caught-up in rhetoric, or when distorted through the complex politics of indigeneity and bioprospecting. Advocates, often with the over-enthusiasm of the convert, have sometimes 'over-egged the pudding' and underestimated the practical problems of making it work in the ways hoped for. Such blanket over-endorsement of indigenous knowledge systems was evident in how, following the publication of the ICSU (International Council for Science) report, the editorial and correspondence pages of *Nature* in 1987 were given over to a rather pointless jousting between those such as R. E. Johannes arguing in favour of 'indigenous knowledge systems', and Jared Diamond arguing that these same can never be assumed to be unquestionably a good thing when they fail to prevent the extinction of megafaunas or human system collapse. The social sciences, meanwhile, not only took too much for granted in terms of how indigenous systems are self-regulating and adaptive, they also spawned a glut of codification of local environmental knowledge, which curiously undermined our appreciation of the site-specificity, spontaneity and flexibility that are among its fundamental features. Such codifications were not easily translated into development practice, where an overly mechanistic approach to participation and application tended to rule. In addition, the speed with which TEK became acceptable in different sectors of science – development consultancy, government and the general public – varied. Governments, for example, have often been trapped between the 'big science' arguments favouring HYVs (High Yielding Varieties) and GMOs (Genetically Modified Organisms) and the 'Green' science alternatives of high agrobiodiversity and the maintenance of the plethora of local landraces. Similarly, local peoples themselves have been trapped between the temptation of the quick short-term high-tech fix and the mid- to long-term option that builds on local knowledge.

The good news is that the arguments in favour of making use of TEK are now being incorporated into some of the best science, and the best development practice, not through applications of codified knowledge, but by leaving 'a space' for local knowledge to respond to local problems, by not demeaning it, by harnessing both science and local knowledge to the solution of common problems. Local people too (including those who are self-consciously 'indigenous') have identified their environmental know-how as a means of empowerment and of promoting their legitimate interests, equally in the market place, in terms of protecting resources and intellectual property, and in valorizing their patrimony and identity. In that real world, hybridization - the merging of coexisting traditions - and 'glocalization' - the merging of local and global agendas - have increasingly become the fertile norm. And this is only possible because the pragmatism of local people operating in circumscribed ecological and sociopolitical contexts involves generally spontaneous performance and recombination as a key adaptive strategy. The relevance of TEK extends beyond health, food security and poverty alleviation. The lesson we must all learn is that the fanciful modernist notion that one day all local folk knowledge will be replaced by science is clearly untenable, partly because science is always slow to respond and in the meantime people must cope, partly because science must always interface with the real world, in real landscapes; and partly because at that interface tacit, intuitive folk knowledge is subject to a process of constant reinvention.

Roy Ellen
Centre for Biocultural Diversity
University of Kent, Canterbury

Notes

1. Roy Ellen, *Modern crises and traditional strategies; local ecological knowledge in island Southeast Asia* (volume 6, 2007); Andrea Pieroni and Ida Vandebroek, *Travelling cultures and plants: the ethnobiology and ethnopharmacy of migrations* (volume 7, 2008); Miguel Alexiades, *Mobility and migration in indigenous Amazonia: contemporary ethnoecological perspectives* (volume 9, 2008).

Chapter 1

Introduction

Serena Heckler

TEK and Change

The majority of chapters in this book were first presented during a panel entitled 'Traditional Environmental Knowledge (TEK) and Change' at the Ninth
International Congress of Ethnobiology in June 2004 at the University of Kent
in Canterbury, England. The title was intended to refer to the use of TEK methods to assess changes in the way that local peoples interact with the natural
resources around them: some speakers in the panel reported on changing socio-
economic systems, while others spoke about changing environments. It soon
became apparent, however, that another kind of change was being exemplified,
that of a changing field of study. The contributions to this volume are written by
researchers from a range of disciplines who have seen the term TEK, or
whichever related term they are using, challenged, deconstructed, and reinvented
in a wide variety of ways. And yet, despite different methodological approaches
and different ideas about what TEK is, the speakers at the conference, and the
authors of this book, hit upon similar issues and made similar statements about
the nature and role of TEK in the lives of local people around the world. This
book, then, represents a diversity of current approaches to TEK research, as well
as demonstrating how those approaches are developing and seem to be converg-
ing onto a few interrelated themes, namely landscape, power and process. In
encapsulating this diversity and convergence, and by presenting a summary of
the development of TEK in each of its contributing disciplines, this book is a
synthesis of a field of study that has expanded beyond its original boundaries.

In the new millennium, researchers have become more nuanced and critical in
situating TEK alongside other types of knowledge and in particular social, political and economic contexts, contexts which themselves are changing. Gone are
the days when TEK could be considered 'ancestral' or 'timeless' or as simple sys-

tems of classification. Today, it is conceived of as emerging from ecopolitical discourse, practical engagement with the landscape and social relationships all at the same time. As such TEK is acknowledged to be in constant flux and exceptionally difficult to pin down. It certainly cannot be fully elicited using the methodological approaches championed by many TEK researchers of the last millennium, such as rapid rural appraisal, pile sorts, tree trails, decision-making models, etcetera. As many of the contributions to this book demonstrate, in-depth methods, such as participant observation, are necessary to understand how TEK is related to other aspects of people's lives. This has opened up TEK research to incorporate other areas of research that were formerly sidelined, such as gender relations, political economy, pedagogy, cosmology and kinship, among others.

This drastic broadening of the subject, while greatly enriching our understanding of human-environment relations, has led to a crisis of identity. We all feel as though we know what TEK is, but are finding it increasingly difficult to agree on a definition or even a name. We all agree that TEK is important, but there are increasingly heated disagreements about how it should be used and who should decide its use. The political economists are highly critical of the cognitivists, who largely ignore the phenomenologists: all are largely negative about the work of development specialists, who continue to invest vast amounts of money in 'indigenous knowledge (IK) informed' projects around the world. As a result, many TEK specialists have begun to feel stuck, arguing over terms and definitions while marginalised peoples around the world are desperately in need of appropriate and meaningful support.

This book is an attempt to bring some of these diverging strands back together, to accentuate the strengths of such wide-ranging enquiry. Rather than arguing that any one approach is best, this compilation takes the stance that all the approaches can help to elucidate the full complexity of TEK and that, to be accurate descriptors of people's lived experience, we need a phenomenological approach, a political economy approach, a cognitive approach and an applied approach. These different theoretical and methodological stances consider different aspects of human-environment interactions and different levels of discourse, activity and decision-making; hence all are needed to describe the full complexity of TEK. We dismiss the other approaches at our peril.

Traditional, Indigenous, Local? The Problem of Nomenclature

Many recent TEK papers and volumes include a discussion of the terms used to describe this type of research (Ellen and Harris 2000: 2-3; Posey 1999: 9; Sillitoe 2002: 8; Sillitoe and Bicker 2004: 1), giving some indication of how difficult it has been to agree on any particular one. Part of the problem is the development of the concept in separate disciplines and by researchers in different professional networks and different parts of the world. These different groups of researchers soon began to share and integrate their research, assuming, perhaps wrongly, that they were talking about the same thing, even if they called it by a different name. Hence, the terms rural knowledge systems, traditional ecological/environmental knowledge, indigenous knowledge, indigenous knowledge systems, indigenous technical knowledge, local knowledge, folk science, people's science, ethnoscience and any number of related terms were all introduced in the 1980s and soon considered to be more or less equivalent. This gave rise to an extended debate, continuing today, about which of these terms is 'best' to describe this concept.

Many authors have objected to the term 'traditional' because it has connotations of being static, ahistorical and out-dated (Inglis 1993: 3). So the term 'indigenous knowledge' (IK) has become increasingly used. But while 'indigenous' can be a useful and meaningful term in some parts of the world where there is a clearly distinct colonial population and a minority of colonised people, such as the Americas, Australia and much of the Arctic and Sub-Arctic (cf. Wolf 1982; Taussig 1993), it is more problematic in places such as Asia and Africa, where a long (recorded) history of migration makes it more difficult to tease out who are the 'original' residents who can claim indigenous status (Sundar 2000: 79-81; see also Posey 2002: 25-27). Even where the term 'indigenous' is most clear-cut, however, it is highly political and, although the use of the term does not always 'provid(e) both the justification for colonial rule and the means towards it' as Sundar claims (2000: 81), it has been accused of entrenching unequal power relations.

Others argue that the term 'local' is best, because it does not make social divisions between different people, does not have the same negative connotations as the other terms, and does not exclude recent immigrant populations or modernised[1] populations that cannot claim indigenous status, but nevertheless, gain much of their subsistence from the land around them. However, 'local' throws up its own series of problems, including the idea that it is somehow separated from the wider context (Pottier 2003: 3), which, as the contributions by Alexiades, Kassam and Ganya, Gilberthorpe, Carss, Bell and Marzano demonstrate, is a misrepresentation of the nature of such knowledge. Indeed, the term 'local' is often implicitly assumed to be subsumed by and inferior to science, which is often considered to be 'global' knowledge (Sillitoe 2007). As Hobart argues (1993), the term 'local' embeds the hierarchy that privileges science at the expense of the local simply by reifying the difference. Moreover, in its very inclusiveness, the term 'local knowledge' loses some of the distinctiveness that has made this concept useful and appealing.

So, it seems we cannot win, all the terms are problematic and yet we agree that there is something valuable in giving a voice to a different way of knowing in the global and scientific discourse. Indeed, researchers and human rights groups who use 'traditional' are generally clear that they do not mean a knowledge that is or ever has been static, but one that has associations that are meaningful for many local people with a particular, self-conscious, construction of their own identity (Posey 1999: 4). The overtly political nature of 'indigenous' can work for indigenous people, as well as against them: it is increasingly being used as a lever to gain access to resources, such as government grants and land tenure (Alexiades, Chapter Three; Heckler 2007: 101). Similarly, 'local' in today's climate of devolution, participatory development and bottom-up governance is a more powerful term than it may have been previously.

Moreover, each of the terms has a historical component. For instance, the early term 'rural knowledge' was first used by rural sociologists and agronomists, particularly in the 'Farmer First' school (e.g. Chambers 1983; Chambers et al. 1989, Scoones and Thompson 1994), who were concerned with what they considered to be the 'unseen poverty' of rural people (Chambers 1983: viii). 'Indigenous knowledge', 'indigenous knowledge systems', and 'indigenous technical knowledge' came from anthropologists (Brokensha et al. 1980), which is understandable given their concern with ethnicity and culture as a marker of difference. 'Traditional environmental knowledge' was first used by ethnobotanists and conservationists who were slightly more orientated towards conservation and environmental sustainability than agriculture (Inglis 1993: vi; Hadley and Schrekenberg 1995; McNeely 1995). 'Local knowledge' has been used interchangeably with 'indigenous' when the latter term did not fit or seemed politically incorrect (e.g. Rocheleau et al. 1989: 14).

In summary, then, not only does each of the above terms reflect assumptions about the nature of such knowledge and its relationship to an equally problematic dominant paradigm, they also reflect the ways in which the authors, by virtue of their disciplinary perspectives, seek to acknowledge and critique this divide and how they seek to represent the relationship between the two. The truth is that each of these dichotomies – global versus local, colonial versus. indigenous, modern versus traditional, and urban versus rural – reflect and entrench the significant barriers that marginalised people the world over encounter. Interfaces between more powerful and less powerful groups of people involve any number of assumptions based on skin colour, livelihood, cultural or ethnic identity, education, and birthplace. However, the importance of each of these issues in different situations varies in a myriad of ways and to say that any one of the issues illustrated in the terms used is the dominant issue is incorrect. Indeed, they are all flawed and they are all useful, so that if one author has chosen to use 'indigenous knowledge' rather than 'local knowledge', it cannot be said that she or he is necessarily 'wrong'.

For this reason, I have not insisted that the contributors to this volume use one term rather than another. Some authors do not discuss any of these terms at length, but rather talk about landscape (for example Gilberthorpe and Sillitoe) and practice (Vermonden), whereas Zent uses several of the terms to signify slightly different things. As an ethnobotanist heavily influenced by the

'Canadian school' (e.g. Inglis 1993: vi), who thinks that interactions with and perceptions of the natural world are key defining characteristics of this knowledge, I have chosen to use the term 'traditional environmental knowledge' as my preferred gloss that, in this introduction only, includes all the other terms as well. Traditional in this sense does not reflect any idea of stasis, but, as the Four Directions Council of Canada put it, is about a 'way of knowing' rather than 'what is known' (Posey 1999: 4). In other words, it is about a process of transmission, interaction and innovation that is embedded in social relations, rather than a discrete series of 'facts' that can be extracted, scientifically verified and transferred to other settings.

Defining Diversity: The Problem of Definition

As the excesses of postmodernism demonstrated, if we over-deconstruct any topic, we end up with nothing or everything. Indeed the chapters in this book cover such a wide ground that the reader may find themselves asking what TEK actually is. Numerous attempts to define TEK have been made (Posey 1999: 9; Sillitoe 1998; see also Zent, Chapter Two) the most all-encompassing and useful of which is by Ellen and Harris (2000: 4-5), but as Vermonden (Chapter Nine) points out, even this impressive attempt has its shortcomings. Just as with nomenclature, then, there are some seemingly insurmountable problems with developing a definitive and encompassing definition of TEK. The problem lies in the diversity of TEKs that exist, and since our primary concern is to represent other 'ways of knowing' as accurately as possible, any one definition may be overly restrictive. Indeed, Hobart argues that the attempt to define TEK is an attempt to 'domesticate practice by recourse yet again to a hegemonic epistemology' (Hobart 1993: 14). In other words, he argues that by defining it, we risk transforming it to something other than TEK. I will return to this issue below, but for now, rather than attempting to add to the definitions posited elsewhere, I am more concerned here to consider how it is used by the contributors to this volume.

For some contributors, TEK seems to exist mainly in opposition to other types of knowledge, and certainly, people only become self-conscious about it and begin to reflect upon it when they are presented with another way of knowing. In another sense, it is considered to be the way people have learned to operate, to gain their subsistence, to build their communities, to contextualise their social relations and to understand themselves vis-à-vis the natural world around them (Gilberthorpe, Boissière, Vermonden, Kassam and Ganya). This type of knowledge, of course, has a much longer history than science, globalisation, urban lifestyles, economic inequality or any of the other things with which we often contrast it. Hence, in its widest sense, the study of TEK is about comparing different epistemologies of the natural world, starting from the author's viewpoint.[2]

Given that the author's perspective is so significant, it is fitting that each contribution explicitly or implicitly informs researchers' notions of TEK and how they affect our study, description and application of it. Indeed, the majority of the chapters in this book illustrate how particular assumptions and methodological approaches have forced researchers into a narrow perception of TEK. In particular, each contribution, no matter how focussed or general their research question, points out what we have missed by approaching TEK in a particular way. In this respect then, the study of TEK is often more limited by the researcher's intent than by the subject matter itself.

TEK-Shaped Instruments: The Problem of Methodology

The issue of how research changes TEK by virtue of collecting, analysing and applying data is an implicit concern of this compilation. Indeed, it has been a key concern of anthropology for decades. While the cognitive ethnoscientists argue that the human brain structures information in a predetermined fashion, so that a translation of TEK from 'local' knowledge systems to scientific language is largely a matter of superimposing similarly organised cognitive structures (Zent, Chapter Two), others argue that the apparent success in describing TEK in this way is simply an artefact of the method used to collect the data. As Schneider put it for more longstanding analytical categories of anthropology:

> It is said that by smashing the atom we break it into its component parts and thus learn what those parts are and what they are made of. This may hold for atoms. But a smashed culture does not break up into its original parts. A culture which is chopped up with a Z-shaped instrument yields z-shaped parts: a culture which is chopped up with tools called kinship, economics, politics, and religion yields those parts. Schneider (1984: 198).

In this same sense, if one uses the categories that many researchers use to organise knowledge systems, i.e. methods designed to structure data in cognitive, systematic, hierarchical or utilitarian ways, then one will extract evidence of TEK systems being structured in those ways. Although the ideal would be to represent TEK without altering it at all, any analytical perspective, representation or translation will use an instrument that privileges some aspects of TEK over others. Of course, TEK researchers are not just speaking for people, but are also speaking to distinct audiences. To be able to engage these audiences and to increase their understanding of and consideration for different TEKs, natural scientists must use certain instruments and social scientists must use others. Hence, rather than assuming that one method or analytical tool is better than another, it is crucial that researchers are aware of the 'shape' of their instrument and recognise that what they elucidate is but one facet of TEK.

Hence, it is significant that the contributors to this volume use and comment upon a variety of methods and analytical approaches to elicit and describe TEK, notably Sillitoe, Thomas, Boissière, Vermonden and Fujimoto. Fujimoto, for example, uses a combination of ethnobotanical survey methods and participant observation. He describes how an important plant use was not captured by traditional ethnobotanical survey methods. In this case, the oversight was two-fold: first, the researcher did not initially think to ask about indirect uses; second, farmers did not spontaneously mention these uses when freelisting or when presented with a plant specimen and asked to list its uses. It was only when Fujimoto engaged in participant observation that it became clear that farmers were reading different weedy species in and near agricultural fields as indicators of a variety of soil and climatic features. The growth form, colour, and presence or absence of weedy species were informing cultivation practices and patterns. The fact that farmers themselves did not mention these uses during the first survey implies that this kind of knowledge is so embedded in context as to not even be talked about. Indeed, Fujimoto found little evidence that they transmit this knowledge orally. Rather, it is usually 'picked up' over a lifetime of farming practice. This indicates that what is articulated as TEK by local and scientific experts is only a part of the expertise used by farmers. It also demonstrates the limitations of the ethnobotanical survey methods often used to elicit such knowledge.

Vermonden also uses quantitative and qualitative methods, but analyses his data from a phenomenological perspective (note that although Vermonden and Fujimoto both use participant observation and structured interviews, their analytical approaches are quite different). Like Fujimoto, Vermonden demonstrates how TEK is embedded in practice and calls into question the primacy of oral instruction in TEK transmission. However, rather than focussing on the utility of a particular plant use category, as Fujimoto does, he focuses on describing the means by which transmission occurs. By elucidating different features of the extraordinarily rich phenomenon that is human perception of and interaction with the world around them, these two chapters make a strong argument for a multi-disciplinary and multi-pronged approach to TEK research.

Landscape, Power and Process

It is fitting that this book should begin with two comprehensive reviews of TEK: Zent's review of the development of the different strands that comprise TEK research; and Alexiades's review of the development of TEK as a resource to be used by indigenous people, development professionals, corporations, etcetera. As well as providing a background of how different disciplines have approached TEK and what they have added to the subject, Zent's chapter provides a benchmark for the current state of TEK research, the complexity and diversity of his analysis reflecting the diversity of the subject matter. While some may argue that this is a sign of the current confusion over nomenclature and definition, theory and potential application of TEK research, Zent argues that it is a sign of its vigour and dynamism. This chapter will prove a necessary starting point for anyone wishing to know more about TEK research.

In keeping with this interpretation, this compilation gives the contributors wide scope to approach TEK from their own theoretical or disciplinary standpoints. They include anthropologists, wildlife biologists, ecologists, ethnobiologists, botanists and agronomists and they come from Europe, the U.S.A., Africa, and Asia. They offer case studies from Papua New Guinea, Indonesia, Kenya, Ethiopia, the U.K., Lithuania, Romania and Greece. Some of the contributions focus on a particular issue, such as Fujimoto, who points out that many studies overlook plant uses that do not fit into preconceived schema. Others are concerned with broad concepts, such as Alexiades, who discusses the influence of global issues on so-called 'local' knowledge and vice versa. Most are situated in particular landscapes, although Carss, Bell and Marzano compare four cases studies from across Europe and Alexiades considers these issues on a global level. Some analyse attempts to incorporate TEK into particular development schemes (Gilberthorpe, Kassam and Ganya, Carss, Bell and Marzano), others are more general (Sillitoe, Thomas, Alexiades), while others analyse TEK without reference to its application in development (Fujimoto, Vermonden, Boissière). I have endeavoured to bring together these different approaches and contrast them in a complementary manner, rather than a critical one. In some cases, the contributions have come to differing conclusions, but others yield some startling convergences. Furthermore, the juxtaposition of different perspectives throws into relief the approaches and assumptions of the differing disciplines. As such, this book offers a synthesis of TEK research for students first engaging with the field as well as for professionals who are continuing to wrestle with the contradictions and insights that such research yields.

Despite this diversity of methods, areas of expertise and analytical approaches, three key themes run explicitly and implicitly throughout the contributions: power, process and landscape. Of course, these issues often overlap: Alexiades considers the broad socio-political processes from which have emerged particular power differentials and which are continuing to shape the role and expression of TEK in the context of globalisation; Gilberthorpe considers how power differentials affect the situation of knowledge within a particular landscape; while Kassam and Ganya analyse how ecological theory, in its failure to acknowledge power relationships has impacted upon landscape dynamics in counterproductive ways. Landscape and process are so intertwined in many of the chapters that the division of the two is largely arbitrary. For instance, Thomas demonstrates how process is integral to an ecological understanding of landscape, whereas Vermonden shows how understanding of landscape is gained through a lifelong process of enskilment. Indeed, all the contributors to this book combine the themes in a new manner, offering the potential to provide a new direction to TEK studies. It is to this exciting potential that I devote the remainder of this introduction.

Power and Process

Zent concludes his chapter by identifying the most recent phase of TEK research, the processual phase, 'by which researchers have ... begun to focus on the dynamic ... aspects – creation, transmission, transformation and erosion – of IK.' Research in the processual phase removes any suggestion that TEK is somehow a remnant of the past or 'ancient knowledge', but rather demonstrates that it is constantly adjusting as a person, community, society or landscape changes. As all the chapters in this book demonstrate, the process by which knowledge is gained, identified and applied has become central to TEK research. But there is another aspect to the process of knowledge formation and utilisation that is touched upon repeatedly in this compilation: the role of social, political and economic inequality, particularly between local or indigenous peoples and 'global' institutions, in defining knowledge and its use. In his section entitled 'IK as a critical ecopolitical discourse', Zent summarises some of the important critiques that have dealt with this issue. They generally draw heavily on the work of Michel Foucault (e.g. Foucault 1980; Mills 2003), in which he argued that bodies of knowledge are not 'autonomous intellectual structures', but rather are 'essentially tied to systems of social control' (Gutting 2000: 290). In other words, that the determination of what constitutes knowledge (and ignorance, cf. Hobart 1993) and who is qualified to know is related to the established social hierarchy, rather than the elucidation of universal truths. The role of science and development in legitimising and supporting these systems of social control has been a central concern of these critiques (Agrawal 1999, 2002; Briggs and Sharp 2004; Escobar 1995; Baviskar 2000; Sundar 2000; Parkes 2000; Fischer 2004).

These critiques, combined with the failure of sustainable development, and its TEK component, to solve development problems as quickly or effectively as hoped have led to a backlash, leaving development professionals and TEK researchers alike beginning to ask if TEK has any use whatsoever (Sillitoe and Marzano 2006).

TEK and Power: The Indigenous Perspective

The obvious answer to that question is not that it is useful to us, but that it is useful to indigenous peoples. Given repeated indigenous demands that their languages, cultures, cosmologies and connection to the land be respected and maintained, it is a matter of some concern that the perspective of indigenous spokespeople and organisations are not included in the debate on the value and appropriate use of TEK more frequently. Of the twenty charters and declarations made by international indigenous organizations and conferences listed in Posey (1999, Appendix I), all of them include demands for the right to maintain their indigenous culture and language, an important aspect of that being

TEK. These declarations are made by people who are involved in extensive social and economic change and who might think that their TEK has little relevance to their aspirations, but they are clear:

> (We are concerned with the) dominant sector societies' lack of understanding of Indigenous Peoples' values and our special relationship with the Earth, and that we have developed traditional technologies and subsistence systems which are as relevant today as they have been for thousands of years. This demonstrates our deep spiritual connection to our ancestral homelands which is essential to sustainability.
>
> Statement from Indigenous Peoples participating in the Fourth Session of the Commission on Sustainable Development (CSD-4), 1996, in Posey (1999: 579).

The classical development view would hold that this 'special relationship with the Earth' is what has held indigenous peoples back, and the association of this kind of language with the Green and New Age movements has made it easy for many scientists, economists and development professionals to dismiss it. Certainly, the repeated assertion of the 'spiritual value' of local and indigenous peoples' relationships with the landscape (see also Posey 1999; 2002) speaks of a benefit that is difficult to capture using scientific assumptions and methods.

In fact, behind the 'fuzzy' language, there is a politically astute intent. Alexiades (Chapter Three) shows us how TEK has come to be a useful political tool for indigenous and local peoples. He focuses on the context of globalisation, where knowledge has become commodified, and he analyses the processes whereby TEK has come to have significance on the global stage. Although he emphasises the importance of inequality in framing the debate over TEK, he also shows how local and indigenous communities see new opportunities to use their own TEK to help reconfigure these political and social relations. Given that the communication of TEK in a language acceptable to scientists and policy-makers has undermined the image of marginalised peoples as ignorant, irrational savages who needed the tutelage and guidance of others to survive, TEK research has played a crucial role in helping them establish a platform from which they may have these concerns heard. We still have a long way to go in the fight for greater social and economic equality, but to suggest that TEK research has no role in this process, hence should be abandoned, is a step backwards.

Lest we be too quick to congratulate ourselves, however, it must be realised that indigenous peoples have been some of the fiercest critics of the use of TEK in development and bioprospecting projects (Greene 2004). In Venezuela, the criticism is so fierce that 'traditional knowledge' has come to be synonymous with such strong terms as 'biopiracy' and 'imperialism' (Heckler 2007). Indeed a statement by indigenous shamans, transcribed and released by indigenous advocacy groups in Venezuela in 2002, used the following strong language to express their feelings about TEK research:

Just as they conquered our lands with weapons, now they destroy our knowledge with contracts.(Luis Gonzalez, *Wöthïhä* shaman, Tobogán de la Selva Accord in Heckler 2006).

(As a result of bioprospecting) I now feel that when a stranger enters my territory, they are penetrating it to destroy it, to destroy my way of life, to try to rob me (Juan Antonio Bolívar, indigenous shaman, Tobogán de la Selva Accord in Heckler 2006).

The parallel between colonialism and TEK research and application is repeatedly asserted by indigenous peoples. The indigenous university in Ecuador, for example, states as one of its primary aims the 'decolonisation of knowledge', going on to say that 'the methodological proposal (of modern science) excludes the possibility of indigenous self-comprehension. In this way, vast dominions of science do not allow for the inclusion of 'the other' and 'the different' within its frontiers of knowledge' (García et al. 2004: 164; translation from Spanish by the author). Although most academics will disagree with the details of this statement, it behoves us to consider what has led indigenous groups to feel such strong antipathy to science and research that it has become 'an imposition of outside philosophies in order to dominate…convince, impose and sell; we have been subjected to conditions of dependency worse than in Spanish colonial times' (Sarango 2006; translation from Spanish by the author).

Indigenous groups argue that, although TEK is important to them, they do not feel that they have any say over how it is used or who benefits from it (Alexiades, Chapter Three; Heckler 2006). Furthermore, as Alexiades points out (pp. 79), 'the issue is not only whether Europeans and Americans have the right to, or even can, represent or appropriate elements of (indigenous) culture, but the fact that such appropriation follows from a history of abuse, marginalisation and violence directed at (indigenous people)…'. The pertinence of long histories of unequal power relations in the process of TEK are also demonstrated in the contributions by Carss, Bell and Marzano, Gilberthorpe, Kassam and Ganya.

Process and Landscape

The integration of the concerns of socio-political relationships and the dynamic nature of both research and knowledge transmission has greatly improved our understanding of TEK in the last decade or so. Nevertheless, this incorporation of power and process has caused something of a crisis of identity: if everything is TEK, how is it a distinct field of research? As the majority of the contributions to this volume demonstrate, the concept of landscape, currently rising to prominence in social anthropology (Stewart and Strathern 2003: 1), can provide a meaningful analytical frame to coordinate these complex interactions. This focus on landscape represents a means of integrating many of the challenges thrown up by the processual approach, hence offering a potential new direction for TEK study.

Landscape, like so many terms, has come to have a particular, and contested, meaning in environmental anthropology. It has developed from a rather static concept to one incorporating process (Hirsch 1995: 22-23) and productive activities, skills or 'tasks' (Ingold 2000: 195, 198), both of which are inextricable from social relationships (Hirsch 1995: 22; Ingold 2000: 195). In its broadest sense the concept of landscape can be defined as, 'the world as it is known to those who dwell therein, who inhabit its places and journey along the paths connecting them' (Ingold 2000: 193). By providing a contextualising frame for human activities and perception, the concept of landscape 'brings into alignment the local, national and global' (Stewart and Strathern 2003: 2). Because '[landscape's] shape at any given time reflects change and is a part of change' (Stewart and Strathern 2003: 4), it allows a consideration of historicity and process. Hence, it becomes a tool for analysing the relationships between globalisation and TEK and the different sources of change that mark the processual phase of TEK research.

It enables Boissière, for instance, to contextualise the most resilient features of TEK within a history of movement over the landscape. He describes two indigenous groups of West Papua and how their TEKs interact with each other, rather than how they interact with some external environmental knowledge. He finds that, while the two groups have hybridised many features of their TEK, including language, agricultural practice and kinship, the two groups have maintained distinct cosmologies and shamanisms, these being reflected in different patterns of plant use and different origin and migration myths.

Of all the contributors, Gilberthorpe most explicitly ties TEK to landscape. She describes IK of the Fasu people of Papua New Guinea as inextricably tied to a lived landscape, made up of both people and places. This is expressed in a formal sense in which land rights are informed by kinship ties and 'pathways'. Each clan is historically connected to a certain area of land, but also, through affinal relationships, individuals are connected to several pieces of land. The mistake that an oil company made when it set up an agreement with the Fasu was in assuming that these land rights were static. In fact they are fluid, allowing for migration, periodic demographic decline and expansion. In assuming a perception of land ownership commensurable with their own, the oil company have encouraged the Fasu to objectify the landscape and end this fluidity, thereby excluding newly in-marrying men and women from any claim to the land. Gilberthorpe and Boissière both recount myths that tell of movement and pathways, in which 'landscape is constituted as an enduring record of ... the lives and works of past generations who have dwelt within it, and in so doing, have left there something of themselves' (Ingold 2000: 189).

The western assumption that land comprises static areas that can be delineated on maps and apportioned and described in a certain way is at the root of Sillitoe's critique of the concept of carrying capacity. While most carrying capacity calculations assume a variety of constants, he shows that the Was people of Papua New Guinea do not interact with the landscape in a static or bounded way. Was Valley farmers are constantly moving and adapting their agricultural practices while the agricultural properties of the land itself are constantly changing, so that Was conception of the landscape is fundamentally different than those of carrying capacity theorists. Given that the predictions of imminent ecological collapse made by various researchers nearly fifty years ago have failed to materialise, the Was perspective may very well be the more accurate one.

Although Sillitoe is critical of ecologists for their overly static view of landscape in Papua New Guinea, Thomas demonstrates how ecologists, too, have up-dated their ideas of the landscape in the past thirty years or so. He uses as an example the manner in which the concept of homeostasis is often applied to traditional land management practices to support a western myth of indigenous peoples as living in harmony with nature. He describes the rejection by ecologists of this concept of homeostasis, in favour of considering disturbance and dynamism to be a fundamental element in ecological systems. He compares this with the Hewa people's (Papua New Guinea) acceptance of disturbance and their role in creating disturbance as a fundamental aspect of the landscape. He goes on to argue against the assumption that, because indigenous people supposedly live 'in harmony' with the landscape that their stewardship is inherently sustainable. Rather, he argues that the sustainability of Hewa land use is largely a function of low population density and an expansive land tenure system.

For most of the authors, a certain perception of landscape is not only embedded in formalised structures, such as kinship, land tenure or subsistence regime, but also in a phenomenological sense, in which people learn to make sense of their world by moving through it and engaging with it. This is exemplified in the myths recounted by Boissière and Gilberthorpe, but is central to Vermonden's analysis of fishing activities in South Buton (Indonesia). Rather than focussing on the more commonly described transmission methods of oral instruction and imitation, he demonstrates how fishermen learn their skills through a lifetime of practice. However, using the landscape, or in this case seascape, as a frame for analysis does not exclude social interactions, as other people are always the most influential elements of a dynamic, interactive landscape. Vermonden describes how fishing practice is guided by more experienced fishermen, comparisons with peers provide benchmarks and the selection of teams and 'apprentices' who will eventually take over for acknowledged experts is a complex and significant process. Nevertheless, much learning occurs by moving through the seascape, experiencing the significance of certain sea features, and the success or failure of fishing endeavours. This argument critiques the notion that TEK can be passed on to scientists and generalised, because it is neither relatable nor demonstrable, but rather embedded within the practice of the fishermen. How does one integrate instructions to learn alongside one's peers and elders from the time you learn to walk, to feel the subtle differences in water quality, to use one's long education of attention to intuit whether a particular technique will be appropriate for a particular spot of the sea into a UNDP development manual or video?

Carss, Bell and Marzano show the importance of human agency and power relationships in shaping perceptions of landscape. They discuss the conflict between ecologists and local fishers in four European Union countries around cormorant management. As with almost all European wild birds, cormorants are legally protected and, as a result their numbers have increased ten-fold or more in the past fifty years. Some fishers and their representative groups often complain loudly about cormorants depleting fish stocks and demand that they be culled. During their field work, however, the researchers soon found that the fishers have a broader and more nuanced understanding of the causes of fishery depletion. The authors conclude that cormorants have become a flashpoint for larger concerns about wetland management policies over which local fishers have no control, including politically motivated restrictions on their activities, large-scale ecosystem modification and economic difficulties. Because cormorants are conspicuous in the landscape and there is a perception that local fishers can do something about them – unlike their perceived lack of power to influence national and international policy – they focus their sense of frustration and helplessness on demanding a cull. This chapter highlights the importance of the broader political, economic and social context in shaping TEK.

The issue of conflicting ideas about the nature of land management is also central to Kassam and Ganya's contribution. They rebut the central assumption of Garrett Hardin's 'Tragedy of the Commons' that non-privatised land is an unregulated free-for-all that inevitably leads to ecological collapse, by describing a coherent, intricate and appropriate land use regime used by nomadic camel herders in northern Kenya. They argue that the common property regime used by these herders is flexible and historically grounded, but also fundamentally connected to their ability to move through, exploit and interact with the landscape. This contribution is also reflexive of the role of science in the process, arguing that 'the application of a framework is not an end in itself, but must further goals of social justice, by analysing and critiquing scholarly models that have led to the implementation of inappropriate policies.'

All three conceptual strands come together in several of the contributions, for instance Carss, Bell and Marzano, Sillitoe and Gilberthorpe. It is fitting that Kassam and Ganya close the book (Chapter Eleven), however, as their analysis is most explicit in the interaction of the three. Using emic and etic historical accounts, they analyse the manner in which colonial policies and warfare amongst neighbouring groups have effected change in Gabra camel herders' sense of landscape and, by extension, the manner in which they manage their common resources.

Conclusion

The contributors to this book, from their diverse starting points contribute to critiques that present a thematically coherent body of work. TEK emerges as an interaction of movement through and engagement with a particular landscape (e.g. Ingold 2000) and the socio-economic context in which this knowledge is developed, evaluated, transmitted and applied. This, perhaps overly reified, perspective is inherently historical, with people's past land use and social relationships informing current TEKs. In so doing, they represent a new phase of TEK research, with a broader and more dynamic analytical frame (the landscape) in which change and the processes that engender it are central features.

Kassam and Ganya suggest that analytical frameworks, such as common property regime, should be taken as heuristic tools rather than prescriptive and predictive models. It is in this sense, too, that I suggest landscape as an analytical framework for both quantitative and qualitative researchers. By moving away from considering a person, a family, a household or a particular agricultural plot as the primary unit of study, and moving towards a unit consisting of people, relationships and a dialectic interaction with the non-human environment, I believe we are offered the opportunity to describe TEK much more accurately.

Notes

I wish to thank Paul Sillitoe and Roy Ellen for invaluable comments on earlier drafts of this chapter. I also thank Roy for his work in organising the Ninth International Congress of Ethnobiology and editing the series of which this volume is part. Finally, I would like to thank Robin Wilson for his editorial assistance during the early stages of the process.

1. Here I use the term 'modernised' as it is defined by Alexiades in Chapter Three.
2. Paradoxically, this type of analysis is only made possible from the author's viewpoint: usually a particular western notion of a division between nature and culture, upon which scientific knowledge is based, that is not reflected in many TEKs. It has been argued that this distinction is at the root of the inequality between science and TEK (Ingold 2000: 13-15).

Bibliography

Agrawal, A. 1999. 'On Power and Indigenous Knowledge' in J. Slikkerveer, ed.,
    Ethnoscience, 'TEK' and its Application to Conservation in Darrell Addison
    Posey, ed., *Cultural and Spiritual Values of Biodiversity*, United Nations
    Environment Program and Intermediate Technology Publications. pp. 177-180.
_____ 2002. 'Indigenous Knowledge and the Politics of Classification', *International
    Social Science Journal* 54(3): 287-297.
Baviskar, A. 2000. 'Claims to Knowledge, Claims to Control: Environmental Conflict
    in the Great Himalayan National Park, India' in R. Ellen, P. Parkes and A. Bicker,
    eds., *Indigenous Environmental Knowledge and its Transformations: Critical
    Anthropological Perspectives*. Amsterdam: Harwood Academic Publishers.
    pp. 101-120.
Briggs, J. and J. Sharp. 2004. 'Indigenous Knowledges and Development: A
    Postcolonial Caution', *Third World Quarterly* 25(4): 661-676.
Brokensha, D., D.M. Warren and O. Werner. 1980. *Indigenous Knowledge Systems and
    Development*. University Press of America, Lanham, MD.
Chambers, R. 1983. *Rural Development: Putting the Last First*. London: Longman.
Chambers, R, A. Pacey and L.A. Thrupp. 1989. *Farmer First: Farmer Innovation and
    Agricultural Research*. Intermediate Technology Productions, London.
Ellen, R.F. and H. Harris. 2000. 'Introduction' in R.F. Ellen, P. Parkes and A. Bicker,
    eds., *Indigenous Knowledge and its Transformations*. Amsterdam: Harwood
    Academic Publishers. pp. 1-33.
Escobar, A. 1995. *Encountering Development: The Making and Unmaking of the Third
    World*. Princeton, N.J.: Princeton University Press.
Fischer, M. 2004. 'Powerful Knowledge: Applications in a Cultural Context' in A.
    Bicker, P. Sillitoe and J. Pottier, eds., *Development and Local Knowledge: New
    Approaches to Issues in Natural Resources Management, Conservation and Agriculture*.
    London: Routledge. pp. 19-30.
Foucault, M. 1980. *Power/Knowledge: Selected Interviews and Other Writings 1972-
    1977*. New York and London: Harvester Wheatsheaf.
García, J., A. Lozano, J. Olivera, César Ruiz. 2004. *Aprender en la Sabiduría y el Buen
    Vivir*. Quito: Imprenta Mariscal and UNESCO.
Greene, S. 2004. 'Indigenous People Incorporated? Culture as Politics, Culture as
    Property in Pharmaceutical Bioprospecting'. *Current Anthropology* 45(2): 211-237.
Gutting, G. 2000. 'Foucault, Michel', p. 290 in *Concise Routledge Encyclopedia of
    Philosophy*. London: Routledge.
Hadley, M. and K. Schrekenberg. 1995. 'Traditional Ecological Knowledge and
    UNESCO's Man and Biosphere (MAB) Programme' in D.M. Warren, L.J.
    Slikkerveer and D. Brokensha, eds., *The Cultural Dimension of Development:
    Indigenous Knowledge Systems*. London: Intermediate Technology Publications, pp.
    464-474.
Heckler, S. 2006. "Just As They Conquered Our Land with Weapons, Now They
    Destroy Our Knowledge with Contracts": The Piaroa Perspective on
    Bioprospecting.' Paper given at the British Academy Festival of Science,
    University of Norwich, 4 September 2006.

_____ 2007. 'On Knowing and Not Knowing: The Many Valuations of Piaroa Local Knowledge' in P. Sillitoe, ed., *Global Science Versus Local Science*. Oxford: Berghahn Books. pp. 91-107.

Hirsch, E. 1995. 'Introduction' in E. Hirsch and M. O'Hanlon, eds., *The Anthropology of Landscape: Perspectives on Place And Space*. Oxford: Clarendon Press.

Hobart, M. 1993. 'Introduction: The Growth of Ignorance?' in M. Hobart, ed., *An Anthropological Critique of Development: The Growth of Ignorance*. London: Routledge. pp. 1-30.

Inglis, J. 1993. *Traditional Ecological Knowledge: Concepts and Cases*. Ottawa: International Program on Traditional Ecological Knowledge and International Development Research Centre.

Ingold, T. 2000. *The Perception of the Environment: Essays in Livelihood, Dwelling and Skill*. London: Routledge.

McNeely, J. 1995. 'IUCN and Indigenous Peoples: How To Promote Sustainable 'Development' in D.M. Warren, L.J. Slikkerveer and D. Brokensha, eds., *The Cultural Dimension of Development: Indigenous Knowledge Systems*. London: Intermediate Technology Publications, pp. 445-450.

Mills, S. 2003. *Michel Foucault*. London and New York: Routledge.

Parkes, P. 2000. 'Enclaved Knowledge: Indigent and Indignant Representations of Environmental Management and Development Among the Kalasha of Pakistan' in R. Ellen, P. Parkes and A. Bicker, eds., *Indigenous Environmental Knowledge and Its Transformations: Critical Anthropological Perspectives*. Amsterdam: Harwood Academic Publishers. pp. 253-292.

Posey, D.A. 1999. *Cultural and Spiritual Values of Biodiversity*. Nairobi and London: United Nations Environment Program and Intermediate Technology Publications.

_____ 2002. 'Upsetting the Sacred Balance: Can the Study of Indigenous Knowledge Reflect Cosmic Consciousness?' in P. Sillitoe, A. Bicker and J. Pottier, eds., *Participating in Development: Approaches to Indigenous Knowledge*. London: Routledge, pp. 24-42.

Pottier, J. 2003. 'Negotiating Local Knowledge: An Introduction' in J. Pottier, A. Bicker and P. Sillitoe, eds., *Negotiating Local Knowledge: Power and Identity in Development*. London: Pluto Press. pp. 1-29

Rocheleau, D., K. Wachira, L. Malaret, and B. Muchiri Wanjohi 1989. 'Local Knowledge for Agroforestry Research and Native Plants' in R. Chambers, A. Pacey and L.A. Thrupp, eds., *Farmer First: Farmer Innovation and Agricultural Research*. London: Intermediate Technology Publications, pp. 14-23.

Sarango, L.F. 2006. 'Hacia la Descolonización de la Educación, el Conocimiento y la Ciéncia'. Boletín Digital Universidad Intercultural Amawtay Wasi, No. 6, Sept. 2006, http://www.amawtaywasi.edu.ec/boletinelectronico/boletin08.htm

Schneider, D. 1984. *A Critique of the Study of Kinship*. Ann Arbor: University Press of Michigan.

Scoones, I and J. Thompson. 1994. *Beyond Farmer First: Rural People's Knowledge, Agricultural Research and Extension Practice*. London: Intermediate Technology Publications.

Sillitoe, P. 1998. 'Defining Indigenous Knowledge: The Knowledge Continuum',
    Indigenous Knowledge and Development Monitor 6(3): 14-15
_____ 2002. 'Participant Observation to Participatory Development: Making
    Anthropology Work' in P. Sillitoe, A. Bicker and J. Pottier, eds., *Participating in
    Development: Approaches to Indigenous Knowledge*. London: Routledge, pp. 1-23.
_____ 2007. *Local Science Versus Global Science: Approaches to Indigenous Knowledge in
    International Development*. Oxford: Berghahn Books
_____ and A. Bicker. 2004. 'Introduction: Hunting for Theory, Gathering Ideology' in
    A. Bicker, P. Sillitoe and J. Pottier, eds., *Development and Local Knowledge: New
    Approaches to Issues in Natural Resources Management, Conservation and Agriculture*.
    London: Routledge. pp. 1-18.
_____ and M. Marzano. 2006. 'What Is The Future for Local Knowledge?'
    Presentation at Ninth Biennial Conference of the European Association of Social
    Anthropologists, Bristol, U.K. 18-21 September 2006.
Stewart, P. and A. Strathern. 2003. *Landscape, Memory and History: Anthropological
    Perspectives*. London: Sterling Press.
Sundar, N. 2000. 'The Construction and Destruction of "Indigenous" Knowledge in
    India's Joint Forest Management Programme' in R. Ellen, P. Parkes and A. Bicker,
    eds., *Indigenous Environmental Knowledge and its Transformations: Critical
    Anthropological Perspectives*. Amsterdam: Harwood Academic Publishers. pp. 79-
    100.
Taussig, M. 1993. *Mimesis and Alterity*. New York: Routledge.
Wolf, E. 1982. *Europe and the People Without History*. Berkeley, CA.: University of
    California Press.

Chapter 2

A Genealogy of Scientific Representations of Indigenous Knowledge

Stanford Zent

Introduction

The anthropological fascination and appreciation for indigenous knowledge has successfully penetrated the popular imagination in recent years. It is now common to find sympathetic references to traditional ecological and cultural wisdom in miscellaneous media, from movies to children's storybooks, from alternative medicine propaganda to New Age religious teachings. Similar to other public trends, the remaking of IK has followed the lead set by advances in scientific research. IK has become incorporated into the research programmes of academic disciplines spanning the social and life sciences, leading some authors to suggest that IK studies deserve to be recognised as a burgeoning interdisciplinary field of research offering many new and exciting theoretical, practical, and ethical insights (Warren et al. 1995; Sillitoe 1998; Grenier 1998). Scientists, politicians, activists and others have stated that this intellectual heritage is valuable and relevant for the modern westernised world and urge that it be documented, preserved, utilised, and integrated with scientific knowledge (Warren et al. 1989; Moock and Rhoades 1992; Williams and Baines 1993; Warren et al. 1995; Posey 1999; Maffi 2001). Despite the mounting accolades, the attitudes of the scientific community towards IK are still marked by considerable ambiguity, scepticism, contention, and debate. The opinions of the 'experts' diverge rather widely in regards to the definition, epistemology, methodology, separation from global science, codification, contextualisation, sustainability, contemporary importance, jurisprudence, and rhetorical representation of IK (cf. McCorkle 1989; Berkes 1993; Williams and Baines 1993; Dewalt 1994; Warren et al. 1995; Agrawal 1995; Brush 1996; Cleveland and Murray 1997; Sillitoe 1998; Ellen et al. 2000; Sillitoe et al. 2002). I would argue that such cognitive dissonance is actually a sign of strength, rather than weakness, because it reflects the current lively and dynamic state of IK research and the active attempts of scientists to understand better this complex phenomenon. The present essay contributes to this debate by providing some genealogical perspective of the evolution of scientific representations of IK during approximately the last half century.

Phases of IK Development

The study of IK systems has passed through several discernible developmental phases from the 1950s up to the present day, distinguished on the basis of shifting research foci, methods, theoretical constructs, and objectives. In this chapter I will review seven phases: (a) environmental ethnoscience; (b) theorisation of folk biological classification; (c) modelling the relationship between knowledge and behaviour; (d) the significance of indigenous knowledge for sustainable development and conservation of nature; (e) debates about the valuation, exploitation, and compensation of IK; (f) IK as a critical ecopolitical discourse; and (g) processual perspectives of IK. Discussion of each phase will focus on the problem orientations, research contexts, methodologies, conceptual biases, and seminal bibliographic sources of each of these phases, as well as some of the implicit or explicit contributions to scientific thought that have emerged from this work. Although the order of presentation of the different phases is intended to reflect the chronology of their appearance, there is a certain degree of overlap in time sequence, case studies, and authorship. But more than just a diachronically-ordered typology of distinct academic traditions, the intention here is to convey a sense of the genealogy, or derivation and development, of families of ideas, scholarship, purpose and practice, with each phase recombining selected characteristics of preceding phases, both strengths and criticisms of weaknesses, along with new information and concepts drawn from elsewhere, thereby creating novel forms. As a review article of previous literature, the treatment provided here is decidedly descriptive, motivated by the goal of providing an introductory-level accounting of the growth of the field for the interested reader who may or may not be well versed in the research. For the expert, I remind him or her that the object of our understanding is a fragmented and moving target, even while some aspects come into sharper focus, and, for the novice, I hope to encourage further interest through a basic grasp of some of the key issues surrounding its development and some of the primary works that have been produced.

Before proceeding on to the genealogical exposition, it might be helpful to make a clarification with respect to terminology. Indigenous knowledge (IK) is presently the most popular term used to refer to the central subject matter treated in this paper and is the term that I use most frequently throughout. An abundance of alternative labels have been used to refer to this topic at different times and places[1], and although each one may evoke slightly different connotations, they have enough focal meaning in common to permit a reasonable level of intersubjective understanding and communication (Ellen and Harris 2000). The (de)merits of the different terms have already been scrutinised and several working definitions have been elaborated to formalise the concept (Kloppenburg 1991a; Hunn 1993; Dewalt 1994; Antweiler 1998; Grenier 1998; Purcell 1998; Semali and Kincheloe 1999; Ellen and Harris 2000; Sillitoe 2002b): I see no need to revisit these issues here (see Heckler, Chapter One). However, my main focus will be on indigenous environmental knowledge, which is to say the locally distinctive, situated and learned knowledge by which a particular society or community apprehends the biotic and abiotic components of the environment and their interrelationships and engages them in a practical sense for sustenance, health, shelter, tools and other survival needs and wants. Given the inherent difficulty (and arbitrariness) of demarcating environmental knowledge from other kinds of knowledge, and not wanting to contribute to the further proliferation of terms, I have chosen to stick with the appellation indigenous knowledge.

Environmental Ethnoscience

Environmental ethnoscience refers to the application of the theory and method of the anthropological perspective known as 'ethnoscience' to the study of cultural-ecological relations. Ethnoscience, also referred to as ethnosemantics or folk classification, is an approach to ethnographic description based on the study of terminological systems and other mostly verbal data, an ideational model of culture, and the epistemological privilege of specifying cultural experience and behaviour from an emic (i.e. insider's) perspective. Inspired by the rigorous inductive discovery procedures employed in structural linguistics, ethnoscientific research typically entailed the elicitation of lexical sets in the local language that were analysed in terms of their basic semantic components and relationships (i.e. distinctive features of meaning and their overall structural organisation), with the goal of revealing what the native needs to know in order to act appropriately in specified cultural contexts. This approach began to take definite shape in the 1950s and early 1960s mostly as a result of field studies of kinship, pronominals, colour terminologies, and folk biology (ethnobotany and ethnozoology). As the popularity of the ethnoscientific approach grew, the range of topics studied and the methodological techniques used expanded to include the description of several domains of environmental or ecological interest, such as natural objects or processes (e.g. soils, land use types, ecological communities, topographic surfaces, meteorological features, seasons, diseases), resource types (e.g. foods, firewood, medicine), and practical activities (e.g. cultivation tech-niques, food preparation, curing, settlement pattern) (Conklin 1954a, 1954b, 1957, 1961, 1967, 1972; Frake 1961, 1962; 1964; Metzger and Williams 1966; Bulmer 1967; Fowler and Leland 1967; Morrill 1967; Bulmer and Tyler 1968; Basso 1972; Berlin et al. 1974; Johnson 1974; Fowler 1977).

An ethnoscientifically informed approach to the study of human-environmen-tal relationships was pioneered by Harold Conklin in the 1950s with monograph-length field studies of the ethnobotany (1954) and shifting cultivation (1957) of the Hanunóo people (Philippines). Conklin's work highlighted sophisticated treatment of native terminologies, categories, and interpretations of various envi-ronmental components (what he labelled 'ethnoecological factors'), but his ethno-graphic reports were remarkably well balanced and gave ample consideration to other cultural and environmental factors through the participant observation of behaviour and other interdisciplinary field methods. The Hanunóo research was revolutionary in the sense of breaking with previous depictions of non-western mentality as primitive or childlike (i.e. less developed, less intelligent), magical or pre-logical (i.e. irrational, non-empirical), and static (i.e. tradition-bound). Instead, Conklin's work effectively demonstrated that such knowledge systems can be complex, systematically organised and well adapted to prevailing environmen-tal conditions, that economic and social activities are closely integrated and inter-dependent with environmental categorisations, and that such people are indeed capable of possessing an incredibly robust and encyclopaedic comprehension of their local environment. His ethnobotanical study documented that the number of terminal plant taxa recognised by the Hanunóo exceeds the number of scien-tific species found in this area, thus suggesting that this non-western folk main-tain a more acute taxonomic appreciation of their local floral environment than do western scientists. His agricultural study depicted Hanunóo swidden farming practice as a highly structured, well organised, ecologically balanced activity, thus was instrumental in overturning pejorative notions of shifting cultivation, held by many western scientists at the time, as haphazard, wasteful, destructive, and underproductive forms of tropical land use.

The primary objective of ethnoscientific research was academic in the sense of seeking to improve the ethnographic enterprise of the discipline of anthro-pology through the employment of more rigorous, replicable and emically accu-rate methods of data collection and analysis which would produce more detailed and culturally valid ethnographic accounts. The basic objective behind the method is translation from native (i.e. cognised world) to scientific (i.e. opera-tional world) categories, in which a sharp epistemological distinction is main-tained between the two knowledge forms. Instead of achieving a new type of ethnography, however, perhaps the most lasting impact of this body of work was to alter scientific attitudes towards non-western, non-literate peoples and their knowledge systems. On one hand, it began to raise questions about the supposedly superior intellect and training of the scientific observer, especially when it came to their grasp of ecologically-complex, poorly-studied local environments (e.g. tropical forests). On the other hand, by demonstrating the sharp detail, empirical accuracy and sheer complexity of ethnoscientific classifications, it became clear that the 'primitive naturalist' controls a trove of potentially useful information which can be tapped by scientists, for example to catalogue the biodiversity in specific locations (cf. Schultes 1994b; Lewis 1993; Leigh 1993).

The conceptual strengths and weaknesses of ethnoscientific research have received a great deal of comment in the years since its inception (D'Andrade 1995) and it is impossible to summarise this complex discussion in the space available. It will suffice to point out that this approach, as understood in its classic and more extreme forms, was based on a concept of culture as knowledge that was (mis)represented as being synchronic (i.e. no concept of change), homogeneous (culturally uniform), holistic (all parts are interrelated and interdependent), homeostatic (internally regulated), closed (bounded from other knowledge systems), relativistic (comprehensible only in its own terms, hence not comparable to other knowledge), formal (analogous to language) and ideal (assumed to be homologous with behaviour). Furthermore, its exclusive reliance on linguistic data effectively excludes non-verbalised forms of knowledge which are embedded in social and ecological behaviours and learned through participant or peripheral observation, individual practice and experimentation (Keesing 1972). Finally, more attention was given to methodological explication rather than theoretical issues. This last criticism was addressed with considerable vigour in the next phase, especially when studies of folk biology began to turn up startling similarities in biological nomenclature and classification, not only among different cultural groups but also between ethnoscientific and scientific biologists.

Theorisation of Folk Biological Classification

Descriptively orientated ethnoscientific studies gave way to more theoretically inclined cognitive research during the 1970s as more investigators became interested in exploring the connections among language, cultural representations, and cognitive processes (Casson 1981; D'Andrade 1995). Paradoxically the study of the relationships between human groups and their organic environments quickly emerged as a cutting edge of this cognitive revolution within anthropology. Whereas earlier studies of ethnobotany or ethnozoology focused on describing the economic or cultural contexts of people's knowledge and use of plants or animals, the primary interest of the field christened as ethnobiology, or folk biology, was in discovering the basic perceptual, cognitive and linguistic underpinnings of the folk (i.e. non-scientific) classification of living things (Bulmer 1970, 1974; Berlin 1973, 1976, 1992; Berlin at al. 1973, 1974; Hunn 1975, 1976, 1977, 1982; Hays 1976, 1982; Dougherty 1978; Randall 1976; Brown 1977, 1979, 1984; Randall and Hunn 1984; Ellen 1979; 1986; Atran

1985, 1990; Boster et al. 1986). Ethnobiology is an interdisciplinary mode of inquiry that incorporates theory, method and data from several different disciplines, including: field biology, biosystematics, cultural anthropology (including ethnoscientific methods), linguistics, cognitive psychology, and logic theory. Study techniques include the collection of voucher specimens (especially plants, birds, reptiles, and insects) in the field, the identification of scientific names by taxonomic specialists, the systematic recording of local names, uses and other cultural significances, the definition of semantic content and structure within and between categories, the exploration of perceptual stimulus recognition, the experimental testing of taxonomic grouping/splitting behaviour as well as category-based reasoning, and the modelling of categorical relationships by means of diagrammatical or quasi-mathematical expressions.

While the growth of this specialised interdisciplinary field has been marked by minute and comprehensive ethnographic descriptions of the knowledge and use of natural organisms by numerous peoples, the main thrust of this work has been comparative and theoretical: to develop a theory of the psychological and biological bases of folk biological classification, their universality and evolution. Much of the credit for establishing this theoretical development should go to Brent Berlin and his collaborators who carried out detailed field studies of Tzeltal (Mexico) ethnobotany and Aguaruna and Huambisa (Peru) ethnobotany and ethnozoology. Comparing their data with other studies, they went on to propose several general principles (i.e. universal tendencies) of classification and nomenclature in folk biology (Berlin et al. 1973; 1974). In the decades following this theoretical breakthrough, many high quality ethnobiological investigations were performed among diverse traditional peoples throughout the world, including many by Berlin's doctoral students, which created a rich empirical database for comparative analysis. This accumulated evidence is reviewed by Berlin in his book *Ethnobiological Classification* (1992), in which he sets out to define and defend a number of structural and substantive typological regularities which are purported to be found in all ethnobiological classification systems. The key tenets can be very briefly summarised as follows: (1) a large but finite subset of the locally present flora and fauna are recognised and named as distinct taxa and this subset is comprised of the most biologically distinctive species as determined by factors such as phylogenetic uniqueness, relative size, prevalence, and ease of observation; (2) the general purpose classification of natural organisms is based on observable morphological and behavioural affinities and is independent of cultural significance; (3) the classification system is organised as a shallow taxonomy consisting of a few (4-6) hierarchically ordered ranks; (4) taxa belonging to the same rank exhibit similar degrees of internal variation/external separation from each other, and thus the concept of rank is conceived as comparably-sized perceptual gaps that really exist in nature; (5) taxa of folk generic rank are by far the most numerous (upper limit of 500-600), the first ones learned by children, and the most quickly and effortlessly recognisable by virtue of their unitary configurational (i.e. gestalt) pattern, and thus are considered to comprise the core of the classification system; (6) generic and specific taxa exhibit a graded internal structure characterised by a central prototype member and one or more peripheral members; and (7) the lexical structure of names given to groups of living organisms, consisting of primary (simple, productive, unproductive) or secondary (i.e. binomial) lexemes, is closely tied to the rank of the group. Such regularities, it is argued, support the notion that there exists a panhuman cognitive disposition for recognising and organising the complex natural diversity presented by the living world. While Berlin's theory suggests that the universal features of ethnobiological classification are at least partly determined by cognitive capacities that are an innate property of the human mind function, he seems to place more emphasis on the imposition of 'nature's basic plan', by which he refers to real discontinuities (i.e. well-defined clusters of plants and animals) in the natural world that simply cannot be ignored.

The identification of cross-cultural regularities and elaboration of theoretical models of ethnobiological classification, among other developments, was instrumental in overturning the dominant Boasian concept of local culture as rela-tivistic, historic particularistic entity. But in addition to making a notable contribution to the scientific understanding of anthropology, ethnobiological research has advanced the anthropological understanding of science in the sense of revealing the deep affinities between folk biological classification and western systematics, the science of biological classification. Such affinities encompass the sharing of formal-structural properties, such as taxonomic organisation, proto-type specimens and binomial nomenclature, as well as substantive correspon-dences in terms of the delineation of the same groups or clusters of organisms and the recognition of the same pattern of resemblance among organisms (Berlin et al. 1974; Hunn 1975; Berlin et al. 1981; Boster et al. 1986; Boster 1987). The discovery of these correspondences has led to a number of interest-ing conclusions regarding the biological and psychological origins of the human classification of nature. For biologists, the fairly close mapping of core ethnobi-ological taxa (usually folk generics) onto Linnaean species is cited as evidence of the objective reality, discreteness, and evolutionary stability of biological species (Gould 1979; cf. Diamond 1966).[2] At the same time, the finding of striking similarities in judgments of biological content and structure across different cul-tural and ecological systems as well as between ethnoscientific and scientific knowledge traditions has induced the hypothesis that biological classification is rooted in an innate, species-specific, hard-wired, mental modular faculty, much like first language learning (Atran 1990; 1998; Hirschfeld and Gelman 1994; Pinker 1994; Boster 1996; Hunn 2002). This idea began to take shape follow-ing Scott Atran's (1990) provocative analysis of the development of natural his-tory and later scientific taxonomic studies in which he argues that scientific

biosystematics share the same cognitive foundations as folk biological classification. Atran points out that scientific taxa such as families, genera and even
species are not entirely natural categories. Their genesis derives more from the
logic imposed by common-sense, which he defines as the universal, spontaneous, domain-specific cognitive schema employed in the apprehension of living kinds, rather than from modern evolutionary theory.

Theoretical cognitive ethnobiological research has mostly been conducted by
anthropologists in collaboration with botanists or zoologists, or, more recently,
by cognitive psychologists and anthropologists either working together or
informed by each others' research, with a highly specialised academic audience
in mind. However, similar to the phase that preceded it, a collateral outcome of
this work has been to raise the stock of IK in the broader public opinion in that
it has provided scientific credibility to the notion that non-western knowledge
of the biological environment is characterised by systematic organisation,
remarkable attention to detail, and empirical accuracy. Nevertheless, this phase
of research has also been punctuated by sharp criticisms of the dominant theoretical, ethnographic, and methodological tendencies of the field which, critics
charge, have led to biased and distorted representations of such knowledge. The
overriding concern for demonstrating perceptual and cognitive universals and
the tightly controlled format for data elicitation have forced the artificial
abstraction and isolation of rigidly formalised taxonomies out of the flow and
flux of the dynamic socio-cultural and material contexts, which also provide
structure and meaning to classificatory behaviour (Ellen 1986). Such distortion
has led to the privileging of shared properties across cultures over variation
between and within cultures, individual cognitive processes over collective symbolic representations, referential/mundane over symbolic/ritual meanings, gen-
eral-purpose over special-purpose classifications, and hierarchical over
non-hierarchical (i.e. cross-cutting, graded) types of categorical relationship. By
contrast, alternative relativist approaches, such as Eugene Hunn's (1982, 1990)
methodological proposal for recording the "activity signatures" of folk biological
taxa or Roy Ellen's (1986, 1993) concept of "prehension", put more weight on
the thick and textured ethnographic description of the multiple local significances of many taxa, the social and material situations in which they are
expressed, the pragmatic or communicative goals which stimulate their usage,
and the different social actors that know and convey them – i.e. a more holistic
and experientially authentic account. The case for a relativistic, contextualised
account of classification is well exemplified by Ralph Bulmer's (1967) classic
explanation of why the cassowary is not classified as a bird by the Kalam of New
Guinea. Bulmer shows that in order to understand why cassowaries (as well as
dogs and pigs) hold a special taxonomic status for this group, it is not enough
to look at morphological and behavioural characters. One must also consider the
special relationship of those animals to people in Kalam social and cosmological

thought, such as how, when, and by whom they are hunted, how they are used, and how their hunting and use are ritually regulated.

Another key debate has pitted intellectualist against utilitarian explanations of the prolific classification abilities of folk peoples. The former, which amounts to a form of psychological reductionism, holds that people are motivated by an instinctual and unconscious intellectual drive to recognise, categorise and name large numbers of plants and animals, many of them without any apparent use or cultural significance, whereas the latter, which amounts to a functionalist interpretation, contends that no group discriminates all of the biological organisms in their surrounding habitat and a truly exhaustive examination of the (direct or indirect) use- or avoidance-value of this subset would find that the selection process was mostly determined by utilitarian or adaptive criteria. This disagreement has faded from active academic discussions without any clear resolution, since the intellectualists were able to identify taxa with no known significance among the groups they studied while the utilitarians could point to salient species which their informants consistently fail to discriminate. However, this exchange served to cast a spotlight on the issue of the adaptive significance of ethnobiological classifications. If the cognitive faculty for classifying the natural world was selected for and persists under evolutionary pressure throughout the entire human species, then what adaptive function(s) does it perform? Yet most ethnobiological research was focused inwardly on the relationship between classification and the human mind (or thought process) rather than outwardly on the relationship between classification and the environment per se (or ecological interaction). Even though it was sometimes noted in passing that classification constitutes a prior step or necessary precondition for effective interaction, the prevailing theoretical agenda mostly excluded the question of how cognition is related to adaptive behaviour. This gap has stimulated proposals to consider more seriously the operational influence of classification on resource procurement and management behaviours and, by extension, on the flow of energy, matter and information within human-occupied ecosystems (cf. Ellen 1982). The related problem of adaptive change in ethnobiological classification and nomenclature and the cultural or environmental factors which cause or condition it is another neglected topic, with the exception of very general and unilineal evolutionary reconstructions (Berlin 1973; Brown 1977, 1979; Dougherty 1978).

Modelling the Relationship Between Knowledge and Behaviour

While ethnoscientific and ethnobiological research were duly recognised as raising the standards of ethnography and cognitive theory respectively, they also drew criticism from cultural ecologists and others, who argued that structural ethnosemantic treatments of folk classifications failed to address the questions of (1) why some taxa are selected for recognition while other potential categories were not; (2) the material effect of such knowledge on ecological behaviours and adaptive processes (Vayda and Rappaport 1968; Harris 1974; Keesing 1974; Hunn 1982; Benfer 1989; Nazarea 1999). In contradistinction, the method of cultural ecology was faulted for being inadequate for studying the adaptive patterns of modern day societies whose dependence on the local environment is mediated or complicated by their insertion in larger social, political, economic, and institutional contexts, who are characterised by considerable socio-economic stratification and behavioural variation within populations, and who are experiencing phases of rapid social and technological transformation (Netting 1974; Bennett 1976). In the wake of these countervailing reviews, more attention was given to bridging the gaps between cognitive and behavioural approaches, individual and collective behavioural adjustments, and short versus long-term adaptive processes. Accordingly, some researchers attempted to reconcile cognition with behaviour by developing testable models of the mental operations by which, it may be inferred, local perceptions and understandings get translated into patterned activity. The key theoretical task of this phase has been to chart the causal chain linking abstract cognitive representations with concrete physical movements, cerebral with embodied activity.

The body of literature in which the relationship between IK and adaptive ecological behaviour is explored is somewhat diffuse and heterogeneous, but here I refer mainly to those works that fall under the rubric of decision-making (also known as rational choice) models, especially of peasant farmers. A number of source materials spanning the disciplines of anthropology, rural sociology, economics, mathematics, and game theory can be identified as contributing directly to the development of decision-making models. Limiting this discussion to those provided by anthropologists, the first set concerns efforts to integrate formalist notions of economic behaviour (i.e. individual cost-benefit maximization) with substantivist models of economic processes (institutional provision of goods and services) to make better models of economic production strategies (Cook 1973; Orlove 1977; Gudeman 1978). Second is John Bennett's (1969) comparative study of the adaptive strategies (short-term adjustments) and adaptive processes (long-term changes) of different segments of a rural society in Saskatchewan, Canada. Bennett shows the complex interplay of environmental, economic, and social factors as different actors attempt to resolve problems and manipulate their fortunes, weigh options, and take decisions in their pursuit of multiple objectives. Third, William Geoghegan (1970) and Alan Johnson (1974) carried out separate empirical tests of the correspondence between expressed ethnoscientific categories and rules on one hand and observed behavioural alternatives on the other in regards to residential choices and crop planting practices respectively. Both studies found a fairly high correlation between the expected behaviour predicted from the category or rule and actual practices.

Building on these precedents, a number of researchers sought to investigate how farmers go about processing environmental information and making decisions, especially in the context of agricultural development, as they respond to the challenges of new technology, shifting market forces, governmental policies, political movements, changing environmental conditions, population growth, etcetera (Cancian 1972; Dewalt 1975, 1979; Anderson et al. 1977; Barlett 1977, 1980a, 1980b, 1982; Gladwin 1979a, 1979b; Roumasset et al. 1979). Under these circumstances, farmers must confront, capture and act upon information coming not only from the natural environment but also from the social-political-economic milieus in which their activities take place. The general focus is on how farmers choose between alternative strategies with respect to primary production, for example: selection of crop/livestock types, mixes and rotations; adoption/non-adoption of new varieties; seed handling; cultivation timing and technique; application of fertilizers and pesticides; plot cultivation, fallowing or abandonment; subsistence farming versus cash cropping versus wage labour; sharecropping arrangements; hired versus family labour; purchase and use of machinery; credit versus cash financing; etcetera. The typical research design often encompasses a mix of emic and etic types of data. For example, structured and semi-structured interview formats record farmers' knowledge of folk categories of landscape units and features, practical knowledge of crop/livestock species and their growing habits, soils, pests and diseases, weather patterns and customary cultivation practices; open-ended queries or questionnaires designed to elicit verbal statements and judgments about alternative production strategies and their associated limitations and opportunities; and informal conversations touching on any technical, social, personal, or institutional aspect of farming practice (e.g. crop experimentation, market experiences, family situation, opinion of development programmes or crop insurance). At the same time, etic data is collected through household censuses, socio-economic surveys, land use mapping, soil analysis, crop measurements, labour time sampling, cost analysis, and description of institutional actors and factors. The key variables found to affect decisions, such as land availability and tenure, labour resources and costs, capital, transportation, risk, yield, profits, consumption needs, family size, information uncertainty and others, are then analysed and incorporated into a schematic model, often depicted in the form of decision matrices, flow-charts, or tree diagrams. Finally, the model may be compared and tested against observations of actual performance in order to assess its predictive power. Much emphasis has been placed on developing models that are capable of representing the decision strategies of individuals (i.e. at the household level), rather than simply normative accounts, by identifying the key variables (e.g. altitude of landholdings, social class, number of dependents, etcetera) that correlate statistically with divergent patterns of choice-making. This attention to individual detail has helped to illuminate not only how factual and procedural knowledge is effectively linked to coping behaviour in the short-term, but also what environmental factors cause or condition local diversity of choice, how such diversity can lead to more marked changes and divergences over time, and therefore why knowledge is directly implicated in adaptive behaviour in an evolutionary (i.e. long-term) sense.

While some approaches have inferred decision processes through the statistical analysis of behavioural outcomes or by using mathematical tools borrowed from microeconomics (e.g. production function, internal rate of return, linear programming), some authors have explicitly attempted to produce more psychologically realistic, or natural, decision models that supposedly follow more closely what environmental information farmers are taking into consideration and the stepwise elimination process that leads to final choices (Gladwin 1979b, 1980; Gladwin and Murtaugh 1980; see also Quinn 1978). Although such emic-based models are intended to represent the rational decision procedures specific to local ethnographic situations, some generalised conclusions have also come out of this work. For example, farmers often make unconscious, non-verbalised distinctions in regards to environmental constraints and framing a sense of their situation before moving on to a more conscious stage involving the deliberate pondering of production choices. Another finding is that farmers tend to make deterministic, rather than probabilistic, logical assessments, through the use of traditionally learned scripts, heuristics, or rules of thumb (i.e. simplifying procedures), to tell them what to do.

The most recent IK decision-making models draw from the insights of artificial intelligence research in using so-called 'expert systems', also referred to as 'knowledge based' systems (Benfer 1989; Guillet 1989a, 1989b; Furbee 1989; Benfer et al. 1991; Schoenhoff 1993). An expert system (ES) is a symbolic-reasoning computer software programme that is designed to mimic human decision-making in a restricted domain of knowledge, such as soil management or health care choices (Guillet 1989b: 57). Rule-based ES consists of a knowledge base of domain-specific facts and procedures, and an inference engine of fixed procedures for manipulating the facts and rules, such as a chained series of 'if...then ...', operations. Proponents of ES tout several advantages of this approach over other decision-making models: (1) it enables more complex and information packed models; (2) the machine-generated model can be presented to local consultants for their evaluation in the field, thus permitting validation, refinement, and translation into an appropriate language and then used to advise local actors on management practices; (3) by requiring the formalisation of usually tacit and implicit procedural knowledge in explicit rule-based form it enhances knowledge capture; (4) through the use of confidence factors (i.e. degree of confidence that a conclusion is valid) it is able to handle incomplete or ambiguous information more adequately; (5) by incorporating variables that may account for individual variation, it is able to provide multiple decision pathways and thus explain how and why different results may be arrived at although starting from the same knowledge base; and (6) used in combination with computer simulation methods, in which production rules are varied and manipulated, it can be directed towards the creation of more dynamic models in anticipation of future changes in circumstances and strategies (Guillet 1989b; Benfer 1989).

Besides the rational choice models applied mainly to the study of agricultural decision-making, there have also been some other notable attempts to elaborate conceptual frameworks for understanding the relationship between environmental cognition and behaviour which may be relevant for agricultural and non-agricultural societies. Ellen (1978, 1982) proposes a generative scheme according to which the end states of patterned sets of ecological relationships (e.g. settlement patterns, garden site selection) are traced back through the formative scheduling sequences, thus revealing how cultural rules interact with ecological givens to generate actual behaviour. Hunn (1989) distinguishes between two basic kinds of knowledge: image – 'cultural information organised by similarity' (models of); and plan – 'cultural information organised by contiguity' (models for). He shows how the two can be integrated through an exhaustive elicitation and analysis of the 'activity signatures' of environmental taxa, referring to the total set of predicated statements containing the taxa. Victor Toledo (1992, 2002) advocates ethnoecology as an integrative, interdisciplinary approach to the study of the process of human appropriation of nature, in which the total complex of *kosmos* (the belief system or cosmovision), *corpus* (the whole repertory of knowledge or cognitive systems), and *praxis* (the set of practices as executed by the producer) are carefully observed and recorded. He argues that the articulation of interpretation (kosmos and corpus) and action (*praxis*) can be revealed by a thorough investigation of the structural (ethnotaxonomies), dynamic (patterns and processes), relational (linkages among natural elements or events), and utilitarian (practical uses) dimensions of knowledge about natural resources. While these approaches lack the methodological rigour characteristic of the rational choice school, a less formalistic or structured research design would permit the construction of models which are more flexible, more holistic, less observer-biased, and more valid empirically (Johnson 1980).

It might be said that the focus of this phase of IK research has been equally academic and applied, theoretical and practical. Besides contributing to a more holistic emic-etic approach to the undertaking of ecological anthropological research, it offers advisory and communicative enhancements to applied development work by making explicit what is tacit or unconscious, and often nonverbalised, knowledge, thus facilitating understanding of the vast complexity of the natural decision-making processes employed by local populations. It also serves to point out key differences in farmers' versus agronomists' perceptions and understandings of production issues. Meanwhile the research, design, testing and redesign of expert system computer models in folk contexts has also begun to have a positive impact on more general applications in the artificial intelligence field, such as contributing towards the development of computerised knowledge acquisition and questioning the universality of western modes of reasoning (Read and Behrens 1989). One of the key conceptual advances achieved during this phase was in recognising and representing IK as a dynamic process instead of a static structure. However, this process is entirely conceived in cognitive psychology terms. That is, IK in most decision-making perspectives is presented as a rather complex formal calculus residing in the head of a hypothetical individual which motivates him or her to react to a particular stimulus with a specific course of action. This approach may be criticised for being overly formal and rational, and for ignoring the social psychology of decision making. Social psychology contends that perception, decisions and actions are structured at supra-individual levels of integration and therefore it is necessary to take into account the social process by which actors observe, communicate, negotiate and acquire different kinds of information through interaction with other community members. Thus information and technology transmission may be explained as much by conformist bias (following what the majority do) and prestige bias (adopting practices associated with successful actors) as much as by performance or payoff information (Henrich 2001; Stone 2004).

The Significance of Indigenous Knowledge for Sustainable Development and Conservation

The agricultural decision-making research described above helped to dispel the myths of peasant farmer irrationality and the impracticality of peasant knowledge in the face of economic and technological modernisation. Moreover, by revealing why individuals choose to adopt or forgo new technologies or managerial strategies and why individuals may respond differently to the same set of global conditions it also implied that IK and IK research have a positive role to play in rural development schemes, for example facilitating communication between outside experts and local practitioners. Yet the focus on farmers as economising, though not necessarily optimising, actors and knowledge as rational logic did not call into question the conventional model of development, built on the core propositions of imported technology transfer and export market expansion, which had dominated the international development scene since the close of the Second World War. However, by the end of the 1970s a radical shift in rural development philosophy was taking hold that highlighted indigenous technical knowledge (ITK) as an essential ingredient for social and economic growth in third world settings. This sea change of policy direction was forced by the growing consensus that the top-down technocratic and economistic approach to development had failed to alleviate the widespread problems of food shortage and poverty, despite supposed success stories like the green revolution, and in some cases might be exacerbating them. This, in turn, led to the loss of confidence in the scientific foundations that supported it. Paul Richards (1985) provides a brilliant analysis of the 'systematic failure' of development policies in colonial Africa, tracing their downfall to the fallacy of scientific universalist thinking that certain principles are true for all times and places and the misplaced pursuit of environmental management problems at an overly abstracted and generalised level. He argues that development strategies in ecologically diverse tropical regions are better guided by the doctrine of ecological particularism – the belief that many environmental problems are localised and specific, thus require local, ecologically particular, responses. This is precisely the guiding principle embodied in many traditional agricultural systems. Furthermore, Richards, along with others (Box 1987; Rhoades 1989), effectively debunks the conventional image of indigenous farmers as being incapable of independent experimentation and innovation.

Western science and technology had by no means been eliminated from development initiatives, but an alternative, and in some ways rival, paradigm began to take shape and win over advocates from within and without the development establishment. This paradigm has been labelled variously as farmer-system, farmer first, farmer-back-to-farmer, populist, participatory or agro-ecological development, and, as the names suggest, it features the local farmer and his or her traditional farming knowledge and practices as the most sensible starting points for intervention (Brokensha et al. 1980; Gliessman 1981; Rhoades and Booth 1982; Chambers 1983; Norgaard 1984; Altieri 1987; Chambers et al. 1989; Farrington and Martin 1987; Warren et al. 1989; Moock and Rhoades 1992; Dewalt 1994; Sillitoe 1998; Warren et al. 1995). Several key principles define this approach: (1) sustainability – achieving long term growth by balancing technological, economic, ecological, and social concerns; (2) appropriate technology – adopting fragmented and locally adapted, usually low input, energy-efficient, diversity-maintaining native technologies which are incrementally modified; (3) bottom-up planning – starting with the knowledge, problems, analysis and priorities of farmers themselves; aware that the diversity of situations and constraints requires diverse, locally specific solutions; (4) local participation – seeking to involve the active participation of local farmers in all phases of the R and D process; and (5) dialogue – fomenting dialogue between development agent and local farmers. With increasing emphasis placed on the intellectual contributions of traditional farmers to new technology generation and implementation, technical IK (or ITK) came to be seen as an undervalued resource that needed to be studied, understood, and incorporated into formal research, development, and extension practice. This led to a surge of IK research conducted mainly by scientists employed by international and national agricultural research centres and development agencies (Brokensha et al. 1980; Biggs 1988; Chambers et al. 1989; Warren et al. 1989;

Moock and Rhoades 1992; Pottier 1993; Warren et al. 1995; see also various issues of Indigenous Knowledge and Development Monitor). An important component of this work has been the creation of specialised IK libraries and databases where the data and results produced in numerous studies are compiled, stored, and disseminated as well as organisational structures dedicated to this task, such as the U.S.-based Center for Indigenous Knowledge for Agricultural and Rural Development (CIKARD), Holland-based Leiden Ethnosystems and Development Programme (LEAD), Canada-based International Development Research Centre (IDRC), among others (Warren 2001). Another measure of success can be found in the extent to which it has penetrated top-down institutions like the World Bank, which in 1998 launched the Indigenous Knowledge for Development Programme in its African department. Based on the idea that IK constitutes the key element of the social capital of the poor and is the main asset they control, the purpose of the programme is 'to leverage global and local knowledge systems to adapt the design of Bank-supported projects and programmes to local conditions' (Gorjestani 2000). A participatory approach has also had a major impact on the field of environmental conservation, where governmental agencies and nongovernmental organisations have embraced the idea of treating indigenous and local peoples as crucial partners in their efforts to preserve natural ecosystems and to promote the sustainable use of natural resources. This can be seen in the proliferation during the past couple of decades of people-inclusive, use-based projects, especially in tropical countries, as an alternative to people-exclusive parks and protected areas (e.g. the Biodiversity Support Program's Integrated Conservation and Development Project initiative, Brown and Wyckoff-Baird 1995). In support of this approach, some analysts have advised that the IK of biodiversity and ecological relationships and indigenous resource management skills constitute valuable tools for conservation planning, implementation, and monitoring, and therefore recommend that these be documented and incorporated into such programmes (Posey et al. 1984; Plotkin and Famolare 1992; Moran 1993; Clay 1988; Posey 1999).

Under the banner of a populist perspective, IK is portrayed as dynamic, experimental, innovative, adaptive, intelligent (but not perfect), locally-specific, and therefore a vital component of development strategy. However, this position is also open to embracing the merits of scientific research and in fact advocates that folk and scientific knowledge be treated as complementary resources which are most effectively used in tandem. In a similar vein, the participatory component sees western scientists and local farmers ideally as mutually dependent collaborators, both sides actively participating in the planning, research, implementation, and monitoring phases. The team approach described here would seem to imply the blurring of the distinction between western scientist and ethnoscientist, between scientific and indigenous knowledge, in the context of agricultural innovation research. Yet experienced observers have confided that such merger of minds actually entails a 'false closeness' because western science is held up as the standard bearer against which the effectiveness of IK is judged, and because the scientist enjoys greater clout, resources and prestige, hence the partnership is not equal (Fairhead 1993; cf. Scoones and Thompson 1994; Agrawal 1995). Nevertheless, the ideal of balanced and equitable collaboration defines the spirit, if not always the practice, of participatory research (Sillitoe 2002b).

This phase of IK research is marked by an applied orientation, the overall objective being to achieve sustainable development through the design and implementation of technologically appropriate, ecologically harmonious, economically viable, and socially equitable development schemes. The research itself is interdisciplinary and carried out by researchers from diverse academic backgrounds. The ideal setup is to work in teams of specialists composed minimally of a social scientist (e.g. an anthropologist or a rural sociologist), a biologist or agronomist, and an economist. A notable feature is the apparent lack of concern for theory building. Rather the research design addresses the practical objectives of basic ethnographic and ecological description, technology assessment through scientific experimentation (both on- and off-site), communication of technological options to local farmers, ideally through an iterative process, managed implementation of new technologies, and evaluation of the results (with the farmer being the final judge). However, certain theoretical-epistemological assumptions are implicit in much of this research, including a positivist, hard-systems approach focusing on discrete elements and structural integration. Thus IK is viewed as a stock of uniform, systematic, site-specific information, open to incorporating external knowledge elements, potentially fractionable and transferable to non-native contexts, and legitimated by scientific verification (cf. Scoones and Thompson 1994).

This mode of representation has of course drawn its fair share of criticism, especially from post-structuralist quarters (e.g. Hobart 1993). For example, the general systems framework depicts knowledge as an abstract, formally constituted, internally coherent entity that can be logically separated from its particular social, economic, political, and ecological contexts. This, in turn, leads to several dubious, and seemingly contradictory, assumptions regarding knowledge documentation, evaluation, and use. On one hand, it has compelled an overemphasis on discovering or falsely attributing the one-to-one knowledge counterpart (or 'hidden reason') behind each observed practice, which of course implies a questionable conflation of knowledge and practice (Fairhead 1993). Richards (1993) challenges the notion that cultivation practices reflect the simple application of a predetermined, fixed, and abstractly conceived stock of knowledge, rather they are improvised and adjusted to fit momentary circumstances which may be dictated by ongoing observations of weather patterns, crop performance, and so on (see also Sillitoe 1996). On the other hand, the imaginary dissection of IK into so-called 'technical' and 'non-technical' sectors serves as a sleight of hand by which knowledge itself can be severed from culturally situated practice and belief. This severance makes it accessible for documentation, codification, and *ex situ* preservation in scientific databases with an eye towards isolating specific 'technical' elements of it and transporting them to other settings. Critics charge that if the broader social, political, religious, aesthetic, moral and other dimensions are ignored or eliminated, the resulting extracted knowledge base is so transformed and distorted as to have little value or meaning (Fairhead 1993; Agrawal 1995, 2002; Ellen and Harris 2000; cf. Warren et al. 1995). The results of much IK research, especially those involving rapid appraisal techniques, have been questioned by members of the anthropological establishment on the grounds that adequate understanding of the practices and the motives behind them, much less the ability to communicate effectively between scientists and locals, cannot be achieved over the short term. The conclusion is that anthropologists with long-term commitments to their study communities need to take on a greater role in applied research and development projects (Hobart 1993; Sillitoe 1998, 2002a; Ellen 2002).

Debates about the Valuation, Exploitation, and Compensation of IK

During the 1980s, growing concerns over environmental degradation along with the advancement of biotechnology would add even greater value to IK and usher in a new phase of rhetorical representation and debate. The rise in value was fuelled by the combination of diminishing supply of biological resources, due to the advancing pace of tropical deforestation, agricultural modernisation and attendant loss of biodiversity, and increased demand as a result of the greater capacity to identify, manipulate and utilise genetic material (Brush 1993). A number of prominent ethnobotanists and pharmacologists began to extol the virtues of ethnobiological and agro-ecological knowledge for natural product development in the sense of providing leads for the elaboration of new foods, condiments, medicines, cosmetics, pesticides, fibres, crop germplasm, etcetera (Elisabetsky 1986; Schultes 1988, 1992, 1994a, 1994b; Plotkin 1988; Soejarto and Farnsworth 1989; Schultes and Raffauf 1990; Balick 1990; Cox and Balick 1994; Balick et al. 1996). Richard Evans Schultes, for example, proclaimed that the Amazon forest constitutes 'an untapped emporium of germplasm for new economic plants (1980: 259)' and proposed that indigenous people be regarded as 'a kind of rapid-assessment team already on the ground, which could help to locate the most promising plants for chemical and pharmacological evaluation' (1994: 24). Schultes's former student, Mark Plotkin, asserted that there is an urgent need to document disappearing ethnobotanical knowledge of tropical forest peoples in order to avert a 'serious economic and scientific loss for mankind' (1988: 87). An explicit motivation behind these arguments was to capture and harness the enormous power of international capital and industry for the service of achieving conservation objectives. Both the species-rich forests and the biocultural integrity of indigenous forest peoples are increasingly eroded and endangered by predatory forms of development. By contrast, biotech-based development depends on the survival and use of living organisms and information about them, which means that safeguarding the forests and salvaging the traditional knowledge and practices of its native inhabitants will (at least potentially) produce more material benefit than by destroying them (cf. Peters et al. 1989). A research agenda aimed at the expanded collection and documentation of biological resources and economic ethnobiological knowledge was thus defined, which theoretically would produce a win-win outcome of environmental conservation, protection of cultural diversity, and economic growth.

This agenda was embraced by the agricultural seed and pharmaceutical industries which found IK to be a valuable tool for bioprospecting, the search for commercially valuable genes and chemical compounds in biological organisms. Folk crop varieties developed and maintained over long time periods by local farmers were already an important component of global crop genetic resources. Large numbers of accessions were stored in the extensive network of international and national gene banks and these were made freely available to both local farmers and industrial plant breeders (Brush 1996; Cleveland and Murray 1997). By the 1980s, more emphasis was placed on the *in situ* conservation of folk varieties through the study and encouragement of farmers' perception, selection, propagation and utilisation of biodiversity within traditional agroecosystems (Altieri and Merrick 1987; Oldfield and Alcorn 1987; Brush 1991; Moock and Rhoades 1992; Cleveland et al. 1994). Justifications for this approach included the need to maintain supplies of crop genetic diversity in the face of environmental change and to provide specific information about folk varieties as well as their wild and weedy relatives that can be used as raw material for breeding modern commercial varieties (MVs). With the continued expansion of industrially produced MVs (hybrids, transgenics) around the world, the traditional cultivars therefore constitute a vital resource for food supply as well as agricultural commerce (Cleveland and Murray 1997).

Pharmaceutical applications of IK deal mainly with the ethnomedical uses of wild plant species. The significance of culturally-specific ethnopharmacopoeias for commercial drug discovery was hinted at by the large number of prescription drugs sold worldwide containing active compounds derived from plants and the fact that there is a high correlation between the therapeutic uses of such plants in traditional medicine and medical science (Farnsworth 1988). Accordingly, some researchers argued that ethnographic-directed investigations could be used to improve the time and cost efficiency of screening plants for bioactivity (Balick 1990; Cox 1990; Daly 1992; King 1992). Putting this logic into practice, IK-based bioprospecting research mushroomed during the late 1980s and 1990s, financed by private corporations or public institutions having direct ties (i.e. sell-

ing patent rights) to industry, and carried out by scientists affiliated with botanical gardens, universities, or research institutes located in the donor or recipient
countries.[3] The research chain involved here is complex and costly and requires a
disciplinary division of labour, whereby anthropologists or ethnobotanists consult with native healers to document the medicinal plant taxa, preparations and
treatments; botanists collect the plant specimens and identify the species;
chemists/pharmacologists perform the bioassays and extract or synthesise the
active compounds; and medical doctors oversee the clinical trials. Another screening strategy has been to comb the published literature on ethnopharmacology for
information about promising medicinal species. However, the lofty expectations
initially attached to ethnodirected bioprospecting would not last very long, due
partly to the lack of big commercial 'hits' after a decade of intensive search and
improvements in random screening techniques (*The Economist* 1999), but more
importantly because of the controversy generated over the economic, ethical and
legal implications of exploiting biodiversity and IK for commercial purposes.

The purpose and practice of bioprospecting was severely criticized for com-
mitting economic injustice against the nations that contain a large portion of the
biodiversity and the communities that possess information about it. Darrell Posey
(1990a, 1999) wrote that the biotechnology industry has 'mined' biogenetic
resources via IK for many years and returned only a miniscule proportion (less
than 0.001%) of profits to indigenous peoples. The recent frenzy of collection
replicates this exploitative habit by considering the knowledge and resources of
indigenous peoples to be 'intellectual *terra nullius*', which is to say ascribed no
value and assumed to be free for the taking. Vandana Shiva (1996) branded industrial bioprospecting as biopiracy, signifying the misappropriation or unauthorised
use of biological resources and information, and frames the discussion in geopolitical terms. For this author, bioprospecting is the modern 'high tech' equivalent
of the old colonial habit of the northern nations, which are capital-rich but bio-
diversity-poor, plundering the natural and human resources of the southern
nations, which are capital-poor but biodiversity-rich.[4] It also amounts to biological and intellectual piracy in the sense that both the genetic material and the traditional knowledge are treated as 'global commons' (i.e. open-access, free goods)
and therefore not duly compensated while, at the same time, scientific and corporate claims of invention are rewarded with patents under western-dominated
national and international property laws. If local communities and tropical
nations receive no substantial benefits from biotechnology, they would have no
incentive to preserve biodiversity or knowledge. These criticisms and others like
them effectively shifted the locus of debate from academic and business circles to
policy, legal, and advocacy forums where the focus has been on the issues of intellectual property rights (IPR), equitable benefit sharing, customary property rights,
social versus economic benefit, rights of refusal, prior informed consent, ethical
behaviour by researchers, the meaning of the term 'indigenous', and the broader

plights affecting indigenous peoples such as self-determination and defence of cultural and human rights (Cunningham 1991, 1993; Brush 1992, 1993; Kloppenburg 1991b; Swanson 1995; Brush and Stabinsky 1996; Posey and Dutfield 1996; Cleveland and Murray 1997; Moran 1999). A large part of this debate has dealt with the quandary of reconciling existing concepts and uses of IPR, built on the precepts of identifiable invention, exclusive rights over profit by private parties, direct compensation for investment and exchange, and market-determined value, with IK which is characterised by uncertain inheritance, shared use rights by collectivities, creativity through free exchange of information, and socially-determined value (Brush 1996; Posey and Dutfield 1996).

The storm generated over the protection and compensation issues and its impact on law and policy matters has shaken up the field of IK studies and altered the roles and conduct of different participants more deeply than anything else in recent years. Although the international legal framework is still evolving and no broad consensus has yet been achieved, it is precisely the dynamic and often contentious nature of this process that has opened up the field of research, policy and action to new players, including intergovernmental bodies, national governments, NGOs, indigenous organisations and local communities. The Convention on Biodiversity (CBD) has had a huge impact on policymaking at national levels, by: (1) enjoining the contracting governments to preserve traditional knowledge, of innovations and practices that are relevant to the conservation and sustainable use biodiversity; (2) recognising the sovereignty of nation-states over genetic resources and their right to regulate access to them; (3) promoting the wider application (i.e. biotechnological development) of such resources and knowledge in support of conservation goals; and (4) encouraging the equitable sharing of benefits arising from such utilisation. Guided by this precedent, many national governments in biodiversity-rich regions have enacted strict access regulations, for example, requiring researchers and bioprospectors to comply with prior informed consent and full disclosure rules and to sign benefit-sharing and technology transfer agreements with government agencies and/or local groups. This has not eliminated bioprospecting however. Instead, in some countries it has fomented partnerships among public institutions, researchers and business groups (e.g. Brazil's autochthonic medicine programme, cf. Lapa 2002), which raises questions about the fair representation of local communities' interests by distant national governments. Presently there are far more nominally 'non-profit' NGO's than profit-seeking companies working with local communities on IK-related projects, funded by private as well as public donors. One important trend in their work has been to seek to build local-level capacities for documenting, managing, using, and transmitting their own knowledge, such as through the creation of community registers and exchanges among different local experts (cf. Gupta 1997). Indigenous organisations and local communities in many places have become increasingly sensitive to the political and economic implications of scientific research and thus have asserted a much more active role in deciding and controlling who and what kind of study or applied programme is done on their lands and knowledge systems, requiring researchers/managers to sign formal agreements and accept greater local input into the study. Moreover, it is increasingly common to find communities refusing to cooperate with outside researchers and some indigenous organisations have gone so far as to declare moratoriums on all research until IPR and other outstanding matters (e.g. land claims) are resolved to their satisfaction. Important effects of the increased militancy are that preconceived research agendas are becoming less and less viable, the topics and questions of investigation are becoming more closely aligned with locally-defined problems and the data and information produced are being more controlled by the study groups.

This phase of research has emphasised the economic, and by extension the ecological and ethical, significance of IK from a world systems perspective. By placing a market value on IK, recognising property rights, and ensuring that fair compensation is paid, it is believed that environmental governance and social justice will be served. However, the act of reducing IK to a mere commodity, as a resource to be exploited, patented, or bought and sold in the global marketplace, also signifies its decontextualisation and deculturation. A divisible, particularistic, objectivistic conception of knowledge is implicit in this perspective, focusing on those discrete bits of information that stand up to external verification and so provide leads to novel and valuable genes or molecules. The scientific validity of IK is acknowledged but only to the extent that it has become an input for biotechnological scientific research. However, the finding of intercultural consistency in the therapeutic applications of particular taxonomic groups (cf. Trotter and Logan 1986) as well as the high degree of correspondence between traditional medicinal plants and commercial drugs derived from plants provides evidence that at least certain portions IK are developed through an empirical trial and error process, much like the scientific method. This debate has also exposed the close economic and political links between science and industry, undermining the pretension that ethnobiological research is a politically neutral activity, tarnishing the image of scientists as so-called disinterested truth-seekers and confusing the distinction between public and private information.

IK as a Critical Ecopolitical Discourse

Although the value of IK for the contemporary western world had become firmly established by converting it into a commodity for the agricultural development and biotechnology industries, critics of these perspectives contended that it still suffered inferior treatment as compared to scientific knowledge from a world political-economic system that did not offer sufficient compensation nor adequate legal protection for its use. Thus in the 1990s a new critique emerged that blamed the previous perspectives with failing to address the root causes of this fundamental inequality, which were thought to stem from the lesser epistemological authority accorded to unscientific types of knowledge as well as the subordinate position of the non-scientific knowledge holders in power relationships with outsiders (Agrawal 1995; Shiva 1996; Dei et al. 2000). Added to this were disenchanted assessments of the rational planning establishment's attempts to systematise and scientise – abstract, extract, evaluate, recodify and disseminate – IK to promote rural development without considering the social and political effects of this act of intellectual conquest (Thrupp 1989a, 1989b; Hobart 1993; Agrawal 1995; 2002; Escobar 1995). Meanwhile many of the marginalised and oppressed peoples of the Third and Fourth Worlds were also re-evaluating their own positions and attitudes towards native versus foreign knowledges in reaction to the social tensions and contradictions stirred up by cultural modernisation, market penetration and habitat degradation, a situation described by George Dei (Dei et al. 2000) as the 'crisis of knowledge' in an age of globalisation. In response to perceived threats coming from the outside, some local groups have questioned the authority of science-based education and development and instead expressed renewed faith in traditional beliefs, values and institutions as a means for defending their cultural identity, political independence, economic security, spiritual wellbeing, ecological integrity, and other basic rights (Dei at el. 2000; Posey 2004). Arising from these critiques, IK was recast as an eco-political discourse in the sense of constituting a totality of language, meaning and agency (i.e. intentional actions) which structures and (re)produces peoples' relationships to each other and to nature. A recurrent theme of the discursive orientation is the revalidation of IK vis-à-vis global science especially in regards to the projects of environmental conservation and sustainable development. This phase is heavily influenced by the postmodernist and poststructuralist intellectual paradigms and is largely concerned with the themes of: knowledge pluralism (there are many systems of knowledge, science being one of them), the cultural construction of knowledge (knowledge of the world is the product of specific cultural and historical contexts), the power relations of knowledge (e.g. hegemonic, subordinate, resistant), textual representations (e.g. valid/non-valid, rational/irrational), polyvocality (expression of different points of view), and cultural critique (by exposing hidden assumptions and forcing self-reflection).

Two general tendencies in the treatment of IK from a discursive point of view can be identified, constructive and deconstructive. Constructive treatments involve the articulation of images of IK as rhetorical devices and conceptual propositions in environmental discourses that are intended to promote social and political change. Such representations have been routinely employed, in literature and speech, by different factions of the radical environmentalist movement (Shiva 1988; Callicott 1989; Mander 1991; Durning 1992; Merchant 1992; Drengson 1995), and by indigenous rights advocates (cf. Posey 1999: 555-601). The master narrative appearing in these accounts is the 'ecologically noble savage', according to which indigenous people are stereotyped as wise and gentle stewards of nature who live(d) in ecological and spiritual balance with their environment prior to the disrupting impact of western industrialism. Critics point out that this stereotype depends on oversimplification and distortion of a diverse and complex indigenous cultural panorama, and more closely resembles western ideas and fantasies (Brosius 1997; Grande 1999; Whelan 1999). Nevertheless, this idea was popularised during the 1970s and 1980s, asserting that supporting the land rights of indigenous peoples is fully compatible with environmental justice, thereby seemingly uniting the goals of the environmentalist and indigenous rights movements (Bunyard 1989; Perrett 1998). However, this alliance appears to be unravelling in recent years due to a clash of priorities (ecocentric versus socio-centric respectively). On one hand, the contemporary as well as historical accuracy of the notion that indigenous peoples are always and essentially conservationists came under severe questioning by ecologists (Diamond 1987; Redford 1991; Krech 1999; Whelan 1999). Consequently, many environmentalists have become sceptical about leaving conservation policy in the hands of indigenous groups, especially now that they are experiencing population growth, using machine technology and adopting consumerist habits (Redford and Stearman 1993; Soulé 1995; Perrett 1998). On the other hand, indigenous activists and their defenders continue to appropriate the ecosavage narrative but the meanings they attach to key concepts such as biodiversity, conservation and sustainable management diverge from those given by scientists: the conservation objective is often subordinated to a larger political agenda in which social justice goals (e.g. self-determination, resource rights, human rights) are the first priorities (Redford and Stearman 1993; COICA 1999; Benton and Short 1999).

Deconstructive treatments entail the analysis of the social and historical constructions of IK in particular ethnographic settings, especially in the context of conservation and development projects and experiences. Such studies examine the linkages among competing categorisations and representations of knowledge, the agencies of distinctively positioned social actors, and the prevailing contests over power, resources, identity, cultural patrimony and other goals. This approach has been increasingly employed to evaluate the (manipulative) communication, (discriminatory) assumptions and (poor) performance characteristic of many conventional technoscientific and participatory oriented development histories, and to suggest alternative engagement strategies (Kloppenburg 1991a; Hobart 1993; Escobar 1995; 1997; Apffel-Marglin and Marglin 1996; Haen 1999; Ellen et al. 2000; Sillitoe et al. 2002; Bicker et al. 2004). The perspective labelled Beyond Farmer First (BFF), which views agricultural development as an ideological and political process, provides a pertinent example (Scoones and Thompson 1994). As an applied research strategy, BFF supersedes the populist strategy by focusing attention on four main areas:

(1) analysis of difference in knowledge, according to gender, ethnicity, class, age, religion, etcetera; (2) examination of the power relationships between different social actors who have divergent, often conflicting, interests with regard to access to and control of resources; (3) exploration of new participatory approaches that would give local people more control over the research and development process; and (4) transformation of institutions and policies in the direction of greater democracy, decentralisation, and diversification. The general objective here is to achieve a socio-politically and gender differentiated type of development based on the tenets of active participation, empowerment, and poverty alleviation.

The discursive phase of IK research and writing evinces an intellectual programme that is geared overtly or covertly towards ideological criticism and socio-political activism (or advocacy). It is critical in the sense of exposing and challenging the hidden premises and truth assumptions that sustain environmental idioms, ideologies and practices. It is action oriented to the extent that it seeks to effect revolutionary change in the social, political and ecological status quo (e.g. empower the poor and underprivileged; decentralise legitimacy; break dependency, foster self-determination, restore healthy ecological relationships) (Alexiades, Chapter Three). These principles are evident in discussions of the problematic relationship between scientific and indigenous knowledge. Lori Ann Thrupp (1989a; 1989b), for example, argues that western scientific knowledge is a powerful ideological force that provides the rationality of exploitative capitalist and modernist institutions, delegitimises and displaces IK through domination of education and development policies, and appropriates and scientises particular bits of IK to further its hegemonic spread around the world (see also Agrawal 2002). She urges development agents and institutions to abandon their faith in scientific superiority and instead to recognise and appreciate the intrinsic value of IK, as seen from local people's own points of view. This type of legitimisation can be a potential source of empowerment for marginalised people, enhance their self-esteem and confidence, and lead to more effective and sustainable local-level actions.

Critical expositions of eco-political policies and discourses have advanced the study, theory and applications of IK in several ways, of which only a few can be mentioned here. Some writers (Cashman 1991; Rocheleau 1991; Fernández 1994; Mishra 1994; Simpson 1994) have called for greater attention to the gendered nature of rural people's knowledge because this division, and especially the crucial contribution made by women to the survival of their families and communities, is too often ignored by outside researchers and development agents. Such blindness and deafness towards women elicits the recommendation that special efforts be made to study and incorporate female expertise, skills and opinions in development interventions to the benefit of women as well as their communities. Arun Agrawal (1995) rejects the polar separation of IK and global science on substantive, methodological and contextual grounds, and points out that the two 'classes' of knowledge have been in intimate interaction since at least the fifteenth century. The demystification and demolition of this binary construct is considered a first step towards levelling the value judgments that denigrate IK and reforming political relationships that discriminate against indigenous peoples. The dissolution of essentialist conceptual dichotomies also paves the way for the concept of hybrid knowledges (natures/cultures), which refers to the creative synthesis of local and global, insider and outsider, traditional and modern, forms of knowledge. It is proposed that most, if not all, societies perpetually incorporate and fuse selected elements of spatially and temporally heterogeneous knowledges peculiar to their location and history, transforming the knowledges and recreating themselves in the process (Escobar 1999; Gupta 1998). The hybrid nature(s) of IK is thought to constitute a potential source of agency and empowerment for marginalised peoples in the sense of constituting a strategy for resistance to external hegemonic discourses and for alliance with alternative discourses and their corresponding social actors.

Epistemologically, this phase is broadly defined as poststructuralist, anti-positivist, anti-essentialist, relativist, constructivist and subjectivist. However, this characterization needs to be qualified by noting that strict versus constrained forms of constructivism can be distinguished (Hayles 1995; cf. Escobar 1999). According to the strict version, all descriptions or representations of the real world 'out there' are so distorted by cultural and perceptual filters that we cannot attain certain or objective knowledge about it. Therefore the study of peoples' comprehension and engagement of nature reveals more about human society and history than it does about the biophysical environment. An environmentalist critique of this position warns that if nature is nothing more than a figment of the human imagination, then it can also be argued that environmental problems are not real and no concrete actions need be taken to address them (Soulé and Lease 1995). By contrast, the constrained version recognises that everybody's understanding of the world is shaped by language, history, and social position but that the real (i.e. pre-social) world imposes certain objective limits on the accuracy and consistency of these representations and therefore some viewpoints are more/less truthful than others. This position suffers from ambiguity in drawing the line between what is subjectively constructed versus objectively real (Soulé 1995). What constraints does a politicised, constructivist approach impose on the specific understanding of IK? First and foremost, we are reminded that knowledge is power, which focuses our attention on the larger political and economic contexts, but at the expense of technical or ecological comprehension (Vayda and Walters 1999). Second, the view of nature as social construction obliges us to look at the historically-framed webs of meaning and action that constitute and transform it. At the same time, if nature has no essential, objective or pre-social status, then the knowledge of it cannot be described or assessed in terms of the criteria of empirical reliability, specificity, comparability or adaptive utility. Finally, the rejected paradigm of revamping IK systems through technological engineering, implied by the critique of science-based development, is replaced by the even more dubious faith in social engineering by political reform or revolution (Sillitoe 2002b).

Processual Perspectives of IK

The social constructivist critique of the supposed ontological and epistemological divide between global science and IK implies as corollary that neither one should be conceived as static, bounded and indifferent systems. The emphasis on interactive engagement, whether oppositional or mutualistic, shifts the investigative gaze to the dynamic (re)constitutive processes and properties of it in fragmented socio-historical contexts marked by encroaching global interconnections of people, material goods and information. However, most deconstructive studies are relatively unconcerned about the particular facts and details of particular knowledge systems and more interested in knowledge *per se* (Ellen 2002). By the mid-1990s, another group of interlocutors was voicing alarm that biological, cultural and linguistic diversities around the world were all rapidly declining, giving rise to the hypothesis that the different types of diversity are interdependent and the degenerative trends are interlocking processes (Nietschmann 1992; Harmon 1996; 2002; Nettle and Romaine 2000; Maffi 2001; 2005). At the local scale, the extinction or erosion of traditional environmental language, knowledge and practices may explain a significant degree of this linkage. Confronted with these disturbing revelations, several researchers were motivated to begin exploring the dynamic or processual aspects – creation, transmission, transformation, conservation, and loss – of IK, but this time on a more empirical footing. The core questions addressed by this work include: how it is created, what the learning process entails, who passes it on to whom, in what situations and contexts transmission occurs, why it is lost or changed, what is the social organisation of knowledge, how social relationships regulate the flow of information, how use patterns and contexts affect knowledge, and what social and ecological factors promote its conservation or extinction. This phase is quite recent, little more than a decade old, still incipient, eclectic, and has not yet coalesced into an easily recognisable body of work. Nevertheless, a process-oriented approach to IK is plainly evident in the growing number of case studies that focus on the ebb and flow, agreement and diversity, transmission and acquisition, retention and transformation of knowledge in specific groups, places and time frames. Much of this research can be conveniently grouped into the following four problem issues or themes: the social organisation of knowledge, knowledge as socially situated performance, the transmission and acquisition of knowledge, and cultural modernisation and the intergenerational retention/loss of knowledge.

(1)   Social organisation of knowledge: cognitive variation was long considered a problem for representations of cultural knowledge in general (D'Andrade 1987) and ethnobiological classification in particular (Gardner 1976, Ellen 1979), but several researchers working with traditional ecological knowledge during the last twenty years have highlighted such variation and used it as a guide map for reconstructing historical processes of knowledge change (Boster 1980, 1984, 1986; Nazarea 1995, 1997; Kempton et al. 1995; Atran 1999; Zent 1999a, 2001; Osseweijer 2000; Zent and Zent 2004). This work has advanced a processual perspective of IK by establishing that social organisation constrains and patterns knowledge distribution synchronically (according to social variables of age, gender, occupation, education, class, ethnicity, etcetera) and diachronically (by regulating the exchange and flow of information over time). To the extent that knowledge is distributed among social segments and transferred through social relationships, any changes in the surrounding physical or cultural environment that impact on social organisation will exert a collateral effect on knowledge. The distribution of IK has also been modelled in terms of social information networks, which broadens our perspective of the flow of information from a micro scale (individual or dyadic levels) to a more macro scale (community or intergroup levels) (Ford 1976; Box 1990; Hanyani-Mlambo and Hebinck 1996; Atran and Medin 1997; Atran 1999; Ross 2002). A focus on networking is useful for identifying the following: (a) the community's propensity to encounter, spread and assimilate new information; (b) the community's capacity for adapting cognitively to changing technological and environmental conditions; (c) the extent and shape of information sharing; and (d) the degree to which expert ecological information is bound to other patterns of social life.

(2)   Knowledge as socially situated performance: a common criticism of scientific (etic) and ethnoscientific (emic) approaches to the description and analysis of IK has been the tendency to decontextualise it, thus not taking into consideration its context-indexed meanings, uses, purposes and variations (Ellen 1986; Ellen and Harris 2000). Addressing this problem, some researchers have focused precisely on the situational, performance-embedded aspects of IK (Borofsky 1987, 1994; Murphy 1992; Ellen 1993; Richards 1993). Richards' (1993) demonstration that the knowledge displayed by African farmers is better understood as concrete practice rather than abstract competence points to the sequential and contingent effect over time of many small and momentary fluctuations in growing conditions, labour supply and market factors as leading the way to knowledge/practice change. Robert Borofsky's (1987) ethnography of Pukapukan (Micronesia) knowledge shows how situational variables (e.g. social relationships between participants) structure, modify, and ultimately transform expressions and referential contents in the course of practice events.

(3)   Transmission and acquisition of knowledge: studies of enculturation or informal education in traditional societies have dealt mainly with the socialisation of values, attitudes and personality traits (Scribner and Cole 1973), but a building trend in IK studies is to focus on the transmission and acquisition of practical ecological knowledge and skills (Stross 1973; Ruddle and Chesterfield 1977; Dougherty 1979; Hewlett and Cavalli-Sforza 1986; Lave and Wenger 1991; Ohmagari and Berkes 1997; Hunn 2002; Zarger 2002; Casagrande 2002; Wilbert 2002; Zent n.d.). These studies have provided descriptive and statistical accounts of the IK learning/teaching process in different cultural settings. Key topics covered include: the types and rates of knowledge accretion by age; the effects of education, occupation, community, and other dynamic variables on individual acquisition; the interpersonal relationships that are more or less responsible for knowledge transmission; and the particular methods and contexts in which learning occurs. Results so far indicate that much learning occurs informally (outside school) and unconsciously, begins at a very early age and is nearly complete by adolescence, takes place in customary activity contexts (work, play and rest), involves observation and experience (e.g. peripheral participation, trial and error), depends somewhat on local language fluency, is obtained from primary care-givers and is usually initiated by the novice and not the expert (i.e. learner-directed). Socio-cultural and economic changes that affect these variables, such as time spent in traditional versus non-traditional activities, with peers versus adults and higher valuation of extra-local knowledge, can disrupt the transmission continuity over time and are manifested locally as a knowledge generation gap (Ross 2002a; Zent n.d.). The question of intergenerational IK transmission is presently a hot issue in environmental policy circles because little is known about it and long-term maintenance depends on it (Nakashima 2005).

(4)   Cultural modernisation and intergenerational retention/loss of knowledge: for years, observers of indigenous groups have reported and lamented the rapid decay or total loss of slowly accumulated ecological knowledge, but such observations were largely anecdotal or impressionistic and not backed up by hard data or precise understanding of the kinds, rates and causes of knowledge erosion (Linden 1991; Schultes 1994a). A recent wave of research is specifically geared to addressing this information gap through the systematic investigation of the impact of modernisation and acculturation on diachronic processes of knowledge retention/loss (Nabhan and St. Antoine 1993; Chipeniuk 1995; Nabhan 1997, 1998; Ohmagari and Berkes 1997; Godoy et al. 1998; Rosenberg 1998; Zent 1999a, 2001; Lee et al. 2001; Heckler 2002; Ross 2002a, 2002b; Byg, A. and H. Balslev 2004; Zent and Zent 2004; Reyes-García 2005). This body of work is noteworthy for empirically confirming and documenting that IK is indeed undergoing drastic changes in many groups where cultural modernisa-

tion is taking place, thus appearing to confirm the hypothesis of generalised erosion. Some of the change indicator variables observed to correlate with variations of IK level include: age, gender roles, personal and parental schooling, bilingualism, market involvement, habitat degradation, distance to forest or town, contact with other groups, availability of western medicines, occupational focus, wealth, religious belief and public economic assistance. However, the direction and strength of these effects on knowledge vary considerably across the different study sites. Moreover, a recent study of the Tzeltal Maya by Rebecca Zarger and John Stepp (2005) found remarkable persistence of knowledge after three decades of progressive socio-economic change (see also Hunn 2002; Sowerine 2004). These results suggest that the erosion process is culture- and site-specific and that complex (and still poorly understood) interactions among cultural and environmental variables determine whether knowledge is discarded or retained. But they may also reflect methodological variance and only the Zarger and Stepp study used time-series data. More such diachronic studies and a better idea of the normal or background rates of knowledge variation, along spatial and temporal dimensions, are needed before general tendencies can be clearly discerned.

Processual IK studies have typically employed integrative methodologies, combining cognitive experimental techniques (structured interviews, cognitive games, sorting and ranking tasks, projective tests), standard anthropological field methods (elicitation of folk classifications, ethnosemantic analysis, participant observation, kinship and social network analysis, socio-economic surveys, life and community histories), bio-ecological data collection (plant trails or plots, plant or animal collections), and different types of statistical analysis (consensus analysis, correspondence analysis, cluster analysis, regression, analysis of variance). However, one of the chief criticisms of the processual perspective has been the lack of standardised methodologies which in turn inhibits comparisons across case studies and generalisation of broader trends. One can envision that further development of this approach hinges upon achieving greater methodological sophistication and clarity.

Theoretical integration of processual studies of IK is presently underdeveloped, due in part to the methodological limitations mentioned above. Some authors have developed potentially useful theoretical frameworks centred around the concepts of process, interactivity and contextuality, notably Tim Ingold's (2000) notion of 'dwelling' and Paul Sillitoe's (2002b) four-dimensional 'global domains model', but it is presently unclear how these may be applied to organise and interpret the expanding empirical database on IK change and variation. To begin this task of conceptualisation, it will be useful to extract the most obvious theoretical-epistemological principles that are reflected in this body of work. Generally speaking, the processual approach implies a shift of descriptive and explanatory focus from structure, classification, function, and content to process, genesis, variation, and context. Knowledge is conceived not simply as an abstract, self-contained, inert body of useful technical and symbolic information but rather as the active, open, somewhat fluid cognitive fabric of observable social and ecological interactions. Other key tenets of this approach are: (1) an explicit sense of history, which considers the production and reproduction of IK in specific cultural and ecological contexts as problematic (rather than automatic) and therefore a central focus of the investigation (cf. Zent 1999b); (2) anti-essentialism, which makes variations, context-embeddedness, and historical contingency the main objects of description and explanation (cf. Vayda 1994); and (3) a pro-positivist bias, which holds that positive statements alleging knowledge change or conservation must be sustained by empirical evidence, which should be obtained through systematic, operationally explicit, replicable, and often quantitative methods of data collection (cf. Martin 1995; Alexiades 1996).

The problem orientation of the processual phase of IK studies is applied as well as academic. Clearly a primary stimulus of the paradigmatic turn towards studying knowledge dynamics, distributions, and contexts has been the concern for the progressive and pervasive trend of local knowledge erosion or change and the desire to develop more effective *in situ* and *in vivo* conservation measures. Whether implicit or openly stated, a common theme throughout much of this work is that a more sophisticated general-theoretical and local-empirical understanding of IK dynamics can enhance the design and success of intervention efforts aimed at local knowledge preservation, such as ethnoenvironmental education or revitalisation programmes. Thus one of the main contributions of this phase is the potential support it provides to scientists and planners working in knowledge-based conservation and development projects.

Conclusion

My main motivation for undertaking this review has been to celebrate the dynamic variety and fertility of scientific views and approaches to local ecological knowledge during the past half century. The diversity of methodological and theoretical orientations has enriched our appreciation and understanding of IK, but also made it increasingly difficult for the scientific community to reach consensus concerning the proper role and significance of the many locally-situated, tradition-rooted, culturally-embedded knowledges in relation to the so-called universal, transcultural scientific disciplines. This is to be expected and even healthy but also disconcerting to policymakers and the public at large who are demanding greater clarity and definition (i.e. simplification) regarding the epistemological, social, ethical and utilitarian status of local knowledge as judged from a 'scientific perspective' (see *Nature* magazine, 1999, Vol. 401: 623, 631). The stakes of this call for unity out of diversity are not merely academic. For example, some educators are striving to open spaces for IK-related studies and modes of learning in the academy (Semali and Kincheloe 1999), a goal that has great significance for the increasingly multicultural urban society as well as the increasingly globalised rural societies. Yet if no scientific agreement exists about how IK is to be understood, then how would it be possible to draw the line for any non-scientific knowledge form, for example the Christian theory of divine creation, prejudicial racist or sexist doctrines or beliefs in little green men from Mars. A major challenge therefore is to integrate the useful insights provided by the different phases while at the same time overcoming or correcting the narrow conceptual biases that each one inevitably entails. What principles provided by the previous approaches might be incorporated into a broadly acceptable, synthetic perspective of IK? The ethnoscientific phase has taught us of the culturally organised and rationalised nature of local environmental classifications, and ethnoscientific methods of data collection and analysis have been widely adopted as standard investigative procedure in most empirical IK studies. The discovery of close affinities of folk and scientific biological classification through research in theoretical cognitive ethnobiology has ratified the claim that folk biologists possess very extensive and accurate knowledge of a large portion of the biodiversity of their surrounding habitats and therefore are valuable sources of scientific information about local biodiversity. Research on formal models of the relationship between cognition and behaviour has established that the path from apprehension of environmental information to concrete action is operationalised through a complex logical process that we may characterise as fundamentally rational yet extremely intricate and conditioned by a vast array of surrounding environmental factors. The research phase dealing with IK as input for sustainable development and environmental conservation has highlighted the ecological wisdom of many traditional resource practices and the practical utility of counting on local peoples as active, intellectually astute participants in and contributors to agricultural research and development initiatives. The literature devoted to debates about the valuation, exploitation, and compensation of IK has raised our consciousness of the contradictory, unequal and seemingly unethical treatment accorded to non-scientific forms of knowledge within the dominant world political-economic system: on one hand, it is recognised to have scientific validity and economic value; on the other hand, it is devalued and discriminated against from a juridical-political point of view. The discursive phase counsels us to be aware of the political dimensions of IK, especially the power plays behind supporting or refuting it, and the sometimes antagonistic relationship between scientific and local knowledge. Finally, the processual phase has revealed that the normal state of local knowledge is change, that it is variably distributed, that it is eminently adaptable and responsive to changing environmental conditions, and therefore it may be fragile and can only be sustained through active effort.

Notes

Oral presentations that later evolved into this chapter were presented at the Seminar on 'Innovative Wisdom', held at White Oak Plantation, Yulee, Florida, From October 19 to 22, 2000 and at the VII International Congress of Ethnobiology, held at Athens, Georgia, October 23 to 27, 2000. I wish to thank all of the participants of those events for their perceptive comments, especially Roy Ellen, Gary Martin, Javier Caballero, Jan Slikkerveer and Victor Toledo. I am also indebted to Elena Gonzalez, Egleé Zent, Jenny Navas, Serena Heckler and Janet Chernela for constructive criticisms of the written version. Serena Heckler edited and improved the redaction. All deficiencies are my own. The Instituto Venezolano de Investigaciones Científicas and the University of Maryland at College Park provided institutional support.

1. These include: folk science, people's science, citizen science, ethnoecology, traditional knowledge, traditional ecological (or environmental) knowledge (TEK), indigenous environmental knowledge, rural people's knowledge (RPK), and local knowledge.

2. Boster's (1987) test showing that novices, or untrained biologists, exhibit a high level of agreement with scientists and folk biologists in sorting bird specimens provides further confirmation of the objective reality of phylogenetic relationships.

3. The close ties between private and public institutions in the recent wave of bioprospecting research are demonstrated by a few well-known examples. In 1986, the U.S. National Cancer Institute hired several botanical gardens to collect plants and screen extracts from the neotropics for anti-HIV and anti-cancer activity. In 1990, the multinational corporation Merck Co. signed a contract with the Costa Rican government and the National Biodiversity Institute (INBio), a non-profit organisation set up by the government, for the right to screen samples of that country's biodiversity. The International Cooperative Biodiversity Groups (ICBG) grant programme is coordinated by the U.S. National Institutes of Health (NIH). Created in 1993, the programme was designed to foster bioprospecting partnerships among local communities, academic researchers, and biotechnology businesses.

4. Brush (1993) points out that this criticism is somewhat unfair in the sense of choosing to ignore that plenty of plant material has been exchanged within and between tropical countries and regions. Local populations in the American tropics have also benefited from medicinal and other utilitarian plants introduced from the Old World (Bennett and Prance 2000).

Bibliography

Agrawal, A. 1995. 'Dismantling the Divide between Indigenous and Scientific Knowledge', *Development and Change* vol. 26: 413-439.

Agrawal, A. 2002. 'Indigenous Knowledge and the Politics of Classification', *International Social Science Journal* vol. 54, no. 3: 287-297.

Alexiades, M.N. ed. 1996. *Ethnobotanical Research: A Field Manual.* Bronx, NY: The New York Botanical Garden.

Altieri, M.A. 1987. *Agroecology: The Scientific Basis of Alternative Agriculture.* Boulder, Co.: Westview Press.

Altieri, M.A. and L.C. Merrick. 1987. 'In Situ Conservation of Crop Genetic Resources Through Maintenance of Traditional Farming Systems' *Economic Botany* vol. 41, no. 1: 86-96.

Anderson, J.R., J.L. Dillon, and J.B. Hardaker. 1977. *Agricultural Decision Analysis.* Ames, IA.: Iowa State University Press.

Antweiler, C. 1998. 'Local Knowledge and Local Knowing: An Anthropological Analysis of Contested 'Cultural Products' in the Context of Development' *Anthropos* vol. 93, no. 4-6: 469-494.

Apffel-Marglin, F. and S.A. Marglin, eds., 1996. *Decolonizing Knowledge: From Development to Dialogue.* Oxford: Oxford University Press.

Atran, S. 1985. 'The Nature of Folk-Botanical Life-forms' *American Anthropologist.* vol. 87, no.2: 298-315.

Atran, S. 1990. *Cognitive Foundations of Natural History: Towards an Anthropology of Science.* Cambridge: Cambridge University Press.

Atran, S. 1998. 'Folk Biology and the Anthropology of Science: Cognitive Universals and Cultural Particulars' *Behavioral and Brain Sciences* vol. 21: 547-609.

Atran, S. 1999. 'Managing the Maya Commons: The Value of Local Knowledge' in V.D. Nazarea, ed., *Ethnoecology: Situated Knowledge/Located Lives.* Tucson: University of Arizona Press, pp. 190-214.

Atran, S. and D. Medin. 1997. 'Knowledge and Action: Cultural Models of Nature and Resource Management in Mesoamerica', in M.H. Bazerman, D.M. Messick, A.E. Tenbrunsel, and K.A. Wade-Benzoni, eds. *Environment, Ethics, and Behavior: The Psychology of Environmental Valuation and Degradation.* San Francisco: The New Lexington Press, pp. 171-208.

Balick, M. 1990. 'Ethnobotany and the Identification of Therapeutic Agents from the Rainforest' *American Botanical Council Classic Botanical Reprint* no. 229: 2-11.

Balick, M.J. and P.A. Cox. 1996. *Plants, People, and Culture: The Science of Ethnobotany.* New York: Scientific American Library.

Barlett, P.F. 1977. 'The Structure of Decision Making in Paso' *American Ethnologist* vol. 4, no. 2: 285-307.

Barlett, P.F. 1980a. 'Adaptive Strategies in Peasant Agricultural Production' *Annual Review of Anthropology* vol. 9: 545-573

Barlett, P.F., ed. 1980b. *Agricultural Decision Making: Anthropological Contributions to rural Development.* New York: Academic Press.

Barlett, P.F. 1982. *Agricultural Choice and Change: Decision Making in a Costa Rican Community.* New Brunswick, N.J.: Rutgers University Press.

Basso, K. 1972. 'Ice and Travel among the Ft. Norman Slave: Folk Taxonomies and Cultural Rules' *Language in Society* vol. 1: 31-49.

Benfer, R.A. 1989. 'Individual Differences in Rule-Based Systems of Knowledge with Behavioral Implications' *Anthropological Quarterly* vol. 62, no. 2: 69-81.

Benfer, R.A., E.E. Brent Jr., and L. Furbee. 1991. *Expert systems.* London: Sage.

Bennett, B.C. and G.T. Prance. 2000. 'Introduced Plants in the Indigenous Pharmacopoeia of Northern South America' *Economic Botany* vol. 54: 90-102.

Bennett, J.W. 1969. *Northern Plainsmen: Adaptative Strategies and Agrarian Life.* Chicago, Aldine.

Bennett, J.W. 1976. *The Ecological Transition: Cultural Anthropology and Human Adaptation.* New York: Pergamon Press Inc.

Benton, L.M. and J.R. Short. 1999. *Environmental Discourse and Practice.* Oxford, U.K.: Blackwell Publishers Ltd.

Berkes, F. 1993. 'Traditional Ecological Knowledge in Perspective' in J.T. Inglis, ed. *Traditional Ecological Knowledge: Concepts and Cases.* Ottowa, Ontario: International Development Research Centre, pp. 1-9.

Berlin B. 1973. 'The Relation of Folk Systematics to Biological Classification and Nomenclature' *Annual Review of Ecology and Systematics* vol. 4: 259-71.

Berlin, B. 1976. 'The Concept of Rank in Ethnobiological Classification: Some Evidence from Aguaruna Folk Botany' *American Ethnologist.* vol. 3, no. 3: 381-99.

Berlin, B. 1992. *Ethnobiological Classification: Principles of Categorisation of Plants and Animals in Traditional Societies.* New Jersey: Princeton University Press.

Berlin, B., D. Breedlove and P. Raven. 1973. 'General Principles of Classification and Nomenclature in Folk Biology' *American Anthropologist* vol.75, no. 1: 214-42.

Berlin, B., D. Breedlove and P. Raven. 1974. *Principles of Tzeltal Plant Classification.* New York: Academic Press.

Berlin, B., J. Boster and J.P.O'Neill. 1981. 'The Perceptual Bases of Ethnobiological Classification: Evidence from Aguaruna Folk Ornithology' *Journal of Ethnobiology* vol. 1: 95-108.

Bicker, A., P. Sillitoe, and J. Pottier. 2004. *Investigating Local Knowledge: New Directions, New Approaches.* Hants, U.K.: Ashgate.

Biggs, S.D. 1988. *Resource-poor Farmer Participation in Research: A Synthesis from Nine National Agricultural Research Programs.* The Hague: International Service for National Agricultural Research.

Borofsky, R. 1987. *Making History: Pukapukan and Anthropological Constructions of Knowledge.* Cambridge: Cambridge University Press.

Borofsky, R. 1994a.' On the Knowledge and Knowing of Cultural Activities' in R. Borofsky, ed., *Assessing Cultural Anthropology.* New York: McGraw-Hill, pp. 331-348.

Boster, J. 1980. *How the Exceptions Prove the Rule: An Analysis of Informant Disagreement in Aguaruna Manioc Identification.* Ph.D. Dissertation, Berkeley: University of California.

Boster, J. 1984. 'Classification, Cultivation, and Selection of Aguaruna Cultivars of *Manihot Esculenta* (Euphorbiaceae)' in G.T. Prance and J.A. Kallunki, eds. *Ethnobotany in the Neotropics. (Advances in Economic Botany* vol. 1). Bronx, N.Y.: The New York Botanical Garden Press. pp. 34-47.

Boster, J. 1986. 'Exchange of Varieties and Information between Aguaruna Manioc Cultivators' *American Anthropologist* 88(2): 428-436.

Boster, J. 1987. 'Agreement between Biological Classification Systems Is Not Dependent on Cultural Transmission', *American Anthropologist* vol. 89: 914-920.

Boster, J. 1996. 'Human Cognition as a Product and Agent of Evolution' in R. Ellen and K. Fukui, eds., *Redefining Nature: Ecology, Culture and Domestication.* Oxford and Washington, D.C.: Berg, pp. 269-289.

Boster, J., B. Berlin, and J. O'Neill. 1986. 'The Correspondence of Jivaroan to Scientific Ornithology' *American Anthropologist* 88(3): 569-583.

Box, L. 1987. *Experimenting Cultivators: A Methodology for Adaptive Agricultural Research.* ODI Agricultural Administration (Research and Extension) Network Discussion Paper 23. London: Overseas Development Institute.

Box, L. ed., 1990. *From Common Ignorance to Shared Knowledge: Knowledge Networks in the Atlantic Zone of Costa Rica.* Wageningen Studies in Sociology No. 28. Wageningen: Wageningen Agricultural University.

Brokensha, D., D.M. Warren, and O. Werner, eds. 1980. *Indigenous Knowledge Systems and Development.* Lanham, MD.: University Press of America.

Brosius, J.P. 1997. 'Endangered Forest, Endangered People: Environmentalist Representations of Indigenous Knowledge' *Human Ecology* vol. 25, no. 1: 47-69.

Brown, C. 1977. 'Folk Botanical Life-Forms: Their Universality and Growth' *American Anthropologist* vol. 79: 317-342.

Brown, C. 1979. 'Folk Zoological Life-Forms: Their Universality and Growth' *American Anthropologist* vol. 81: 791-817.

Brown, C. 1984. *Language and Living Things: Uniformities in Folk Classification and Naming.* Brunswick, New Jersey: Rutgers University Press.

Brown, M. and B. Wyckoff-Baird. 1995. *Designing Integrated Conservation and Development Projects.* Washington, D.C.: Biodiversity Support Program.

Brush, S.B. 1991. 'A Farmer-Based Approach to Conserving Crop Germplasm' *Economic Botany* vol. 45: 153-66.

Brush, S. 1992. 'Farmers Rights and Genetic Conservation in Traditional Farming Systems' *World Development* vol. 20, no. 11: 1617-1630.

Brush, S. 1993. 'Indigenous Knowledge of Biological Resources and Intellectual Property Rights: The Role of Anthropology' *American Anthropologist* vol. 95: 653-686.

Brush, S. 1996. 'Whose Knowledge, Whose Genes, Whose Rights?' in S. Brush and D. Stabinsky, eds., *Valuing Local Knowledge: Indigenous People and Intellectual Property Rights.* Washington, D.C.: Island Press. pp. 1-21.

Brush, S. and D. Stabinsky, eds. 1996. *Valuing Local Knowledge: Indigenous People and Intellectual Property Rights.* Washington, D.C.: Island Press.

Bulmer, R.N.H. 1967. 'Why Is the Cassowary Not a Bird? A Problem of Zoological Taxonomy among the Karam of the New Guinea Highlands' *Man* vol. 2: 5-25.

Bulmer, R.N.H. 1970. 'Which Came First, the Chicken or the Egg-Head?' in J. Pouillon and P. Maranda, eds., *Echanges et communications.* The Hague: Mouton, pp.1069-1091.

Bulmer, R.N.H. 1974. 'Folk Biology in the New Guinea Highlands' *Social Science Information* vol. 13, no. 4/5: 9-28.

Bulmer, R.N.H. and M. Tyler. 1968. 'Karam Classification of Frogs' *Journal of the Polynesian Society* vol. 77: 333-385.

Bunyard, P. 1989. 'Guardians of the Forest: Indigenist Policies in the Colombian Amazon' *The Ecologist* vol. 19, no. 6: 255-258.

Byg, A. and H. Balslev. 2004. 'Factors Affecting Local Knowledge of Palms in Nangaritza Valley, Southeastern Ecuador' *Journal of Ethnobiology* 24(2): 255-278.

Callicott, J.B. 1989. 'American Indian Land Wisdom? Sorting out the Issues' in J.B. Callicott, ed., *In Defence of the Land Ethic: Essays in Environmental Philosophy.* Albany, N.Y.: State University of New York Press, pp. 203-219.

Cancian, F. 1972. *Change and Uncertainty in a Peasant Economy.* Stanford, CA.: Stanford University Press.

Casagrande, D.G. 2002. *Ecology, Cognition and Cultural Transmission of Tzeltal Maya Medicinal Plant Knowledge.* Ph.D. Dissertation. Athens, GA.: University of Georgia.

Cashman, K. 1991. 'Systems of Knowledge as Systems of Domination: The Limitations of Established Meaning' *Agriculture and Human Values* vol. 8, no. 1 and 2: 49-58.

Chambers, R. 1983. *Rural Development: Putting the Last First.* London: Longman.

Chambers, R., A. Pacey, and L.A. Thrupp, eds., 1989. *Farmer First: Farmer Innovation and Agricultural Research.* London: Intermediate Technology Publications.

Chipeniuk, R. 1995. 'Childhood Foraging as a Means of Acquiring Competent Human Cognition about Biodiversity' *Environment and Behavior* vol. 27, no. 4: 490-512.

Clay, J. 1988. *Indigenous People and Tropical Forests: Models of Land Use and Management for Latin America.* Cambridge, MA.: Cultural Survival Report 27.

Cleveland, D.A. and S.C. Murray. 1997. 'The World's Crop Genetic Resources and the Rights of Indigenous Farmers' *Current Anthropology* vol. 38, no. 4: 477-514.

Cleveland, D.A., D. Soleri, and S.E. Smith. 1994. 'Do Folk Crop Varieties Have a Role in Sustainable Agriculture?' *BioScience* vol. 44, no. 11: 740-751.

COICA. 1999. *Biodiversidad, Derechos Colectivos y Régimen sui generis de Propiedad Intelectual.* Quito: COICA-OMAERE-OPIP.

Conklin, H.C. 1954a. *The Relation of Hanunóo Culture to the Plant World.* Ph.D. Dissertation, New Have, CT: York University.

Conklin, H.C. 1954b. 'An Ethnoecological Approach to Shifting Agriculture' *Transactions of the New York Academy of Sciences* vol. 17, no. 2: 133-142.

Conklin, H.C. 1957. *Hanunóo Agriculture: AReport on an Integral System of Shifting Cultivation in the Philippines.* FAO Forestry Development Paper No. 12.

Conklin, H.C. 1961. 'The Study of Shifting Cultivation' *Current Anthropology* vol. 2, no. 1: 27-61.

Conklin, H.C. 1967. 'Some Aspects of Ethnographic Research in Ifugao' *Transactions of the New York Academy of Sciences* Series 2 vol. 30, no. 1: 99-121.

Conklin, H.C. ed., 1972. *Folk Classification: A Topically Arranged Bibliography of Contemporary and Background References.* New Haven, CT: Department of Anthropology, Yale University.

Cook, S. 1973. 'Production, Ecology, and Economic Anthropology: Notes Toward an Integrated Frame of Reference' *Social Science Information* vol. 12, no. 1: 25-52.

Cox, P. 1990. 'Ethnopharmacology and the Search for New Drugs' in D.J. Chadwick and J. Marsh, eds., *Bioactive Compounds from Plants.* Ciba-Geigy Symposium No. 154. New York: John Wiley and Sons, pp. 40-55.

Cox, P. and M. Balick. 1994. 'The Ethnobotanical Approach to Drug Discovery' *Scientific American* vol. 270, no. 6: 82-87.

Cunningham, A.B. 1991. 'Indigenous Knowledge and Biodiversity: Global Commons or Regional Heritage?' *Cultural Survival Quarterly* vol. 15, no. 3: 4-8.

Cunningham, A.B. 1993. *Ethics, Ethnobiological Research, and Biodiversity.* Switzerland: WWF International Publication.

D'Andrade, R.G. 1987. 'Modal Responses and Cultural Expertise' *American Behavioral Scientist* vol. 31, no. 2: 194-202.

D'Andrade, R.G. 1995. *The Development of Cognitive Anthropology.* Cambridge: Cambridge University Press.

Daly, D. 1992. 'The National Cancer Institute's Plant Collections Program: Update and Implications for Tropical Forests' in M. Plotkin and L. Famolare, eds., *Sustainable Harvest and Marketing of Rain Forest Products.* Washington, D.C.: Island Press, pp. 224-230.

Dei, G.J.S., B.L. Hall, and D.G. Rosenberg; eds. 2000. *Indigenous Knowledges in Global Contexts* Toronto: University of Toronto Press.

DeWalt, B.R. 1975. 'Inequalities in Wealth, Adoption of Technology, and Production in a Mexican Ejido' *American Ethnologist* vol. 2, no. 1: 149-168.

DeWalt, B.R. 1979. 'Alternative Adaptive Strategies in a Mexican Ejido: A New Perspective on Modernisation and Development' *Human Organisation* vol. 38, no. 2: 134-143.

DeWalt, B.R. 1994. 'Using Indigenous Knowledge to Improve Agriculture and Natural Resource Management' *Human Organization* vol. 53, no. 2: 123-131.

Diamond, J.M. 1966. 'Zoological Classification System of a Primitive People (Fore, New Guinea)' *Science* vol. 151, no. 3714: 1102-1104.

Diamond, J.M. 1987. 'The Environmentalist Myth' *Nature* vol. 324: 19-20.

Dougherty, J.W.D. 1978. 'Salience and Relativity in Classification' *American Ethnologist* vol. 5: 66-80.

Dougherty, J.W.D. 1979. 'Learning Names for Plants and Plants for Names' *Anthropological Linguistics* vol. 21: 298-315.

Drengson, A. 1995. 'The Deep Ecology Movement' *Trumpeter* vol. 12, no. 3: 143-145.

The Economist. 1999. 'Shaman Loses Its Magic' *The Economist* vol. 350, no. 8107: 77.

Elisabetsky, E. 1986. 'New Directions in Ethnopharmacology'. *Journal of Ethnobiology* vol. 6, no. 1: 121-128.

Ellen, R.F. 1978. *Nuaulu Settlement and Ecology: An Approach to the Environmental Relations of an Eastern Indonesian Community.* The Hague: Martinus Nijhoff.

Ellen, R.F. 1979. 'Omniscience and Ignorance: Variation in Nuaulu Knowledge, Identification and Classification of Animals' *Language in Society* vol. 8: 337-364.

Ellen, R.F. 1982. *Environment, Subsistence and System: The Ecology of Small-Scale Social Formations.* Cambridge: Cambridge University Press.

Ellen, R.F. 1986. 'Ethnobiology, Cognition, and the Structure of Prehension: Some General Theoretical Notes' *Journal of Ethnobiology* vol. 6: 83-98.

Ellen, R.F. 1993. *The Cultural Relations of Classification: An Analysis of Nuaulu Animal Categories from Central Seram.* Cambridge: Cambridge University Press.

Ellen, R.F. 1996. 'The Cognitive Geometry of Nature: A Contextual Approach'.in P.
    Descola and G. Pálsson, eds., *Nature and Society: Anthropological Perspectives*.
    London: Routledge. pp. 103-123.
Ellen, R.F. 2002. 'Déjà Vu, All Over Again' in P. Sillitoe, A. Bicker and J. Pottier, eds.,
    Participating in Development: Approaches to Indigenous Knowledge. ASA
    Monographs 39. London and New York: Routledge. Pp. 235-258.
Ellen, R. and H. Harris. 2000. 'Introduction' in R. Ellen, P. Parkes, and A. Bicker,
    eds., *Indigenous Environmental Knowledge and its Transformations*. Amsterdam:
    Harwood Academic Publishers, pp. 1-33.
Ellen, R.F., P. Parkes, and A. Bicker, eds. 2000. *Indigenous Environmental Knowledge
    and its Transformations*. Amsterdam: Harwood Academic Publishers.
Escobar, A. 1995. *Encountering Development: The Making and Unmaking of the Third
    World*. Princeton, N.J.: Princeton University Press.
Escobar, A. 1997. 'Cultural Politics and Biological Diversity' in R.G. Fox and O.
    Starn, eds., *Between Resistance and Revolution: Cultural Politics and Social Protest*.
    New Brunswick, N.J.: Rutgers University Press, pp. 40-64.
Escobar, A. 1999. 'After Nature: Steps to an Antiessentialist Political Ecology' *Current
    Anthropology* vol. 40, no. 1: 1-30.
Fairhead, J. 1993. 'Representing Knowledge: The "New Farmer" in Research Fashions'
    in J. Pottier, ed., *Practising Development: Social Science Perspectives*. London and
    New York: Routledge, pp. 187-204.
Farnsworth, N.R. 1988. 'Screening Plants for New Medicines' in E.O. Wilson, ed.,
    Biodiversity. Washington, D.C.: National Academy Press. pp. 83-97.
Farrington, J. and A. Martin. 1987. *Farmer Participatory Research: A Review of Concepts
    and Practices*. ODI Agricultural Administration (Research and Extension)
    Network, Discussion Paper 19. London: Overseas Development Institute.
Fernández, M.E. 1994. 'Gender and Indigenous Knowledge' *Indigenous Knowledge and
    Development Monitor* vol. 2, no. 3: 4pp.
Ford, R.I. 1976. 'Communication Networks and Information Hierarchies in Native
    American Folk Medicine: Tewa Pueblos, New Mexico' in W. Hand, ed., *American
    Folk Medicine*. Berkeley: University of California Press,pp. 143-157.
Fowler, C.S. and J. Leland. 1967. 'Some Northern Paiute Native Categories' *Ethnology*
    vol. 6: 381-404.
Fowler, C.S. 1977. 'Ethnoecology' in D.L. Hardesty, ed., *Ecological Anthropology*. New
    York: Alfred A. Knopf, pp. 215-243.
Frake, C.O. 1961. 'The Diagnosis of Disease among the Subanun of Mindanao'
    American Anthropologist vol. 63: 113-132.
Frake, C.O. 1962. 'Cultural Ecology and Ethnography' *American Anthropologist* vol.
    64: 53-59.
Frake, C.O. 1964. 'Notes on Queries in Ethnography' *American Anthropologist* vol. 66,
    no.3: 132-145 .
Furbee, L. 1989. 'A Folk Expert System: Soils Classification in the Colca Valley, Peru'
    Anthropological Quarterly vol. 62, no. 2: 83-101.
Gardner, P.M. 1976. 'Birds, Words, and a Requiem for the Omniscient Informant'
    American Ethnologist vol. 8: 446-468.

Geoghagen, W.H. 1970. 'Residential Decision Making among the Eastern Samal' Paper presented to the Symposium on Mathematical Anthropology, 69th Annual Meeting of the American Anthropological Association, San Diego.

Gladwin, C.H. 1979a. 'Production Functions and Decision Models: Complementary Models' *American Ethnologist* vol. 6, no. 4: 653-674.

Gladwin, C.H. 1979b. 'Cognitive Strategies and Adoption Decisions: A Case Study of Nonadoption of an Agronomic Recommendation' *Economic Development and Cultural Change* vol. 28, no. 1: 155-173.

Gladwin, C.H. 1980. 'A Theory of Real Life Choice: Applications to Agricultural Decision' in P. Barlett, ed., *Agricultural Decision-Making: Anthropological Contributions to Rural Development.* New York: Academic Press, pp. 45-85.

Gladwin, H. and M. Murtaugh. 1980. 'The Attentive–Pre-attentive Distinction in Agricultural Decision Making' in P. Barlett, ed., *Agricultural Decision Making: Anthropological Contributions to Rural Development.* New York: Academic Press, pp. 115-136.

Gliessman, S. 1981. 'The Ecological Basis for the Application of Traditional Technology in the Management of Tropical Agroecosystems' *Agro-ecosystems* vol. 7: 173-185.

Godoy, R., N. Brokaw, D. Wilkie, D. Colón, A. Palermo, S. Lye, and S. Wei. 1998. 'On Trade and Cognition: Markets and the Loss of Folk Knowledge among the Tawahka Indians' *Journal of Anthropological Research* 54: 219-33.

Gorjestani, N. 2000. *Indigenous Knowledge for Development: Opportunities and Challenges.* http://www.worldbank.org/afr/ik/default.htm.

Gould, S.J. 1979. 'A Quahog is a Quahog' *Natural History* vol. 88: 18-26.

Grande, S.M.A. 1999. 'Beyond the Ecologically Noble Savage: Deconstructing the White Man's Indian' *Environmental Ethics* vol. 21, no. 3: 307-320.

Grenier, L. 1998. *Working with Indigenous Knowledge: A Guide for Researchers.* Ottawa, Ontario: International Development Research Centre.

Gudeman, S. 1978. *The Demise of a Rural Economy: From Subsistence to Capitalism in a Latin American Village.* Boston: Routledge and Kegan Paul.

Guillet, D.W. 1989a. 'Expert-Systems Applications in Anthropology' *Anthropological Quarterly* vol. 62, no. 2: 57-58.

Guillet, D.W. 1989b. 'A Knowledge-based-systems Model of Native Soil Management' *Anthropological Quarterly* vol. 62, no. 2: 59-67.

Gupta, A.K. 1997. 'The Honey Bee Network: Linking Knowledge-rich Grassroots Innovations' *Development* vol. 40, no. 4: 36-40.

Gupta, A. 1998. *Postcolonial Developments: Agriculture in the Making of Modern India.* Durham, NC.: Duke University Press.

Haen, N. 1999. 'The Power of Environmental Knowledge: Ethnoecology and Environmental Conflicts in Mexican Conservation' *Human Ecology* vol. 27, no. 3: 477-491.

Hanyani-Mlambo, B.T. and P. Hebinck. 1996. 'Formal and Informal Knowledge Networks in Conservation Forestry in Zimbabwe' *Indigenous Knowledge and Development Monitor* vol. 4, no. 3: 1-8.

Harmon, D. 1996. 'Losing Species, Losing Languages: Connections between Biological and Linguistic Diversity' *Southwest Journal of Linguistics* vol. 15: 89-108.

Harmon, D. 2002. *In Light of Our Differences: How Diversity in Nature and Culture Makes Us Human.* Washington, D.C.: Smithsonian Institution Press.

Harris, M. 1974. 'Why a Perfect Knowledge of All the Rules One Must Know to Act Like a Native Cannot Lead to a Knowledge of how Natives Act' *Journal of Anthropological Research* vol. 30: 242-251.

Hayles, N.K. 1995. 'Searching for Common Ground'.in M.E. Soulé and G. Lease, eds., *Reinventing Nature? Responses to Postmodern Deconstruction.* Washington, D.C.: Island Press, pp. 47-63.

Hays, T. 1976. 'An Empirical Method for the Identification of Covert Categories in Ethnobiology' *American Ethnologist* vol. 3, no. 3: 489-507.

Hays, T. 1982. 'Utilitarian/Adaptationist Explanations in Folk Biological Classification: Some Cautionary Notes' *Journal of Ethnobiology* vol. 2: 89-94.

Heckler, S. 2002. 'Traditional Ethnobotanical Knowledge Loss and Gender among the Piaroa' in J. Stepp, F.S. Wyndham, and R.K. Zarger, eds., *Ethnobiology and Biocultural Diversity.* Athens, GA.: International Society of Ethnobiology, pp. 532-548.

Henrich, J. 2001. 'Cultural Transmission and the Diffusion of Innovations; Adoption Dynamics Indicate that Biased Cultural Transmission is the Predominate Force in Behavioral Change' *American Anthropologist* vol. 103: 992-1013.

Hewlett, B.S. and L.L. Cavalli-Sforza. 1986. 'Cultural Transmission among Aka Pygmies' *American Anthropologist* vol. 88, no. 4: 922-934.

Hirschfeld, L.A. and S. Gelman. 1994. *Mapping the Mind: Domain Specificity in Cognition and Culture.* New York: Cambridge University Press.

Hobart, M. 1993. Introduction: The Growth of Ignorance?'in M. Hobart, ed., *An Anthropological Critique of Development: The Growth of Ignorance.* London and New York: Routledge, pp. 1-30.

Hunn, E.S. 1975. 'A Measure of the Degree of Correspondence of Folk to Scientific Biological Classification' *American Ethnologist* vol. 2, no. 2: 309-328.

Hunn, E.S. 1976. 'Towards a Perceptual Model of Folk Biological Classification' *American Ethnologist* vol. 3, no. 3: 508-28.

Hunn, E.S. 1977. *Tzeltal Folk Zoology.* New York: Academic Press.

Hunn, E.S. 1982. 'The Utilitarian Factor in Folk Biological Classification' *American Anthropologist* vol. 84: 830-47.

Hunn, E.S. 1989. 'Ethnoecology: The Relevance of Cognitive Anthropology for Human Ecology' in M. Freilich, ed. *The Relevance of Culture.* New York: Bergin and Garvey pp. 143-160

Hunn, E.S. 1990. 'Nch'i-wána, "The Big River": Mid-Columbia Indians and Their Land' Seattle, WA.: University of Seattle Press.

Hunn, E.S. 1993. 'What Is Traditional Ecological Knowledge?' in N. Williams and G. Baines, eds., *Traditional Ecological Knowledge: Wisdom for Sustainable Development.* Canberra: Centre for Resource and Environmental Studies, National Australian University, pp. 13-15

Hunn, E.S. 2002. 'Evidence for the Precocious Acquisition of Plant Knowledge by Zapotec Children' in J. Stepp, F.S. Wyndham, and R.K. Zarger, eds., *Ethnobiology and Biocultural Diversity.* Athens, GA.: International Society of Ethnobiology, pp. 604-613.

Johnson, A.W. 1974. 'Ethnoecology and Planting Practices in a Swidden Agricultural System' *American Ethnologist* vol. 1, no. 1: 87-101.

Johnson, A.W. 1980. 'The Limits of Formalism in Agricultural Decision Research' in P. Barlett, ed., *Agricultural Decision-Making: Anthropological Contributions to Rural Development.* New York: Academic Press, pp. 17-43.

Keesing, R. 1972. 'Paradigms Lost: The New Ethnography and the New Linguistics' *Southwestern Journal of Anthropology* vol. 28: 299-332.

Keesing, R. 1974. 'Theories of Culture' *Annual Review of Anthropology* vol. 3: 73-98.

Kellert, S.R. 1985. 'Attitudes towards Animals: Age-Related Development among Children' *Journal of Environmental Education* vol. 16, no. 3: 29-39.

Kempton, W., J.S. Boster, and J.A. Hartley. 1995. *Environmental Values in American Culture.* Cambridge, MA.: The MIT Press.

King, S. 1992. 'Pharmaceutical Discovery, Ethnobotany, Tropical Forests, and Reciprocity: Integrating Indigenous Knowledge, Conservation, and Sustainable Development' in M. Plotkin and L. Famolare, eds., *Sustainable Harvest and Marketing of Rain Forest Products.* Washington, DC: Island Press. pp. 231-238.

Kloppenburg Jr., J. 1991a. 'Social Theory and the De/Reconstruction of Agricultural Science: Local Knowledge for an Alternative Agriculture' *Rural Sociology* vol. 56: 519-548.

Kloppenburg Jr., J. 1991b. 'No Hunting! Biodiversity, Indigenous Rights, and Scientific Poaching' *Cultural Survival Quarterly* vol. 15, no. 3: 14-18.

Krech, S. 1999. *The Ecological Indian: Myth and History.* New York: W.W. Norton and Co.

Lapa, A.J. 2002. *Bioprospecting in Brazil: Alternative Approaches towards producing Autochthonic Medicines.* http://sciencecareers.sciencemag.org/career development/previous issues/articles/1820.

Lave, J. and E. Wenger. 1991. *Situated Learning: Legitimate Peripheral Participation.* Cambridge: Cambridge University Press.

Lee, R.A., M.J. Balick, D. Lee Ling, F. Sohl, B.J. Brosi and W. Raynor 2001. 'Cultural Dynamism and Change – An Example from the Federated States of Micronesia' *Economic Botany* vol. 55, no. 1: 9-13.

Leigh Jr., E.G. 1993. 'Epilogue: Comments on the Paris Symposium by a Concerned Biologist' in C.M. Hladik, A. Hladik, O.F. Linares. H. Pagezy, A. Semple and M. Hadley, eds., *Tropical Forests, People and Food. Biocultural Interactions and Applications to Development.* (*Man and the Biosphere Series,* vol. 13) Paris: UNESCO and the Parthenon Publishing Group, pp. 829-838.

Lewis, H.T. 1993. 'Traditional Ecological Knowledge – Some Definitions' in N.M. Williams and G. Baines, eds., *Traditional Ecological Knowledge: Wisdom for Sustainable Development.* Canberra: Centre for Resources and Environmental Studies, Australian National University, pp. 8-12.

Linden, E. 1991. 'Lost Tribes, Lost Knowledge' *Time* vol. 138, no. 12: 32-40.

Maffi, L. ed., 2001. *On Biocultural Diversity: Linking Language, Knowledge, and the Environment.* Washington, DC: Smithsonian Institute Press.

Maffi, L. 2005. 'Linguistic, Cultural, and Biological Diversity' *Annual Review of Anthropology* vol. 34: 599-617.

Mander, J. 1991. *In the Absence of the Sacred: The Failure of Technology and the Survival of the Indian Nations*. San Francisco, CA.: Sierra Club Books.

Martin, G. 1995. *Ethnobotany: A Methods Manual*. London: Chapman and Hall.

McCorkle, C.M. 1989. 'Towards a Knowledge of Local Knowledge and its Importance for Agricultural RD and E'. *Agriculture and Human Values* vol. 6, no. 3: 4-12.

Merchant, C. 1992. *Radical Ecology: The Search for a Liveable World*. New York: Routledge.

Metzger, D. and G. Williams. 1966. 'Some Procedures and Results in the Study of Native Categories: Tzeltal Firewood' *American Anthropologist* vol. 68, no. 2: 389-407.

Mishra, S. 1994. 'Women's Indigenous Knowledge of Forest Management in Orissa (India)' *Indigenous Knowledge and Development Monitor* vol. 2, no. 3: 5pp.

Moock, J. and R. Rhoades. 1992. *Diversity, Farmer Knowledge and Sustainability*. Ithaca, N.Y.: Cornell University Press.

Moran, E. 1993. 'Managing Amazonian Variability with Indigenous Knowledge' in C.M. Hladik, A. Hladik, O.F. Linares. H. Pagezy, A. Semple and M. Hadley, eds., *Tropical Forests, People and Food. Biocultural Interactions and Applications to Development*. (*Man and the Biosphere Series*, vol. 13) Paris: UNESCO and the Parthenon Publishing Group, pp. 753-766.

Moran, K. 1999. 'Towards Compensation. Returning Benefits from Ethnobotanical Drug Discovery to Native Peoples' in V.D. Nazarea, ed., *Ethnoecology: Situated Knowledge/Located Lives*. Tucson: University of Arizona Press, pp. 249-262.

Morrill, W.T. 1967. Ethnoicthyology of the Cha-Cha *Ethnology* 6: 405-416.

Murphy, I.I. 1992. *'And I, in My Turn, Will Pass It on': Indigenous Education among the Kayapó Amerindians of Central Brazil*. Ph.D. Dissertation. Pittsburgh: University of Pittsburgh.

Nabhan, G. 1997. *Cultures of Habitat: On Nature, Culture, and Story*. Washington, D.C.: Counterpoint.

Nabhan, G. 1998. 'Passing on a Sense of Place and Traditional Ecological Knowledge between Generations: A Primer for Native American Museum Educators and Community-Based Cultural Education Projects' *People and Plants Handbook* 4: 30-33.

Nabhan, G. and S. St. Antoine. 1993. 'The Loss of Floral and Faunal Story, the Extinction of Experience' in S.R. Kellert and E.O. Wilson, eds,. *The Biophilia Hypothesis*. Washington, DC: Island Press, pp. 229-250.

Nakashima, D. 2005. Safeguarding the Transmission of Local and Indigenous Knowledge of Nature. *UNESCO Working Document. Paris: UNESCO*.

Nature. 1999. 'U.S. Keeps a Watchful Eye from the Sidelines' *Nature*, World Conference on Science News. June 1999, http://www.nature.com/wcs/1news/30-1b.html

Nazarea-Sandoval, V.D. 1995. *Local Knowledge and Agricultural Decision-Making in the Philippines: Class, Gender, and Resistance*. Ithaca, N.Y.: Cornell University Press.

Nazarea, V.D. 1997. *Cultural Memory and Biodiversity*. Tucson: University of Arizona Press.

Nazarea, V.D. 1999. 'Introduction. A View from a Point: Ethnoecology as Situated Knowledge' in V.D. Nazarea, ed., *Ethnoecology: Situated Knowledge/Located Lives.* Tucson: University of Arizona Press, pp. 3-20.

Netting, R. McC. 1974. 'Agrarian Ecology' *Annual Review of Anthropology* vol. 3: 21-56.

Nietschmann, B. 1992. *The Interdependence of Biological and Cultural Diversity.* Occasional Paper no. 21, Center for World Indigenous Studies, December 1992.

Norgaard, R. 1984. 'Traditional Agricultural Knowledge: Past Performance, Future Prospects, and Institutional Implications' *American Journal of Agricultural Economics* vol. 66: 874-878.

Ohmagari, K. and F. Berkes, 1997. 'Transmission of Indigenous Knowledge and Bush Skills among the Western James Bay Cree Women of Subarctic Canada' *Human Ecology* vol. 25, no. 2: 197-222.

Oldfield, M.L. and J.B. Alcorn 1987. 'Conservation of Traditional Agroecosystems' *Bioscience* vol. 37: 199-208.

Orlove, B.S. 1977. 'Integration through Production: The Use of Zonation in Espinar' *American Ethnologist* vol. 4, no. 1: 84-101.

Osseweijer, M. 2000. ' "We Wander in our Ancestor's Yard": Sea Cucumber Gathering in Aru, Eastern Indonesia' in R. Ellen, P. Parkes, and A. Bicker, eds., *Indigenous Environmental Knowledge and its Transformations.* Amsterdam: Harwood Academic Publishers, pp. 55-78.

Perrett, R.W. 1998. 'Indigenous Rights and Environmental Justice' *Environmental Ethics* 20(4): 377-391.

Peters, C.M., A.H. Gentry, and R. Mendelsohn 1989. 'Valuation of an Amazonian Rainforest' *Nature* 339: 655-656.

Pinker, S. 1994. *The Language Instinct: How the Mind Creates Language.* New York: Harper Collins.

Plotkin, M. and L. Famolare, eds., 1992. *Sustainable Harvest and Marketing of Rain Forest Products.* Washington, D.C.: Island Press.

Plotkin, M.J. 1988. 'Ethnobotany and Conservation in the Guianas: The Indians of Southern Suriname' in F. Almeda and C. Pringle, eds. *Tropical Rainforests: Diversity and Conservation.* San Francisco: California Academy of Sciences, pp. 87-109.

Posey, D.A. 1990a. 'Introduction to Ethnobiology: Its Implications and Applications' in D.A. Posey and W.L. Overal, eds., *Ethnobiology: Implications and Applications.* Vol. I. Belem: Museu Paraense Emilio Goeldi, pp. 1-7.

Posey, D.A. 1990b. 'The Application of Ethnobiology in the Conservation of Dwindling Natural Resources: Lost Knowledge or Options for the Survival of the Planet' in D.A. Posey and W.L. Overal, eds., *Ethnobiology: Implications and Applications.* vol. I. Belem: Museu Paraense Emilio Goeldi, pp. 47-59.

Posey, D.A. 1992. 'Traditional Knowledge, Conservation, and "The Rain Forest Harvest" ' in M. Plotkin and L. Famolare, eds., *Sustainable Harvest and Marketing of Rain Forest Products.* Washington, DC: Island Press, pp. 46-50.

Posey, D.A. 1999. 'Safeguarding Traditional Resource Rights of Indigenous Peoples' in V.D. Nazarea, ed. *Ethnoecology: Situated Knowledge/Located Lives*. Tucson: University of Arizona Press, pp. 217-229.

Posey, D.A. ed. 1999. *Cultural and Spiritual Values of Biodiversity.* London: Intermediate Technology Publications.

Posey, D.A. 2004. 'The "balance sheet" and the "sacred balance": Valuing the Knowledge of Indigenous and Traditional Peoples'.in D. Posey, and K. Plenderleith, ed., *Indigenous Knowledge and Ethics: A Darrell Posey Reader*. New York: Routledge,pp. 195-205.

Posey, D.A. and G. Dutfield. 1996. *Beyond Intellectual Property: Towards Traditional Resource Rights for Indigenous Peoples and Local Communities.* Ottowa: International Development Research Centre.

Posey, D.A., J. Frechione, J. Eddins, L.F. da Silva, D. Myers, D. Case, and P. MacBeath. 1984. 'Ethnoecology as Applied Anthropology in Amazonian Development' *Human Organization* vol. 43: 95-107.

Pottier, J. ed., 1993. *Practising Development: Social Science Perspectives.* London and New York: Routledge.

Purcell, T.W. 1998. 'Indigenous Knowledge and Applied Anthropology: Questions of Definition and Direction' *Human Organisation* vol. 57, no. 3: 258-272.

Quinn, N. 1978. 'Do Mfantse Fish Sellers Estimate Probability in their Heads?' *American Ethnologist* vol. 5, no. 2: 206-226.

Randall, R. 1976. 'How Tall is a Taxonomic Tree? Some Evidence of Dwarfism' *American Ethnologist* vol. 3, no. 3: 543-55.

Randall, R. 1977. *Change and Variation in Samal Fishing: Making Plans to 'Make a Living' in the Southern Philippines.* Ph.D. Dissertation, Berkeley: Unversity of California.

Randall, R. and E. Hunn. 1984. 'Do Life Forms Evolve or Do Uses for Life? Some Doubts about Brown's Universals Hypotheses' *American Ethnologist* vol. 11: 329-349.

Read, D. and C. Behrens. 1989. 'Modeling Folk Knowledge as Expert Systems' *Anthropological Quarterly* vol. 62, no. 3: 107-120.

Redford, K.H. 1991. 'The Ecologically Noble Savage' *Cultural Survival Quarterly* vol. 15, no. 1: 46-48.

Redford, K.H. and A.M. Stearman. 1993. 'Forest-Dwelling Native Amazonians and the Conservation of Biodiversity: Interests in Common or in Collision?' *Conservation Biology* vol. 7, no. 2: 248-255.

Reyes-García, V., V. Vadez, E. Byron, L. Apaza, W.R. Leonard, E. Pérez and D. Wilkie 2005. 'Market Economy and the Loss of Folk Knowledge of Plant Uses: Estimates from the Tsimane of the Bolivian Amazon' *Current Anthropology* 46(4): 651-656.

Rhoades, R. 1989. 'The Role of Farmers in the Creation of Agricultural Technology'.in R. Chambers, A. Pacey, and L.A. Thrupp, eds., *Farmer First: Farmer Innovation and Agricultural Research*. London: Intermediate Technology Publications, pp. 3-9.

Rhoades, R. and R. Booth. 1982. 'Farmer-back-to-Farmer: A Model for Generating Acceptable Agricultural Technology' *Agricultural Administration* vol. 11: 127-137.

Richards, P. 1985. *Indigenous Agricultural Revolution: Ecology and Food Production in West Africa.* Boulder, CO.: Westview Press.

Richards, P. 1993. 'Cultivation: Knowledge or Performance?' in M. Hobart, ed., *An Anthropological Critique of Development.* London: Routledge, pp. 64-78.

Rocheleau, D.E. 1991. 'Gender, Ecology, and the Science of Survival: Stories and Lessons from Kenya' *Agriculture and Human Values* vol. 8, no. 1 and 2: 156-165.

Rosenberg, J. 1998. 'Documenting and Revitalizing Traditional Ecological Knowledge: Seri Survey' *People and Plants Handbook* vol. 4: 34-35.

Ross, N. 2002a. 'Cognitive Aspects of Intergenerational Change: Mental Models, Cultural Change, and Environmental Behavior among the Lacandon Maya of Southern Mexico' *Human Organization* vol. 61, no. 2: 125-138.

Ross, N. 2002b. 'Lacandon-Maya Intergenerational Change and the Erosion of Folkbiological Knowledge' in J. Stepp, F.S. Wyndham, and R.K. Zarger, eds., *Ethnobiology and Biocultural Diversity.* Athens, GA.: International Society of Ethnobiology, pp. 585-592.

Roumasset, J.A., J.-M. Boussard and I. Singh, eds. 1979. *Risk, Uncertainty, and Agricultural Development.* New York: Agricultural Development Council.

Ruddle, K. and R. Chesterfield. 1977. *Education for Traditional Food Procurement in the Orinoco Delta.* Ibero-Americana 53. Berkeley and Los Angeles: University of California Press.

Schoenhoff, D.M. 1993. *The Barefoot Expert: The Interface of Computerized Knowledge Systems and Indigenous Knowledge Systems.* Westport, CT.: Greenwood Press.

Schultes, R. E. 1979. 'The Amazonia as a Source of New Economic Plants' *Economic Botany* vol. 33, no. 3: 259-266.

Schultes, R.E. 1988. 'Primitive Plant Lore and Modern Conservation' *Orion* vol. 7, no. 3: 8.

Schultes, R.E. 1992. 'Ethnobotany and Technology in the Northwest Amazon: A Partnership' in M. Plotkin and L. Famolare, eds., *Sustainable Harvest and Marketing of Rain Forest Products.* Washington, D.C.: Island Press, pp. 7-13.

Schultes, R.E. 1994a. 'Burning the Library of Amazonia' *The Sciences* vol. 34, no. 2: 24-31.

Schultes, R.E. 1994b. 'The Importance of Ethnobotany in Environmental Conservation' *American Journal of Economics and Sociology* vol. 53, no. 2: 202-06.

Schultes, R.E. and R.F. Raffauf. 1990. *The Healing Forest: Medicinal and Toxic Plants of the Northwest Amazonia.* Portland, OR: Dioscorides Press.

Scoones, I. and J. Thompson. 1994. 'Knowledge, Power and Agriculture – Towards a Theoretical Understanding' in I. Scoones and J. Thompson, eds., *Beyond Farmer First.* London: Intermediate Technology Publications, pp. 16-32.

Scribner, S. and M. Cole. 1973. 'Cognitive Consequences of Formal and Informal Education' *Science* vol. 182: 553-559.

Semali, L. and J.L. Kincheloe. 1999. 'What is indigenous knowledge and why should we study it?' in L. Semali and J.L. Kincheloe, eds., *What is Indigenous Knowledge? Voices from the Academy.* New York: Falmer Press, pp. 3-57.

Shiva, V. 1988. *Staying Alive: Women, Ecology and Development.* London: Zed Books.

Shiva, V. 1996. *Biopiracy: The Plunder of Nature and Knowledge.* Boston: South end Press.

Sillitoe, P. 1996. *A Place Against Time: Land and Environment in the Papua New Guinea Highlands.* Amsterdam: Harwood Academic Publishers.

Sillitoe, P. 1998. 'The Development of Indigenous Knowledge' *Current Anthropology* vol. 39, no. 2: 223-252.

Sillitoe, P. 2002a. 'Participant Observation to Participatory Development: Making Anthropology Work' in P. Sillitoe, A. Bicker and J. Pottier, eds., *Participating in Development: Approaches to Indigenous Knowledge.* ASA Monographs 39. London and New York: Routledge. pp. 1-23.

Sillitoe, P. 2002b. 'Globalising Indigenous Knowledge' in P. Sillitoe, A. Bicker and J. Pottier, eds., *Participating in Development: Approaches to Indigenous Knowledge.* ASA Monographs 39. London and New York: Routledge, pp. 108-138.

Sillitoe, P., A. Bicker and J. Pottier, eds. 2002. *Participating in Development: Approaches to Indigenous Knowledge.* ASA Monographs 39. London and New York: Routledge.

Simpson, B.M. 1994 'Gender and the Social Differentiation of Knowledge' *Indigenous Knowledge and Development Monitor* vol. 2, no. 3: 5 pp.

Soejarto, D.D. and N.R. Farnsworth. 1989. 'Tropical Rain Forests: Potential Source of New Drugs?' *Perspectives in Biology and Medicine* vol. 32, no. 2: 244-256.

Soulé, M.E. 1995. 'The Social Siege of Nature'.in M.E. Soulé and G. Lease, eds. *Reinventing Nature? Responses to Postmodern Deconstruction.* Washington, D.C.: Island Press, pp. 137-170.

Soulé, M.E. and G. Lease, eds., 1995. *Reinventing Nature? Responses to Postmodern Deconstruction.* Washington, DC: Island Press.

Sowerine, J. 2004. 'The Socio-Ecological Landscape of Dao Traditional Botanical Medicine: A Tradition in Process'in T. Carlson and L. Maffi, eds., *Ethnobotany and Conservation of Biocultural Diversity. (Advances in Economic Botany vol. 15).* New York: Botanical Garden Press, pp. 235-262.

Stone, G. 2004. 'Biotechnology and the Political Ecology of Information in India' *Human Organization* vol. 63, no. 2: 127-140.

Stross, B. 1973. 'Acquisition of Botanical Terminology by Tzeltal Children' in M.S. Edmonson, ed., *Meaning in Mayan Languages.* The Hague: Mouton, pp. 107-141.

Swanson, T., ed. 1995. *Intellectual property rights and biodiversity conservation.* Cambridge: Cambridge University Press.

Thrupp, L.A. 1989a. 'Legitimizing Local Knowledge, Scientized Packages, or Empowerment for Third World People' in D.M. Warren, L.J. Slikkerveer and S.O. Titilola, eds., *Indigenous Knowledge Systems: Implications for International Development.* Technology and Social Change Studies 11, Ames, IA.: Iowa State University, pp. 138-153.

Thrupp, L.A. 1989b. 'Legitimizing Local Knowledge: From Displacement to Empowerment for Third World People' *Agriculture and Human Values* vol. 6, no. 3: 13-24.

Toledo, V.M. 1992. 'What is Ethnoecology? Origins, Scope and Implications of a Rising Discipline' *Etnoecológica* vol. 1, no. 1: 5-21.

Toledo, V.M. 2002. 'Ethnoecology: A Conceptual Framework for the Study of Indigenous Knowledge of Nature' in J. Stepp, F.S. Wyndham, and R.K. Zarger, eds., *Ethnobiology and Biocultural Diversity*. Athens, GA.: International Society of Ethnobiology, pp. 511-522.

Trotter, R.T. and M.H. Logan. 1986. 'Informant Consensus: A New Approach for Identifying Potentially Effective Medicinal Plants' in N.L. Etkin, ed.' *Plants in Indigenous Medicine and Diet: Biobehavioral Approaches*. Bedford Hills, NY: Redgrave Publishing Company, pp. 91-111.

Vayda, A.P. 1994. 'Actions, Variations, and Change: The Emerging Anti-Essentialist View in Anthropology'.in R. Borofsky, ed., *Assessing Cultural Anthropology*. New York: McGraw-Hill, pp. 320-330.

Vayda, A. and R. Rappaport. 1968. 'Ecology, cultural and noncultural'in J.A. Clifton, ed., *Introduction to Cultural Anthropology*. Boston: Houghton-Mifflin. Pp. 477-497.

Vayda, A.P. and B.B. Walters.1999. 'Against Political Ecology' *Human Ecology* vol. 27, no. 1: 167-179.

Warren, D.M. 2001. 'The Role of the Global Network of Indigenous Knowledge Resource Centers in the Conservation of Cultural and Biological Diversity' in L. Maffi, ed., *On Biocultural Diversity: Linking Language, Knowledge, and the Environment: The Interdependence of Biological and Cultural Diversity*. Washington, DC: Smithsonian Institution Press.

Warren, D.M., L.J. Slikkerveer and D. Brokensha, eds,. 1995. *The Cultural Dimension of Development: Indigenous Knowledge Systems*. London: Intermediate Technology Publications, pp. 446-461.

Warren, D.M., L.J. Slikkerveer and S.O. Titilola, eds., 1989. *Indigenous Knowledge Systems: Implications for International Development*. Technology and Social Change Studies 11, Ames, IA: Iowa State University, .

Whelan, R. 1999. *Wild in the Woods: The Myth of the Noble Eco-Savage*. IEA Studies on the Environment. no. 14 London: Coronet Books, Inc.

Wilbert, W. 2002. 'The Transfer of Traditional Phytomedical Knowledge among the Warao of Northeastern Venezuela' in J. Stepp, F.S. Wyndham, and R.K. Zargar, eds., *Ethnobiology and Biocultural Diversity*. Athens, GA.: International Society of Ethnobiology. pp. 336-350.

Williams, N.M. and G. Baines, eds., 1993. *Traditional Ecological Knowledge: Wisdom for Sustainable Development*. Canberra: Centre for Resources and Environmental Studies, Australian National University.

Zarger, R. 2002. 'Acquisition and Transmission of Subsistence Knowledge by K'ekchi Maya Children in Belize' in J. Stepp, F.S. Wyndham, and R.K. Zarger, eds., *Ethnobiology and Biocultural Diversity*. Athens, GA.: International Society of Ethnobiology. pp. 593-603.

Zarger R.K. and J.R. Stepp. 2004. 'Persistence of Botanical Knowledge among Tzeltal Maya Children' *Current Anthropology* 45(3): 413-18.

Zent, S. 1997. 'Reinventando los sistemas de atención médica para las comunidades indígenas: el papel de las medicinas tradicionales' in J. Chiappino and C. Ales, eds., *Del Microscopio a la Maraca*. Caracas: Editorial Ex Libris. Pp. 339-349.

Zent, S. 1999b. 'Los elementos paradigmaticos de la ecología histórica: Pautas para la renovación de la etnobotánica' *Memorias del Instituto de Biología Experimental* vol. 2, no. 1: 27-30.

Zent, S. 1999a. 'The Quandary of Conserving Ethnobotanical Knowledge: A Piaroa Example' in T. Gragson and B. Blount, eds. *Ethnoecology: Knowledge, Resources, Rights.* University of Georgia Press, pp. 90-124.

Zent, S. 2001. 'Acculturation and Ethnobotanical Knowledge Loss among the Piaroa of Venezuela: Demonstration of a Quantitative Method for the Empirical Study of TEK Change' in L. Maffi, ed. *On Biocultural Diversity: Linking Language, Knowledge, and the Environment,* pp. 190-211, Washington, D.C.: Smithsonian Institution Press.

Zent, S. n.d. Traditional Ecological Knowledge (TEK) and Biocultural Diversity: A Close-up Look at Linkages, Delearning Trends, and Changing Patterns of Transmission' in M. Chiba, S. Kube and D. Nakashima, eds., *Safeguarding the Transmission of Local and Indigenous Knowledge of Nature.* Paris: UNESCO. (in press)

Zent, S. and E.L. Zent. 2000. 'Inferring Processes of Ethnobotanical Knowledge Acquisition from Patterns of Knowledge Acquisition.' Paper presented at the VII International Congress of Ethnobiology. Athens, GA, October 23-27, 2000.

Zent, S. and E.L. Zent. 2004. 'Ethnobotanical Convergence, Divergence, and Change Among the Hoti' in T. Carlson and L. Maffi, eds,. *Ethnobotany and Conservation of Biocultural Diversity. (Advances in Economic Botany* vol. 15) Bronx, N.Y.: Botanical Garden Press, pp. 37-78.

Chapter 3

The Cultural and Economic Globalisation of Traditional Environmental Knowledge Systems

Miguel N. Alexiades

Introduction

In 1999, participants of the World Conference on Science for the Twenty-First Century called for a new 'social contract' between science and society on the grounds that science had entered a new phase in which the nature of the problems it faces, and therefore its function, have changed (World Conference on Science 1999). In this chapter I explore some of the broad implications of this 'new phase' – which includes massive technological change, widespread economic and political re-structuring and the dramatic increase in the transnational flows of ideas, goods, people, capital and services – for both indigenous knowledge and its relationship to science. I suggest that traditional environmental knowledge (TEK) has undergone unprecedented validation, commoditisation and politicisation, and that these interrelated processes can be instructively examined in the context of technological, social and political changes following the re-organisation of the global economy during the end of the twentieth century. As local, and especially traditional and indigenous knowledge,[1] acquires new meanings as an economic and political resource, opportunities are created for its flow, transmission, incorporation and transformation, opening spaces for both cooperation and conflict between the actors who claim ownership or representation over different kinds of knowledge.

Before examining the complex interrelationships between TEK and global processes, it is instructive to define and qualify a few terms and concepts. Globalisation, broadly defined as 'the intensification of economic, political, social and cultural relations across borders' (Holm and Sorensen 1995: 1) is by no means a novel process. A world economy linking Europe and Asia through trade dates back to the thirteenth century (Abu-Lughod 1989), and even before then there were extensive movements of peoples, goods, ideas and technologies among different regions of the world. This world economy has undergone successive phases of expansion and contraction with occasional collapses (Hall 2000, Holton 1998). The rise of capitalism in the sixteenth century marked a new wave of expansion and the creation of a particular form of global economy (Wallerstein 1974).[2]

Globalising processes have clearly increased in scope and intensity over the past century. Robertson (1992), for example, identifies several distinct phases, the latest of which is characterised by 1) the replacement of a bipolar international geopolitical system – itself linked to the Cold War – with a more fluid and uncertain one; 2) an unparalleled 'time-space compression' due to the revolution in communications technology; 3) the growth of the information and service sectors; 4) the spread of economic neoliberalism; and 5) the growth of transnational social or environmental movements. It is this syndrome of interrelated yet distinct processes, encompassed by the term 'globalisation' (cf. Mittelman 2000), that I focus on in this chapter.

There is some confusion in the use of the terms 'international', 'multinational', 'transnational' and 'global', as these are sometimes used interchangeably or interpreted differently. I follow the simple convention that 'international' refers to relationships between nation-states, in contrast to transnational processes, which operate at a level above or beyond national determination and control (Holton 1998: 10). While transnationalism overlaps with globalisation, the latter has a broader connotation: global processes take place in a global space and are in effect de-centred from specific national territories. While transcending individual nation-states, transnational processes may still be anchored to one or more nation-states (Kearney 1995). The international economy of the nineteenth and early twentieth centuries was largely based on exchanges between national economies, carried out by actors and institutions based within particular nations, and mostly involved trade. Since the 1960s, economic globalisation has been increasingly transnational in kind: greater integration of the world's financial markets and de-regulation of capital transfers means that flows of capital by far exceed flows of goods. In a transnational economy, capital investment, marketing and manufacturing are structured according to optimal profitability and a growing number of transnational companies are in effect no longer necessarily tied to any one particular nation-state (Holton 1998: 52, Neef 1999: 13). This transformation in the nature and organisation of global capitalism is, I suggest, instructive to our understanding changes in the meanings, values and struggles linked to indigenous environmental knowledge and its transformations.

Because globalisation is by definition a complex and heterogeneous process with distinct, yet clearly overlapping and linked economic, political, social and cultural aspects, its effects are not experienced in the same way everywhere or by everyone (Long 1996). My analysis regarding the commoditisation and politicisation of indigenous knowledge – including a discussion of 'biopiracy' and questions relating to struggles over the rights for control, representation and use of knowledge – draw mostly on experiences from the Americas, though even within this region the processes I describe are not universal nor do they have the same effects everywhere (see also Alexiades 2003).

Modernisation, Globalisation and the Changing Role of Traditional Knowledge

Throughout much of recent history, the paradigm of modernisation retained a hegemonic presence in the development ideology of nation-states throughout the world (Norgaard 1994).[3] Three conceptual cornerstones underlie the modern project: scientism, the belief that the scientific worldview is the only way to a true understanding of the world; developmentalism, the belief in progress based on certain patterns of consumption; and statism, the emphasis on the modern nation state as the legitimate form of political authority (Ekins 1992: 207). Modern education, the expansion of the market and in particular, the promotion of wage labour and mass consumption are all critical elements of this modernising project (Phillips 1998).

In the decades after the Second World War, 'Third World' countries, aided and abetted by 'First World' countries, embarked on a massive project of modernisation. This period of social engineering, characterised by nation-building, urbanisation and industrialisation subordinated rural 'peripheral' populations – including their subsistence practices, traditions and knowledge – to those of political and economic 'cores'. This led to the logical superposition of universalist ideals espoused by modernity and the marginalisation of all that is considered 'primitive', including, of course, traditional environmental knowledge. Under the aegis of modernity, tradition became 'something to be overcome, to be subverted rather than encouraged, its legitimacy questioned' (Ellen and Harris 2000: 11).

In recent decades, and particularly since the 1970s, modernisation has given way to a new historical project, globalisation or neo-modernisation (Phillips 1998). Like modernisation, globalisation seeks to stabilise global capitalism, only through global – as opposed to national – economic management. Moreover, rather than suggesting that poor nation-states 'develop' by replicating the paths of industrialised countries, globalisation encourages actors to 'position' themselves in the global economy through regional specialisation (McMichael 1996). Amidst de-centralised production and consumption and constantly shifting markets, diversity has become, in the words of Klein (1999: 115, cited in Edelman 2001: 300) 'the mantra of global capital.' The transition from modern to post-modern capitalism, therefore, has signified a shift in the value – symbolic, political and economic of cultural and biological diversity.

The Validation and Valuation of Indigenous Knowledge

Above, I have argued that broad technological, social and political changes have signalled a shift in the meanings and values attached to 'peripheral' places, peoples and knowledge. The revitalisation of TEK is evident in the extent to which it has become validated and valued in the context of scientific research and in economic and social development.

Science, TEK and the Rise of Cultural Relativism

Ethnocentric views of indigenous cultures have been used consistently throughout the past centuries as a means to justify their colonisation, submission and forced integration. Columbus's failure to recognise the existence of an indigenous language during his first encounters with Amerindians (Todorov 1984: 30), illustrates a crude ethnocentrism which prevails in the modernist discourse and its denial of the value, and at times even the existence, of indigenous knowledge. While still prevalent, modernist views of cultural diversity and the value of local knowledge became increasingly questioned in the late twentieth century. Local, especially indigenous environmental, knowledge has in fact undergone a process of unprecedented validation and recognition within such centres of political and economic power as government and multilateral development agencies, international donors, international and national non-governmental organisations (NGOs), scientific institutions, private corporations and the media (Anani 1999, Sillitoe 1998: 223-224).

The validation of indigenous knowledge can in turn be seen to be part of a broader tendency towards cultural relativism, the notion that all cultures, no matter how idiosyncratic or strange they might appear to an outsider, are internally coherent, meaningful and intrinsically worthy of respect (Winthrop 1991). Influential nineteenth- and twentieth-century social scientists, such as Boas, Durkheim, Evans-Pritchard and Malinowski, were instrumental in spreading a relativist perspective of culture in and beyond academia. Ethnoscience's emphasis on the complexity and systematic nature of local knowledge, particularly environmental knowledge, has been particularly influential in changing perceptions of traditional, and especially indigenous, knowledge

(Nazarea 1999, Winthrop 1991). Within this field, particularist approaches emphasise that, as a social product, environmental knowledge is necessarily embedded in specific situational, social or environmental contexts (Conklin 1969, Ellen 1993), whereas universalist perspectives suggest that different societies perceive key aspects of reality in ways that are fundamentally similar (Atran 1990, Berlin, Breedlove and Raven 1974).

A third, utilitarian, approach, distinct from the particularist and universalist orientations outlined above, is exemplified by economic botanists such as Schultes (1980) and others (Balick 1979, Prance et al. 1994). These scholars, mostly botanists, have highlighted the practical value of environmental knowledge for conservation and developing new commodities. Yet another approach emphasises the value of traditional environmental knowledge systems in resource management, land planning, poverty alleviation and environmentally and socially sound development (Bentley 1992, Brokensha et al. 1980, Posey 1983, Warren et al. 1995). Despite differences in their approaches, these various strands within ethnoecology and ethnobotany all question a fundamental premise of modernisation: that traditional knowledge is rudimentary, naive or lacking intrinsic merit or value (Nazarea 1999).

Ethnobotanists, ethnoecologists, anthropologists and others have produced detailed accounts of the sophisticated resource management strategies developed by rural non-industrial societies, suggesting that important lessons can be inferred from these knowledge systems and applied to contemporary health, development and conservation problems (Alcorn 1995, Berkes et al. 2000, DeWalt 1994, Posey et al. 1984). These messages resonated among sectors of the public, media and the development community during the 1980s (Brokensha et al. 1980, Chambers 1983, Howes 1980). By then it was clear to many that postwar modernist development programs had failed not only to reduce poverty amidst increasing affluence, but had also crippled many Third World countries with massive debt, while creating social and environmental havoc (Banuri 1990, Norgaard 1994). The prominence of environmental problems, such as acid rain, ozone depletion and climate change, whose cause and effect clearly surpass political boundaries, further propelled the environment into the mainstream and international political arena, helped by the ability of a growing environmental movement to capture public opinion through the media.

The concept of sustainability, with its emphasis on long-term economic, environmental and social well-being, grew out of this period of crisis. Developed at the UN Conference on the Human Environment in 1972 and popularised amongst policy makers by the United Nations-sponsored Brundtland Commission Report in 1987 (World Commission on Environment and Development 1987), the notion of sustainable development was formally legitimised as a development strategy during the 1992 United Nations Conference on Environment and Development (Little 1995).

Similar developments were taking place around the same time in the context of international health. For example, the Alma Ata Conference of 1978 organised by the World Health Organisation proclaimed that adequate health for the world's poor could only be achieved by integrating traditional medicine into primary health care delivery programs (Bannerman et al. 1983, WHO 1988). Several years later, the notion that indigenous medicinal plant knowledge could help identify cures for diseases such as cancer and AIDS was widely popularised by some ethnobotanists and the media (Balick et al. 1994, Plotkin 1993). As a result, European and American audiences commonly associate the rainforest as a source of 'miracle cures' (Alexiades 2004). Despite this widespread perception and the renewed interest in some scientific circles regarding the promising role of indigenous knowledge in drug development (Heinrich 2000, Prance et al. 1994), indigenous knowledge continues to play a fairly minor role in commercial drug discovery (ten Kate and Laird 1999: 62).

While rhetoric about the environment and traditional knowledge has clearly not always translated into practice, its emergence nonetheless signals a shift in how indigenous environmental knowledge is viewed and represented within centres of power. This in turn has created new opportunities for the utilisation of indigenous knowledge in the context of development (Sillitoe et al. 2002, Warren et al. 1989).

Sustainability, the Rise of the Information Economy and the Revitalisation of TEK

In contrast to the modernist development paradigm, the concept and rhetoric of sustainable development privileges rather than discriminates against local forms of environmental knowledge, organisation and participation. The 1987 Brundtland report, the 1992, the United Nations Conference on the Environment and Development (UNCED) Rio Declaration on Environment and Development and Agenda 21, for example, all specifically identify indigenous knowledge as a critical resource for achieving sustainable development. While the degree to which indigenous or traditional resource management regimes are 'sustainable' is clearly a complex question, the integration of development and environmental agendas has in some instances helped reposition 'peripheral' knowledge in relation to centres of economic and political power (Wilmer 1993). It has also made indigenous knowledge an important political resource in indigenous claims to territory and rights (Muehlebach 2001).

The popularisation and validation of indigenous knowledge has also been facilitated by the environmental justice movement and its wide network of contacts in government, and among multilateral development agencies, scientists, the media and local communities (Ribeiro and Little 1998). Within this revisionism lies a long legacy of idealising and romanticising indigenous cultures, even if these representations reveal more about the anxieties and fantasies of modernity and its discontents than about indigenous peoples themselves (Ellen 1986, Krech 1999). As noted by Ellen and Harris (2000: 13), 'In this new vision, indigenous peoples are given central focus because of rather than in spite of their cultural differences'.[4]

At a broader level, the emergence of sustainable development of the 1980s reveals a new awareness of the importance of diversity to social wellbeing:

> Awareness of such heterogeneity is reflected in the questioning, in certain policy circles, of standardised solutions to problems of economic development, employment and welfare, in favour of what are described as more flexible, localised and 'sustainable' strategies. This shift implies, at least in public rhetoric, a greater recognition of the strategic contribution that local knowledge, organisation and participation can make to development. (Long 1996: 39)

The shift in development from 'standardised solutions' to 'flexible and localised strategies' resonates with a broader shift in the structure of economic organisation. During the first half of the twentieth century the industrial phase of capitalism emphasised the development of the industrial sector, centralisation, mass production and consumption. As such, the industrial age was structured around vertically integrated organisations with high costs of communication, information and transportation. The second half of the twentieth century, on the other hand, gave way to a new form of economic organisation, referred to as postmodern or network phase of capitalism, where economic growth is propelled by the knowledge industries and the service sector. Today, revolution in communications technology has dramatically reduced costs of communication, information and transportation, leading to decentralised production and consumption, emphasising horizontal networks and the development of specialised, or 'niche', markets – the so called 'flexible accumulation' model of late capitalism (Harvey 2000: 294, Oman 1997).

These trends were intensified by the recession of the world economy in the late 1970s, which had devastating effects on the economies of countries that had become heavily indebted following ambitious industrialisation and modernisation projects. As the prices received for their products declined, many countries – in Latin America particularly – were forced to default on their loans. The extension of further loans, deemed essential for economic recovery, was made contingent on the acceptance of drastic structural adjustment policies imposed by the International Monetary Fund (IMF) and the World Bank (Phillips 1998). This, coupled with the collapse of the Soviet block in the 1990s, gave huge impetus to the spread of free-market economics.

The renewed interest in market processes as mechanisms to achieve development and conservation goals (Coker and Richards 1992, Edwards 1995, Freese 1998), and the growing influence of non-state actors, including the private sector and NGOs (Fisher 1993, 1996) in development resonate with these post-

1980s free market economic policies and the concomitant dismantling of the welfare state. In a similar vein, Ribeiro and Little (1998) suggest a causal relationship between the shift towards an information and service based economy and the growth of the environmental movement.

The economic, moral and philosophical importance projected onto diversity is most clearly revealed in the popularisation of the terms 'biological diversity' and 'cultural diversity' (Wilson 1988), sometimes referred to as biocultural diversity (Maffi 2001). The following statement by Marglin (1990) echoes similar arguments made by scientists and environmentalists, and reflected by the media (see for example, Linden 1991):

> Cultural diversity may be the key to the survival of the human species. Just as biologists defend exotic species like the snail darter in order to maintain the diversity of the genetic pool ... so should we defend exotic cultures in order to maintain the diversity of forms of understanding, creating and coping that the human species has managed to generate (Marglin 1990: 6).

The Commoditisation of Knowledge

Capitalism is inherently expansionist and self-enlarging (Prugh et al. 2000: 71). The continuous development of new commodities, products of human activity with an assigned market price, is one of the ways to maintain such growth. Not surprisingly then, commoditisation is a particularly noticeable trend in modern capitalism (Grimes 2000). While demand for such cultural commodities as 'ethnic art' can be traced to the colonial era (Thomas 1987), the recent surge in interest and mass marketing of this and other cultural commodities, including 'native spirituality,' 'world music' and 'cultural tourism' suggest that in post-colonial times culture has become 'a primary field of entrepreneurial and capitalistic activity' (Harvey 2000: 296). The consumption of culture in the global 'cultural supermarket' has become an important means through which post-industrial citizens define their identity (Mathews 2000). This increased commodification of culture, and by implication of cultural diversity, suggests, once more, an economy in which the importance of diversity, heterogeneity and difference is emphasised, both in terms of supply (niche marketing) and demand (lifestyle choices).

In addition, the shift towards an information-based economy has profoundly altered the social, political and economic value and meaning of information and knowledge (Castells 1993, Long 1996). The technological revolution in communications and computing make it possible to 'generate information that was heretofore unattainable, transmit it instantaneously around the globe, and – in a rapidly growing number of instances – sell it in information markets' (Melody 1994: 21). Advances in automation, computing and biotechnology have fundamentally transformed the commercial potential of biological and genetic resources (Verpoorte 2002) and contributed to an informational perspective of nature and the world (Alexiades 2003, Alexiades in preparation).

This perspective is particularly palpable in many of the discussions on biological and cultural diversity. Nazarea's remark, for example, that 'genes and cultures have something very important in common: both are repositories of coded information essential to adaptation and survival' (Nazarea 1998: 73), illustrates the extent to which the informational view of diversity has been normalised, both conceptually and in a utilitarian sense. This informational dimension of local environmental knowledge is especially significant in the context of science and its goal of producing, in the words of Latour (1986, cited in DeWalt 1994) 'immutable mobiles', or trans-local knowledge. The flow of knowledge across social spheres, particularly in the context of commoditisation, entails its disassociation from its social context and its re-incorporation into new, often geographically and culturally remote, social and economic settings. Just as commodities are defined and redefined as they flow between different spheres of social and economic exchange (Haugerud et al. 2000), the flow of knowledge within the global network is inevitably transformed, in terms of its meaning, roles and context in which it is produced and reproduced (Ellen et al. 2000).

As knowledge becomes appropriated, circulated, commoditised and transformed, questions regarding rights to access, representation, ownership and control become paramount. Not surprisingly, the issue of intellectual property rights has moved to the forefront of international and national regulatory agendas during the past two decades. The Trade-Related Intellectual Property Rights (TRIPS) agreement issued in the Uruguay round of GATT is indicative of three interrelated processes: the growing importance of the knowledge and the information sector, including the software, entertainment and biotechnology industries; the increased commoditisation of genetic resources; and the globalisation in the flow of these different products, largely through the expansion of transnational corporate activity. The Convention on Biological Diversity also responds to this new context by seeking to establish a regulatory framework through which nation-states can control access to genetic resources and develop material transfer and benefit-sharing agreements (Dutfield 2002, Monagle and Gonzales 2001). [5]

Pistorius and van Wijk (2000) discuss these changes in the context of agriculture and the historical development of what they identify as three major production strategies. The first of these, non-industrial agriculture, was the main global agricultural production strategy until the end of the nineteenth century, and continues to form the basis of the agriculture practiced by the world's majority of economically and socially marginalised farmers. These farmers depend on free access to a wide range of plant genetic resources as a means to guarantee their families' food security and oppose patenting of plant varieties and intellectual property rights regimes.

During much of the twentieth century, the Organisation for Economic Co-operation and Development (OECD) countries and their multilateral agencies (World Bank, the Future Harvest Centres of the Consultative Group on International Agricultural Research and others) actively promoted agro-industrialisation via plant genetic resource collection and conservation, emphasising plant breeding and plant breeder's rights as mechanisms to guarantee national, as opposed to family, food security. This period of agricultural development coincides with the period of modernisation and nation building outlined earlier.

The 1980s marked the beginning of what Pistorius and van Wijk refer to as market-led agro-industry, with an emphasis in crop development through the application of revolutionary biotechnologies, which rely on the use of genetic information from biodiversity and not simply from crop genetic resources. In contrast to the family-level and state-level of control of the two previous production strategies, production is now controlled by large transnational corporations, which in turn is facilitated by national de-regulation and economic liberalisation, and extended to non-OECD countries through such institutional mechanisms as the World Bank and the WTO. Changes in U.S patent law in the 1980's allowing patents on life forms (Mooney 1997), and the internationalisation of intellectual property rights regimes through TRIPS, reflect a shift in the strategic and economic role of genetic information and, more generally, biodiversity.[6]

New powerful conflicts of interest arise from the dual status of knowledge as a public resource, whose value depends on it being shared, and as a private resource, whose value depends on it being guarded. Indigenous leaders and activists in Latin America, for example, have expressed concern that the value of indigenous knowledge as a tool for cultural revival and self-determination, a process known as *revalorización*, is being increasingly frustrated by fears that once diffused, such knowledge will be misappropriated (Alexiades 2003). Scientists too are increasingly torn between their obligation to disclose the results of their research to the scientific community and to the general public, and their obligations to either corporate or indigenous partners, who may require withholding certain kinds of information from publication (Laird et al. 2002). The privatisation of science (Busch et al. 1999), the rapid growth of agribusiness and biotechnology, and the increased mobilisation of indigenous and environmental watchdog organisations concerned with the social and environmental impacts of these industries (Feder 1999, McCarthy 1999, Shiva 1997) are likely to continue generating conflicts of interest as different forms of environmental knowledge fulfil diverse, often contradictory, roles.

The Politicisation of Knowledge

The revitalisation of traditional environmental knowledge bears distinct, inter-secting and often conflicting social and economic dimensions – in the form of ethnic revitalization and commoditisation, for example. Traditional environ-mental knowledge has thus become politicised in new ways, at times serving as an arena where struggles over representation, control, authenticity, property and equity are played out in an increasingly interconnected world.

New Social Movements and the Politics of Identity

Economic liberalisation and the dismantling of the welfare state have eroded the presence of the state in the service sector, including health, education and devel-opment. Coupled with a global tendency towards democratisation (Clark 1997), this in turn has created new spaces for the growth of civil society[7] (Edel-man 2001), as evidenced by the rapid growth in the number and influence of non-governmental and grass-roots organisations (Blunt and Warren1996, Esco-bar and Alvarez 1992).

The revitalisation of 'tradition' and the re-emergence of indigenous political agency is evidenced by the growing number of peoples who define themselves as indigenous, the proliferation of indigenous associations, federations, commu-nity-based organisations and NGOs, the recognition of indigenous collective rights in national and international jurisprudence and the increasing presence of indigenous delegates within the United Nations (Colchester 2002; Muehlbach 2001; Nagel 1996; Warren 1998; Wilmer 1993: 5). This 're-indigenisation' reflects the importance of identity, based on ethnicity, locality or religion, as a form of cultural and political renewal in an era of increasingly globalised exchanges (Cornell 1998; Clark 1997; Turner 1993; McMichael 2000: 286).

Like environmental activism, indigenous and human rights activism have become increasingly transnational (Brysk 2000; Varese 1996), often involving strategic alliances between different organisations and movements (Poole 1990; van de Fliert 1994). These 'new social movements' have emerged as collective form of resistance amidst globalisation in the same way as trade unions formed in response to the industrial phase of capitalism (Clark 1997; Falk 1993; Finger 1994; Sklair 2000). Not surprisingly, the commercial, political, ethical, legal and moral issues surrounding use, access and control of local environmental knowl-edge and genetic resources lie at the core of a number of social movements (Edelman 1999; Mooney and Majka 1995) and international organisations such as the Indigenous People's Biodiversity Network and the Indigenous Knowledge Program (Muehlebach 2001: 435).

As an instance of 'globalisation from below' (Falk 1993) these movements have shifted, even if at times only temporarily and partially, the balance of power between indigenous peoples and national governments (Burger 1987; Kearney

1995; Wilmer 1993). A rapidly growing indigenous movement has not only succeeded in blocking of large-scale hydroelectric development projects in Brazil and Canada (Fisher 1994; Aubry and Mcilroy 1994), but has also pushed constitutional reform in the Philippines, Ecuador and Bolivia (Maybury-Lewis 1984), and led to indigenous self-government in many parts of Eurasia, Asia and the Americas (Cordillera Peoples Alliance et al. 2005; Dahl et al. 2000; Wessendorf 2005).

The crisis of modernity, the growth of civil society and the emergence of identity as a vehicle for political and spiritual renewal, have created new opportunities for indigenous political organisation. Cultural knowledge, including environmental knowledge, is particularly important as a means of legitimising claims to secondary resources, such as land or natural resources. As knowledge becomes increasingly valued, circulated and transformed, it becomes increasingly contested. As a result, struggles over rights of access and representation of knowledge serve as means through which broader and deeper conflicts are expressed and negotiated.

Disputes over the appropriation of Native American spirituality by non-native actors, for example, not only revolve around questions of authenticity and legitimacy, but also of justice. Brown (1998: esp. 201-202) provides an insightful critique of the notion that any minority group can claim collective property rights over culture, and the legal, political and social implications of treating culture as property, given culture's unbounded and dynamic nature. However, the issue is not only whether Europeans and Americans have the right to, or even can, represent or appropriate elements of Native American culture (Joralemon 1990), but the fact that such appropriation follows from a history of abuse, marginalisation and violence directed at native Americans in general, and against native American spirituality in particular (Hall 2000: 257-258).

Science, TEK and the Crisis of Representation

The Enlightenment, with its emphasis on individualism, materialism, rationalism, universalism and the role of science as the privileged source of truth, has come under increased scrutiny and reflexive criticism (Inayatullah 1997; Roberts and Hite 1999: 18; Touraine 1989). Concomitantly, a preoccupation with heterogeneity, uncertainty, and subjectivity is evident in much of contemporary science, philosophy and aesthetics. For some, this emphasis on fragmentation, ephemerality, difference and 'otherness' reflects a 'crisis of representation' brought about by the radical transformation of the experience of time and space following the dramatic advances in communications technology and the re-organisation of capitalism (Harvey 2000: 294), with the concomitant plurality of power and heightened economic competition this has entailed (Bergsen 2000: 181; see also Friedman 1998).

One facet of the crisis of representation is the questioning of authority, both with regards to what is established as 'the truth' and the procedures used to determine that truth. An important dimension of this debate concerns the power relationship between scientific and other knowledge systems, including local knowledge. While many scholars, environmentalists and development workers note the importance of considering the 'local perspective', in practice this perspective is afforded an inferior status to the 'scientific perspective'. The subordination of local to scientific knowledge is evident in the ways that 'local' views of the environment are presented as illusory and incomplete, in contrast to the presumed objectiveness and totality of the 'global' view (Ingold 1993: 31). Campbell (2002), for example, provides an elegant example of how scientific knowledge and technology, in this case linked to the use of Geographical Information Systems (GIS), was used to subordinate or block local forms of knowledge and understanding. In practice such distinctions often serve to legitimate the disempowerment of local people in the management of their environments (Brosius 2002, Fairhead and Leach 1996).

In other instances, the value of traditional knowledge is presented as contingent upon its scientific validation. An example of this position was articulated by U.S. officials during the World Conference of Science, who expressed concern that traditional knowledge should be considered as a science, a demand heard from a variety of developing countries, suggesting instead that traditional knowledge 'be studied more – to be scientifically validated' (Nature 1999). By characterising Western sciences as transcultural and universal and indigenous knowledge systems as culturally and locally grounded, the latter are implicitly relegated to a lower order of knowledge production (Semali and Kincheloe 1999: 21). Making the validation of traditional knowledge contingent on scientific testing reveals a power relationship between both systems of knowledge (Viergever 1999). Agrawal (1995, 2002) further suggests that the distinction between 'scientific' and 'indigenous' knowledge reifies a false dichotomy and ultimately serves to further marginalise disadvantaged groups.

The issue of power relations is particularly important in the context of local environmental knowledge given the common observation that the groups 'that control the greatest wealth of traditional knowledge and biological resources may be the most marginalised by nation-states' (Brush 1993: 664). Similarly, Alcorn (1995: 1) identifies the status difference between bearers of ethnobotanical knowledge and development specialists as one of the barriers for implementing and incorporating such knowledge in development. The following statement by Robbins (1999) clearly articulates the fundamental importance of power relations in structuring contact and exchange along the local-global continuum:

> Given the terrible inequalities of power and wealth that continue to structure the world of nations, no version of worldliness – wherever it is located, however close it remains to the grassroots – cannot be accused of depending and benefiting from these inequalities ... Even human rights activism involves actions of unequal power and mobility and can thus be classified as a form of the "aerial global view". This is no

truer of the inequalities between First and Third World governments than of the inequalities between a metropolitan and a Third World NGO. It also distinguishes activists in a Third World capital from the rural population they are trying to help. The differentials of power and privilege are equally dramatic at every scale. No good intention, no democratic scrupulosity, can wish them away. (Robbins 1999: 5)

Globalisation has also profoundly reshaped the social, political and economic fields in which scientific knowledge is produced, and hence the relationship between science and society and between 'scientific' and other forms of knowledge. For one thing, the relationship between science, technological innovation and the economy has changed in fundamental ways (Castells 1993). The great technological advances of the nineteenth and early twentieth century, including steel, electric power, telegraph, telephone, automobiles and aviation, were mainly the creation of 'talented tinkerers' such as Bell, Edison, Kelly and Bessmer, who 'were indifferent to science and the fundamental laws underlying their investigations' (Bell 1999: 20). In contrast, the new industries of the twentieth century, including computing, fibre optics and biotechnology, all emerge from within the core of the great scientific advances of the twentieth century, notably relativity theory and genetics.

The changing role of science in the new economy, the advent of potentially destructive and widely feared technologies such as nuclear energy and genetic engineering, and a widespread crisis of authority and representation, have all contributed to a growing distrust of science within certain sectors of society, as exemplified by the 'science wars' of the 1990s (Ross 1996). This coupled with a decrease in public funding and the widespread privatisation of science has created new challenges and conflicts of interest for its practitioners.

Accusations of 'biopiracy', levelled against many scientists and scientific institutions in the recent past, highlight some of the new and complex economic, legal and political dimensions of the revolution in biotechnology, and illustrate how science increasingly operates under public scrutiny (Riordan 1995, Weinberg 2001). The level of suspicion directed towards scientists may be perplexing to some, particularly in instances and regions where highly predatory resource extraction schemes operate apace and largely unchallenged (Laird et al. 2000).

One way of reconciling this apparent paradox is by considering bioprospecting, linked as it is to new technologies and to an increasingly globalised economy, as emblematic of a new order of social, political and economic relations and its concomitant tensions (Clement and Alexiades 2000, Mooney 1997). As a social phenomenon, biopiracy thus expresses the collective memory of a colonial and neo-colonial past, as well as the fear of a new technological and economic order in which notions of national, subnational and individual sovereignty or integrity are threatened (Alexiades in preparation, Jackson 2002).

In a discussion of the rediscovery, reification and reinvention of indigenous knowledge within the environmental and development sector, Ellen and Harris (2000) note a clear tendency towards decontextualising and disaggregating indigenous knowledge. Escobar has expressed scepticism about the appropriation of local knowledge of biodiversity:

> 'Modern biology is beginning to find local knowledge systems to be useful complements. In these discourses, however, knowledge is seen as something that exists in the 'minds' of individual persons (shamans, sages, elders) about external 'objects' (plants, species), the medical or economic 'utility' of which their bearers are supposed to 'transmit' to the modern experts. Local knowledge is not seen as a complex cultural construction, involving not objects but movements and events that are profoundly historical and relational' (1995: 204).

The 'universalising discourse' of indigenous knowledge as homogeneous, systemic and static, runs the risk of repeating the errors of past development projects by 'ignoring specific local experience in favour of a generalisable and universal solution' (Harris 1996: 14, cited in Ellen and Harris 2000: 15). Such an approach is in turn unlikely to be effective in addressing social and environmental problems 'on the ground', possibly discrediting the value of local knowledge as an effective tool for development.

A central question then, is not whether indigenous environmental knowledge has value and application outside of its own particular context, but rather how it is used, represented or appropriated, by whom, to what ends, for whose benefit, and under what conditions. Likewise, it is not the appropriation, circulation and transformation of local environmental knowledge that is novel; it is the economic, social and especially political significance that such knowledge has acquired, and concomitantly, the spaces for cooperation and conflict that such a shift has created.

Globalisation, Integration and Fragmentation

Contemporary globalisation has given way to two fundamental, interrelated yet apparently contradictory processes: integration and fragmentation. The simultaneous occurrence of these two processes is revealed in all aspects of social life affected by globalisation. In economic terms, for example, while increased capital flows and foreign direct investment have led to economic integration at one level, regional specialisation and the creation of an international division of labour have led to new and simultaneous forms of economic fragmentation (Gereffi 2000, Petras 1999: 15). This fragmentation is evidenced by increasing social and economic polarisation within and between countries (Cox 1997: 26, Böröcz and Smith 1995).

In geopolitical terms, the interplay of integration and fragmentation is exemplified by the tendency for some regions and nations to become simultaneously unified and disaggregated at different levels. Some analysts suggest that regionalisation represents a more significant form of geopolitical and economic integration than globalisation (Fernández and Mommen 1998), whereas others see it as a facet or a stage in globalisation (Cox 1994). Western Europe is a case in point, where countries like the United Kingdom and Spain are being integrated 'from above' into the European Union, while simultaneously experiencing a fragmenting pull 'from below', in the form of separatist or autonomy movements. The end of the Cold War and the collapse of the Soviet Block has also contributed to the fragmentation of nation-states. The tendency for geo-political fragmentation is also particularly evident in regions where political boundaries were laid down in recent colonial or post-colonial contexts, and within which claims to sovereignty based on race, religion or ethnicity are effectively being articulated in a post-Cold-War context.

In the realm of culture, the interplay between integration and fragmentation is expressed as the simultaneous processes of homogenisation and heterogenisation: 'Just as globalisation gives impetus to cultural homogenisation, so too does a global thrust undermine state power and unleash subterranean cultural pluralism' (Mittelman 1997: 8). Appadurai (1994) sees the tension between these two as the central problem of today's global interactions. Just as fragmentation occurs as a reaction to integration, heterogenisation also emerges as a response to homogenisation (Mittelman 1997).

Amid this tension, products become increasingly valued in terms of local variation as opposed to, and in response to, standardisation. For example, renewed interest in heirloom varieties of fruits and vegetables and in locally grown and processed food products occurs as a response to increased transnationalisation, industrialisation and homogenisation of food products (Bérard and Marchenay 1996, Norberg-Hodge 1998). The 'Appelation Controlée' denomination, geographical indications and the 'Slow Food' network are among the legal mechanisms and business initiatives which respond to the demands by consumers who reject mass-produced food for reasons of quality, health or environment (Downes and Laird 1999, Stille 2001). Widespread interest and revival in local, traditional and indigenous arts and crafts can clearly also be understood in this context.

The engagement of particular localities within a global field leads to a unique interpenetration of the global and the local, to the localisation of the global, or to 'glocalisation' (Robertson 1995). These global-local interchanges, epitomised by the slogan 'Think Globally: Act Locally', are a defining aspect of contemporary social life, and are particularly important in the context of how local environmental knowledge is circulated and transformed. The notion that local medicinal knowledge has considerable potential and application in curing such 'global' ailments as AIDS or cancer is an example of one type of global-local interchange, the globalisation of the local (Brosius 2000).

International property rights regimes, particularly TRIPS, are in effect globalising and extending market notions of property into locally managed resources, be these environmental knowledge or genetic resources, that until recently were shared according to other principles. At the same time, some forms of local environmental knowledge, or its representation, are becoming a powerful vehicle through which individuals and groups establish identity on the basis of ethnicity, religion or locality, distancing themselves from other groups. Brosius (2000) provides an example of the opposite type of global-local interchange, the localisation of the global, describing how the Penan people in Borneo have appropriated 'globalised' views of indigenous knowledge in their own representations of environmental, and specifically medicinal, knowledge.

The interplay between both tendencies does not necessarily mean that there is equivalence in scale. With regards to linguistic diversity, the overall global tendency is clearly towards homogenisation, including the loss of a large number of indigenous oral languages (Kane 1997), even though in some areas particular languages are in the process of revaluation and recovery (Schmidt 1990). Likewise, the overall tendency in the world is homogenisation of agro-biodiversity, despite the above mentioned exception, in which there is a concomitant counter tendency towards heterogenisation. In corporate terms, the valuation of diversity generates a form of 'mono-multiculturalism' (Klein 1999: 115, cited in Edelman 2001: 300) across a myriad differentiated markets.

Traditional Environmental Knowledge in a Post-September 11 World: A New Phase?

Never static, the world economy is always in a state of flux. In this chapter I have focused on the transition between the industrial and the network phases (cf. UNDP 2002) of modern capitalism. The violent political and social events that have unfolded since 11 September 2001 highlight the degree of contingency and uncertainty in the world, and may suggest a turning point, if not in the organisation of the world economy, then certainly in the political and social context in which different social, economic and knowledge systems engage with each other. On the one hand, the experience of ethnonationalist violence in the Balkans and post-colonial Africa, and of post 9/11 'Islamic terrorism', have crystallised fears of social breakdown through the assertion of religious, ethnic or ethnonationalist difference. Ethnonationalist and religious violence may clearly damage agendas that strive to facilitate multiculturalism in its various forms, or indeed the appetite for cultural commodities, based as they are on the fascination with the 'other'.

This, coupled with a tendency for political unilateralism and closing of borders, seems to run counter to the tendency for increased interpenetration and flow of peoples, goods, ideas and capital, which have all so clearly been favoured by economic globalisation and underpinned by the revolution in communications technology. While the long or even medium-term impacts of these political changes on the form of the world economy are uncertain, they could foreseeably help reshape the social meanings projected on local forms of being and knowing and, more generally cultural diversity. This shift could easily be accelerated by the way in which the 'war on terrorism', hinging as it does on a strategically unde-fined term, be seized by central governments as a way of suppressing movements of ethnic resistance, particularly given the conflicts that underlie indigenous and State simultaneous claims to sovereignty (Wilmer 1993: 2). In other words, cur-rent political events may signal a shift in the power balance between local and central forms of knowledge, organisation and control, which in turn will have an impact on how local knowledge is construed internally and engaged with exter-nally. In addition, the post-September 11 wars are subjecting academics, in the U.S at least, to new and more intense levels of public and political scrutiny by special interest groups, interest groups which are deeply suspicious of the kinds of agendas that support indigenous rights to self-determination (Jackson 2002).

In the specific context of conservation, a renewed tendency away from rely-ing on local forms of knowledge, organisation and control is already evident in the backlash against community-based resource management strategies. The growth of an environmental surveillance industry in parts of the world and the privatisation of areas of conservation (Brockelman et al. 2002; Oates 1999; Spinage 1998; Srikosamatara and Brockelman 2002; Terborgh 1999) may also undermine – or at least redefine – how local people and knowledge are drawn upon in development and conservation agendas, which, as we have seen, have become important arenas for the validation of such knowledge systems.

Conclusions

In the introduction to this volume, Heckler makes a plea for pulling together the different strands and approaches to the study of TEK. In this chapter I have sought to link the revitalisation of TEK, and more generally of local forms of environmental knowledge, organisation and control, to the broad political, social, economic and technological transformations that unfolded after the 1970s. In effect, the reorganisation of the world economy in the late twentieth century entailed a shift away from centralised modes of organisation, control, production and consumption and from an industrial model of development model based on replication to one emphasising decentralisation and regional specialisation, themselves underpinned by a revolution in communications tech-nology and the emergence of a networked knowledge and service economy. This shift has taken place amidst a global environmental crisis, the growth of civil society and of local and indigenous social movements, the increased interpene-tration of local and global processes and actors, and the heightened presence of the market in almost every aspect of social life. In this new context, local and traditional knowledge, and more generally cultural diversity, have often acquired new and powerful meanings: rather than an obstacle to modern development, they have been redefined as potentially valuable resources in political, social, ecological, economic and spiritual renewal.

The increased commodification and politicisation of culture, knowledge and information coupled with the increased means and opportunities for information sharing and exchange have raised complex questions regarding authenticity, control and benefit-sharing resulting from the flow and transformation of indigenous environmental knowledge in the context of commerce, development and science.

As the entire world becomes increasingly interconnected, inequity becomes increasingly apparent and its effects increasingly destabilising. There is some evidence to suggest that while inequity has decreased in some cases, in others it has actually increased. The income gap between the world's richest and poorest almost tripled between 1960 and 1998 (UNDP 2001: 16-17), reflecting sharp new divisions between those who have the capital, mobility and skills to flourish in global markets and those who do not.[8] One concern is that attempts to achieve international economic integration will create domestic social disintegration (Rodrik 2000), feeding a cycle of instability and conflict. Contributing to this are the destabilising effects of global media, which bring into bold relief the ideological, social and economic differences that exist between 'the strong and weak, rich and poor, young and old, and educated and undereducated' (Westmacott 1999). Growing inequality will further contribute to the generation of social tension, some of which may be discharged precisely at those who – such as many anthropologists or ethnobotanists – operate at the interface between political, economic and intellectual elites and disenfranchised groups (Zarembo 2001). It is easy to envision how the increased uncertainty, polarisation and conflict of a post-September 11 world may heighten these tensions, placing new ethical and moral burdens on anthropologists and practitioners of sister disciplines (Price 2002).

The problems addressed by science have themselves become inherently more complex and explicitly linked to social, political and economic processes (Kay et al. 1999). Issues such as global warming, pollution, deforestation or loss of biodiversity are not only challenging from a technical standpoint, but are also embedded in complex, dynamic, inherently indeterminate and somewhat unpredictable social and political systems, involving local and global actors, events and trends (Funtowicz and Ravetz 1991). Additionally, scientists are increasingly being encouraged, if not pressured, to define and operationalise such problematic concepts as sustainability in a scientific manner, as well as to inform policy (Lélé and Norgaard 1996).

As scientists enter arenas where 'facts are uncertain, values are in dispute, stakes are high, and decisions are urgent' (Prugh et al. 2000: 94), the contradictions of pursuing an objective science amidst a value-loaded and socially charged reality become evident (Shrader-Frechette and McCoy 1993). One can anticipate these challenges will continue to grow, as the world becomes increasingly interconnected through mass media and telecommunications, and as scientists become accountable to – or at least scrutinised by – an increasingly diverse range of stakeholders.

Minimally, this will require an awareness of the broader political and social ramifications of one's practice, particularly in terms of how this is represented to and perceived by communities outside of academia. The developing new context of science is thus pushing those in academia to dynamically engage with other spheres of social life such as politics, public relations, business and media, simultaneously incorporating new and often contradictory forms of knowledge, approaches and methodologies. This in turn presents new challenges and opportunities for those who practice or teach science and its articulation with other systems of knowledge (Alexiades and Laird 2002). Recognising that 'scientific' and 'indigenous' knowledge are more 'an active verb than a noun' (Gardner 1995: 187) may be a significant first step, allowing one, as the different chapters in this book illustrate, to consider the processual and contextual aspects of knowledge systems, including how knowledge systems develop over time, respond to changing realities, and interface with other knowledge systems.

The re-organisation of capitalism, coupled with increased transnational flows of peoples, ideas, goods and capital, has unleashed powerful centripetal and centrifugal forces of integration and fragmentation, of homogenisation and heterogenisation, of democratising information and guarding knowledge, of exploitation and liberation, of division and interconnectedness, of ethical absence and moral assertion (Trevor 1999). The interplay of these conflicting forces is reshaping the junctures between different social bodies and their knowledge systems. Herein lies a central challenge for those wishing to help articulate 'scientific' and 'traditional' knowledge systems: to help redefine the relationship between different societies, between different forms of knowledge and knowing, in a social environment characterised by contingency, uncertainty and conflict, and concomitantly by opportunities to articulate alternative world views, establish new forms of political agency and develop new alliances. For the communities that generate and manage 'traditional' knowledge, these changes may also provide new opportunities for reconfiguring power and social relations, for hybridisation, innovation and organisation, while simultaneously implying challenges in their ability to maintain some control over their ways of life and modes of thought.

Acknowledgements

I am grateful to the Global Diversity Foundation and to Gary Martin for inviting me to the Innovative Wisdom symposium at White Oak Plantation, Yulee,

Florida, in October 2000, where I presented the original version of this chapter. I am also grateful to Serena Heckler for the opportunity to publish this chapter here. Anthony Cunningham, Robin Goodman, Sarah Laird, Daniela Peluso, Steve Rubinstein and, most especially, Gary Martin, also provided helpful comments on earlier versions of this article. Charles Clement drew my attention to the volume by Pistorius and van Wijk, and to its salient points.

Notes

1. The terms 'indigenous knowledge' and 'traditional knowledge' reify the false dichotomy of 'modern' versus 'traditional', obscuring the degree to which local forms of knowledge have been historically appropriated and incorporated into scientific knowledge and vice versa (Ellen and Harris 2000; Semali and Kincheloe 1999). These blanket terms include a broad range of very different, fluid and continuously changing systems of local, shared, empirical, holistic and integrative forms of knowledge, itself embedded in practice and 'situated within broader cultural traditions' (Ellen and Harris 2000: 3; Hobart 1993). For a review of the different terms, including a discussion of their history and meaning, see the introduction by Heckler and the chapter by Zent (Chapter Two).
2. Using the plural form of the term, 'capitalisms' would better convey the multiple ways in which this economic system is structured over time and across regions and contexts (see Blim 2000 for an overview of some of the regional and historical variations of capitalism in different regions and over time).
3. Hegemony refers to a structure of order that gains enough acceptance and stability so as to remain unquestioned, appearing as the natural order to most actors. Such systems of meaning are underpinned by a structure of power in which one nation state is usually, but not necessarily, dominant (Cox 1981, cited in Connor 1994: 4).
4. As some have repeatedly noted, although these idealised, romanticised and essentialised representations have been effectively used by environmentalist and indigenous activists, they may in the long-term backfire, particularly if indigenous people 'fail' to meet these unrealistic expectations on the ground (Brosius 1997; Conklin and Graham 1995; Goodman 2001; Redford 1991).
5. While both TRIPS and CBD are examples of regulatory globalisation (cf. Drahos 2001), their approach to a series of common issues, including the role and rights extended to traditional knowledge, is quite different, creating several conflicts of interest among signatories (Dutfield 2000; Monagle and Gozales 2001).
6. This shift is also evident within the OECD in its extension to the field of biodiversity and economic development (OECD 1999, 2002).
7. Civil society is here defined as the organisations and individuals who work to promote a public good from a civilian standpoint (Yamamoto 1995, cited in Win 1998: 101).
8. In 1993, the richest 1% of the world's people received as much income as the poorest 75% (Milanovic 1998, cited in UNDP 2001). Inequality has also increased within countries: a study of 77 countries with 82% of the world's population shows that inequality rose in 45 countries and declined in 16 countries, between the 1950s and the 1990s (Cornia 1999, cited in UNDP 2001).

Bibliography

Abu-Lughod, J. 1989. *Before European Hegemony The World System AD1250-1350.* New York: Oxford University Press.

Agrawal, A. 1995. 'Indigenous and Scientific Knowledge: Some Critical Comments' *Indigenous Knowledge Monitor* 3(3): 3-6. http://www.nuffic.nl/ciran/ikdm/3-3/articles/agrawal.html

_____ 2002. 'Indigenous Knowledge and the Politics of Classification'. *International Social Science Journal* 54 (173): 287-297.

Alcorn, J.B. 1995. 'Ethnobotanical knowledge systems – A Resource for Meeting Rural Development Goals' Pages 1-12 in D. Warren, L.J. Slikkerveer and D. Brokensha, eds., *The Cultural Dimension of Development. Indigenous Knowledge Systems.* London: Intermediate Technology Publications.

Alexiades, M.N. 2003. 'Ethnobotany in the Third Millennium: Expectations and Unresolved Issues' *Delpinoa* 45: 15-28.

_____ 2004. 'Ethnobotany and Globalisation: Science and Ethics at the Turn of the Century' in: T.J.S. Carlson and L. Maffi, eds., *Ethnobotany and Conservation of Biocultural Diversity.* Bronx: The New York Botanical Gardens Press, pp. 283-305.

_____ and S.A. Laird. 2002. 'Laying the Foundation: Equitable Biodiversity Relationships' in S.A. Laird, ed., *Biodiversity and Traditional Knowledge: Equitable Partnerships in Practice.* London: Earthscan, pp.3-15.

Anani, Kofi. 1999. 'Sustainable Governance of Livelihoods in Rural Africa: A Place-Based Response to Globalism in Africa' *Development* 42(2): 57-63.

Appadurai, A. 1994. 'Disjuncture and Difference in the Global Cultural Economy' in Williams and L. Chrisman (eds.), *Colonial Discourses and Postcolonial Theory.* New York: Columbia University Press, pp. 324-339.

Atran, S. 1990. *Cognitive Foundations of Natural History: Towards an Anthropology of Science.* Cambridge: University Press.

Aubry, J. and A. Mcilroy. 1994. 'PQ Halts Great Whale Hydro Project: Cree Chief Celebrates Victory' *The Ottawa Citizen,* Saturday November 19, 1994, final edition, A1.

Balick, M. J. 1979. 'Amazonian Oil Palms of Promise: A Survey' *Economic Botany* 33: 11-28.

_____ E. Elisabetsky and S. Laird. 1996. *Medicinal Resources of the Tropical Forest: Biodiversity and Its Importance to Human Health.* New York: Columbia University Press.

Bannerman, R.H., J. Burton, and C. Wen-Chieh, eds., 1983. *Traditional Medicine and Health Care Coverage: A Reader for Health Administrators and Practitioners.* Albany: World Health Organization.

Banuri, T. 1990. 'Modernization and Its Discontents: A Cultural Perspective on Theories of Development' in Marglin, F.A. and S.A. Marglin (eds), *Dominating Knowledge: Development, Culture and Resistance.* Oxford: Clarendon Press, pp. 73-101.

Bell, D. 1999 [1973]. *The Coming of Post-Industrial Society: A Venture in Social Forecasting.* Special Anniversary Edition. New York: Basic Books.

Bentley, J. 1992. 'Alternatives to Pesticides in Central America: Applied Studies of Local Knowledge' *Culture and Agriculture* 44: 10-13.

Bérard, L. and P. Marchenay. 1995. 'Tradition, Regulation, and Intellectual Property: Local Agricultural Products and Foodstuffs in France' in S.B. Brush and D. Stabinsky, eds., *Valuing Local Knowledge. Indigenous People and Intellectual Property Rights.* Washington DC: Island Press, pp. 230-243.

Bergsen, A.J. 2000. 'Postmodernism Explained' in T.D. Hall, ed., *A World Systems Reader.* New York: Rowman and Littlefield Publishers, pp.181-192.

Berkes, F., J. Colding and C. Folke. 2000. 'Rediscovery of Traditional Ecological Knowledge as Adaptive Management' *Ecological Applications* 10: 1251-1262.

Berlin, B., D.E. Breedlove and P.H. Raven. 1974. *Principles of Tzeltal Plant Classification; An Introduction to the Botanical Ethnography of a Mayan-Speaking People of Highland Chiapas.* New York: Academic Press.

Blim, M. 2000. 'Capitalisms in Late Modernity' *Annual Review of Anthropology.* 29: 25–38

Blunt, P. and D.M. Warren. 1996. *Indigenous Organizations and Development.* London: Intermediate Technology Press.

Böröcz, J. and D.A. Smith. 1995. 'Introduction: Late Twentieth-Century Challenges for World-System Analysis' in D.A. Smith and J. Böröcz, eds., *A New World Order? Global Transformations in the Late Twentieth Century.* Westport: Greenwood Press, pp.1-15.

Brockelman, W.Y., M. Griffiths, M. Rao, R. Ruf, and N. Salafsky,2002. 'Enforcement mechanisms' in J. Terborgh, C. van Schaik, L. Davenport and M. Rao, eds., *Making Parks Work. Strategies for Preserving Tropical Nature.* Washington DC: Island Press, pp. 265-278.

Brokensha, D., D.M. Warren and O. Werner. 1980. *Indigenous Knowledge Systems and Development.* Lanham: University Press of America.

Brosius, J.P. 2000. 'Endangered forest, endangered people: environmentalist representations of indigenous knowledge' in R.F. Ellen, P. Parkes and A. Bicker, eds., *Indigenous Knowledge and Its Transformations: Critical Anthropological Perspectives.* Amsterdam: Harwood Academic Publishers, pp. 293-317. (Originally published in *Human Ecology* 25(1): 47-69).

_____ 2002. *'Seeing Natural and Cultural Communities: Technologies of Visualization in Contemporary Conservation.' Paper presented at the Society for Conservation Biology 16th Annual Meeting 14-19 July 2002, Canterbury, Kent.*

Brown, M.F. 1998. 'Can Culture Be Copyrighted?' *Current Anthropology* 39(2): 193-222.

Brush, S.B. 1993. 'Indigenous Knowledge of Biological Resources and Intellectual Property Rights: The Role of Anthropology' *American Anthropologist* 95(3): 653-686.

Brysk, A. 2000. *From Tribal Village to Global Village: Indian Rights and International Relations in Latin America.* Stanford: Stanford University Press.

Burger, J. 1987. *Report from the Frontier: The State of the World's Indigenous Peoples.* London: Zed.

Busch, L., W.B. Lacy, J. Burkhardt, and L.R. Lacy. 1999. *Plants, Power and Profit. Social, Economic and Ethical Consequences of the New Biotechnologies*. Cambridge and Oxford: Basil Blackwell.

Castells, M. 1993. 'The Information Economy and the New International Order' in M. Carnoy, M. Castells and S.S. Cohen, eds., *The Global Economy in the Information Age*. University Park: Pennsylvania State University Press, pp. 15-44.

Chambers, R. 1983. *Rural Development: Putting the Last First*. London, Longman.

Clark, A.K. 1997. 'Globalisation Seen from the Margins: Indigenous Ecuadorians and the Politics of Place' *Anthropologica* 39: 17-26.

Clement, C.R. and M.N. Alexiades. 2000. 'Etnobotânica e biopirataria na Amazônia'. in T.B. Cavalcanti and B.M. Teles Walter, eds., *Tópicos Atuais Em Botânica – Palestras Convidadas do 51º Congresso Nacional de Botânica*. Brasília: Sociedade Botânica do Brasil, pp.250-252.

Coker, A. and C. Richards, eds., 1992. *Valuing the Environment: Economic Approaches to Environmental Evaluation*. Boca Raton: CRC Press.

Colchester, M. 2002. 'Indigenous Rights and the Collective Conscious' *Anthropology Today* 18(1): 1-3.

Connor, E.A. 1994. 'The Global Political Economy of Communication and International Political Economy' in E.A. Connor, ed., *The Global Political Economy of Communication: Hegemony, Telecommunications and the Information Economy*. New York: St. Martin's Press, pp.1-19.

Conklin, H.C. 1969. 'An Ethnoecological Approach to Shifting Agriculture' in P. Vayda, editor, *Environment and Cultural Behavior: Ecological Studies in Cultural Anthropology*. Austin: University of Texas Press, pp.221-233.

Conklin, B.A. and L.R. Graham. 1995. 'The Shifting Middle Ground: Amazonian Indians and Eco-politics' *American Anthropologist* 97(4): 695-710.

Cordillera Peoples Alliance (CPA), PACOS Trust, Center for Orang Asli Concerns (COAC), and Anthrowatch. 2005. *Indigenous Peoples and Local Government: Experiences from Malaysia and the Philippines*. IWGIA Document No. 113. Copenhagen: International Work Group for Indigenous Affairs, IWGIA.

Cornell, S. 1988. *The Return of the Native: American Indian Political Resurgence*. New York, Oxford University Press.

Cox, R.W. 1994. 'Global Restructuring: Making Sense of the Changing International Political Economy' in R. Stubbs and G.R.D. Underhill, eds., *Political Economy and the Changing Global Order*. New York: St. Martin's Press, pp. 45-59.

_____ 1997. 'A Perspective on Globalisation' in J.H. Mittelman, ed., *Globalisation: Critical Reflections*. Boulder and London: Lynne Rienner Publishers, pp. 21-30.

Dahl, J., J. Hicks and P.J. Nunavut, eds., 2000. *Inuit Regain Control of their Lands and Their Lives*. IWGIA Document No. 102. Copenhagen: International Work Group for Indigenous Affairs, IWGIA.

DeWalt, B.R. 1994. 'Using Indigenous Knowledge to Improve Agriculture and Natural Resource Management' *Human Organization* 53(2): 123-131.

Downes, D. and S.A. Laird, 1999. *Innovative Mechanisms for Sharing Benefits of Biodiversity and Related Knowledge: Case Studies on Geographical Indications and Trademarks*. Report Prepared for UNCTAD Biotrade Initiative.

Drahos, P. 2001. 'Negotiating Intellectual Property Rights: between Coercion and Dialogue.' Paper presented at the Oxfam-International Seminar on 'Intellectual Property and Development: What Future for the WTO TRIPs Agreement?,' Brussels, 20 March 2001. Unpublished draft circulated on BIO-IPR with the permission of the author, April 2001.

Dutfield, G. 2002. *Intellectual Property Rights, Trade, and Biodiversity.* London, Earthscan.

Edelman M. 1999. *Peasants Against Globalisation: Rural Social Movements in Costa Rica.* Stanford: Stanford University Press.

_____ 2001. 'Social Movements: Changing Paradigms and Forms of Politics.' *Annual Review of Anthropology* 30: 285–317.

Edwards, V.M. 1995. *Dealing in Diversity: America's Market for Nature Conservation.* Cambridge and New York: Cambridge University Press.

Ekins, P. 1992. *A New World Order: Grassroots Movements for Global Change.* London and New York: Routledge.

Ellen, R. F. 1986. 'What Black Elk Left Unsaid: On the Illusory Images of Green Primitivism.' *Anthropology Today* 2(6): 8-12.

_____ 1993. *The Cultural Relations of Classification: An Analysis of Nualu Animal Categories from Central Seram.* Cambridge: Cambridge University Press.

_____ and H. Harris. 2000. 'Indigenous Knowledge and Its Transformations. Critical Anthropological Perspectives' in R.F. Ellen, P. Parkes and A. Bicker, eds., *Indigenous Knowledge and its Transformations: Critical Anthropological Perspectives.* Amsterdam: Harwood Academic Publishers, pp. 1-29.

_____ P. Parkes and A. Bicker, eds., 2000. *Indigenous Knowledge and its Transformations: Critical Anthropological Perspectives.* Amsterdam, Harwood Academic Publishers.

Escobar, A. and S.E. Alvarez, editors. 1992. *The Making of Social Movements in Latin America: Identity, Strategy, and Democracy.* Boulder: Westview.

Falk, R. 1993. 'The Making of Global Citizenship' in J. Brecher, J.B. Childs and J. Cutler eds., *Global Visions: Beyond the New World Order.* Boston: South End Press, pp. 39-50.

Fairhead, J. and M. Leach. 1996. *Misreading the African Landscape: Society and Ecology in a Forest-Savanna Mosaic.* Cambridge: Cambridge University Press.

Feder, B.J. 1999. 'Plant Sterility Research Inflames Debate on Biotechnology's Role in Farming'. *The New York Times* April 19, 1999: Section A, Page 18, Column 1; National Desk.

Fernández J., A.E. and A. Mommen. 1998. 'Globalisation versus Regionalization' in A.E. Fernández J. and A. Mommen, *Regionalization and Globalisation in the Modern World Economy: Perspectives on the Third World and Transitional Economies.* London and New York: Routledge, pp.1-26.

Finger, M. 1994. 'NGOs and Transformation: Beyond Social Movement Theory' in T. Princen and M. Finger, eds., *Environmental NGOs in World Politics: Linking the Local and the Global.* London and New York: Routledge, pp. 48-66.

Fisher, J. 1993. *The Road from Rio: Sustainable Development and the Nongovernmental Movement in the Third World.* Westport: Praeger.

_____ 1996. 'Grassroots Organizations and Grassroots Support Organizations: Patterns Of Interaction' in E. Moran, ed., *Transforming Societies, Transforming Anthropology*. Ann Arbor: University of Michigan Press, pp.57-102.

Fisher, W.H. 1994. 'Megadevelopment, Environmentalism, and Resistance: The Institutional Context of Kayapó Indigenous Politics in Central Brazil' *Human Organization* 53(3): 220-232.

van de Fliert, L., compiler. 1994. *Indigenous Peoples and International Organizations*. Nottingham: Spokesman.

Freese, C.H. 1998. *Wild Species as Commodities: Managing Markets and Ecosystems for Sustainability*. Washington DC: Island Press.

Friedman, J. 1998. 'Transnationalization, Socio-Political Disorder and Ethnification as Expressions of Declining Global Hegemony' *International Political Science Review* 119(3): 233-250.

Funtowicz, S. and J. Ravetz. 1991. 'A New Scientific Methodology for Global Environmental Issues' in R. Costanza, ed., *Ecological Economics: The Science and Management of Sustainability*. New York: Columbia University Press, pp.137-152.

Gardner, K. 1995. 'An Anthropological Critique of Development: The Growth of Ignorance,' book review. *Journal of the Royal Anthropological Institute* 1(1): 186-187.

Gereffi, G. 2000 [1994]. 'Rethinking Development Theory: Insights from East Asia and Latin America' in J.T. Roberts and A. Hite, eds., *From Modernization to Globalisation: Perspectives on Development and Social Change*. Oxford: Blackwell Publishers, pp.228-254.

Goodman, R.T. 2001.' The Rainforest Rape' in *Infertilities: Exploring Fictions of Barren Bodies*. Minneapolis: University of Minnesota Press, pp.165-190.

Grimes, P. 2000. 'Recent Research on World-Systems'. in T.D. Hall, ed., *A World-Systems Reader. New Perspectives on Gender, Urbanization, Cultures, Indigenous Peoples, and Ecology*. New York: Rowman and Littlefield, pp. 29-55.

Hall, T.D. 2000. 'Frontiers, Ethnogenesis and World-Systems: Rethinking the Theories' in T.D. Hall, ed., *A World Systems Reader*. New York: Rowman and Littlefield, pp. 237-270.

Harvey, D. 2000 [1992]. 'Capitalism: The Factory of Fragmentation' in J.T. Roberts and A. Hite, eds., *From Modernization to Globalisation: Perspectives on Development and Social Change*. Malden: Blackwell Publishers, pp. 247-291.

Haugerud, A., M.P. Stone, and P.D. Little. 2000. *Commodities and Globalisation: Anthropological Perspectives*. Lanham: Rowman and Littlefield Publishers.

Heinrich, M. 2000. "Ethnobotany and Its Role in Drug Development" *Phytotherapy Research* 14: 479-488.

Holm, H.-H. and G. Sorensen. 1995. *Whose World Order? Uneven Globalisation and the End of the Cold War*. Boulder: Westview Press.

Holton, R.J. 1998. *Globalisation and the Nation-State*. New York: St. Martin's Press.

Howes, M. 1980. 'The uses of indigenous technical knowledge in development' in D.W. Brokensha, D.M. Warren and O. Werner, eds., *Indigenous Knowledge Systems and Development*. Lanham: University Press of America, pp. 341-357.

Inayatullah, S. 1997. 'Global Transformations' *Development* 40(2): 33-37.

Ingold, T. 1993. 'Globes and Spheres: The Topology of Environmentalism' in K. Milton, ed., *Environmentalism: The View from Anthropology*. New York: Routledge, pp. 31-42

Jackson, J. 2002. 'ACTA Report Criticizes Professors' *Anthropology News*, March 2002: 7.

Jackson, M. 2002. 'Biotechnology and the Critique of Globalisation' *Ethnos* 67(2): 141-154.

Joralemon, D. 1990. 'The Selling of the Shaman and the Problem of Informant Legitimacy' *Journal of Anthropological Research* 46(2): 105-117.

Kane, H. 1997. 'Half of Languages Becoming Extinct' in L.R. Brown, M. Renner and C. Flavin, eds., *Vital Signs, 1997: The Environmental Trends That Are Shaping Our Future*. New York: W.W. Norton, pp. 130-131.

ten Kate, K. and S.A. Laird. 1999. *The Commercial Use of Biodiversity: Access to Genetic Resources and Benefit-Sharing*. London: Earthscan.

Kay, J.J, J.A. Regier, M. Boyle and G. Francis. 1999. 'An Ecosystem Approach for Sustainability: Addressing the Challenge of Complexity' *Futures* 31: 721-742.

Kearney, M. 1995. 'The Local and the Global: The Anthropology of Globalism and Transnationalism' *Annual Review of Anthropology* 24: 547-65.

Krech, S. 1999. *The Ecological Indian: Myth and History*. New York: W.W. Norton.

Laird, S.A., M.N. Alexiades, K.P. Bannister and D.A. Posey. 2002. 'Publication of Biodiversity Research Results and the Flow of Knowledge' in S.A. Laird, ed., *Biodiversity and Traditional Knowledge: Equitable Partnerships in Practice*. London: Earthscan, pp. 77-101.

Lélé, S. and R.B. Norgaard. 1996. 'Sustainability and the Scientist's Burden' *Conservation Biology* 10(2): 354-365.

Little, P.E. 1995. 'Ritual, Power and Ethnography at the Rio Earth Summit' *Critical Anthropology* 15(3): 265-288.

Linden, E. 1991. 'Lost Tribes, Lost Knowledge' *Time*, September 23, 138(12): 46-56.

Long, N. 1996. 'Globalisation and Localization: New Challenges to Rural Research' in H. Moore, ed., *The Future of Anthropological Knowledge*. London and New York: Routledge, pp. 37-59.

Maffi, L. 2001. 'On Biocultural Diversity: Linking Language, Knowledge, and the Environment' Washington DC: Smithsonian Institution Press.

Marglin, S.A. 1990. 'Towards a Decolonization of the Mind' in F. Appfel-Marglin and S.A. Marglin, eds., 1990. *Dominating Knowledge: Development, Culture and Resistance*. Oxford: Clarendon Press, pp. 1-28.

Mathews, G. 2000. *Global Culture/Individual Identity: Searching for Home in the Culture Supermarket*. New York and London: Routledge.

Maybury-Lewis, D. 1984. 'Indian and Pro-Indian Organizations in Brazil' *Cultural Survival Quarterly* 8(4): 19-21.

McCarthy, R. 1999. 'Mayans Oppose UGA Research' *The Atlanta Journal and Constitution*. December 7, 1999: 8C.

McMichael, P. 2000 [1996]. 'Globalisation: Myths and Realities' in J.T. Roberts and A. Hite, eds., *From Modernization to Globalisation: Perspectives on Development and Social Change*. Malden: Blackwell Publishers, pp. 274-291.

Melody, W.H. 1994. 'The Information Society: Implications for Economic Institutions and Market Theory' in E.A. Comor, ed., *The Global Political Economy of Communication: Hegemony, Telecommunications and the Information Economy.* New York: St. Martin's Press, pp. 21-36.

Mittelman, J.H. 1997. 'The Dynamics of Globalisation' Pages 1-19 in J.H. Mittelman, ed., *Globalisation: Critical Reflections.* Boulder and London: Lynne Rienner Publishers.

Mittelman, J.H. 2000. *The Globalisation Syndrome: Transformation and Resistance.* Princeton: Princeton University Press.

Monagle, C. and A.T. Gonzales. 2001. 'Biodiversity and Intellectual Property Rights: Reviewing Intellectual Property Rights in Light of the Objectives of the Convention on Biological Diversity' Joint Discussion Paper. Washington DC: CIEL, WWF.

Mooney, P.R. 1997. 'Biopiracy and the Life Industry' *Development* 40(2): 27-30.

Mooney, P.H and T.J. Majka. 1995. *Farmers' and Farm Workers' Movements: Social Protest in American Agriculture.* New York: Twayne.

Muehlebach, A. 2001. '"Making Place' at the United Nations: Indigenous Cultural Politics at the U.N. Working Group of Indigenous Populations". *Cultural Anthropology* 16(3): 415-448.

Nagel, J. 1996. *American Indian Ethnic Renewal: Red Power and the Resurgence of Identity and Culture.* Oxford and New York: Oxford University Press.

Nature. 1999. 'US Keeps a Watchful Eye from the Sidelines' *Nature,* World Conference on Science News. June 1999, http://www.nature.com/wcs/1news/30-1b.html.

Nazarea, V.D. 1998. *Cultural Memory and Biodiversity.* Tucson: University of Arizona Press.

_____ 1999. Introduction. 'A View from a Point: Ethnoecology as Situated Knowledge' in V.D. Nazarea, ed., *Ethnoecology. Situated Knowledge/Located Lives.* Tucson: University of Arizona Press, pp. 3-20.

Neef, D. 1999. *A Little Knowledge is a Dangerous Thing. Understanding Our Global Knowledge Economy.* Boston: Butterworth Heinemann.

Norberg-Hodge, H. 1998. 'Think Global – Eat Local! Delicious Ways To Counter Globalisation' *The Ecologist* 28(4): 208-214.

Norgaard, R.B. 1994. *Development Betrayed: The End of Progress and a Coevolutionary Revisioning of the Future.* New York: Routledge.

Oates, J. F. 1999. *Myth and Reality in the Rain Forest: How Conservation Strategies Are Failing in West Africa.* Berkeley: University of California Press.

Oman, C.P. 1997. 'The Policy Challenges of Globalisation and Regionalization' *Development* 40(2): 43-53.

Organization for Economic Co-Operation and Development, OECD. 1999. *Handbook of Incentive Measures for Biodiversity: Design and Implementation.* Paris: Organization for Economic Cooperation and Development.

Organization for Economic Co-Operation and Development, OECD. 2002. *Handbook of Biodiversity Valuation: A Guide for Policy Makers.* Paris: Organization for Economic Cooperation and Development.

Petras, J. 1999. 'Globalisation: A Critical Analysis' *Journal of Contemporary Asia* 29(1): 3-37.

Phillips, L. 1998. 'Introduction: Neoliberalism in Latin America' in L. Phillips, ed., *The Third Wave of Modernization in Latin America. Cultural Perspectives on Neoliberalism.* Wilmington, Scholarly Resources, pp. 11-14.

Pistorius, R. and J. van Wijk. 2000. *The Exploitation of Plant Genetic Information: Political Strategies in Crop Development.* Wallingford and New York: CABI Publishing.

Plotkin, M.J. 1993. *Tales of a Shaman's Apprentice. An Ethnobotanist Searches for New Medicines in the Amazon Rainforest.* New York: Penguin Books.

Poole, P. 1990. *Desarrollo de trabajo conjunto entre pueblos indigenas, conservacionistas y planificadores del uso de la tierra en America Latina.* Turrialba: CATIE.

Posey, D.A. 1983. 'Indigenous ecological knowledge and the development of the Amazon' in E.F. Moran, ed. *The dilemma of Amazonian development.* Boulder: Westview Press, pp. 225-250.

_____ and J. Frechione, J. Eddins, L.F. da Silva, D. Myers, D. Case and P. Macbeath. 1984. 'Ethnoecology as Applied Anthropology in Amazonian Development'. *Human Organization* 43(2): 95-107.

Prance, G.T., D.J. Chadwick and J. Marsh, eds. 1994. *Ethnobotany and the Search for New Drugs.* New York: John Wiley and Sons

Price, D. 2002.' Past Wars, Present Dangers, Future Anthropologies' *Anthropology Today* 18(1): 3-5.

Prugh, T., R. Costanza and H. Daly. 2000. *The Local Politics of Global Sustainability.* Washington, DC: Island Press.

Redford, K.H. 1991. 'The Ecologically Noble Savage' *Cultural Survival Quarterly* 15(1): 46-48.

Ribeiro, G.L. and P.E. Little. 1998. 'Neoliberal Recipes, Environmental Cooks: The Transformation of Amazonian Agency' in L. Phillips (ed.) *The Third Wave of Modernization in Latin America: Cultural Perspectives on Neoliberalism.* Wilmington: Scholarly Resources, pp. 175-191.

Riordan, T. 1995. 'Patents: A Recent Patent On A Papua New Guinea Tribe's Cell Line Prompts Outrage and Charges of "Biopiracy" '. *The New York Times,* November 27, 1995, section D, p. 2.

Robbins, R. 1993. *Feeling Global: Internationalism in Distress.* New York: New York University Press.

Roberts, J.T. and A. Hite. 1999. *From Modernization to Globalisation: Perspectives on Development and Social Change.* Malden, Massachusetts: Blackwell Publishers.

Robertson, R. 1992. *Globalisation: Social Theory and Global Culture.* London: Sage.

Robertson, R. 1995. 'Globalisation: Time-Space and Homogeneity-Heterogeneity' in M. Featherstone, S. Lash and R. Robertson (eds.) *Global Modernities.* Newbury Park: Sage Publications, pp. 25-44.

Rodrik, D. 2000 [1997]. 'Has Globalisation Gone Too Far?' in J.T. Roberts and A. Hite (eds.) *From Modernization to Globalisation: Perspectives on Development and Social Change.* Oxford: Blackwell Publishers, pp. 298-305.

Romero, S. 2000. 'Industry and Nature Meet Along the Amazon' *The New York Times*, June 17, 2000.

Ross, A. 1996. *Science Wars*. Durham, N.C.: Duke University Press.

Schmidt, A. 1990. *The Loss of Aboriginal Language Heritage*. Canberra: Aboriginal Studies Press.

Schultes, R.E. 1980. 'The Amazonia as a Source of New Economic Plants' *Economic Botany* 33: 259-266.

Semali, L. and J.L. Kincheloe, eds. 1999. 'What is Indigenous Knowledge and why should we study it?' in L. Semali and J.L. Kincheloe (eds.), *Indigenous Knowledge? Voices from the Academy*. New York and London: Falmer Press, pp. 3-57.

Shiva, V. 1997. *Biopiracy: The Plunder of Nature and Knowledge*. Boston: South End Press.Shrader-Frechette, K. and E.D. McCoy. 1993. *Method in Ecology: Strategies for Conservation*. New York: Cambridge University Press.

Sillitoe, P. 1998. 'The Development of Indigenous Knowledge: A New Applied Anthropology' *Current Anthropology* 39(2): 223-252.

_____ A. Bicker, J. Pottier, eds., 2002. *Participating in Development: Approaches to Indigenous Knowledge*. London: Routledge.

Sklair, L. 2000 [1995]. 'Social Movements and Global Capitalism' in J.T. Roberts and A. Hite, eds., *From Modernization to Globalisation: Perspectives on Development and Social Change*. Oxford: Blackwell Publishers, pp. 340-352.

Spinage, C. 1998. 'Social Change and Conservation Misrepresentation in Africa.' *Oryx* 32(4): 265-276.

Srikosamatara, S. and W.Y. Brockelman. 2002. 'Conservation of Protected Areas in Thailand: A Diversity of Problems, A Diversity of Solutions' in, J. Terborgh, C. van Schaik, L. Davenport and M. Rao, eds., *Making Parks Work. Strategies for Preserving Tropical Nature*. Washington DC: Island Press, pp.218-231.

Stille, A. 2001. 'Slow Food' *The Nation, August 20, 2001*.
http://www.thenation.com/doc.mhtml?i=20010820ands=stille

Terborgh, J. 1999. *Requiem for Nature*. Washington, DC: Island Press/Shearwater Books.

Thomas, N. 1987. *Possessions: Indigenous Art/Colonial Culture*. London: Thames and Hudson.

Todorov, T. 1984. *The Conquest of America*. New York: Harper Torchbooks.

Touraine, A. 1989. 'Is Sociology Still the Study Of Society?' *Thesis Eleven* 23: 5-34.

Trevor, H. 1999. 'Globalisation and the Trade in Human Parts' *The Canadian Review of Sociology and Anthropology* 36(1): 21-35.

Turner, T. 1993. 'Anthropology and Multiculturalism: What Is Anthropology That Multiculturalists Should Be Mindful of It?' *Cultural Anthropology* 8(4): 411-429.

UNDP, United Nations Development Program. 2001. Human Development Report 2001. *Making New Technologies Work for Human Development*. New York and Oxford: Oxford University Press.

Varese, S. 1996. 'The New Environmentalist Movement of Latin American Indigenous People' in S.B. Brush and D. Stabinsky, eds., *Valuing Local Knowledge. Indigenous People and Intellectual Property Rights*. Washington DC: Island Press, pp. 122-142.

Verpoorte, R. 2002. 'Pharmacognosy in the New Millenium: Leadfiding and Biotechnology' in J. Fleurentin, J.-M. Pelt and G. Mazars (eds.) *From the Sources of Knowledge to the Medicines of The Future.* Paris: Institut de Recherche pour le Developpment, IRD: 253-262.

Viergever, M. 1999. 'Indigenous Knowledge: An Interpretation of Views from Indigenous Peoples' in L.M. Semali and J.L. Kincheloe, eds., *What is Indigenous Knowledge? Voices from the Academy.* New York and London: Falmer Press, pp. 330-360.

Wallerstein, I. 1974. *The Modern World System.* New York: Academic Press.

Warren, D.M. 1995. *The Cultural Dimension of Development: Indigenous Knowledge Systems.* London: Intermediate Technology Publications.

_____ L.J.Slikkerveer and D. Brokensha, eds.,1989. *Indigenous Knowledge Systems: Implications for Agriculture and International Development.* Ames: Iowa State University.

Warren, K. B. 1998. *Indigenous Movements and Their Critics: Pan-Maya activism in Guatemala.* Princeton: Princeton University Press.

Weinberg, B. 2001. 'Bio-piracy in Chiapas' *The Nation,* August 20, 2001. http://www.thenation.com/doc.mhtml?i=20010820&s=weinberg

Wessendorf, K. ed., 2000. 'An Indigenous Parliament? Realities and Perspectives in Russia and the Circumpolar North.' IWGIA Document No. 16. Copenhagen: International Work Group for Indigenous Affairs, IWGIA.

Westmacott, T.I. 1999. Culture, Capital and Communications. *Research Technology Management* 42(1): 48-51.

World Health Organization (WHO). 1988. *From Alma-Ata to the Year 2000: Reflections at the Midpoint.* Geneva: WHO.

Wilmer, F. 1993. *The Indigenous Voice in World Politics Since Time Immemorial.* Newbury Park: Sage Publications.

Wilson, E.O., ed., 1988. *Biodiversity.* Washington DC: National Academy Press.

Win, A.A. 1998. 'The Growing Civil Society in Asi'. *Development* 41(1): 101-106.

Winthrop, R.H. 1991. *Dictionary of Concepts in Cultural Anthropology.* New York: Greenwood Press.

World Commission on Environment and Development. 1987. *Our Common Future.* New York: Oxford University Press.

World Conference on Science. 1999. *Science Agenda: A Framework for Action.* Paris: UNESCO/ICSU (http://www.unesco.org/opi/science/).

Zarembo, A. 2001. 'Magnet for Globophobes' *Newsweek,* Atlantic Edition. April 9, 2001: 29.

Chapter 4

Competing and Coexisting with Cormorants
Ambiguity and Change in European Wetlands

David N. Carss, Sandra Bell
and Mariella Marzano

Introduction

This chapter explores issues surrounding environmental change or, more precisely, local peoples' experiences and perceptions of environmental change, in relation to a particularly virulent conflict that exists across European wetlands between commercial and recreational fishermen[1], the fish-eating bird, the Great Cormorant, and those responsible for wildlife conservation and management. This conflict is embedded in two important global environmental challenges: the conservation of biodiversity and the sustainable management of natural resources. However, as with most human-wildlife conflicts, cormorant-fisheries conflicts are acted out at the local level (Anderson and Berglund 2004; Croll and Parkin 1992).

Wetland environments are historically recognised as "shifting landscapes", large sectors being either temporarily or permanently under water creating conditions where inhabitants must adapt to the natural fluctuations of their watery worlds. However, there is evidence that many groups of people are finding it increasingly difficult to negotiate the rapid environmental changes that are occurring across many European wetlands (Bell 2004; Tonder 2005). On the surface, local assessments of environmental change are usually articulated in a relatively straightforward manner, for example, people claim that more and more cormorants are feeding on declining fish stocks in direct competition with fishermen. The simple explanation that assumes a direct causal relationship between increased numbers of cormorants and reduced amounts of commercial species of fish is attractive but flawed. As we shall show, prolonged conversations even with those most predisposed to espouse this view often reveal significant ambiguities. Such underlying uncertainties point to the presence of much wider social, economic and environmental concerns, particularly in relation to hydrological factors and top down approaches to natural resource management. Nevertheless, with their highly visible fish capture techniques, their distinctive pose when drying their wings and their clustering together in roosting and breeding colonies, cormorants are a highly conspicuous feature of wetland landscapes. So, if fishing and keep nets are empty, or full of the 'wrong' species and the reasons are too complex and difficult to change, cormorants are easy to blame.

Experiences of economic hardship and people's consequent anxieties about the security of the natural resource base are commonly reported as major influences on people's perceptions of and attitudes to the natural environment (Lewicki et al. 2003).Where livelihoods are not at issue and the fishery is a focus for recreational angling feelings also run deep. Anglers are also prone to blaming cormorants for fish losses (particularly of fish stocked artificially for subsequent recapture) despite poor statistics on yields and stocking (Adamek et al. 1997). So, while studies have shown that cormorants are increasing in numbers and do eat a lot of fish, the intense conflict over 'the cormorant problem' often masks more complex concerns over changes in the ecological and social environment (cf. Rotmans et al. 2000).

This chapter thus explores the multidimensional perspectives of cormorant-fisheries conflicts, incorporating the material dimensions of wildlife predation as well as the social and cultural dimensions (Knight 2000). Previous attempts to resolve cormorant-fisheries conflicts have relied largely on the work of biologists and biological understanding is obviously important, especially because the ambition of most wildlife management plans is to incorporate the best scientific evidence. However a purely biological approach is usually inadequate to the task of trying to address why human-wildlife conflicts occur and why they can remain contentious for decades (cf. Lewicki et al. 2003). Knight (2000: 20) suggests that many apparent human-wildlife conflicts actually have more to do with 'tensions, divisions and antagonisms' between humans.

Here we will draw upon four specific case studies from the U.K., Greece, Lithuania and Romania to emphasize the need to broaden the focus beyond biology to examine the wider context within which cormorant-fisheries conflicts are set. Although these places have different social, political and economic histories, all are facing problems with cormorants. While it is recognised that the 'cormorant problem' is occurring on a pan European scale, attempts to manage conflicts may be most effective at the local level. For example, examinations of how local people assess environmental change demonstrates how fishermen tend to localise the cause of problems, partly because they consider themselves more capable of assessing what can be done to remedy problems closest to home (Bell 2004). To add weight to the view that interdisciplinary approaches to human-wildlife conflicts require cultural contextualisation, we therefore focus on tensions surrounding cormorant-fisheries interactions at the local level. Socio-cultural issues help to fuel conflicts and need to be carefully unravelled before they can be tackled. Thus, we have a situation where science is moving away from the premise that it can deliver a 'solution', to more collaborative endeavours involving information exchange and greater involvement of local people in decision-making and planning: relationships, collaborations and dialogues are intensifying between the research community, practitioners, and policy makers as science moves closer to applications (Marzano et al. 2006: 186). Furthermore, by drawing attention to local people's fears and concerns over environmental changes, encapsulated in their attitudes towards the cormorant, we also help to clarify how environmental managers and policy makers might embark on more sensitive, informed and inclusive interventions.

Background

This chapter brings together findings and explorations from two EU-funded Fifth Framework Programme projects, REDCAFE [2] and IMEW [3], both of which considered cormorant-fisheries conflict in four countries (Figure 1). The REDCAFE project (taking a natural science perspective) was designed to complement and develop previous biological work by addressing several of the main uncertainties highlighted during the development of an *Action Plan for the Management of the Great Cormorant in the African-Eurasian Region* (see van Dam and Asbirk 1997 and also below). The project synthesised available cormorant-fisheries information, identified methods of reducing the current Europe-wide conflict between cormorants and fisheries interests, and collated expert evaluations of their practical use. REDCAFE took a novel approach (in relation to cormorant-fisheries issues at least) by, for the first time, bringing together avian, fisheries and social scientists and many relevant 'stakeholders' [4] to discuss and report on these issues. The project also included a cormorant-fishery conflict management case study focussing on the Lea Valley in southeast England. This case study formed the first phase of the development of a local Fisheries Action Plan, a government agency-led initiative to address and prioritise local social as well as biological issues affecting inland fisheries at a catchment scale. Some of the workshop outputs are presented here.

The IMEW project (taking a primarily social science perspective) set out to understand the role of people in relation to biodiversity conservation and focused on four sensitive European wetland regions, three of which (Kerkini Lake, Greece; Nemanus Delta, Lithuania; Danube Delta Romania) are included here. IMEW's research focused on (1) perceptions of nature among adults and children, (2) the informal and formal social institutions that mediate between people and natural resource use, (3) how aspects of local people's livelihoods relate to, and impact upon, natural resource use, and (4) the development of responsible tourism. Interviewees were not asked specifically about cormorants at the start of this research but, if they mentioned these birds, we then explored their feelings and concerns over them in more depth. Finally, ecologically based work also attempted to quantify natural fish predation and collate fisheries statistics.

Despite their different disciplinary perspectives, both projects considered the 'cormorant problem' as experienced by local people, uncovering how fishermen are reacting to the rapid transformation of their social and natural environments, which has coincided with the increase in cormorant numbers.

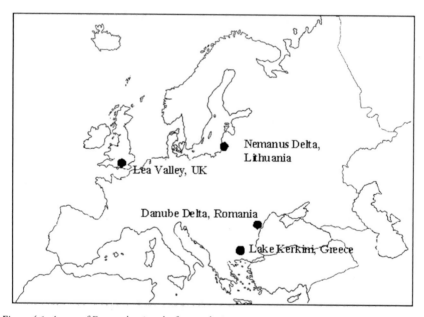

Figure 4.1: A map of Europe showing the four study sites

The Expansion of European Cormorant Populations

Two subspecies of Great Cormorant (hereafter 'cormorant') occur in Europe: the 'Atlantic' subspecies *Phalacrocorax carbo carbo* and the 'Continental' subspecies *P. c. sinensis*. Latest (1995) breeding estimates for *P.c. carbo* are of 40,000 pairs, mostly on the coasts of Norway, U.K., Ireland and northern France, representing over 80 percent of the world population of the *P.c. carbo* race (Debout et al. 1995).

Although there are no estimates for *P.c. sinensis* populations during the nineteenth century or the first half of the twentieth, it is likely that numbers in the remainder of Europe had declined to an unprecedented level of around 800 breeding pairs in the Netherlands in the early 1960s. Thereafter, numbers increased dramatically to over 150,000 pairs throughout the region in 1995 (van Eerden and Gregersen 1995) and it is likely that the species is now more numerous than ever before. The geographical range of these populations has expanded with cormorants returning to some areas after a long absence whilst also moving into areas previously never occupied. Moreover, birds spread all over Europe outside the breeding season, breeding birds from one country may spend the winter in others and *vice versa*. For example, a Mediterranean country may have a cormorant problem in winter caused by birds that breed in Scandinavia during the summer.

The reasons for such expansion are unclear but possible causal factors include a 'non-limiting food supply' (i.e. populations are not limited by a lack of food), protection of breeding sites and reduction in persecution throughout Europe (van Eerden and Gregersen 1995, Bregnballe and Gregersen 1997). Undoubtedly, protective legislation, particularly the EEC Directive 79/409 on the Conservation of Wild Birds (but also others), [5] has also been an extremely important factor in the increase of cormorant populations throughout the region (van Eerden et al. 1995) and is seen by many as a conservation success story. However, as we shall argue in this chapter, the expansion of the European cormorant population must also be considered in the context of environmental and social changes unprecedented during the late twentieth century.

The 'Cormorant Problem'

Cormorants are 'generalist' fish-eating predators, taking a wide variety of species in shallow coastal seas, freshwater fisheries (natural and stocked artificially) in lakes and rivers, and both traditional/extensive and intensive aquaculture systems (Cramp and Simmons 1977). In many wetland regions across Europe, fish stocks, particularly of commercially valuable species, have become depleted. In almost all countries where cormorants occur, their increasing numbers and geographical spread has led to a growing number of conflicts with commercial fisheries and recreational angling interests (e.g. Bildsøe et al. 1998 and Suter 1995, respectively). The main argument for the conflict is that cormorants impact on fisheries through direct consumption of commercial or rare fish species. Best scientific estimates for the daily food requirement of cormorants range between 400g and 800g per bird per day [6], depending on subspecies and reproductive status (for instance in the breeding season birds will also be foraging to provision their chicks) (Wilson et al. 2003). Cormorant predation is also thought to result in indirect effects such as injury to fish and the spread of diseases and/or parasites that increase fish mortality and reduce their market value.

Quantifying the impact of cormorant predation on fish stocks and catches is notoriously difficult to do in a rigorous scientific manner (see endnote 6 and Wires et al. 2003 for review). Nevertheless, there are clear cases of cormorant damage to fishing gear and ensnared fish, as well as documented cases of considerable stock depletion at fish farms and small lakes and ponds (cf. van Dam and Asbirk 1997). However, demonstrating any ecological impact of cormorants on fish stocks or catches in large rivers, lakes and coasts is difficult because of ecological complexities. Similarly, demonstrating an economic impact is also difficult often because of a lack of information (Carss 2003: 153-154). Despite the difficulties in quantifying the biological or economic impact of cormorants in most situations, and because, like all wild birds in Europe, the cormorant is subject to protection, there have been attempts to minimise the conflict between fisheries interests and cormorants at the continental scale through legislation.

International Legislation, Conservation and Management Plans

In order to understand why cormorant-fisheries conflicts are still prevalent and to show why it is so difficult to manage the problem across Europe, we present a brief review of the current legislation and management. Under a derogation of the EU Birds Directive it is possible to kill a small number of cormorants under certain circumstances at a specific fishery as a 'crop protection measure'. Although this, or a national equivalent, have been applied on a local scale, the calls for further measures to reduce the population size of cormorants made by some fisheries interests, particularly those in regions where cormorants overwinter, increased during the 1990s. After a lengthy political process (see van Dam and Asbirk 1997), and mindful of calls to take effective action to restore depleted fish stocks and ensure that the Common Fisheries Policy maintains fish at levels that can support both human fisheries and natural predators, an *Action Plan for the Management of the Great Cormorant in the African-Eurasian Region* was drawn up in 1998 (Bonn Convention document Jnr.SN1996-885/29-0001). This document included population models which were used to estimate the numbers of cormorants that would have to be killed in order to reduce the then current cormorant population. With important reservations (see van Dam and Asbirk 1997: 75-78), estimates suggested that several tens of thousands of cormorants would have to be killed across Europe every year in order to begin to reduce the cormorant population. The Action Plan aimed to minimise the conflict between fisheries interests and the cormorant by "*ensuring that best practice is followed in mitigating, preventing and reducing their reported impacts on fisheries, while maintaining a favourable conservation status for the species.*" The Action Plan also stated that Range States should try to achieve this, in the following order of preference, through (a) appropriate site-specific fisheries management, (b) local management and control of cormorants, and (c) co-ordinated management and control of cormorants between Range States.

The Action Plan was sent to all European Range States with a request to implement the recommendations included therein. Any response to the Action Plan was left to the discretion of individual Range States who appeared to continue with their own regional or national cormorant mitigation policies based on their interpretations of national and international legislation. Countries did not integrate their mitigation policies and there was little evidence of advice on the implementation of the Action Plan being made available to Range States nor was there facilitation or funding to co-ordinate its implementation at the international level. Perhaps most importantly, many local people (e.g. commercial fishermen, recreational anglers, fish farmers) felt excluded from the process, suggesting that it did not address their concerns over cormorant numbers and cormorants' impact on fisheries (Carss 2003: 132-133). Thus, for many fishermen and anglers most affected by the 'cormorant problem', the Action Plan appears to be ineffectual, fuelling the perception at the local level, that nothing is being done to help them protect the fish but much is being done to protect the cormorant. The case study examples presented here also show the growing frustrations fishermen feel as their livelihoods or leisure pursuits are increasingly constrained by forces of change which are out of their control.

Local Perceptions of Environmental Change

In each of the four study wetlands, local people's views that fish stocks and quarry species from both commercial and recreational fisheries have declined considerably are commonplace and widely expressed, most often by comparing the present against times within living memory (see also Minnegal et al. 2003). Local people also considered that cormorant numbers had increased in these four wetlands, since the early 1990s or before, and this is corroborated by biological counts. Cormorants are cited by many as the culprits for these fish declines but the association between increased numbers of cormorants and reduced fish catches does not necessarily mean that there is a cause-and-effect relationship (van Dam and Asbirk 1997) and deeper discussions in our study areas reveal widespread concerns over other environmental, socio-political and economic changes. Here we offer a brief summary of local perceptions of these changes in relation to fish catches (and cormorant impacts) for each wetland.

Lea Valley, England

The extensively managed River Lea (sometimes spelled 'Lee') runs some ninety kilometres roughly north to south, from rural Bedfordshire to the River Thames in east London. Much of the upper river is natural or semi-natural, the lower catchment is a mosaic of countryside areas, urban green spaces and completely urban areas. Some 3 million people live within thirty minutes drive of the Lea Valley. Cormorant predation on rivers is often perceived to be a major issue. As one local angling representative wrote:

> 'If one asks those anglers who have stopped fishing the Lee "why?" – they will say catch rates and cormorants. In their eyes they see hundreds of these birds in the sky over the Lee Valley every day and they are surviving. Therefore they must still be feeding on fish. They have personally witnessed fish of all sizes taken or killed and to the anglers' perception there are no fish left and it is a waste of time trying. The Lee Bridge Road area, which produced many 20lb. plus bags [of fish] every winter weekend, was wiped out by cormorants in just two winters. Cormorants are in the Lee Valley twelve months of the year.'

However, the workshop revealed that cormorant predation is only one of several problems facing the Lea Valley, though for those involved it remains the most conspicuous. Other biological issues were cited by local stakeholders, including changes in water quality and levels and the threat of the invasive, alien signal crayfish (*Pacifastacus leniusculus*). Moreover, further problems cited stem from social issues including poaching of carp (*Cyprinus carpio*) for the table, the influence of private angling enterprises (that provide stocked fish in man-made water bodies), the loss of angling 'hotspots' as a result of poor planning (e.g. development encroaching on river banks), and several access and safety issues.

Indeed, during the workshop, a number of key issues affecting the Lea Valley emerged from our discussions with local people. For example, many believe that the main problem facing the Lea Valley is an economic one. Economic measures of angling 'effort' (i.e. day and season ticket sales and angling club membership) have all fallen considerably in the last decade: people have either stopped fishing or now fish elsewhere. This has had a knock-on effect on the local economy such as the closure of tackle shops.

Local people consider that these economic problems are the result of too few anglers catching too few fish in the Lea Valley. Several lines of evidence suggest that many fish stocks and/or catches there have declined dramatically (see Lea Valley draft consultation document, Environment Agency). The perception is that most small fish – both small individuals and small species – have declined whilst there may still be fisheries containing large individuals (i.e. 'specimen' fish) of some species such as barbel (*Barbus barbus*) and carp. However, even for these latter species, the concern is that once these larger individuals die, the capacity for the species to breed successfully and sustain viable populations will be greatly reduced. In some cases, such perceptions have been confirmed by fish surveys (Environment Agency, pers. comm.). There is also some evidence that the distribution of fish has changed within the Lea Valley (Environment Agency, pers. comm.). Anglers often choose to fish adjacent to bridges in the belief that these structures are now the only places were fish aggregate in any numbers.

According to local people, the lack of fish, and the related economic decline, have both local ecological and social implications. There are concerns at the species and genetic levels in relation to the stocking of non-indigenous fish. Some anglers are also concerned that other fish-eating birds will suffer as a result of the lack of small fish or due to the 'aggression' of cormorants. As the fishery declines, it becomes uneconomical to pay bailiffs to maintain riverbanks, with resulting declines in littoral growth and associated fauna and increases in litter and pollution.

There is also a wider social impact. Local angling clubs are considered critical social partners with the National Federation of Anglers (NFA), the Environment Agency (EA) and central government. The NFA operates a coaching scheme that teaches coaches to train young people in all aspects of angling and associated environmental issues, whilst the EA and central government operate an Angling Participation Scheme. This scheme aims to re-establish derelict urban fisheries and develop properly trained, motivated young people. Such 'stewardship' schemes, and the recreational opportunities associated with them (as well as things like local employment and transport demand) all decline as the number of local angling clubs, and anglers, declines.

Finally, local people also told us of planning and policy implications resulting from the economic decline. With the demise of local angling clubs, organised citizens groups lose key players with their associated conservation and financial benefits. Moreover, falling motivation levels as a result of declining angling clubs mean that other Government initiatives suffer (e.g. angling/environmental awareness schemes) and vital community links may be lost. The Lea Valley case thus raises a number of important social issues in relation to young people, community livelihoods and traditions. The problem is related both to institutions and their survival.

Lake Kerkini, Greece

Lake Kerkini is an artificial lake created in 1932 after the construction of a dam across the Strymon River. The lake was intended as a source of irrigation, a means of flood control, and to promote fisheries and biodiversity. However, this multiplicity of purposes turned into sources of conflict (Bell et al. in press). In 1982 a bigger dam was constructed in order to increase the carrying capacity for irrigation and the water levels now fluctuate seasonally by around 7 metres. By 2001 a population of 26,000 people lived in the twenty-three villages around the lake. Hydrological work has led to increased water levels and shrinkage of shallow water areas important for fish spawning, and reduced grazing areas for cattle and water buffalo (Crivelli et al. 1995a). There are also associated changes in the fish composition of the lake in favour of species with low economic value, particularly the gibel carp (*Carassius auratus*). Fish species valued by local people as a food source and mainstay of the commercial fishery (such as carp, wells *Silurus glanis* and eel *Anguilla anguilla*) are in serious decline (Crivelli et al. 1995b). Reed bed habitats have also declined through a combination of increased grazing pressure in riparian areas and alterations in water level. Furthermore, changing water levels have altered the structure and distribution of aquatic vegetation, whilst riparian forests to the north of the lake now suffer prolonged inundation.

Lake Kerkini is an important site for many waterbirds although rising water levels have had a serious impact on many of the 300 local bird species (Crivelli et al. 1995b). By contrast, numbers of (breeding) cormorants have increased from 500 pairs in 1990 to reach 3,500 pairs in 2002 (Carss and Marzano 2005: 154). Both amateur and commercial fishermen appear unanimous in fierce denunciation of cormorants. As an official from a local fisher association stated: 'Cormorants on the other hand are the lake's black sheep. They wipe out everything in their way.' His colleague explained: 'I like birds but I don't like cormorants. Dirty birds, birds of Satan they call them. Wherever they go, the place stinks. Fish don't go near. How could I like birds like these?'

Generally, cormorants were acknowledged as having a rightful place in the natural world, though they were categorised as pests. Knight (2000: 8) believes that the discourse of wildlife pestilence is often subjective with claims that are 'inaccurate, exaggerated or ill-founded'. He also suggests that many wildlife pests may serve as the 'scapegoats of human society'. The majority of fishermen interviewed described cormorants as particularly harmful and around 40 percent claimed that their numbers should be reduced. Fishermen were certain that the cormorant population had increased over the past few years and this, together with the bird's perceived preference for carp fry, had resulted in economic decline of the fishery creating social ills. One fisherman said that without cormorants 'there would be carp and I would have a better life….Another 500 families could make a living from the lake. Young people would stay here rather than look for ways to go away.' Many fishermen and other locals said hopelessly that they just wanted cormorants to 'go away' because, in combination with problems caused by fluctuating water levels, the odds became too greatly stacked against the fishery.

Although local people are passionately attached to this wetland ecosystem, they are disappointed over recent environmental change which they blame on the authorities. A 70-year-old retired fisherman told us: 'The lake has become a sea. Fish used to hide among the reed beds and the forest. This all perished since the dam was built. There is nothing left. Since then the lake has been left bare and we have lost what we had in the past'. A currently active fisherman expressed a similar view: 'Within four years the reed beds were lost and only water lilies were left. Ten years later water lilies were lost too.' Fishermen at Kerkini value fishing as part of their identity and a means of relating to nature but many describe it now as a 'useless' job because of its poor economic return. Fishermen also feel powerless and neglected by the authorities that control water levels as one highlighted: 'The first thing to do would be to keep the water level stable during April and May until the fish spawn. This is impossible though because thousands of fields in the Serres Plain depend on this water…The result of all this is we have no power to speak. Their voice is stronger.'

Nemanus Delta, Lithuania

The inhabitants of the Nemanus Delta have similar concerns to those around Lake Kerkini in relation to hydrological change but they also face the uncertainty associated with the socio-political and economic transition confronting Eastern Europe [7]. The Delta, a dense network of waterways formed at the mouth of the Nemanus River, is located on the eastern shore of the Curonian Lagoon, a shallow freshwater body with some influx of brackish water from the adjacent Baltic Sea. The area contains twenty-five villages and a population of around 4,000 people. Informants from the Nemanus Delta viewed fish-eating birds as significant predators threatening fish stocks. The cormorant figured prominently as the most voracious of all. The following exchange, in a focus group with staff at a local fish-breeding institute, is typical: 'A: Cormorants are worse than anglers, B: Worse than poachers, A: The quarry of an angler is 12 tonnes per year. The quarry of a cormorant is 120 tonnes, C: They don't pay taxes!'

In the above quote, the latter figure for annual cormorant consumption of fish (120 tonnes) is over 410 times the maximum scientific estimate for the food requirements of the species and is thus biologically nonsensical. However, the main point of interest here is that a cormorant is claimed to take ten times the amount of fish annually that an angler would catch. Having said that, the value given for an angler's annual catch is also a gross overestimate – requiring the angler to catch almost 33kg of fish every day of the year.

A commonly aired view of cormorants is that they should be killed. Furthermore, cormorants were seen as originating from 'outside' the area and representing a new threat to local fisheries. For local people, this 'new' threat is associated with other uncertainties ushered in since the end of the Soviet period, their alien status rendering them fair game for vilification. Hampshire et al. (2004) note that privatisation of the marketing system in Lithuania (and Romania) has led to the expansion of black market trading and to over-fishing of certain species. For example, the opening up of free-markets in the fish farm sector has also caused conflicts between fisheries and cormorants in both Poland and the Czech Republic (Carss 2003), whilst associations between open markets, changes in livelihood strategies, over-fishing and cormorants have also been made in Estonia [8]. The dislike of cormorants seems to go beyond direct competition for fish and often appears to be linked to the consequences of major international changes in market economies operating on local fisheries embodying, perhaps, local people's frustrations concerning lack of prosperity more generally.

Water management is a major concern of villagers in the Nemanus Delta. They maintain that the rivers are silting because of reduced dredging during the post-Soviet period. People fear this impedes the movement of fish. There is also a widespread opinion that the Curonian Lagoon is becoming more saline due to the impact of engineering works at its northern end. These works have opened the lagoon to intake of brackish water from the Baltic Sea and people hold them partly responsible for perceived decreases in fish stocks. As one local fisherman said: 'The situation is changing rapidly, especially because of the recent deepening of the Curonian Lagoon. Before that it took two to three days for the wind to blow from the west to get sea water over here and now it takes one day. This pushes all the [freshwater] fish away from here.' Fishermen also connect the decline of available fish stocks to the imposition of a national boundary across the lagoon between Kalingrad (Russian Federation) and Lithuania. They argue that a combination of currents, winds, and fish-feeding habits mean that desirable species are present in greater numbers on the Russian side of the Lagoon. These waters, once valuable fishing grounds, are now lost within Russian territory; a fact that contributes to the general belief that there are fewer fish for capture. The perception that fish stocks are decreasing is widely expressed, though the extent, its cause, and future prognosis of the depletion are typically a matter of conjecture and uncertainty. This situation breeds an air of pessimism and insecurity about the future and is encapsulated in comments from commercial fishermen: 'We expect nothing. We are afraid about the future of our children. Fish will not remain for them.'; 'The situation is worsening.'; 'The only aim is to survive.'

As in the Lea Valley and Lake Kerkini, the mounting presence of cormorants, in addition to the aforementioned changes facing fishermen, leads to increasing conflict. However, while cormorants are ostensibly to blame for fish decline, local understanding of environmental change also implicates other, human adversaries. Here we have a vivid example of the assertion that in some cases, conflicts are effectively projected onto wildlife which becomes a symbolic vehicle 'for the expression of a social conflict' between people or between people and the state (Knight 2000: 21). The Danube Delta case provides further evidence of this people-state conflict.

Danube Delta, Romania

In the Romanian Danube Delta local inhabitants feel powerless against powerful institutions such as the Danube Delta Biosphere Reserve, accusing them of misunderstanding the natural environment while imposing restrictions, in the name of wildlife conservation, on how the inhabitants can live and work.

The Danube Delta comprises three major channels, 400 lakes and a network of interconnected waterways. It is Europe's largest delta and has a unique pattern of closely interconnected habitats and ecosystems. There are twenty-six human settlements within the Delta and a population of around 14,000 people. The activities of cormorants and pelicans are seen as particularly damaging when set beside the hydrological and ecological changes affecting the Romanian Danube Delta. Informants judged these birds to be feeding less frequently in lakes, the birds' once favoured foraging grounds, because these water bodies are shrinking and forcing fish to retreat into channels, where they are followed by the birds. These environmental observations by local people heighten the sense of competition between fish-eating birds and fishermen especially because fishermen's licences usually permit fishing in lakes rather than channels. There is also widespread opinion that the currently low water levels make it easier for these birds to catch fish. The majority of informants consider that cormorants consume 'too much fish.'

Nevertheless, like the inhabitants of the Nemunas Delta, Danube Delta inhabitants' perceptions of the natural environment are heavily coloured by economic hardship and anxieties about the security of the natural resource base. As in all the case study wetlands presented, they are also worried about what they consider to be the most elementary aspect of the Delta's ecosystem – water volume, flow regime, and water quality. There is a solid consensus that water levels are dropping, marshes and channels drying out, silting up or becoming clogged with vegetation: 'Now around Caraorman it is like the Sahara desert...the balta [local term for the Delta's marshes and swamps] is drying up. Nature is suffering.'; 'Alluvia has come and covered the lakes with mud.'; 'The level of the water is decreasing and fish are dying.'

Although some informants mention lack of rain (two explicitly mention climate change) as being the cause of these changes, by far the majority blame what they see to be incompetent hydrological management. This relates to a common source of cormorant-fisheries conflict which stems from feelings of exclusion among local people, to which poor communications and simplistic understandings of information transfer needs have contributed. For example, feelings towards the Danube Delta Biosphere Reserve Authority (concerned with conservation and management of the Delta) are largely negative. There is acknowledgement that the Danube Delta must be managed and agreement that species and habitats require protection, especially against poachers and outsiders who seek to exploit the Delta's resources. In addition to suffering economic deprivation, isolation and lack of basic facilities such as piped drinking water and sewage facilities, local people feel that the authorities also blame them for failing to care for nature. Yet local people regard themselves as the most worthy champions of the natural world which is their daily reality. Historical and chronic lack of trust is a serious obstacle to the close collaboration between Delta inhabitants and members of the DDBRA essential for sustainable management of this wetland.

In discussing their intrinsic suspicion of the DDBRA, inhabitants point to the hydrological changes they believe to be pertinent to the decline of the Delta's fishery, the size and composition of the fish stock being affected by 'reduced water levels', 'the clogging of channels', 'the silting up of lakes', and 'the growth of weeds and algae'. One species has increased to the point of becoming what people describe as 'dominant' – the gibel carp. This is a non-native species and an escapee from the now abandoned Soviet-era fish farms in the Delta but the fish makes inferior eating and is of low economic value. Poor water quality is also considered to have affected fish stocks more adversely than fish-eating birds. As a retired helmsman remarked: 'It is said that the pelicans and cormorants eat more fish, but when there were large numbers of fish there was enough food for local people and birds too. The birds are not the principle cause for diminishing fish.'

Indeed, a fisherman from the village of Mila 23 cites poor water quality to explain the lack of carp: 'The common carp has died because he rests in winter, just like bears. His gills filled with mud. He couldn't breathe and when it got warmer he still had mud in his gills, so he didn't make it.' While a younger fisherman says: 'It would be better if they opened the channels to bring fresh water. Because of dirty water the fish die.' Traditionally, reeds were burned in winter to allow for more rigorous new growth in spring, which was cut and dried to provide animal fodder for winter. This practice is now severely restricted by local authorities (see Bell 2004: 62) but local people claim that important ecological benefits once came of it. As one fisherman said: 'Prior to 1989, the water was clean and the channels were clean. In winter and early spring people burned the reed from the bank and the floating reed islets. When fish spawned the water ways were clear…This is a most important thing not only for fish but for vegetation too.' Another stated: 'When the reed is burned it regenerates the fish and birds and everything else. Otherwise during the summer the water becomes foul.'

The Danube Delta case adds another perspective to why conflicts occur. There is a disparity in opinion between the DDBRA, representing nature conservation interests and those involved in the fisheries. Indeed, fishing is always potentially in conflict with conservation. In ecological terms, humans who fish are predators, albeit ones who respond to and reflect upon their role as predators, whilst conservation is a set of ideas and measures intended to ensure the maintenance, and possible enhancement, of populations of fauna and flora within their natural habitats. In the Danube Delta, local villagers feel that the fishing economy has taken second place to conservation efforts to preserve wildlife (including cormorants). Part of the problem is how different species are valued by the different stakeholders, especially fish-eating species such as cormorants (Bell et al. 2001). For example, cormorants are commonly held in contempt by fishermen across Europe but are considered important by others (such as scientists, conservationists and many lay people) as the top predators in many aquatic systems (Bell et al. 2001).

Fisheries Management Is More Than Managing Fish

Like anglers in the Lea Valley, the case studies from wetlands in Greece, Lithuania and Romania illustrate the changing circumstances fishermen find themselves in, where the increased abundance of cormorants becomes the object of dissatisfaction with degraded environments (and decreasing fish stocks), political and social change as well as the pressures of top-down management of the natural resources. It is clear that when attempting to better understand the nature of cormorant-fishery conflicts it is also useful to consider other, more wide-ranging issues that lead to conflicts over fisheries resources. These issues, both ecological and social, are often closely linked (Daniels and Walker 2001) and thus are perhaps best approached through an integrated framework that includes people's lived experiences within these dynamic environments. In this chapter we have highlighted how local people described their fears and concerns in relation to their fishing businesses or recreational angling pursuits as well as voicing their specific worries over fish-eating birds, particularly the numbers of cormorants and how much fish they are eating. In all study locations, perceptions of environmental change were similar and involved large-scale anthropogenic habitat and hydrological modification with concomitant changes in water levels, water quality, the distribution of aquatic vegetation, and the abundance and structure of fish communities. Moreover as fish stocks become more obviously affected by these changes, ultimately manifesting themselves in lower fish catches, two things often happen as a consequence: fish become more 'valuable' to local people, and fish-eating birds – especially cormorants – are increasingly seen as competitors for these fish.

One overlying issue affecting all fisheries, and certainly our local informants, is the long-held concern over increasing pressure on limited aquatic resources, particularly within the current climate of calls for sustainable management of natural resources. Symes (1996) notes that overfishing has been acknowledged by fishermen, administrators and scientists for over a hundred years and that by the mid-1990s the Food and Agriculture Organisation had estimated that some 70 percent of the world's fish stocks were overfished. Fishing takes place in uncertain and diverse environments, including both the biological and the social setting in which these activities are undertaken (Acheson 1981). This not only relates to commercial fisheries but also to aquaculture, another income producing fisheries activity (see Noakes et al. 2003), and to recreational angling. Thus, attempts to create 'sustainable' fisheries must extend to all aspects of the fishery system, from the fish stocks and ecological considerations to the social, cultural and economic structure of fishing groups and management institutions (Symes 1996, Charles 2001). Furthermore, as Rotmans et al. point out 'the increasing complexity of European society means that sustainable development cannot be addressed from one perspective, one country or one scientific discipline' (2000: 810).

However, another concern voiced by local people is the fact that they often have little control over how legislation is interpreted by national and regional authorities or how the wetlands in which they live are managed. Until recently, academic contributions to fisheries management have usually been dominated by biologists and economists, whose understanding is influenced by their own discipline (Couper and Smith 1997). Now scientists and policy-makers are also paying attention to the human element in fisheries management by including an appreciation of fishermen's perspectives.

Many commercial fish stocks are now no longer plentiful and fisheries management must take into account the 'uncertainty factor' resulting from the behaviour of fishermen (individually and collectively through organisations), which is increasingly influenced by growing insecurity surrounding their livelihoods base (Symes 2001). In many societies around the world, fishing rights are controlled. Acheson (1981: 281) believes such rights-based systems operate to reduce uncertainty: 'if fishermen cannot control the fish, at least they can control who will be allowed to fish for them and how they will do so'. Seen in this context, local fishermen view cormorants as another 'fisherman' in the system, albeit one whose access to the fishery they currently have no, or very little, control over. Moreover, as in all the field sites discussed here, many fishermen feel that cormorants are given unduly high conservation status or legal protection, and that current legislation works against them (see also Marquiss and Carss 1997). Thus, as a consequence, local people often feel that other 'stakeholders' (e.g. nature conservationists, biologists, policy-makers) have too much control over rights of access to their fisheries and over the fisheries management decision-making process. Cormorants become a symbol of environmental but also social and political 'realities' facing local fishermen. Tensions are inevitable.

In this chapter we have shown how local people speak perceptively of the environmental changes affecting their wetland and fisheries and the resulting frustration they feel, indicating that despite the inclination to scapegoat the cormorant, they do understand the multiple factors involved in their complaints. Similarly, Pinkerton (1989) considers several major fisheries conflict issues that also emerged through our discussions with local people, identifying three relevant factors congruent with our own research. First, there is often a lack of faith in the ability of governments to solve management problems. Second, fishermen want a voice in the decision-making process to ensure more appropriate and equitable management. Both suggest the necessity for collaborations between the research community, practitioners and policy-makers. Third, there is an evident lack of trust: fishermen do not feel that they can depend on the reliability of scientific data, or that governments (or the scientists they commission) have adequate data. Most field biologists would agree: often their data are incomplete, provisional, and have a considerable level of uncertainty. For their part, local and national governments can regard fishermen as unrelenting predators who, in many cases, have overfished through inadequate understanding of fish biology (cf. Jentoft et al. 1998, Hardin 1968, Clover 2004). This strongly suggests the need for greater collaboration between local people and scientists. The sharing of local knowledge and scientific information and the inclusion of local knowledge (in the form of perspectives, concerns and experiences) in decision-making and planning are both essential if fisheries management strategies are to be successful and sustainable.

Integrating Local Knowledge into Fisheries and Cormorant Management

There has long been a growing movement towards the development and implementation of effective, 'holistic' fisheries management programmes which include local knowledge (cf. Mackinson and Nøttestad, 1998). In order to avoid inadequate fisheries policies and management systems that tend to treat the symptoms (in this case, the observation of increasing cormorants and the perception that there are too many) rather than address underlying problems (widespread anthropogenic changes in wetland hydrology and ecology), broader environmental and institutional factors should be taken into account and fundamental socio-cultural conditions must also be given high consideration (Symes 1996). Rettig et al. (1989) suggest that participatory co-management in fisheries, where fishermen and managers co-operate in drafting policy, may facilitate successful management and reduce conflicts (see also Jentoft et al. 1998; Pitcher and Hollingworth 2002).

One particular benefit of co-management relates specifically to the formation of relationships. Pinkerton (1989: 8) states: 'Once the relationship among actors is changed by establishing an area of co-operation, enlarging co-operation to other management functions becomes easier.' In relation to incorporating the knowledge and experience of local people into some form of co-ordinated assessment and management of the European 'cormorant problem', the process of 'establishing an area of cooperation' is proving difficult (Carss and Marzano 2005). The REDCAFE and IMEW projects gave local people some opportunity to describe their concerns over environmental change, and specifically cormorants, and also allowed natural scientists to consider social, cultural, political and economic perspectives to what were once considered 'biological issues'. They have also given both fishermen and natural scientists the opportunity of framing the cormorant-fisheries conflict in a wider context of complex 'social' issues and wide-scale environmental change. However, these two projects also revealed the current disparity between many local people's felt needs of fewer cormorants and the current 'reality' of scientific understanding of both the impact of cormorant predation on fish populations, stocks and catches, and of the ecological systems within which the birds exist.

Given the difficulties in managing many of the other biological and social issues affecting fisheries, many people believe they could have some control over cormorant numbers. For many, the 'cormorant problem' could be addressed by a reduction in bird numbers through a widespread cull across Europe. However, as mentioned earlier, because population reduction on such a scale would require the killing of tens of thousands of cormorants each year (van Dam and Asbirk 1997: 86-88), there would undoubtedly be logistical, political, and perhaps ethical, issues to address. Moreover, biologists point out that:

'A best professional judgement suggests that a substantial reduction in population size does not necessarily lead to a substantial reduction in the number of cormorants foraging in so-called problem areas. Furthermore, economic losses would not necessarily decline proportionately with a decline in the number of cormorants foraging in a problem area' (van Dam and Asbirk 1997: 89).

This situation is causing continued, if not heightened, friction between fisheries interests, scientists and policy makers and it is still proving difficult to incorporate local people and their knowledge into cormorant management processes and strategies.

Indeed, the involvement of local people in fisheries planning and decision-making can be fraught with difficulties as there is rarely a single 'public discourse' and, in the majority of situations, there is likely to be a range of contested views and values in relation to natural resources (Hampshire et al. 2004, Minnegal et al. 2003). The present synthesis has shown a range of contested views and values specifically in relation to cormorant-fishery conflicts, just one area of concern for fisheries management. We have shown how concerns over the sustainability of the natural resource influences how local people perceive and experience the environment but research into human-wildlife conflicts must also include an examination of the role of power (for example: who has control over decision-making) in fuelling conflicts.

As well as a contextualising frame, which links the local with the national and global, environmental problems are repeatedly identified as presenting the most urgent need for the benefits conferred by interdisciplinary research (Kinzig 2001, Brewer 1999, Turner and Carpenter 1999, Stewart and Strathern 2003). We think that the examples discussed above, though not perfect in their interdisciplinary balance, demonstrate the truth of this assertion. Certainly the interpenetration of researchers across the two projects, REDCAFE and IMEW, created new understandings about the cormorant issue and about obstacles to interdisciplinary research (Marzano et al. 2006). In addition there have been strong calls for the involvement in environmental management issues of a full range of stakeholders, particularly local participants (cf. Chambers 1997, Pound et al. 2003, Sillitoe 2004). Either one of these approaches requires people to break down barriers and is difficult enough to achieve in its own right, but we would add that neither will succeed alone. In the case of cormorant-fisheries conflicts, it is plain that a diverse range of solutions are the only ones likely to begin to remedy a wildlife conflict afflicting so many European countries, and which others are preparing for.

Acknowledgements

This chapter draws on our research in two EU-funded Framework 5 projects: REDCAFE (Reducing the conflict between cormorants and fisheries on a pan-European scale) Concerted Action Q5CA-2000-31387 and IMEW (Integrated Management of European Wetlands) Research Project EVK2-CT-2000-00081. We offer our heartfelt thanks to all those involved in these two endeavours – both local people and researchers.

Notes

1. Here we use the word 'fishermen' to describe men and women who catch or farm fish for commercial gain, use commercial fishing gear to catch fish as a hobby, and angle for fish with rod-and-line as a recreational pursuit.
2. REDCAFE (Reducing the conflicts between cormorants and fisheries on a pan-European scale), EU Framework 5 Concerted Action Q5CA-2000-31387. Synthesised current understandings of cormorant conflicts with fisheries, cormorant ecology, potential management tools and organised a conflict-resolution case study workshop involving researchers and other stakeholders.
3. IMEW (Integrated Management of European Wetlands) EU Framework 5 Research Project EVK2-CT-2000-00081. Conducted comparative natural and social science research in four European wetlands. http://www.dur.ac.uk/imew.ecproject/.
4. The word 'stakeholders' was used in the REDCAFE project and is a difficult one: it means different things to different people and it is not easily translated into some languages. In the context of this chapter the term 'stakeholders' is taken to mean (a) people who are affected (either positively or negatively) by a particular problem or activity or (b) people who can influence (either positively or negatively) the outcome or end result of a particular process. For further details see Ramírez (1999).
5. Other important protective legislation in the EU includes the Bern Convention on the Conservation of European Wildlife and Natural Habitats and the Bonn Convention on the

Conservation of Migratory Species of Wild Animals and, in the EU and elsewhere, the Ramsar Convention on Wetlands of International Importance especially as waterfowl habitat.

6. It is difficult to put this daily food requirement into context for several reasons. First, during its daily foraging a cormorant may eat one or two large fish or several dozen small ones, thus without knowledge of the size of predated fish it is impossible to estimate the numbers of them being eaten per day. Second, the numbers of cormorants visiting foraging sites can vary from a single bird to flocks of several thousand (depending on the size of the water body involved). Even at a specific feeding site a mere count of the numbers of birds present is not a rigorous quantification of the numbers feeding there as it takes no account of the turnover of birds arriving to fish and leaving again throughout the day. Third, without an adequate estimate of the numbers of fish within a particular fishery, it is not possible to speculate on the likely consequences of the removal of those lost to cormorants. Adequate estimates of fish numbers are exceptionally difficult to make with current technology for all but the smallest and simplest fishery systems. Finally, such considerations assume some relatively simple relationship between the ultimate size of a fish 'population', the 'stock' of fish in a particular sector of a water body, and the actual 'catch' of fish by people from that same sector – the simplistic assumption being that a fish lost to a cormorant is one lost to the fish catch. There are numerous reasons why this might not be the case. Similarly there is some evidence that predators will select 'unhealthy' fish that are likely to die 'naturally' anyway and thus be unavailable to the fishery, and that at least some of the fish that are not predated 'compensate' for reduction in competitors with higher growth rates (and possibly ultimate survival).

7. Our research was carried out before Lithuania joined the European Union on 1 May 2004.

8. Vetemaa et al. (2000) detail how, during the Soviet period, all Estonian water bodies were state owned and commercial fishing was carried out by collectives mostly serving the markets of socialist countries. Following independence there was a high demand for fish and a rapid increase in exports so that fish prices rose dramatically. Most fishermen formally connected to collectives were given the chance to privatise fishing boats and gear at low cost, whilst the abandonment of an oppressive border regime allowed fishermen free access to the sea. Fishing quickly became an important livelihood strategy and resulted in unsustainable pressure on fish stocks. Profitability has declined in recent years, exacerbated by increasing costs and declining stocks. Within the troubled fishing industry, the debate over cormorant predation has highlighted potential conflict and, in certain regions, many commercial fishermen now believe that cormorants are to blame for declining catches (Eschbaum et al. 2003).

Bibliography

Acheson, J.M. 1981. 'Anthropology of Fishing'. *Annual Review of Anthropology* 10: 275-316.

Adamek, Z., H. Klinger and E. Staub.1997. 'Cormorants in Europe – The Evaluation Of EIFAC/FAO Questionnaire Campaign' *Supplemento alle Richerche di Biologia della Selvaggina* XXVI: 347-353.

Anderson, D.G. and E. Berglund. 2004. *Ethnographies of Conservation: Environmentalism and the Distribution of Privilege*. New York and Oxford, Berghahn Books.

Bell, S. 2004. *Integrated Management of European Wetlands.* Final Report EVK2-CT-2000-00081.

_____ K. Hampshire and S. Topalidour (in press) 'The Political Culture of Poaching: A Case Study from Northern Greece' *Biodiversity and Conservation.*

_____ I. Nichersu, L. Ionescu and E. Iacovici. 2001. 'Conservation versus Livelihood in the Danube Delta' *Anthropology of Eastern Europe Review* 19: 11-15.

Bildsøe, M., I.B. Jensen and K.S. Vestergaard. 1998. 'Foraging Behaviour of Cormorants *Phalacrocorax Carbo* in Pound Nets in Denmark: The Use of Barrel Nets to Reduce Predation' *Wildlife Biology* 4: 129-136.

Bregnballe, T. and J. Gregersen.1997. 'Changes in Growth of the Breeding Populations of Cormorants *Phalacrocorax carbo sinensis* in Denmark'. *Supplemento alle Ricerche di Biologia della Selvaggina* XXVI: 31-46.

Brewer, G. D. 1999. 'The Challenges of Interdisciplinarity' *Policy Sciences* 32: 327-337.

Carss, D.N., ed., 2003. 'Reducing the Conflict between Cormorants and Fisheries on a Pan-European Scale. Final Report on EC Concerted Action Q5CA-2000-31387' Available at: http://www.intercafeproject.net

_____and M. Marzano, eds., 2005. 'Reducing the Conflict between Cormorants And Fisheries on a Pan-European Scale. Summary and National Overviews. Report Developed from EC Concerted Action Q5CA-2000-31387' Available at: http://www.intercafeproject.net

Chambers, R. 1997. *Whose Reality Counts? Putting the First Last.* London: Intermediate Technology Development Group Publishing. London.

Charles, A.T. 2001. *Sustainable Fisheries Systems: an Interdisciplinary Approach to Fisheries Analysis.* Oxford, Blackwell Sciences.

Clover, C. 2004. *The End of the Line: how overfishing is changing the world and what we eat.* London: Ebury Press.

Couper, A.D. and H.D. Smith.1997. 'The Development of Fishermen-Based Policies' *Marine Policy* 21: 111-119.

Cramp, S. and K.E.L. Simmons eds., 1977. *The Birds of the Western Paleartcic. Vol. 1.* Oxford, Oxford University Press.

Crivelli, A.J., P. Grillas, H. Jerrentrup, T. Nazirides. 1995a. 'Effects on Fisheries and Waterbirds of Raising Water Levels at Kerkini Reservoir, a Ramsar Site in Northern Greece' *Environmental Management* 19: 431-443.

_____ Grillas, P. and B. Lacaze. 1995b. 'Environmental Auditing: Responses of Vegetation to a Rise in Water Level at Kerkini Reservoir (1982-1991), a Ramsar Site in Northern Greece' *Environmental Management* 19: 417-430.

Croll, E. and D. Parkin eds.,. 1992. *Bush Base: Forest Farm.* London: Routledge.

van Dam, C. and Asbirk, S. eds.,. 1997. *Cormorants and Human Interests.* Wageningen: IKC natuurbeheer.

Daniels, S.E. and G.B. Walker. 2001. *Working through Environmental Conflict: The Collaborative Learning Approach.* Connecticut: Praeger.

Debout, G., N. Røv and R.M. Sellers.1995. 'Status and Population Development of Cormorants *Phalacrocorax Carbo Carbo* Breeding on the Atlantic Coast of Europe' *Ardea* 83: 47-59.

van Eerden, M.R. and J. Gregersen 1995. 'Long-term Changes in the Northwest European Population of Cormorants *Phalacrocorax carbo sinensis*' *Ardea* 83: 61-79.

_____ Koffijberg, K. and M. Platteeuw. 1995. 'Riding the Crest of the Wave: Possibilities and Limitations for a Thriving Population of Migratory Cormorants *Phalacrocorax carbo* in Man-Dominated Wetlands' *Ardea* 83(1): 1-9.

Environment Agency. *River Lee FAP consultation.* Available at http://www.environmentagency.gov.uk/subjects/fish/165773/346898/665025/?lang=_e. Accessed September 2006

Eschbaum, R., T. Veber, M. Vetemaa and T. Saat. 2003. 'Do Cormorants and Fishermen Compete for Fish Resources in the Väinameri (Eastern Baltic) Area?' in *Interactions between Fish and Birds: Implications for Management.* ed., I.G. Cowx. Oxford: Fishing News Books. pp72-83.

Hardin, G. 1968. 'The Tragedy of the Commons', *Science* 162: 1243-1248.

Hampshire, K., S. Bell, F. Stepukonis and G. Wallace. 2004. ' "Real Poachers" and Predators: Shades of Meaning in Local Understandings of Threats to Fisheries' *Society and Natural Resources* 17: 305-318.

Jentoft, S., B.J. McCay and D.C.Wilson. 1998. 'Social Theory and Fisheries Co-Management' *Marine Policy* 22(4-5): 423-436.

Kinzig, A. P. 2001. 'Bridging Disciplinary Divides to Address Environmental and Intellectual Challenges' *Ecosystems* 4: 709-715.

Knight, J. ed.,. 2000. *Natural Enemies: People-Wildlife Conflicts, An Anthropological Perspective.* Routledge, London and New York.

Lewicki, R.J., Gray, B. and M. Elliot. 2003. *Making Sense of Intractable Environmental Conflicts.* Washington: Island.

Mackinson, S. and L. Nøttestad. 1998. 'Combining Local and Scientific Knowledge' *Reviews in Fish Biology and Fisheries* 8: 481-490.

Marquiss, M. and D.N. Carss. 1997. 'Fish-eating Birds and Fisheries' *BTO News* May-June/July-August 1997: 201-211.

Marzano, M., Carss, D.N. and S. Bell. 2006. 'Working to Make Interdisciplinarity Work: Investing in Communication and Interpersonal Relationships' *Journal of Agricultural Economics.* 57 (2): 185-197.

Minnegal, M., T.J. King, R. Just and P.D. Dwyer. 2003. 'Deep Identity, Shallow Time: Sustaining a Future in Victorian Fishing Communities' *The Australian Journal of Anthropology.* 14 (1): 53-71.

Noakes, D.J., L. Fang, K.W. Hipel and D.M. Kilgour. 2003. 'An Examination of the Salmon Aquaculture Conflict in British Columbia Using the Graph Method for Conflict Resolution' *Fisheries Management* 10: 123-137.

Pinkerton, E. 1989. 'Attaining Better Fisheries Management through Co-Management – Prospects, Problems and Propositions' in E. Pinkerton, ed., *Co-operative Management of Local Fisheries: New Directions for Improved Management and Community Development.* University of British Columbia Press, Vancouver: 7-33.

Pitcher, T.J. and C. Hollingworth eds., 2002. *Recreational Fisheries: Ecological, Economic and Social Evaluation.* Oxford: Blackwell.

Pound, B., S. Snapp, C. McDougall and A.Braun. 2003. *Managing Natural Resources for Sustainable Livelihoods: Uniting Science and Participation.* London: Earthscan.

Ramírez, R. 1999. 'Stakeholder Analysis and Conflict Management' in D. Buckles, ed., *Cultivating Peace*. Washington DC: International Development Research Centre, World Bank Inst.

Rettig, R.B. and F. Berkes. 1989. 'The Future of Fisheries Co-Management: A Multi-Disciplinary Assessment' in E. Pinkerton, ed., *Co-operative Management of Local Fisheries: New Directions for Improved Management and Community Development*. Vancouver: University of British Columbia Press, pp. 273-289.

Rothman, N. Rijkens. 2000. 'Visions for a Sustainable Europe' *Futures* 32: 809-831.

Rotmans, J., M. van Asselt, C. Anastasi, S. Greeuw, J. Mellors, S. Peters, D. Rothman, N. Rijkens. 2000. 'Visions for a Sustainable Europe' *Futures* 32: 809-831.

Sillitoe, P. 2004. 'Interdisciplinary Experiences: Working with Indigenous Knowledge in Development' *Interdisciplinary Science Reviews* 29 (1): 6-23.

Stewart, P., A. Strathern. eds., 2003. *Landscape, Memory and History: Anthropological Perspectives*. London: Pluto Press.

Suter, W. 1995. 'The Effect of Predation by Wintering Cormorants *Phalacrocorax Carbo* on Grayling *Thymallus Thymallus* and Trout (*Salmonidae*) Populations: Two Case Studies from Swiss Rivers' *Journal of Applied Ecology* 32: 29-46.

Symes, D. 1996. 'Fishing in Troubled Waters' Crean, K. and D. Symes, eds., *Fisheries Management in Crisis*. Fishing News Books: 3-16.

—2001. 'The Future of Europe's Fisheries: Towards a 2020 Vision' *Geography* 86: 318-328.

Tonder, M. 2005. *Anatomy of an Environmental Conflict– A Case Study of the Conservation of the Saimaa Ringed Seal*. Joensuu: University of Joensuu Publications in Social Sciences.

Turner, M.G. and S.R. Carpenter. 1999. 'Tips and Traps in Interdisciplinary Research' *Ecosystems* 2: 275-276.

Vetemaa, M., R. Eschbaum, R. Aps and T. Saat. 2000. 'Collapse of Political and Economical System as a Cause for Instability in Fisheries Sector: An Estonian Case' *Proceedings of the IIFET 2000 International Conference. Microbehaviour and Macroresults*. Oregon State University, Corvall, USA. Available at: http://www.orst.edu/Dept/IIFET/2000/papers/vetemaa.pdf.

Wilson, B.R., Feltham, M.J., Davies, J.M., Holden, T., Britton, J.R., Harvey, J.P. and I.G. Cowx. 2003. 'Increasing Confidence in Impact Estimates – The Monte Carlo Approach' in T. Keller and D.N. Carss, eds., *Cormorants: Ecology and Management at the Start of the 21st Century. Die Vogelwelt* 124 (2003) Supplement, pp. 375-387.

Wires, L.R., Carss, D.N., Cuthbert, F.J. and J.J. Hatch. 2003. 'Transcontinental Connections in Relation to Cormorant-Fisheries Conflicts: Perceptions and Realities of a "Bête Noire" (Black Beast) on Both Sides of the Atlantic' in T. Keller and D.N. Carss, eds., *Cormorants: Ecology and Management at the Start of the 21st Century. Die Vogelwelt* 124 (2003) Supplement, pp. 389-397.

Chapter 5

Pathways To *Developmen*
Identity, Landscape and Industry in
Papua New Guinea

Emma Gilberthorpe

Introduction

When isolated indigenous populations are faced with global intrusions they are
forced in one way or another to act on deep-seated indigenous knowledge to
make sense of things. In Papua New Guinea extractive industry is one such
intrusion that forces populations to consciously acknowledge their historical
connection to the place they live in order to be recognised as landowners and
receive compensation, equity and, in some cases, royalties. As hosts to the
Kutubu branch of the Kutubu-Gobe-Moran oil fields in Papua New Guinea the
Fasu people are required to present themselves as landowning clans in order to
collectively receive two percent of the total commercial value of petroleum. The
conflict between traditional and Western perceptions of land in this region has
been summed up by Weiner who writes:

> From the point of view of the single person in this region of Papua New Guinea, land
> is not viewed as a discrete parcel of territory with clear borders. Rather, land is the
> culmination of the historical and temporal travel over a particular person's bush tracks
> through specific areas that he (or she) has laid claim to during his or her lifetime. It
> is this view of land, so at odds with the Western view of enclosed and em-bordered
> plots of property, that is truly Melanesian (or at least Papuan), and which resource
> companies and government ministries must come to terms with if it is to understand
> land-ownership and disputes over land in the Kutubu and Gobe oil projects area at
> all (Weiner 2002: 10).

Since project inception in 1992 operations have become part of the landscape, and whilst infrastructure is unimposing it is clearly segregated through the construction of compounds and productive enclaves. The enclosure not only transmits perceptions of property and power (see also Bender 1999), but also represents modernity and *developmen* (Pidgin term for development). Perception of the Western enclave as a symbol of development (cf. Ferguson 2005; Polier 1996) has filtered into Fasu villages where one sector of society in particular has, through a combination of historical and traditional processes, been able to seize *developmen* by forging links with both the operators and clans in perceptively more developed regions such as the provincial capital Mendi and the national capital Port Moresby. This sector, comprising a number of young males educated during the period of missionisation in the 1980s, are beginning to view the landscape and their relationship to it and within it in terms of historical connectivity, mirroring the categorising needs of Western industry described by Weiner. This has caused a number of problems between gender and age sets at the village level generating a rift between those who are able to tap into development agendas and those who are not.

However, whilst young, entrepreneurial males grasp development they do so through a conduit of cultural processes grounded in deep-seated indigenous knowledge so that the attainability of *developmen* is conceived along traditional lines of interaction. The activities of young men emerge within a context of pre-industrial sensibilities revealing a conflict of continuity and change at the village level.

This conflict came to light during my doctorate fieldwork in the Hekari region of Fasu territory (2000 to 2001). Data showed that Fasu relations with land are based on a division of male and female identity after puberty, and reinforced through analogies between male and female biogenetic substances (semen and menstrual blood) and nature. Male and female identities are informed by what I refer to here as 'rooted identity' and 'extended identity' (cf. O'Hanlon and Frankland 2003); complementary forms that ensure a regional network of interrelations and interactivity. Rooted identity refers to cultural processes of being and becoming; a deep-seated sense of belonging to place and natal kin. Extended identity refers to experience, travel and distance; connections with land and individuals beyond place of origin. Rooted and extended identities differ for males and females; whilst both have a sense of belonging to the place they were born by virtue of shared substance with their parents, this is either strengthened or weakened at the time of puberty. Male connectivity to place is strengthened through the transference of substance (semen and meat) and transmission of sago palms at the time of, during and immediately following puberty, whilst female connectivity is weakened as they leave their natal clan on marriage (just prior to puberty). Male rooted identity is central to their ongoing connectivity with place, whilst to many females it becomes a distant memory. Perceptions of maleness and femaleness are reified in the natural environment; in permanent tree crops such as sago palms, in running rivers, and in still pools. Natural symbols of maleness and femaleness are also represented in pathways, roads trodden into the rainforest, or rivers that provide access between communities. These pathways represent extended identity and connectivity between natal clan and allied groups.

Pathways are created by females when they leave their natal clan on marriage, their movement establishing physical links between two clans. Obligatory gifts and trade goods continue to traverse pathways along with other females, establishing inter-clan connectivity over several generations. Male extended identity is realised through the paths of connectivity created by wives, mothers, and sisters, whilst female extended identity is realised through the very experience of moving from natal to marital group, a pattern that can occur several times in a female's life time as the result of divorce, widowhood and remarriage. Whilst pathways represent extended identity over a broad landscape, they also represent connectivity of a more regional nature. Inter-clan relations are created through permanent transfers of land and maintained through ongoing exchanges along connective pathways ensuring a regional network of support.

The construction of pathways and the conceptual foundation underlining their significance are important elements of Fasu knowledge that inform the integration of development agendas. Roads linking villages with the company headquarters on Iagifu Ridge represent new paths of regional connectivity along which royalties, compensation and equity flow. Larger roads connecting the Fasu with Mendi, and air travel connecting them to Port Moresby, further symbolise pathways extending beyond the region, representing a medium for establishing relations on a broader national scale (Gilberthorpe 2007). As the recipients of royalties (see below) and fluent in Pidgin and in most cases English, some young men have been able to take advantage of new pathways, extending their spheres of connectivity to perceptively more developed regions; a process which reveals the bourgeoning conflict between continuity and change at the village level. The incident that brought this conflict to light involved a dispute between two landowning clans – Karopai and Fasu Sanemahi – over the area of land housing company headquarters and operations, Iagifu Ridge. Iagifu was inherited by Karopai's head-man (the eldest, living male) when his wife's natal clan died out in the early 1980s. When land is inherited along affinal lines it is common for the inheritor to break from his clan and occupy the inherited land to create supportive links between two clans over an extended area. However, with no living brothers to transfer his own clan land to, the Karopai head-man transferred Iagifu Ridge to a cousin who had recently returned to the village after a decade's absence, during which time he had lost head-man status within his own clan (Fasu). Once complete, the permanent transfer marked an important link between Karopai and the newly formed clan of Fasu Sanemahi.

Since the resident oil company began the commercial production of petroleum in 1992 the Karopai head-man's male children have grown, had children of their own and are now in a position to split and form their own clans. The sons see Iagifu Ridge as their maternal land and are asking for it back. They say 'this is our mother's land. She worked sago there and our ancestors are there'. The introduction of a landowner mentality and royalty payments has engendered a shift not only in how land is perceived within this generation of males but also how ties are devised and maintained. No longer seen as a medium for establishing necessary links between clans to ensure a network of support and interaction in an environment dominated by warfare, sorcery and cannibalism, land is now seen as a mechanism for attaining development. Iagifu Ridge does not generate extraordinary land rentals, the area being on an economic par with other owned territory, but as site of the main production facility and employee camp its owners are aligned with the development landscape, living just outside the company enclosure. The road connecting them with the company provides a channel for developing links and they have devised contracts becoming powerful and wealthy in the process.

What has emerged is a series of competitive manoeuvres between the young men of both clans, each establishing and strengthening ties on a national and international scale to participate in *developmen*.[1] In this chapter I examine this phenomenon in relation to the indigenous knowledge base from which it has emerged to show how industry has augmented male extended and rooted identity whilst restricting them for females. I begin with a necessary outline of the Fasu social landscape and contact history, followed by an outline of Fasu identity and finally discussing the implications of the conflict between continuity and change in a resource extraction context.

Fasu Clanship

The Fasu are a small Papuan language group of approximately 1,100 occupying the area of land between the Hekikio (Kikori) and Soro Rivers just south of Lake Kutubu in Southern Highlands Province, Papua New Guinea. Whilst the name Fasu[2] has been adopted by the younger generation as a generic term for the people living between the Hekikio and Soro, elders do not acknowledge such a broad connectivity. They do, however, recognise a shared language, *Namo Me* (literally 'real talk'), between an expansive group of people who speak it, *Namo Aporo* (literally 'real people'). The Fasu conceptually divide to form three geographically and dialectically distinct groups, the Uri, Hekari and Yasuku, each group comprising small totemic clans interlinked along various relational lines often extending beyond Fasu territory to geographically close neighbouring groups, the Foi, Huli, Kasua and Kaluli. Like their fringe highland neighbours the Fasu are predominantly hunter-horticulturists subsisting on a staple of sago complimented by local greens, sweet potato and occasionally small game and fish (Weiner 1988).

As for many Papua New Guineans, the term 'clan' is a recent gloss for characteristically dynamic units of affiliation. For clarity, however, I continue to use the term. Fasu clans are descent-based with a patrilineal bias and kinship terms distinguishing levels of membership and obligation. In the context of endemic warfare, low life expectancy and fear of sorcery, clans were dynamic units that integrated migrants to boost support, and segmented in line with natural growth cycles.

In 1936 the Fasu region was infiltrated by Australian administrators (Schieffelin and Crittendon 1991, Williams 1976) and during the 1970s and early 1980s by missionaries (Wood 1982, Kurita 1988). Missionary influence ensured that a number of children were educated, some going to high school in the provincial capital Mendi. As females were needed for domestic duties at home males were more likely to be educated. Missionary presence has been absent in the Fasu region since the mid-1980s and local church services are now conducted by local pastors in a mixture of the Fasu language and Pidgin.

Prior to 'contact' the Fasu moved around their land in line with gardening and hunting cycles and the maturation of sago palms and other permanent tree crops. Clans maintained communal longhouses, split into male and female sections, and oscillated between longhouse and individually-owned bush houses close to sago palms within shared territory. During the colonial period, scattered longhouse groups were forced together into villages (of which there are currently thirteen), and architecture shifted to a central male longhouse and peripheral, smaller women's houses (cf. Weiner 1991).

As hosts to the Kutubu branch of the Kutubu-Gobe-Moran oil fields the Fasu received in excess of 45 million kina between 1992 and 2000.[3] Benefits are distributed via Incorporated Land Groups, a model of human/land organisation that requires clans to present themselves as landowning units formally linked to fixed, bordered territory (Gilberthorpe 2007, Goldman 2000, Weiner 1998, Sagir 2004, Marru 2002). As clans are units of male affiliation, benefits are accessible only to male members of the Fasu population. The Kutubu Oil Project has basic, largely inconspicuous infrastructure including two employee camps, two production facilities, a number of well-heads, several access roads (including the pipeline road which connects all but one of the Fasu villages), and an underground pipeline that accommodates the oil from its extraction site to an export facility in the Gulf of Papua (Knauft 1993). There is no central township at Kutubu and operations and employee activity are enclosed within secure compounds policed on a twenty-four-hour basis.

The need to demarcate territory to meet landowner status has caused the Fasu to rethink the landscape. For the first time, it is thought of as a resource so that previously interactive, interrelated and interdependent clans are forced to re-evaluate their relationships with each other (Gilberthorpe 2007, see also Ernst

1999, Guddemi 1997). The landowner ideology enforces perceptions of land as the property of a fixed clan, conflicting with the fluid and informal nature of Papua New Guinea traditional land tenure (Weiner 2002; see also Guddemi 1997, Sillitoe 1999). Repercussions of the landowner mentality include the tightening of clan boundaries to acknowledge only descent as criteria for membership, and the prevention of migrant affiliation.

Whilst industry has become part of the landscape it is a part that most Fasu have little interaction with. Industrial activity neither encroaches on nor directly affects everyday subsistence activity and villages remain largely structured from bush materials. Electrical supplies are limited to the occasional generator, and running water is restricted to a single source per village (although not all villages have this luxury). The landscape remains the primary source of subsistence, individual identity and shared history.

Human-to-Land Relations

The connection between individual and landscape is realised through a number of trajectories, most evidently through the conceptualisation of a core, representing rooted identity, and of arteries leading out from the core, representing extended ties and extended identity. Every clan is rooted to the area they inhabit through association with a clan name and a clan totem (cf. Langlas and Weiner 1988). Clan names are generally linked to the landscape, whilst clan totems are fauna and flora associated directly with local ecology (Table 5.1). Naturally, the clan identity (land, name and totem) outlives its members and representatives of any clan at any time may or may not have actual genealogical ties to a clan founder (see Gilberthorpe 2007). Males and females have disparate clan status; males are permanently rooted to their clan whilst females are seen as temporary members moving between clans throughout their life course. A clan is represented by a core kinship grouping known as *kepo* (lit. 'origin'), a group of males headed by its eldest living member who is conceptually a direct lineal descendent of a clan founder. By virtue of inheritance he is at once the *aporo uni hi* (lit. 'head man') and *wafaya hauaka* (lit. 'father of the land').

Table 5.1: Examples of Fasu clan names

Clan Name	Meaning	Totem
Upuko	Name of a mountain	Banana leaf
Nari	Name of 'Tulip' tree	'Tulip' leaf
Kikiri	Name of a type of sago that grows on their land	Kikiri palm leaf
Ekatamayu	Flat, white, oblong stones	White stones
Yafaraka	Name of creek that flows through their land	Bamboo that grows by the creek

The *kepo* comprises a head-man and his younger brothers, or a head-man and his sons (repesented by the black symbols in Figure 5.1), and a clan (*aporo ira*, lit. 'man tree') can be made up of either one *kepo* and dependents (Figure 5.1) or a number of *kepo* represented by a core unit. The kin group are obligated to each other in raising bridewealth and they share resources, whilst individually establishing and maintaining exchange relations with other individuals and clans to ensure a support network spanning a broader region. Males are not considered to be members of the *kepo* until they are productively mature and able to fully contribute to the exchange sphere.

Figure 5.1: A typical Fasu Clan

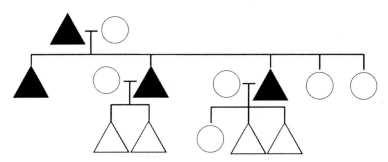

Rooted identity is established at birth when all children, regardless of sex, are connected as dependents of a kin-based clan group. This connectivity is realised through shared substance with both the mother (blood) and father (semen). As children progress through life, connectivity with the father is strengthened through the transference of semen and meat, the former ingested with the mother's milk to ensure the development of bones and teeth, the latter consumed for healthy growth. This nurturing process ensures a permanent rooted identity to place of birth and father's clan (i.e. the land, totem and name) that is only severed on permanent departure. Extended identity is created by females; by sisters who leave their natal clan to marry and by mothers and wives who have entered the region. The pathways created by women between their natal and husband's clans symbolise a link between the two and represent the source of not only her extended identity but also that of her husband and children.

Extended Identity

The importance of pathways (*ikia*) as symbols of connectivity between two distant groups are found throughout the literature on internal Papua New Guinea (see especially Modjeska 1982) and for the Fasu, like others, the notion of pathways connecting individuals and groups is rooted in mythology. According to myth, the Fasu landscape emerged from flood waters as Mount Tipuria. A couple (one male and one female), caught in the floodwaters on their sago boat car-

rying various resources including sago palm shoots, pigs, tree kangaroos and garden produce, found refuge on Mount Tipuria and built a house and made gardens. They bore a number of children who, when grown, were married, each
pair given a gift of either an important resource (sago palm shoots, pigs, tree
kangaroos) or traditional knowledge (knowledge of fire-making, knowledge of
hunting) by their parents. One couple, however, received secret knowledge that
they took with them far away from Fasu land. This 'secret' is now believed to be
the knowledge of writing and the English language, and *developmen* is seen as
the medium for attaining it. As legend goes, all other couples dispersed into the
valley starting their own clans that spread over generations to create new paths
over an ever-increasing area (Gilberthorpe 2004). The Fasu origin myth provides
a collective symbolic centre whilst emphasising the idea of dispersal and connectivity on which all activities and relations, including *developmen*, are judged.

As the origin myth suggests, pathways connect each conceptually central clan
to other individuals and groups, and it is these arteries that represent extended
identity. Extended identity essentially represents distance and externality in
opposition to the internal solidarity represented by rooted identity; the opposition highlights the relational difference between close kin and allies and the status of each to clan land and resources. The opposition between internal (rooted)
and external (extended) identity differs for males and females and the means
through which identity is actually lived out in everyday experience is reversed.
Males are defined by rooted identity, working, sleeping and exchanging within a
specific sphere of male clan solidarity (Gilberthorpe 2007). Their extended identity has been created by their mother, wife/wives and sisters. Identity with
mother's clan represents the primary sphere of male extended ties and the bond
between children and their mother's brothers and father is particularly strong. For
the Fasu, the blood line (links through the mother) is symbolic of ancestral spirits and the exchange items that travel along the pathways connecting children
with their mother's natal clan represent protection and support. Fathers ensure
their children are protected and supported through gifts made to in-laws, receiv-
ing gifts along the pathways their own sisters have travelled to their marital clan.

Whilst males live within the sphere of rooted identity and male kin solidarity,
females live their extended identity, retaining ties with the natal clan they may
never return to. Females are connected to the landscape by virtue of their movement across it, moving from their natal group at the time of marriage and any
number of times thereafter as a result of divorce, widowhood and remarriage. As
all children remain with the father's clan, females may be connected through them
to any number of clans in their lifetime. Female identity therefore can be contained
within a series of pathways that connect her to a number of different groups.

Pathways created by females at the time of marriage are also conduits for
trade activity. The Fasu region is characterised by a flow of trade objects (shells,
pigs, tree oil for body decoration, tobacco, string bags, black-palm bows, sago

and more recently cash and store goods) not only between Fasu clans but also with other language groups, the Fasu region acting as a trade centre between northern highland groups and lowland and coastal groups. The area of land between the Hekikio and Soro Rivers lies between 300 and 1 500 metres above sea level, offering a range of ecological conditions from sago swamp valleys and limestone ridges to dense tropical rainforest. The three Fasu groups therefore inhabit geographically and ecologically distinct regions, the Uri living in the upper grasslands, the Yasuku in the lower rainforest, and the Hekari in the central sago swamp valleys. The three groups are recognised for regional speciality, the Uri for raising pigs, the Yasuku for hunting and the Hekari for fishing and sago production. Specialisation ensures the maintenance of pathways between the three regions, whilst primary wealth items, kina and cowrie shells, enter by way of main watercourses from north and south. The Hekari and Yasuku groups claim 'the best shells come from up-river', from the Huli groups to the north. As suggested in the origin myth above, the practical undertones of this web of activity lie in the need to trade essential resources between specialised groups.

Paths are littered with historical and symbolic markers that hold meaning for the individuals who travel along them. As this would suggest, indigenous knowledge for the Fasu is a series of dynamic narrative histories based on individual experience, movement, activity, and kin connectivity. Pathways within the immediate environment have different meanings for men and women, symbolising fertility, debility, health and history. Paths to garden sites represent fertility as these are the sites of male initiation rites and sexual intercourse, whilst paths to female menstrual and birth huts represent debility and are dangerous to men. These paths are socio-symbolic of male/female relations grounded in perceptions of the male and female life course that are closely bound up in the landscape.

The Source of Identity

For the Fasu, male and female identities are clearly opposed and defined by different criteria. Identity is, however, grounded in shared knowledge that gives cultural meaning to activity and interaction in this part of Papua New Guinea. Knowledge is generated by a belief in opposed male and female biogenetic substances (blood and semen) and analogies of these in the landscape. Across all Papuan cultures the properties of semen and menstrual blood feature prominently in procreative ideologies (see in particular Strathern 1988, Jorgensen 1986, Weiner 1988) and landscape analogies (Weiner 1991). For the Fasu, male semen is said to produce foetal bones and nails whilst female menstrual blood is said to produce foetal flesh and blood.

Procreative ideology is manifested in every-day activities characterised by a strict sexual division of labour and the segregation of male and female habitation and subsequent sociality. Male activities include hunting, trapping, fishing, house building, garden tilling, fence building, tree felling, and exchange activities. Female activities include processing sago and gardening, and collecting bamboo, sago grubs, wild nuts and firewood. Females are also primary carers of infants up until approximately two years of age, after which both males and females share responsibility. Production is highly genderised it being inappropriate for the opposite sex to participate in the other's tasks. This strict segregation of the sexes, not seen in other fringe highland language groups (see Weiner 1988), links to distinct oppositions in all aspects of life. The opposed characteristics of male and female are reified by oppositions of day and night, movement and stillness, and vitality and debility experienced through the landscape. The female activity of sago processing, taking place from dawn to dusk, conceptually links females with light and day, whilst the male activity of hunting, taking place from dusk till dawn, conceptually links males with dark and night.

The opposition of movement and stillness in the numerous watercourses that permeate the Fasu region provide further analogy for masculine and feminine attributes, the movement of water (rivers themselves signifying exchange paths) representing the passage of primary exchange objects (pearl shells) from north to south (from the Huli language group). As exchange is a male concern, the movement of water is analogous to the male activity of exchange, representing life and prosperity via conceptual associations with the passage of wealth. In contrast, still water as stagnant and polluted is associated with menstrual blood (Gilberthorpe 2004, cf. Weiner 1991). The properties of running water (vitality/life) and still water (debility/death) as conceptually transposed characteristics of maleness and femaleness respectively inform a perception of females as potentially harmful and polluting, particularly to males. Women never step over food, tools and equipment and during menstruation they isolate themselves in bush huts. Males build bridges over the dangerous female paths that impinge on their own hunting paths (Kurita 1994).

Children are not considered to be mature adults until they are able to fully contribute to domestic activities. It is at the time of puberty that characteristics of 'male' and 'female' are fully imbued. Until recently young men went through a series of male initiation rituals (see Kurita 1994)[4] during which the transference of semen and meat from elders ensured strength and vitality, both semen and cooked pig fat being seen as essential to bone development. Male semen is a symbol of strength and vitality, and its depletion over the male life course, through sexual intercourse, symbolises the depletion of vitality (cf. Strathern 1972). In opposition females are seen as weak as a result of blood loss at the time of puberty. Both children and the elderly are described as having feminine characteristics of weakness.

There is a close connectivity between humans, animals and spirits within a total interconnected landscape in which the cycle of birth, life and death is intertwined. This cycle is conceptualised through perceptions of bodily constitution and the dissipation of its parts at the time of death. Until relatively recently, bodies were displayed on bamboo platforms at the periphery of villages.[5] Eventually, the female-constituted parts (blood and flesh) dissipated into waterways and the bush to reform as spiritual embodiments, leaving only the male-constituted parts (bones and teeth), which were stored in special burial caves in the past and are buried close to villages today. Spirits are associated with the maternal blood line and are omnipresent in every-day life. A good hunter is believed to be able to communicate with ancestral spirits inhabiting the bodies of fish, wild pig and cassowary, requesting deliverance of their hosts to him. Spirits also inhabit areas of stillness and decay and can be harmful to humans if affinal ties are not maintained with ongoing gifts. Females then are associated with spirits and death (cf. Weiner 1991) whilst males are associated with life and vitality (cf. Strathern 1972).

The Sago Palm

The sago palm is symbolically and metaphorically important to the Fasu and is central to the articulation of status representing at once rooted and extended identity for males and females. Sago palms are the primary sphere of connectivity between males and the landscape they are born into and inhabit. Whilst males never actually harvest palms (as it is a female-only task) they do conceptually own them through transference from their father. The *kepo* kin group is, therefore, characterised by the ownership of sago palms within shared territory inherited along descent lines from a male clan founder (Gilberthorpe 2007).

The method of palm transference from father to son is carried out over an extended period. This begins with a process of 'showing palms' to male children at an early age (Kurita 1988). Males conceptually mature at the same rate as the palms that are 'shown' to them (palms taking about thirty-two years to mature in the local climate). Rights are activated when males become productively mature, at which time female kin (wife, sister, and/or mother) harvest them. Sago palms are individually owned so each owner has the power to transfer them to his own male children and (in the past) to migrant males in order to develop his own network of alliances.

The lineal transference of palms physically and historically connects males to land. As symbols of connectivity palms act as metaphors highlighting the rootedness of male identity in Fasu life. The *kepo*, meaning 'origin' and 'base of tree', is metaphorically aligned to sago palms, representing its base. The spreading palm represents the extension of male relations from this central core, the clan (*aporo ira*, 'man tree') being representative of this (Figure 5.1). The difference between male and female spatial connectivity is founded on the relationship between the *kepo* kin group and sago palms, representing a lineal inheritance that does not exist for women (Gilberthorpe 2007).

For females, the process of sago production is a lengthy task (taking about eight hours of continuous work), during which they vocalise experience, movement and connectivity through 'sago songs' (cf. Feld 1982, Weiner 1991). These songs act as individual mnemonic maps of female movement and history whilst being important mediums for maintaining pathways between groups. Women sing about landmarks along marriage paths and about people they have known. They sing to the landscape and to the spirits inhabiting the swampy areas where sago palms grow, expressing the urgency of completing the task before the light fades and the moon rises (and male hunting begins). The following two songs from the Hekari region are expressions of these characteristics and demonstrate the role sago production plays in expressing female rooted and extended identity.

Song 1

> *Fupe oto harufapo*
> Tree trunk, wait a minute
> *Ira apu karaferapo*
> You are big enough for me to finish but you are delaying my time
> *Tupa huni ne parorare*
> Wash the sago, I will not give in
> *Tupa huni harufapo*
> Wash the sago, wait a minute
> *Sere maiya he yao makeraka apura*
> It is time for the sun to go behind the river and bush, time is running out
> *Fataraku makeraka apura*
> [Name of a type of tree], time is running out
> *Keso maiya kima makeraka apura*
> The moon is coming up, time is running out
> *Putura keame*
> [Name of wild nuts that grow by the river side]
> *Sohoakuku kima makeraka apura*
> [Name of greens that grow by the river side], time is running out
> *Pau kima makeraka apura*
> Wash the sago, time is running out
> *Sereyame he yao makeraka apura*
> The sun is falling on the river and bush, time is running out
> *He tawara oto hinamo*
> Sago hammers from the coast followed women here
> *Ira napaku hinamo*
> Sago from the coast followed women here
> *Pasi kapokoko hinamo*
> [We can] break the coconuts [because they] followed women here
> *Sereyame he yao makeraka apura*
> The sun is falling on the river and bush, time is running out
> *Makaporosasere harufapo*
> [Name of the place where the author washed sago], wait a minute

Song 2

> *Waipa kakaseku erene*
> [Name of a palm leaf], it's getting dark
> *Ira wakaku erene*
> [Name of a tree leaf], it's getting dark
> *Ira tarupuku erene*
> [Name of a tree leaf], it's getting dark
> *Furanameke erene*
> [Name of a palm tree leaf], it's getting dark
> *Puria ope sairo ope*
> Go, come here
> *Ira wakaku erene*
> [Name of a tree leaf], it's getting dark
> *Wayupa kakaseku erene*
> [Name of a palm leaf], it's getting dark
> *Ira soteku erene*
> [Name of a tree leaf], it's getting dark
> *Apu piri kawepo*
> My sister's new sago beater, we are not yet done
> *Ira tarupuku erene*
> [Name of a tree leaf], it's getting dark
> *Maiya apure*
> The sun is going down
> *He Kikiao oto yaoraka apure*
> Swim across the Kikori River, go
> *He Popari yaorakaapure*
> Swim across the Popari River, go
> *He Pakapae yaoraka apure*
> Swim across Pakapae Creek, go
> *Ira wakaku erene*
> [Name of a tree leaf], it's getting dark

The imagery in these songs evokes the movement of women through the land-scape and connection with natal groups. In song 1 the author refers to the sago beaters, coconut palms and sago palms that followed *hinamo* ('women') along marriage paths (cf. Weiner 1991: 118-119). Similar imagery is evoked in song 2 expressing the landmarks that connect the Bosavi and Hekari regions (Kikori River, Popari River, and Pakapae Creek). With both nostalgic and emotive undertones, sago songs play a central role in maintaining paths between differ-ent clans. Sung by males during ceremonial exchanges they evoke nostalgia and emotion in invited guests, inciting them to dispense with more valuable gifts (see also Weiner 1991). Fasu ceremonies take place for marriages and new longhouse openings and are important socio-political events involving large-scale exchange. The songs sung by guest males invited to *keraka* (lit. 'sing and dance') over a twenty-four-hour period along the internal walkway of the male-only longhouse, are actually appropriated from females. As males walk through the rainforest they listen to females singing and commit the songs to memory. They then practise the songs with their *keraka* partners and perform them at ceremonial events to a male-only audience. Songs composed by females are, then, verbal exposés of their extended and rooted identity, appropriated by males to enhance extended ties.

Shifting Identities

At first glance, extractive industry at Kutubu appears to have had little impact on the Fasu and their relationship with the landscape as they remain inalienably connected to and in contact with the environment to which they claim historical links. Women continue to sing the sago songs that represent journeys across territory, men maintain connections to the landscape through descent and the transference of sago palms, and an ideology of male and female movement and activity informed by the landscape and its analogous features is ever-present. The conceptualisation of a central core and extended arteries connected by various pathways retains prominence. The semi-permanent roads that now connect all but one Fasu villages to each other and to the project infrastructure (including the airport) represent exchange paths along which wealth, power and knowledge traverse. The opportunities afforded a sector of males since the early 1980s by way of access to education and knowledge along these extended paths are played out in everyday activity through connections with the operators of industry and in efforts to develop ties in the larger towns. The advocacy of external (as opposed to indigenous) knowledge is reconciled as the 'secret' given to one of the 'original' Fasu couples migrating from Mount Tipuria.

It is the revelation of this secret which, although accounted for by the origin myth, generates conflict at the village level through the restriction and extension of indigenous constructs on a number of levels. Restriction is perhaps most evident in clan membership, where the ban of migrants has meant that clans are represented by core units of father and sons (i.e. the *kepo*) who split in line with natural growth patterns as shown in the Iagifu Ridge case outlined in the introduction. The clan is, then, a much more solid unit than it ever was.[6] What we see here is a shift in the consequences for establishing and maintaining relationships. Migration was integral to group composition and continuity in a climate dominated by warfare, sorcery and low-life expectancy. In a climate dominated by industry, royalties and development benefits (medical centres, schools and so forth), however, relational ties are adjusted to ensure benefit streams are tapped for present and future generations.

At the same time indigenous constructs are extending beyond the region to incorporate larger towns. A number of young males are looking beyond traditional marriage routes to establish ties with perceptively more developed regions such as Mendi and Port Moresby. What we see here is an extension of traditional pathways of connectivity, a process benefiting males by providing them with access rights to land and resources in 'developed' regions, but restricting for females who are often overlooked as marriage partners and become increasingly burdened with domestic chores. A combination of the need to consolidate future claims through land ownership and the male control of the exchange arena mean that females remain external to development activities. As Fasu women become ever-more marginalised their own pathways of connectivity begin to disappear and marital and trade paths established and maintained over generations of activity and intermarriage fade back into the bush. Many of the sago songs females continue to sing are those taught to them by their mothers, representing a pan-generational identity in which they become ever-more isolated, rooted to a landscape they have restricted experience of and limited access to in terms of the economic benefits it provides.

Opposed male and female extended and rooted identities emerge against an altered landscape; one dominated by an ideology of *developmen* that, whilst contained within a limited sector of society, has implications on a much broader scale. The outcome is not conducive to a future without the economic support of the oil project. As oil supplies dry up and the likelihood of an off-shoot gas project decreases (Goldman personal communication) the Fasu face a life without development within the next twelve years. The inevitable outcome of a post-industrial context will see those who have developed pathways between their rural home and urban centres (the small number of males who have been able to access 'the secret' and thus development) leave, whilst those who have not will remain. As such, what the Fasu case shows is that traditional indigenous knowledge lends itself to the generation of new ideologies of *developmen*. And, whilst meanings, identities and values are appropriately refined to incorporate the shift, the phenomenon of social change does not, and cannot, reach every sector of society. In this sense *developmen* is at once restrictive, selective and unsustainable.

This socio-cultural analysis presents the Fasu as a paradigm of human culture articulating change through a lived experience that goes far deeper than knowledge of the immediate environment (Ingold 2000; Hirsch 1995). Movement through the landscape is directed by a cluster of sensory and cognitive applications that determine a future that cannot be assumed by external parties. In this sense indigenous knowledge is understood as historical, processual and dynamic (Sillitoe 2002) through the socio-cultural analysis of the anthropologist. It is this element of indigenous knowledge research that I propose adds gusto to the new synthesis of knowledge-based studies providing but one component for understanding people's lived experience. The purpose of socio-cultural analysis shifts from one used to understand cultural diversity to one that provides a framework for understanding that diversity in a climate dominated by globalisation.

Notes

1. This is just one example of conflict over land in the Fasu region, although this particular case is all-encompassing in the Hekari region where clans align themselves to either Karopai or Fasu Sanemahi.
2. Fasu is, in fact, the name of a single clan in the Hekari region.
3. Kina is the national currency of Papua New Guinea, K1.00 equalling GBP 0.18 in 2006.
4. Male initiation is no longer ritualistically practiced.
5. It is now more common for dead bodies to be contained in wooden coffins and displayed on bamboo platforms within these. A practice encouraged at the time of missionisation in the 1980s.
6. I discuss this issue in more detail in Gilberthorpe 2007.

Bibliography

Bender, B. 1999. 'Introduction' *in* B. Bender, ed., *Landscape, Politics and Perspectives.* Oxford: Berg.

Ernst, T. 1999. 'Discourse and Entification in Onabasulu Modernity' *American Anthropologist* 101(1): 88-97.

Feld, S. 1982. *Sound and Sentiment: Birds, Weeping, Poetics and Song in Kaluli Expression.* Philadelphia: University of Pennsylvania Press.

Ferguson, J. 2005. 'Seeing Like an Oil Company: Space, Security, and Global Capital in Neoliberal Africa' *American Anthropologist* 107(3): 377-382.

Gilberthorpe, E. 2004. *The Fasu, PNG: Analysing Modes of Adaptation through Cosmological Systems.* Unpublished PhD Thesis. University of Queensland.

_____ 2007. 'Fasu Solidarity: A Case Study of Kin Networks, Land Tenure and Oil Extraction in Kutubu, Papua New Guinea' *American Anthropologist* 109(1): 101-112.

Goldman, L. 2000. *Position Paper: ILGs, Zones, Reforms and Rational Reform.* Department of Petroleum and Energy. Konedobu, NCD, Papua New Guinea.

Guddemi, P. 1997. 'Continuities, Contexts, Complexities, and Transformations: Local Land Concepts of a Sepik People Affected by Mining Exploration' *Anthropological Forum* 7(4): 629–647.

Hirsch, E. 1995. 'Introduction' *in* E. Hirsch and M. O'Hanlon eds., *The Anthropology of Landscape: Perspectives on Place and Space.* Oxford: Clarendon Press.

Ingold, T. 2000. *The Perception of the Environment: Essays in Livelihood, Dwelling and Skill.* London: Routledge.

Jorgensen, D. ed.. 1986. 'Concepts of Conception: Procreation Ideologies of Papua New Guinea' in *Mankind* special issue, 14 (1).

Knauft, B. 1993. 'Like Money You See in a Dream: Petroleum and Patrols in South New Guinea' *Oceania* 64: 187-190.

Kurita, H. 1988. 'Place and Personal Names as Markers of History: An Approach to the Historical Consciousness of the Fasu, Papua New Guinea' *The Japanese Journal of Ethnology* 52(4): 299-326.

_____ 1994. 'Blood and Semen Reconsidered: Childbirth and Child Rearing among the Fasu of Papua New Guinea' *in* K. Yamaji, ed., *Gender and Fertility in Melanesia.* Nishinomiya: Kwansei Gakuin University.

Langlas, C. and J. Weiner. 1988. 'Big-men, Population Growth, and Longhouse Fission amongst the Foi, 1965-79' *in* J. Weiner, ed., *Mountain Papuans: Historical and Comparative Perspectives from New Guinea Fringe Highland Societies.* Ann Arbor: University of Michigan Press.

Marru, I. 2002. 'Contemporary Challenges on the use of Customary Corporations in Petroleum Development Projects in Papua New Guinea' South Pacific Land Tenure Conflict Symposium, University of South Pacific. www.usp.ac.fj/landmgmt/SYMPOSIUM/

Modjeska, N. 1982. 'Production and Inequality: Perspectives from Central New Guinea' *in* A. Strathern, ed., *Inequality in New Guinea Highlands Societies.* Cambridge: Cambridge University Press.

O'Hanlon, M. and L. Frankland. 2003. 'Co-present Landscapes: Routed and Rootedness as Sources of Identity in Highland New Guinea' *in* P. Stewart and A. Strathern, eds., *From Landscape, Memory and History.* London: Pluto Press.

Polier, N. 1996. 'Of Mines and Min: Modernity and its Malcontents in Papua New Guinea'. *Ethnology* 35(1): 1-16.

Sagir, B. 2004. 'The Politics of Petroleum Extraction and Royalty Distribution at Lake Kutubu' *in* A. Rumsey and J. Weiner, eds., *Mining and Indigenous Lifeworlds in Australia and Papua New Guinea.* Oxon: Sean Kingston Publishing.

Schieffelin, E. and R. Crittendon. 1991. *Like People You See in a Dream: First Contact in Six Papuan Societies.* Stanford: Stanford University Press.

Sillitoe, P. 1999. 'Beating the Boundaries: Land Tenure and Identity in the Papua New Guinea Highlands' *Journal of Anthropological Research.* 55(3): 331-360.

_____ 2002. 'Participant Observation to Participatory Development: Making Anthropology Work' *in* P. Sillitoe, A. Bicker and J. Pottier, eds., *Participating in Development: Approaches to Indigenous Knowledge.* London: Routledge.

Strathern, A. 1972. *One Father, One Blood: Descent and Group Structure among the Melpa People.* Canberra: Australian National University Press.

Strathern, M. 1988. *The Gender of the Gift: Problems with Women and Problems with Society in Melanesia.* Berkeley: University of California Press.

Weiner J. 1988. *Mountain Papuans: Historical and Comparative Perspectives from New Guinea Fringe Highlands Societies.* Ann Arbor: University of Michigan Press.

_____ 1991. *The Empty Place: Poetry, Space and Being among the Foi of Papua New Guinea.* Indianapolis: Indiana University Press.

_____ 1998. *The Incorporated Ground: The Contemporary Work of Distribution in the Kutubu Oil Project Area, Papua New Guinea.* Working Paper 1998/17, Resource Management in Asia Pacific, Australian National University.

_____ 2002. 'Adverse Possession: Some Observations on the Relation between Land and Land-Based Knowledge in Papua New Guinea' South Pacific Land Tenure Conflict Symposium. University of the South Pacific. www.usp.ac.fj/landmgmt/ SYMPOSIUM/

Williams, F.E. 1976. 'Natives of Lake Kutubu, Papua' *in* E. Schwimmer, ed., *Francis Edgar Williams 'The Vailala Madness' and other essays.* London: C. Hurst and Co.

Wood, M. 1982. *Kamula Social Structure.* Unpublished Ph.D. Thesis, Macquarie University.

Chapter 6

How Do They See It?

Traditional Resource Management, Distrubance and
Biodiversity Conservation In Papua New Guinea

William H. Thomas

Introduction

Traditional societies are often portrayed as stewards of their environment who are living in 'balance' with their natural surroundings. Since much of the planet's remaining wilderness is also the home of an indigenous society (Robles Gil 2002), some nations are hoping to capitalise on traditional management techniques to conserve biodiversity and provide sustainable development options for traditional landowners. The apparent compatibility of traditional land management practices with biological diversity has spawned interest in understanding these management systems (Barrett et al. 2001), collecting traditional ecological knowledge (TEK) (Ludwig, Mangel and Haddad 2001) and potentially using traditional land management practices as templates for biodiversity conservation (Posey 1988). However, while experts from many fields agree both on the need for local participation and the value of TEK (Folke 2004), the inclusion of indigenous people in the conservation process has been problematic (Chatty and Colchester 2002). As forests continue to disappear, prominent conservationists are openly questioning the compatibility of sustainable development with conservation, with some going so far as to describe this experiment as a disaster for nature (Soule 2000). This has caused a backlash among some observers who can usually be counted on as advocates for indigenous people. Some have questioned the usefulness of TEK in the face of global change (du Toit et al. 2004; Walker and Campbell 2004; Terborgh 2001). Others have pointed to the discrepancy between the western perception of a traditional conservation ethic and reality (Salim et al. 2001), as well as the unworkable assumptions concerning local participation in the face of national laws that negate local input in the conservation process (Pierce and Wadley 2001).

I believe that the situation is salvageable, i.e. traditional societies can act as stewards of their biological inheritance, even under the stress induced by globalisation. However, in order to avert a complete disaster for both nature and traditional societies, we need to examine the underpinnings of this latest version of the 'primitive conservationist', by revisiting our assumptions concerning the relationship between tradition and biodiversity. Prior to beginning this experiment of engaging traditional landowners in conservation, no consensus had emerged concerning the relationship between traditional life and biological diversity (West and Brechin 1991). In an attempt to establish some common ground for conservation, I have been recording TEK of the impact of human activity on birds from the Hewa of Papua New Guinea. The Hewa are a traditional society whose homeland is one of New Guinea's most important wilderness areas. Since conservation programs in Papua New Guinea must be generated by the local people, the Hewan understanding of the relationship between tradition and avian/biological diversity will be a vital link in the conservation of this area.

It had been assumed that the most diverse ecosystems were in fact the most stable (Reice 1994). This assumption fit nicely with the traditional western view of the universe as a collection of parts that are connected into a working system or machine that when working properly is controllable, predictable and in balance (Goerner 1994). Accordingly, an ecosystem is said to be in balance when the member species (the parts) produce a system that becomes stable in terms of species abundance and composition over time (Reice 1994). From a mechanistic perspective, the conservation of tropical forests requires the development of a plan to inventory the species in the system, understand how each species is connected to the others, and maintain their system of internal relationships, i.e. their equilibrium.

Yet the natural world has proven to be a frustrating machine to keep in balance. Natural systems are extremely complex and difficult to define. This difficulty has led ecologists to question the 'balance of nature' concept and instead concentrate on the dynamic components of an ecosystem rather than its stability (Pickett et al. 1991). Current ecological research has focused on the role of non-equilibrium factors, i.e. disturbance, in the enhancement of biodiversity (Reice 1994). In an ecological sense disturbance is a 'relatively discrete event that disrupts a population, community or ecosystem and changes resources available' (Pickett et al. 1991). Unlike prediction, disturbance is not intrinsic to the life of the prey species (Reice 1994). Instead disturbance is unpredictable and non-selective, producing effects that will vary from minutes to centuries in duration. Whether it originates outside an ecosystem, like a storm that enhances forest diversity by producing a mosaic of blow-downs or is generated from the

internal dynamics of an ecosystem, disturbance creates the patchiness that char-
acterises many environments and creates the niches that present opportunities
for colonisation by new species (May 1989). To scientists of the non-equilibrium school, every ecosystem is in varying degrees of recovery from a disturbance. Recovery from disturbance, not equilibrium, is the normal state of affairs
in any ecosystem and its response to continual disturbance will determine the
structure of any ecological community (Reice 1994). In terms of its ability to
generate biodiversity, disturbance is a scale-related phenomenon. It enriches
two measures of diversity by creating more habitats (gamma diversity) and containing more organisms (greater alpha diversity) than an unaltered landscape.
Too much or too little disturbance produces environments that are not as
diverse as those that are continually subjected to minor disturbances (Terborgh
1992). As long as disturbances occur frequently enough to prevent the competitive exclusion of poorer competitors, these species can continue to survive along
with more efficient species (Reice 1994). This 'intermediate disturbance
hypothesis' argues that a level of disturbance that is not too severe promotes the
highest degree of species richness by creating a mosaic of environments that, in
turn, prevent the extinction of competing species (Connell 1978).

The shift from balance to disturbance by ecologists has gone unrecognised by
many who continue to portray traditional societies as 'in balance' (Hames
1991). Yet, by factoring disturbance into the relationship between tradition and
biodiversity, researchers have moved beyond the stereotypes of the 'noble savage'
and are beginning to unravel the archaeological evidence of humanity's role in
both historic and prehistoric extinctions (Diamond 1986; Denevan 1992). Historical ecologists have begun to paint a more nuanced picture of the relationship
of traditional societies to biological diversity. The continued disappearance of
wild lands coupled with the coexistence of traditional cultures with biological
diversity, often referred to as biocultural diversity (Maffi 2001), has forced conservationists to reconsider our notions concerning the nature of wilderness (Mit-
temeyer et al. 2003).

Nowhere has this paradigm shift had more impact than in our understanding of the forests of Amazonia. As if peeling an onion, researchers have removed
successive layers of misinformation concerning the relationship between traditional societies and Amazonian biodiversity. They have refuted the theory that
the region's modern societies are primitive remnants that reside in a pristine forest with little understanding of forest management. Instead, research has painted
a picture of an Amazonian landscape that has been through a series of changes
that are a tribute to the 'immense transformative power of prehistoric humans'
(Graham 1998). In fact, the prehistoric Amazon basin once supported larger,
sedentary and more complex societies (Roosevelt 1980; Roosevelt 1989). These
societies and their modern counterparts are now seen as master manipulators of
their forests, intensely managing their lands produce a mosaic of habitats (Posey

1985; Johnson 1989; Balée 1994). They create and then manage vegetative zones using techniques that go beyond clearing and burning (Balée and Gely 1989; Anderson and Posey 1989). While the biological diversity of any plot may initially plummet as it the land is cleared for gardens, this decline in diversity is not necessarily permanent and in many cases will become part of a mosaic with greater diversity than the original landscape (Balée1998). For many analysts, the forests of Amazonia, long considered one of the earth's finest wilderness tracts, can best be understood as an old fallow rather than pristine forest (Balée1995).

The issue here is one of intent (Parker 1992). Armed with the above mentioned findings, some have suggested that traditional life might serve as a template for the conservation of Amazonia (Posey 1984). The realisation that the traditional lives of indigenous people could be compatible with biological diversity opened the possibility of cooperation between two groups that might seem to be natural allies – conservationists and indigenous people (Nabhan 2001). The underlying assumption of many of the advocates for this alliance had been that traditional societies, through their long association with the land, have learned to minimise their impact on the land (Smith 1984).

Yet, the importance of local involvement in conservation may have blinded advocates to the realities of traditional life. In general, traditional systems seem to be incapable of conserving game (Redford 1991). Once it became apparent that their work was being cited as evidence that traditional societies had been conserving biodiversity, historical ecologists were quick point out that such assumptions might be faulty (Sillitoe 1996). Although traditional forest manipulation must be incorporated in modern forest management, one cannot assume that these management practices will be compatible with conservation (Posey and Balée 1989). It may be that the conservation of biodiversity by traditional societies has been their intention. It may also be that biodiversity is an unintentional side-effect of small-scale gardening by mobile peoples moving over a vast landscape. In general, the non-critical acceptance of the compatibility of traditional life with conservation has led to the failure of many conservation-based development schemes in the tropics and has prompted prominent conservationists to call for the reconsideration of conservation-based development schemes (Soule 2000; Terborgh 2001). The fate of the alliance between conservationist and indigenous societies may hang in the balance.

TEK, Habitat Disturbance, Avian Diversity and Conservation

I became interested in the relationship between tradition and biodiversity during my initial fieldwork with the Hewa of Papua New Guinea (PNG). PNG is one of the world's most significant centers of biodiversity and contains large tracts of intact forest (Meyers et al. 2000). The Hewa live in one of PNG's most important wilderness areas, the headwaters of the Strickland River in the Central Range (142 30'E, 5 10' S; elevation 500-3000 meters). They number fewer than 2,000 people and inhabit roughly 65,000 hectares of hilly and sub-montane forest in the uppermost Strickland River. Their region is located on the eastern verges of the 'Great Rivers Headwaters,' a rain-soaked upland zone in the centre of New Guinea that recent analyses have identified as the richest in biodiversity in this island (Beehler 1993). This Headwaters region is where the four great river systems of New Guinea converge (Sepik, Fly, Digul, Idenburg). The Strickland is the major tributary of the Fly and the Hewa inhabit the forests where the Strickland meets the torrential Laigaip River. Within PNG, this region of the Central Range has been identified as a 'major terrestrial unknown,' and a conservation priority (Swartzendruber 1993).

The ability of indigenous societies to coexist with biological diversity is not limited to Amazonia. It has also been described for societies in New Guinea (Sillitoe 1996). However in seventeen years of fieldwork, I have never heard the Hewa use the term 'balance' to describe their relationship to the land. Instead the Hewa describe their traditional activities as creating a mosaic of garden *Agwe*, grassland *Poghali*, old garden *Agwe Teli*, old garden 'true' *Agwe Teli Popi* and primary forest *Nomakale* – each with a set of pollinators and seed dispersal agents that are impacted by the Hewa cutting the forest to establish and maintain gardens. The microclimate associated with altitude and terrain effectively confines Hewa horticulture between the altitudes of 500 metres at the riverbank and the base of the mountain wall at 1500 metres with the majority of these gardens below 1000 metres. The Hewa raise their gardens, relying primarily on sweet potato (*Ipomoea batatas*), yams (*Dioscorea sp.*), banana (*Musa sp.*) and to a lesser degree cassava (*Manihot esculenta*) and pumpkin (*Cucurbita maxima*) as food crops. Scattered throughout the area are several species of Pandanus and *Pangium edule* trees that the Hewa claim individually. The seasonal ripening of these trees, as well as gathering other wild foods and hunting, provides the Hewa with some sustenance. However gardens are the primary source of food. Each year the typical household clears and plants an average of four 100m^2 gardens. This gardening cycle is the most important factor in shaping this environment. Like many New Guineans, the Hewa re-use their gardens. By continually using as much of the fence surrounding an old garden as possible, the Hewa create a chain of old and new gardens. The established gardens seldom lie fallow for more than twenty-five years, upon which time their secondary forest cover is cut, burned and cleared and a new garden planted. The result is a mosaic on the surrounding hillsides comprised primarily of primary forest interspersed with small plots of land in the garden/fallow cycle. In fact, the patchwork the Hewa create of new gardens, grasslands, succession and primary forest increases the number of environments and hence one measure of the biodiversity of this territory.

It is this dynamic – the need to garden for survival, the importance of secondary forest to soil fertility and the effect of gardening on avian diversity that has the greatest implications for conservation. In order to assess the compatibility of the traditional Hewa lifestyle with biodiversity, I have asked my informants to describe the impact of traditional gardening on birds. Birds are accepted indicators of biodiversity and well known to both local and international naturalists. Because New Guinea is east of the Wallace line, the island lacks many of the mammalian agents of seed dispersal found to the west in Indonesia. Therefore, forest conservation in New Guinea is tied to avian conservation (Schodde 1973).

Sillitoe has said that traditional knowledge is about to become the new applied anthropology (Sillitoe 1998). By using the Hewa TEK of birds, I hope to describe the relationship between traditional activities and biological diversity in a manner that will go beyond species inventories (Nabhan 2001) and intelligible to both the Hewa and conservationists. While all ethnobiological studies have to deal with the cultural gaps created by New Guinea vernacular and the genus species system of western science (Diamond and Bishop 1999; Sillitoe 2000; Berkes and Folke 2002), birds are an accepted indicator of ecosystem diversity and health (Azevedo-Ramos, De Carvalho and Nasi 2002). Since birds are the best known organisms in New Guinea, I believe that the following approach allows both the Hewa and conservationist to establish a common ground concerning the impact of human activity on avian diversity. It will assist both parties in the evaluation of their capacity for co-management, overcome major obstacles in communication (Drew 2005), while avoiding some of the more contentious issues surrounding TEK (Ellen and Harris 2000).

Methods

Through a combination of structured interviews, transects, and station surveys, the Hewa TEK concerning the impact of traditional activities on birds was recorded. Working with the field guide, *Birds of New Guinea* (Beehler, Pratt and Zimmerman 1986) each informant was asked to identify the birds to be found in their territory, as well as the altitude and habitat each bird favoured. Habitats were broadly defined using the indigenous categories for garden *Agwe*, grassland *Poghali*, old garden *Agwe teli*, old garden 'true' *Agwe Teli Popi* and primary forest *Nomakale*. The old garden/old garden true distinction described their perception of the differences between the bird life to be found in secondary forest growth that was younger than twenty years (old garden) and secondary growth with more than twenty years (old garden true). The information obtained in interviews was then checked against four months of field surveys.

Results

To date, my research has recorded 170 species of birds corresponding to 128 Hewa bird folk taxa. Like western ornithologists, the Hewa associate species with altitude and habitat. The Hewa indicate that some of the species are associated exclusively with primary forest and that others can make use of forests that the Hewa describe as the oldest secondary forest growth, i.e. forest that has been growing for twenty or more years. Experience has taught the Hewa that cutting the primary forest will eliminate the fifty-six species (33 percent) of birds that can only live in primary forest (Table 6.1). Of particular interest to conservationists is the perceived effect of gardening on the fruit and nectar eating birds. Frugivores are rare in secondary forest growth that is younger than twenty years. According to the Hewa their gardens create an environment that is hostile to the fruit-doves (*Ptilinopus* sp.) and some species of lorikeets *(Charmosyna* sp.). Both species are thought to be vital to forest regeneration. In general, the Hewa report that human disturbance creates environments that are hostile to many species identified exclusively with New Guinea's forests. The vulturine parrot *Psittrichas fulgidus*, pheasant pigeon *Otidiphaps nobis*, blue-collared parrot *Geoffroyus simplex,* wattled brush turkey *Aepypodius arfakianus,* hornbill *Rhyticeros plicatus,* flame bowerbird *Sericulus aureus* and purple-tailed imperial pigeon *Ducula rufigaster* are just a few of the species that the Hewa say will find secondary growth incompatible with their needs.

Table 6.1: Hewa TEK of Birds Found Only in Primary Forest.

Common Name	Genus	Species	Diet1	Altitude2
Northern Scrub Robin	*Drymodes*	*superciliaris*	I	A
Vulturine Parrot	*Psittrichas*	*fulgidus*	F	N,C
Dwarf Whistler	*Pachycare*	*flavogrisea*	I	N,C
Long-tailed Buzzard	*Henicopernis*	*longicauda*	V	A
Belford's Melectides	*Melidectes*	*belfordi*	N/A	C
Palm Cockatoo	*Probosciger*	*aterrimus*	S	A
Red-throated Myzomela	*Myzomela*	*eques*	N/I	C
Papuan King-Parrot	*Alisterus*	*chloropterus*	S	N,C
Pheasant Pigeon	*Otidiphaps*	*nobis*	S/F	N,C
Common Smoky Honeyeater	*Melipotes*	*fumigatus*	F	N,C
White-eared Bronze Cuckoo	*Chrysococcyx*	*meyerii*	I	N,C
Short-tailed Paradigalla	*Paradigalla*	*brevicauda*	F/A	C
Macgregor's Bower Bird	*Amblyornis*	*macgregoriae*	F/I	C
Black-winged Monarch	*Monarcha*	*frater*	A/I	A

Table 6.1: Continued

Common Name	Genus	Species	Diet1	Altitude2
King of Saxony BOP	Pteridophora	alberti	F/I	C
Grey Goshawk	Accipter	novaehollandiae	V	N,C
Sooty Owls	Tyto	tenebricosa	V	A
White-faced Robin	Tregellasia	leucops	I	A
Purple Tailed Imperial Pigeon	Ducula	rufigaster	F	N,C
Ornate Melectides	Melectides	torquatus	N/A	N,C
Black-Billed Cuckoo-Dove	Macropygia	nigrirostris	F	N,C
White-bibbed Ground-Dove	Gallicolumba	jobiensis	F	N,C
Mountain Red-headed myzomela	Myzomela	adolphinae	N/I	C
Black-mantled Goshawk	Accipter	melanochiamys	V	N,C
Spotted Babbler	Ptilorrhoa	leucosticte	A	A
Papuan Mt Pigeon	Gymnophaps	albertisii	F	N,C
Brown Collared Bush Turkey	Talegalla	jobiensis	G	A
Wattled Brush-turkey	Aepypodius	arfakianus	G	N,C
Pink-spotted Fruit-Dove	Ptilinopus	perlatus	F	A
Red-cheeked Parrot	Geoffroyus	geoffroyi	F/S	N,C
Josephine's Lorikeet	Charmosyna	josefinae	N	N,C
Little Red Lorikeet	Charmosyna	pulchella	N	A
Red-flanked Lorikeet	Charmosyna	placentas	N	A
Pygmy Lorikeet	Charmosyna	wilhelminae	N	C
White-breasted Fruit-Dove	Ptilinopis	rivoli	F	N,C
Crested Pithoui	Pithoui	cristatus	A	A
Mountain Owlet-nightjar	Aegotheles	albertisi	I	A
Little Paradise Kingfisher	Tanysiptera	hydrocharis	A/V	N,C
Great Cuckoo-Dove	Reinwardtoena	reinwardtii	F	A
Feline Owlet-nightjar	Aegotheles	insignis	I	A
Dwarf Fruit-Dove	Ptilinopus	nanus	F	A
Yellow-browed Melectides	Melidectes	rufocrissalis	N/A	C
Shovel-billed Kingfisher	Clytoceyx	rex	A/V	A
Flame Bowerbird	Sericulus	aureus	F/A	C
Hornbill	Rhyticeros	plicatus	F/G	A
Gurney's eagle	Aquila	gurneyi	V	N,C
Common Paradise Kingfisher	Tanysiptera	galatea	A/V	N,C
Common Scrub fowl	Megapodius	freycinet	G	N,C

Table 6.1: Continued

Common Name	Genus	Species	Diet1	Altitude2
Wattled ploughbill	*Eulacestoma*	*nigropectus*	I	N,C
Blue-collared Parrot	*Geoffroyus*	*simplex*	S	N,C
Rufous Owls	*Ninox*	*rufa*	V	A
Blue Jewel-Babbler	*Ptilorrhoa*	*caerulescens*	A	A
Ornate Fruit-Dove	*Ptilinopus*	*ornatus*	F	A
Papuan Black Myzomela	*Myzomela*	*nigrita*	N/I	C
Red Myzomela	*Myzomela*	*cruentata*	N/I	C

1) Diet codes: S=seeds, F=fruit, A=arthropods, I=insects, N=nectar, V=vertebrates, L=lichens, G=generalist.
2) Altitude: A=all, H,N=500-1 000m ; N,C'1000-1500m

Discussion

In the short run, the aim of this project was to develop a vehicle for cross-cultural communication between the Hewa and the conservation community. I wanted to portray their traditional knowledge in a positivist light, and establish a baseline for the conservation of their lands. By using an accepted indicator of biodiversity (birds) and focusing on the impact of human disturbance, we established a common ground for co-management, moving beyond the lists of traditional vocabulary, the problems associated with terminology and the politics that have separated parties that should be natural allies – conservationists and traditional societies. Since scientists steeped in the western positivist tradition dominate conservation organisations, I wanted to open a line of communication that would break down the dual prejudices of traditional societies as conservationists or traditional societies as destroyers and allow all parties to use this common language – the impact of human activity on biodiversity – to chart a new course. In the long run, I believe that the basic approach developed here – establishing a common understanding of the relationship between a society and the biological diversity found on its land – will allow more traditional societies to partner with the conservation community to conserve their lands and culture. Although this is certainly not the only valid pursuit for those interested in TEK, it is a practical one with the potential to have an impact on conservation policy and practice.

If the relationship between traditional human activity and biodiversity is one of disturbance rather than balance, this has important implications for the ability of local people to conserve biological diversity in the face of changing conditions. My informants have put Hewa land use in a context that illustrates the perils of conflating a small-scale disturbance regime with sustainable management. Rather than portraying themselves as capable of balancing their needs with the needs of the other organisms in their environment, the Hewa describe their traditional gardening as a source of disturbance on this landscape. When a small human population continually moves across the landscape, cutting gardens, allowing these plots to lie fallow and eventually re-cutting these same garden plots, the product is a landscape with tremendous biological diversity (Balée 1998). This human generated landscape contains more organisms (greater alpha diversity) and more habitats (gamma diversity) than an unaltered landscape. The combination of gardens, grasslands, the various stages of forest regrowth and primary forest are more biologically diverse than the climax forest alone. However, a comparison of the avian diversity found within each of the succession regimes created by gardening, shows that each stage of forest regeneration is less diverse, in terms of birds, than the primary forest. According to the Hewa, the majority of the fruit and nectar eating birds this primary forest depends on for regeneration cannot be found in fallow gardens or secondary growth. Since birds are the primary agents of seed dispersal in New Guinea's forests, the Hewa knowledge of this dynamic provides an important insight into the ability of indigenous people to use the environment without compromising the biological diversity.

As one might expect of a small, mobile society with a surplus of land, the Hewa have developed few cultural mechanisms to limit habitat disturbance. For example, consider their traditional Hewa concept of sacred places. The designation of an area as sacred is an individual matter for the Hewa. Both men and women identify places that appear in dreams to each individual, often prompted by spirits of dead ancestors. These areas have no formal designation. It has been proposed that sacred places might, if large enough to serve as habitat for a viable population, serve as wildlife sanctuaries or reservoirs of biodiversity. Yet, all of the sacred areas that I recorded were no larger than a pool of water or a grove of bamboo. Such areas are too small to be effective reservoirs for all but the smallest species. None of the sacred places I was shown would support a viable population of birds, mammals, reptiles or amphibians. Likewise no taboos have been initiated to limit the number of gardens created, to regulate the fallow cycle or prohibit the killing of any bird or mammal. There has been no effort to limit habitat disturbance at these lower elevations. The only taboo with the potential to be useful in conservation is the traditional post-partum taboo. According to my informants, this prohibition on sex while wives are breast-feeding traditionally spaced children for three years and may limit the number of number of offspring a couple could produce in their lifetime. Combined with a life expectancy of less than forty years (Gillett 1991), it is possible that the post-partum taboo played a role in limiting the scale of disturbance to the primary forest. If this practice can be maintained, it may help to slow the growth of the population as western medicines are introduced. However, people often portray themselves as virtuous even though they do not strictly adhere to taboos. The low population density of this region may in fact be the result of the short life expectancy of the Hewa. Although the Hewa express a reverence for the ancestral spirits that inhabit their lands, my research does not indicate that traditional Hewa religious activities are part of a blueprint for conservation.

Another cultural feature that is often described as integral to sustainable land use is traditional land tenure. In fact, traditional landowners have been described as a 'special form of conservation NGO' (Baines 1990). Customary patterns of land tenure are formally recognised by the state in PNG. Throughout New Guinea, land tenure systems have been identified as important to resource conservation (Cinner et al. 2005a; Cinner et al. 2005b). Conservationists believe that the force of law will reinforce traditional institutions, enabling landowners to continue to conserve the biodiversity currently found on their lands (Swartzendruber 1993). The traditional rules of Hewa land tenure are based on bilateral kinship, i.e. they live and cooperate with both their mother's and father's kin. Although many informants cannot identify the exact linkage between their families, clan names provide a convenient memory device allowing men and women to identify a larger number of co-descendants than they could by using kin terms alone (Steadman 1992). Since clan names are inherited at birth and immutable, there can be no transfer of affiliation to non-kin. All that is necessary to identify distant kin is the sharing of a clan name. In this way, each individual is at the centre of an ever-widening group of kinsmen – to the extent that he or she has a good enough memory to remember the clan names of their ancestors. Traditional marriage rules also prohibit marriage between men and women who can trace a kinship connection between them. With no common co-descendants, the couple and their offspring have access to more lands of various clan affiliations than would be possible if the Hewa married closer kin.

Clan territories are clearly marked by streams. Individuals have the right to use land in any territory to which he or she can trace their ancestry using inherited clan names. A Hewa family must cut, plant and harvest an average of four gardens per year in order to feed themselves. Even after burning the vegetation, hence returning some of the nutrients to the soil, the Hewa can only coax three months of production out of it. The ability to recognise many kin allows the Hewa to identify fertile land for gardening and they often take advantage of more distant clan affiliations to garden. For example, in 1996-97, the 63 percent of males surveyed were using their paternal kin ties to ties to establish their residence. During the same period 24 percent were living on their maternal kin's land and 12 percent were living on spousal land. Traditional land tenure currently has the effect of spreading the Hewa throughout their territory to the empty spaces and fertile soils they require. Conservation is a side-effect of a system operating for a small, scattered population living on relatively infertile ground. Yet, the land tenure system's only criterion for access to land is kinship. There is no recognised authority that prohibits the use of land by kinsmen and soil fertility is a matter of individual judgment. The web of kinship does not limit the number of kinsmen who can ask for access to their ancestral lands. Although the interrelatedness of landowners might prevent a 'tragedy of the commons' scenario from developing, there are yet no provisions to forestall the shortening of the fallow cycle by kinsmen.

If the lifestyle of the Hewa is altered to produce a larger sedentary population, the result, by their reckoning, will be the simplification of this environment. The real threat to biodiversity will likely come with the implementation of a conservation-based development scheme and the health care centre that will likely follow. Better health care should improve life expectancy (Gillett 1991). The population increase that is likely to occur will initially result in the conversion of the land that is within easy walking distance of the health centre into gardens. Once this land has been exploited, the Hewa will probably shorten their fallow period. Although it is hard to imagine that some enterprising gardeners have not tried (and failed) to copy their highland neighbours like the Kopiago, some of the Hewa with land close to the health centre may attempt to establish more permanent mounded gardens. Finally, those unable to secure lands near the health centre will be forced to expand their efforts and garden at higher and less desirable altitudes or exploit their more distant kinsmen to take advantage of available land more distant from the development. At some point that neither the Hewa nor western science have determined, the scale of this disturbance will mean that the Hewa will cease to be a force for the biological diversification of their land. Instead, the scale of human disturbance will be of a magnitude wherein the Hewa will have begun to simplify their environment.

Similar population changes have produced anthropogenic grasslands throughout New Guinea and the tropics (Smith and Wishnie 2000). Much of this environmental simplification was accomplished before the arrival of Europeans and under the traditional rules of land tenure. Although the Hewa are not involved in a sustainable development project, they provide a glimpse of the future and the simplified environment that might follow if development involves an increase in population or permanent settlements. Traditional activities that at one time were sustainable and produced an increase in the number of species could, under slightly different conditions, diminish biodiversity. It is therefore understandable that traditional societies could both promote biodiversity and cause extinctions using the same traditional activities under varying conditions. While societies like the Hewa remain intact and their traditions are compatible with biological diversity, the knowledge exists to develop a land use plan that is truly sustainable for their lands. It may also be possible to use this connection between disturbance and biological diversity for other cultures, helping them to establish the connection between tradition, disturbance and conservation for the planet's remaining forested lands.

Bibliography

Anderson, A. and D. Posey. 1989. 'Management of a Tropical Scrub Savanna by the Gororite Kayapo of Brazil' in D. Posey and W. Balée, eds., *Resource Management in Amazonia: Indigenous and Folk Strategies. (Advances in Economic Botany, vol. 7)* Bronx: New York Botanical Gardens, pp.158-73.

Azevedo, C., O.de Carvalho and R. Nassi. 2002. *Animal Indicators: A Tool to Assess Biotic Integrity after Logging Tropical Forests?* CIFOR report.

Baines, G. 1990. *South Pacific Conservation Program.* World Wildlife Fund, Washington DC.

Balée, W.1992. 'Indigenous History and Amazonian Biodiversity' in H.K. Steen and R.P. Tucker, eds., *Changing Tropical Forests: Historical Perspectives on Today's Challenges in Central and South America.* Durham, NC: Forest History Society

_____ 1994. *Footprints of the Forest: Ka'apor Ethnobotany – The Historical Ecology of Plant Utilization by an Amazonian People.* New York: Columbia University Press

_____ 1995. 'Historical Ecology of Amazonia' in L. Sponsel,ed., *Indigenous Peoples and the Future of Amazonia: An Ecological Anthropology of an Endangered World.* Tucson: University of Arizona Press.

_____ 1998. *Advances in Historical Ecology.* New York: Columbia University Press

Berkes, F. and C. Folke. 2002. 'Rediscovery of Traditional Ecological Knowledge as Adaptive Management.' *Ecological Applications* 10: 1251-1262.

Barrett C.B., K. Brandon, C. Gibson and H.Gjertsen. 2001.'Conserving Tropical Biodiversity amid Weak Institutions.' *Bioscience* 51 497-502.

Beehler, B. 1993. *A Biodiversity Analysis for Papua New Guinea – With an Assessment for Conservation Needs.* Biodiversity Support Program, Washington DC.

-_____ T. Pratt , D. Zimmerman, 1986. *Birds of New Guinea.* Princeton: Princeton University Press.

Chatty, D. and M. Colchester 2002. 'Introduction' in D. Chatty and M. Colchester, eds., *Conservation and Mobile Indigenous Peoples.* New York : Berghahn, pp. 1-20.

Cinner, J.E., M.J. Marnane, T.R. McClanahan. 2005a. 'Conservation and Community Benefits from Traditional Coral Reef Management at Ahus Island, Papua New Guinea.' *Conservation Biology* 19 (6): 1714-1723.

_____ , M.J. Marnane, T.R. McClanahan, T.H. Clark and J. Ben 2005b. 'Trade, Tenure, and Tradition: Influence of Sociocultural Factors on Resource Use in Melanesia.' *Conservation Biology* 19 (5): 1469-1477.

Connell J.H. 1978. 'Diversity in Tropical Rainforests and Coral Reefs.' *Science* 199: 1302-1310.

Denevan, W. 1992. 'The Pristine Myth: The Landscape of the Americas in 1492' *Annals of the Association of American Geographers* 82(3): 369-385.

Diamond, J. 1986. 'The Environmentalist Myth.' *Nature* 324: 19-20.

_____ and K.Bishop. 1999. 'Ethno-ornithology of the Ketengban people, Indonesian New Guinea' in D. Medin and S. Attran, eds., *Folkbiology*. New York: Bradford Books.

du Toit, J.T., B.H. Walker and B.M. Campbell. 2004. 'Conserving Tropical Nature: Current Challenges for Ecologists' *Trends in Ecology and Evolution* 19: 12-17.

Drew, J. 2005. 'Use of Traditional Ecological Knowledge in Marine Conservation' *Conservation Biology* 19(4): 1286-93.

Ellen, R.F. and H. Harris. 2000. 'Introduction' in R.F. Ellen, P. Parkes and A. Bicker, eds., *Indigenous Environmental Knowledge and its Transformations*. Amsterdam: Harwood Academic Publishers.

Folke, C. 2004. 'Traditional Knowledge in Socio-Ecological Systems' *Ecology and Society* 9 (3): 7.

Gillett, J.E. 1991. *The Health of Women in Papua New Guinea*. Papua New Guinea Institute of Medical Research. Monograph No. 9.

Goerner, S.J. 1994. *Chaos and the Evolving Ecological Universe*. Langhorne Pa: Gordon and Breach Publishing. pp. 278-299.

Graham, E. 1998. 'Metaphor and Metamorphism: Some Thoughts on Environmental Metahistory.' in Balée, ed., *Advances in Historical Ecology*. New York: Columbia University Press. pp. 119-137.

Hames, R. 1991. 'Wildlife Conservation in Tribal Societies.' in M. Oldfield and J. Alcorn, (eds., *Biodiversity Culture, Conservation and Ecodevelopment*. Boulder: Westview Press, pp. 172-99.

Johnson, A. 1989. 'How the Machinguenga Manage Resources: Conservation or Exploitation of Nature?' in D. Posey and W. Balée, eds., *Resource Management in Amazonia: Indigenous and folk strategies. (Advances in Economic Botany* series, vol. 7) Bronx: New York Botanical Gardens pp.213-222.

Ludwig D., M. Mangel and B. Haddad. 2001. 'Conservation and Public Policy.' *Annual Review of Ecology and Systematics* 32: 481-517.

Maffi, L.,ed., 2001. *On Biocultural Diversity: Linking Language, Knowledge and the Environment*. Washington: Smithsonian Institute Press.

May, R. 1989. 'The Chaotic Rhythms of Life' *New Scientist*, 18: 37-41.

Meyers, N., R. Mittermeier, C. Mittermeier, G. da Fonseca and J. Kent. 2000. 'Biodiversity Hotspots for Conservation Priorities' *Nature* 403 (6772): 853-58.

Mittermeier, R., C. Mittermeier, T, Brooks, J. Pilgrim, W. Konstant, G. da Fonseca and C. Kormos. 2003. 'Wilderness and Biodiversity Conservation' *PNAS 100 (18)*: 10309-10313.

Parker, E. 1992. 'Forest Islands and Kayapo Resource Management in Amazonia: A Reappraisal of the Apete' *American Anthropologist* 94: 406-428.

Pickett S., V. Parker and P. Fiedler. 1991. 'The New Paradigm in Ecology.' in P. Fiedler and S. Jain, eds., *Conservation Biology*. New York: Chapman and Hall, pp. 65-88.

Pierce, C.J. and R.L. Wadley. 2001. 'From "Participation" to "Rights and Responsibilities" in Forest Management: Workable Methods and Unworkable Assumptions in West Kalimantan, Indonesia' in C.J. Pierce Colfer and Y. Byron, eds., *People Managing Forests: The Links between Human Well-Being and Sustainability*. Resources for the Future: Washington DC.

Nabhan, G. 2001. 'Cultural Perceptions of Ecological Interactions – An Endangered People's Contribution to the Conservation of Biological and Linguistic Diversity.' in L. Maffi,ed., *On Biocultural Diversity: Linking Language, Knowledge and the Environment*. Washington: Smithsonian Institute Press.

Posey, D.A. 1985. 'Indigenous Management of Tropical Forest Ecosystems: The Case of the Kayapó Indians of the Brazilian Amazon' *Agroforestry Systems* 3: 139-158.

_____ 1988. 'Native and Indigenous Guidelines for New Amazonian Development Strategies: Understanding Biological Diversity through Ethnoecology,' in J. Hemming, ed., *Change in the Amazon*. Manchester: Manchester University Press, pp. 156-81.

_____ 1998. 'Diachronic Ecotones and Anthropogenic Landscapes in Amazonia: Contesting the Consciousness of Conservation'. in W. Balée, ed., *Advances in Historical Ecology*. New York: Columbia University Press, pp. 104-118

_____ and W. Balée. 1989. *Resource Management in Amazonia: Indigenous and Folk Strategies*. (*Advances in Economic Botany* series, vol. 7). Bronx: New York Botanical Gardens.

Redford, K.H. 1991. 'The Ecologically Noble Savage' *Cultural Survival Quarterly* 13(1): 46-48.

Robles Gil, P. 2002. *Wilderness*. Japan:Toppan, pp.19-54.

Reice, S.R. 1994.'Nonequilibrium Determinants of Biological Community Structure.' *American Scientist* 82 (5): 424-435.

Roosevelt, A. 1980. *Parmana: Prehistoric Maize and Manioc along the Amazon and Orinoco*. New York: Academic Press

_____ 1989. 'Resource Mangement in Amazonia before the Conquest: Beyond the Ethnographic Projection' in D. Posey and W. Balée, eds., *Resource Management in Amazonia: Indigenous and Folk Strategies*. (*Advances in Economic Botany* series vol. 7) Bronx: New York Botanical Gardens, pp.30-62.

Salim, A. et al. 2001. 'In Search of a Conservation Ethic.' in C.J. Pierce Colfer and Y. Byron, eds.,.*People Managing Forests: The Links between Human Well-Being and Sustainability*. Washington DC: Resources for the Future, pp.155-166.

Schodde, R. 1973.'General Problems of Faunal Conservation in Relation to the Conservation of Vegetation in New Guinea.' in A.B. Costin and R. Groves, eds.. *Nature Conservation in the Pacific*. Canberra: ANU Press, pp. 123-144

Sillitoe, P. 1996. *A Place Against Time: Land and Environment in the Papua New Guinea Highlands*. Amsterdam: Harwood Academic.

_____ 1998. 'The Development of Indigenous Knowledge.' *Current Anthropology* 39 (2): 223-252.

_____ 2000. 'Let Them Eat Cake: Indigenous Knowledge, Science and the Poorest of the Poor.' *Anthropology Today* 16 (6): 3-7.

Smith, E.A. 1984.'Anthropology, Evolutionary Ecology and the Explanatory Poverty of the Ecosystem Concept.' in E. Moran, ed., *The Ecosystem Concept in Anthropology.* Westview Press, Boulder, Colorado, USA, pp. 51-85.

Smith, E.A. and M. Wishnie. 2000.'Conservation and Subsistence in Small-Scale Societies' *Annual Review of Anthropology*, 29: 493-524.

Soule, M. 2000.'Does Sustainable Development Help Nature?' *Wild Earth* 10 (4): 56-63.

Steadman, L.B. 1992. *'Kinship, Religion and Ethnicity.' Human Behavior and Evolution Society Meeting.* Albuquerque, New Mexico 1992.

Swartzendruber, J.F. 1993. *Papua New Guinea Conservation Needs Assessment* Washington DC: USAID Biodiversity Support Program.

Terborgh, J. 1992. *Diversity and the Tropical Rainforest.* New York: Scientific American.

_____ 2001. 'Why Conservation in the Tropics is Failing.' in D. Rothenberg and M. Ulvaeus, eds., *The World and the Wild: Expanding Wilderness Conservation Beyond its American Roots.* Tucson: University of Arizona Press, pp. 80-90.

West, P. and S. Brechin, 1991. 'Introduction.' in P. West and S. Brechin, eds.,. *Resident Peoples and National Parks,* Tucson: University of Arizona Press, pp. 1-28.

Chapter 7

Wild Plants as Agricultural Indicators

Linking Ethnobotany with Traditional Ecological Knowledge

Takeshi Fujimoto

Introduction

Ethnobotanical studies have generally investigated traditional uses of plants by local people, including food, medicinal, and construction uses as well as plant classification (Cotton 1996; Martin 2004). However, such studies may not reflect the entire range of plant uses. Local people have diverse relationships with plants, beyond those of utility and classification. Researchers are increasingly interested in traditional ecological (or environmental) knowledge (TEK), including a more embedded and processual approach to plant knowledge (Zent, Chapter Two). Most recent ethnobotanical studies refer in some way to TEK. However, what is elucidated and described as TEK is defined, not only by what local people know and how they know it, but also by what researchers expect to find, hence what they look for.

I discuss a range of plant uses that are often overlooked by researchers, therefore marginalised in their descriptions of TEK. Specifically, rather than describing direct plant uses, I analyse knowledge of indirect plant uses, with a particular focus on how Malo farmers in southwestern Ethiopia use wild plants as agricultural indicators. In small-scale societies, some people 'read' specific wild plants (and animals) as ecological indicators. Among hunter–gatherers, such ecological inferences are critical to their survival. However, subsistence farmers, especially shifting cultivators, also glean information regarding agro-ecological conditions from wild plants. Despite the obvious centrality of these uses to the successful procurement of food and other basic necessities, previous ethnobotanical studies have often overlooked such indirect uses of wild plants.

To further understand the importance of agricultural indicator plants and why they are so often overlooked in ethnobotanical studies, I have carried out a literature review of shifting and intensive cultivators from around the world and found widespread, but isolated and incompletely described instances of the use of agricultural indicators. The relative rarity of such reports, however, suggests either that farmers have little knowledge of these plant uses, use that knowledge only rarely or that such data is not easily captured using standard ethnobotanical methods. In an attempt to more fully understand whether the state of the literature reflects the true importance of agricultural indicators in small-scale agricultural societies, I consider the case of the Malo, mountain farmers in southwestern Ethiopia, with whom I have conducted fieldwork. I found that farmers, themselves, are unlikely to acknowledge agricultural indicator uses when asked directly about plant uses, but only when discussed in the context of agricultural activities, suggesting that this particular use type is so embedded in local TEK that farmers do not recognise it out of context, nor would it be elicited through standard ethnobotanical survey methods. A finding which indicates that farmer use of agricultural indicators, as an example of subtle, detailed and dynamic understandings of local ecological conditions is only beginning to be understood by TEK researchers.

Ethnobotany of Direct Plant Uses

Researchers from anthropological and other backgrounds have studied the ethnobotany of wild plant uses by farmers. Etkin and Ross (1994), for example, examine the local medicinal uses of wild plants. Other studies have focused on wild plants as foods, including their uses as relishes, supplementary foods, and famine foods (e.g. Huss-Ashmore and Johnston 1997; Turner and Davis 1993). Howard (2003) recently published important work on gender and ethnobotany. Studies have also addressed the use of wild plants in material cultures, such as for house construction (e.g. Cunningham and Gwala 1986; Yamada 1984). Whereas such studies have undoubtedly made substantial contributions to our knowledge of wild plant uses, they have primarily focused on the direct aspects of plant uses. In direct uses, plants are physically employed by people and consumed partially or wholly. The plants are largely considered to be practically useful, although some may also be used for symbolic or religious purposes (e.g. as ritual offerings or talismans). Most ethnobotanical studies have dealt with plant uses in this direct-use category.

Ethnobotany of Indirect Plant Uses

However, more 'indirect' uses of plants, which do not involve the actual physical exploitation of plants, also take place. For example, trees often have symbolic meanings, and rituals or feasts may take place beneath symbolic trees (e.g. Rival 1998). In addition to such religious or symbolic aspects, practical 'indirect' uses are also known. Plants may be thought to serve as fodder for animals or pollen sources for honeybees; in these cases, people relate to the plants indirectly through their livestock or bees. Indirect uses can also include environmental uses. Cook (1995: 6) gives examples of 'environmental' uses: intercrop and nurse crop plants, ornamentals, barrier hedges, shade plants, windbreaks, and soil improvers, plants for re-vegetation and erosion control, waste water puri-fiers, and indicators of the presence of metals, pollution, or underground water. Although not all of these examples of environmental uses are necessarily indi-rect, indicator uses can certainly be considered indirect. Additionally, indicators are not limited to those mentioned. Here, I describe both the uses of wild plants as indicators of agricultural conditions among the Malo, and indirect plant uses in other societies.

Methods

The data presented here were collected largely through participant observation during an on-going study with the Malo of southwestern Ethiopia that began in 1993. In the early stages of my research I also carried out a structured survey of local wild plant uses and names. I showed collected fresh plant specimens to local farmers, asking their names and uses in local Malo language, for example, 'Hanno ab gine (What do you call this)?', 'Abis ekintine (For what is it taken)?', 'Abis ts'ak'k'amine (For what do you use it)?', 'Akko ts'ik'im yene (Are there any uses)?' In the later stages, from October 1998 to August 1999, I used participant observation and unstructured interviews to gather data for an in-depth analysis of their land use systems and agricultural activities covering the full annual cycle. In doing so, however, I learned that some wild plants are 'used' if indirectly as agricultural indicators, which is the topic of this paper.

Finally, a general and informal literature review was undertaken. To carry out the literature review, I visited libraries and reviewed literature on farming societies, mostly in Africa. Where I came across references to indicators, I made notes.

Use of Wild Plants as Agricultural Indicators around the World

The results of the literature review are presented in the appendix. In general, I found that agricultural indicators are widespread around the world, although most references to them are brief. Before examining the case in Malo, I high-light some general features of wild plant agricultural indicators as described in relevant literature.

Pan-Tropical Distribution of Agricultural Indicator Uses

Wild plant agricultural indicators are widely found in regions throughout Africa, Asia, Oceania, and South America (see Appendix). Although I have listed more societies for certain regions than for others, this imbalance may merely reflect my regional research focus on Africa. The point is that such indirect uses are found in various regions of the tropics.

Types of Agricultural Indicator Use

Although there are exceptions, agricultural indicators can be roughly divided into two use categories: field soil conditions and climatic conditions. The former may be further divided into two sub-categories: positive indicators and negative indicators. The positive indicators of field soils, the majority of cases in the Appendix, indicate high soil fertility, hence are helpful in selecting sites to be cleared for cultivation, whereas negative indicators signal fertility decline (or poor fertility), allowing the farmer to judge when to abandon fields for fallow periods.

Seasonal indicators, found in a smaller number, are those that signal the approach or arrival of the rainy season, the start of the sowing period and/or other markers of the agricultural cycle.

Life Forms and Characters of Indicator Plants

The indicator plants listed in the Appendix vary by form (i.e. grass, herb, shrub/tree) and character (annual, perennial), but some tendencies are notable. Annual herbs and grasses are more likely to be used as indicators of soil fertility decline. In contrast, perennial plants ranging from herbs or grasses to shrubs and tall trees are used to indicate fertility recovery or high fertility in a field. Seasonal indicators include several species of herbs and trees, but apparently no grasses are known to serve this purpose.

Regional differences are also apparent. Whereas woody and herbaceous species are predominant indicators in Asia, nearly half of the indicator plants in Africa are grasses, including *Hypparhenia*, *Pennisetum*, *Andropogon*, *Digitaria*, *Eragrostis*, *Melinis*, and *Setaria*. As many studies report, grasses are widely used in Africa as thatching material, animal fodder, and famine food sources. However, their use as indicators deserves further investigation.

Predominance of Indicator Uses in Cereal Cultivation

The literature review also suggests that indicators are mostly related to cereal cultivation. Only a few exceptions involve root-crop cultivation, such as cassava (manioc) cultivation in Africa and Amazonia and taro cultivation in Oceania. This may come from different agricultural characters of cereal and root/tuber cultivation methods. Generally speaking, cereal cultivation requires more strict management as to seasonality and soil conditions than root/tuber cultivation. The yield of cereals can drop dramatically if farmers do not time the cultivation cycle correctly. This difference may explain why many indicators are associated with cereal cultivation. Or it may simply be related to researcher bias: that those who study cereal cultivation are more alert to the possibility of indicator plants, therefore are more likely to record them.

Dominance of Shifting Cultivators as Indicator Users

As a general tendency, it can be pointed out that shifting cultivators are the predominant users of wild plants as agricultural indicators. Why are such users shifting cultivators rather than other agriculturists? Alan (1965), who studied East African agricultural systems, once noted the following:

> The 'shifting' cultivator also has an understanding of his environment suited to his needs. He can rate the fertility of a piece of land and its suitability for one or other of his crops by the vegetation which covers it and by the physical characteristics of the soil; and he can assess the 'staying power' of a soil, the number of seasons for which it can be cropped with satisfactory results, and the number of seasons for which it must be rested before such results can be obtained again. His indicator of initial fertility is the climax vegetation and his index of returning fertility is the succession of vegetational phases that follows cultivation. In many cases his knowledge is precise and remarkably complete. He has a vocabulary of hundreds of names of trees, grasses, and other plants and he identifies particular vegetation associations by specific terms. This fund of ecological knowledge is the basis of 'shifting' cultivation (Alan 1965: 5).

The climax concept may no longer be widely accepted in the ecological sciences (Thomas, Chapter Six), but the essence of the above statement may still hold true for shifting cultivators.

Shifting cultivation is generally considered to be a type of agriculture that demands minimum labour investment with simple tools under low population density conditions. But it is suggested that this system may also require maximum ecological knowledge such as of interpreting agricultural conditions based on elements of the surrounding environment including wild plants. It is probably because most contemporary shifting cultivators live in the tropics that indirect uses of wild plants as agricultural indicators are largely concentrated in this region. However, this tendency may also reflect the attention paid by researchers of shifting versus permanent cultivation agricultural systems, a point to which I will return shortly.

Small Number of Indicator Plants and of Societies Having Such Uses

The literature review suggests a small number of indicator uses are described when compared with the number of direct plant uses described. The number of the societies reported to have indicator plant uses is also quite small relative to the number of societies engaged in shifting cultivation. Do these data suggest that agricultural indicator uses of wild plants are not important for farmers' livelihood and that subsistence farmers have little such knowledge? In the following, I describe the cases in Malo and then discuss the significance of agricultural indicators.

The Malo: Mountain Farmers of Southwestern Ethiopia

The area of present-day southwestern Ethiopia became assimilated into Ethiopia's national territory at the end of the nineteenth century. This area is known for its ethnic and cultural diversity, and has numerous small ethnic groups. Among these, the Malo, with a population of 30,000–40,000, occupy steep mountainous land at the heart of the region. Malo society is hierarchically stratified and includes two minor subordinate artisan groups (potters and blacksmiths) within the majority population of sedentary farmers engaging in subsistence agriculture (Fujimoto 2003).

Malo Land and Settlements

The land the Malo occupy ranges widely in elevation from approximately 600 to 3,400 m above sea level. Afro-montane rainforests probably originally covered this territory before being transformed into crop and fallow fields (Friis 1992). Settlements are distributed between 1,000 and 3,000 m. Three elevational zones are locally distinguished: 'highland' (*gezze*: more than 2,200 m above sea level), 'mid-altitude' (*dollo*: 1,600–2,200 m), and 'lowland' (*gad'a*: less than 1,600 m). It is here that the Malo have their fields and settlements, only excepting mountain ridges, cliffs, and riverine areas. Of the three elevation zones, the highland zone has the smallest area, but is the most densely populated, whereas the lowland zone has the largest area, but is the most sparsely populated. According to my estimates, in 1996 the population density in the highland village, Gaytsa was 252 people/km², whereas that in the lowland village, Ziita was 129 people/km².

Throughout the Malo area, a concentric pattern of land use is evident, with individual homes at the centre. Immediately around the homes are homegardens (*kara kale*), which are carefully tended. Regularly fertilised with manure and sectioned into a number of patches, the homegardens are more or less permanently planted with a wide variety of species. Extensive outlying fields (*gade*) are devoted to a few crops such as cereals (barley, wheat, sorghum, tef, etcetera) and pulses (pea, cowpea, etcetera). Outlying fields, in contrast to homegardens, are unfertilised and monocropped; they are planted for a period and then left fallow for several years before replanting.

However, even the outlying fields are differentiated. Whereas fields located near homegardens are generally prepared using intensive-tillage methods and allowed only short periods of fallow, more distant fields tend to be sown extensively using shallow- or no-tillage methods and are allowed to lie fallow for longer periods. Thus, land use varies from permanent cultivation immediately surrounding the house, to long fallow, shifting cultivation in the farthest fields. Importantly, all of the indicator uses of wild plants occur in the outlying fields, and most of them are found in the most distant, long-fallowed ones.

Agricultural Systems of the Malo

The Malo grow more than one hundred plant species, including roots and tubers, cereals, pulses, vegetables, fruits, condiments, medicinal plants, ornamentals, and plants for house materials. Crops other than cereals are mostly planted in homegardens with each household keeping ten to thirty types. The most important staple food crop, which is planted in the most fertile plots is enset (*Ensete ventricosum*), a perennial of the banana family (Musaceae). More than sixty local varieties of enset have been identified. Starch is extracted from enset's corm and leaf-sheath pulp while other parts of the plant are used for various materials.

In the outlying fields, farmers sow various cereals and some pulses. Whereas barley, wheat, sorghum, and peas are successively cropped in rotation in the highlands, an indigenous fine millet called tef (*Eragrostis tef*) is sown exclusively in the lowlands (Fujimoto 2002). Seasonality is critical for cereal cultivation in the outlying fields. Cereals other than maize are sown at the peak of the rainy season from June to August, and harvested during the dry season from November to February.[1]

Reciprocal male work parties (*zafe*) are organised for labour-intensive tasks, such as field preparation and weeding in the outlying fields. In contrast, homegardens are normally maintained by both male and female household members.

Local Classification of Agricultural Fields, Soils and Plants

Malo farmers classify their fields into three types in relation to land use patterns. *Maasila* designates a relatively fresh field in a short fallow cycle, cultivated for only one to two years followed by a one to three year fallow. A *shook'a* (*shoyk'a*) field follows *maasila*, and is successively sown for four to ten years prior to a short fallow. An *ottse* field follows a long fallow (four to ten years) and is sown only for one to three years. Home gardens are generally regularly fertilised and cultivated nearly permanently as *shook'a*. However, land use in the outlying fields varies between the highlands and the lowlands. In the densely populated highlands , *shook'a* is the most common category of land use, whereas in the more sparsely populated lowlands, *ottse* is the most common field type.

Malo farmers also classify their soils as one of three types: (1) *aradda*, a fertile soil in heavily fertilised homegardens and some outlying fields adjacent to deep forests; (2) *ints'o*, the most common soil with an intermediate level of fertility, which is lightly fertilised by allowing livestock to graze on the stubble left in fields after harvests, thereby leaving manure (known as 'stubble feeding');

and (3) *ts'alda* or *goppo*, a relatively unfertile soil unsuitable for crop cultivation and never fertilised. Some farmers use even more detailed classifications. For example, *aradda* can be classified as *daro arrada* (extremely fertile soil) and *ch'ere aradda* (normally fertile soil). A rich vocabulary is used to describe the effect of various management regimes on soils, for instance the word '*arradiza*' is a verb denoting the process of one type of soil becoming more fertile or suitable for cultivation by fertilisation or being left to fallow; whereas *laddiza* denotes the process of one type of soil becoming less fertile and even unsuitable for cultivation after successive cropping.

Unsurprisingly, a loose association is found between land-use patterns and soil types. Permanent or short-fallowed cultivation is likely to be practiced in fields with relatively high-fertility soils, although long-fallow cultivation is not always practiced in fields of lower fertility soils. And, of course, farmers are keenly aware of soil characters, enabling them to determine the most appropriate land-use patterns. Any tools that will help them to accurately gauge soil fertility are significant in this context.

Malo people commonly classify plants into three categories: 1) *kattsa* which means crops, or more precisely, herbaceous crops as well as food in general and steam-boiled dishes in particular; 2) *maata* which designates wild and often weedy herbs and grasses; 3) *mittsa*, which implies trees and shrubs, cultivated and wild, in general as well as firewood in particular. Climbing or creeping lianas are generically called *tura*, among which herbaceous ones are categorized into *maata*, and woody ones are also categorised as *mittsa*. As discussed below, all the indicator plants are *maata*.

Malo Use of Wild Plants

The Malo grow and use various cultivated crops for daily consumption, but they also retain a rich knowledge of wild plant uses. Out of more than six hundred botanical species thus far identified to the specific or generic levels, over two hundred are used by the Malo. Whereas the majority (74 percent) of crop plants are grown and used for food consumption, wild plants are collected and used primarily for medicines (53 percent), and secondarily for materials for tools and house construction (35 percent). While several species are planted for medicinal or material uses, wild plants are still essential for these purposes, though such uses do not occur frequently. In contrast, wild plants are not used for daily meals at all, but rather, are occasionally eaten by children as snacks, or rarely, as famine foods.

It can be said that, in spite of rich repository of knowledge concerning wild plant uses, people only rarely use them in practice. Viewed from such direct uses, wild plants seem to have a minor role in the livelihood of the Malo. However, if we consider their indirect uses, wild plants are still quite important for the Malo.

Malo Use of Agricultural Indicator Species

The Malo observe wild plant species in order to glean information on a wide variety of ecological conditions in their fields, including: soil types, soil fertility, the degradation of soils, the recovery of soils, and as indicators of seasonal changes.

Table 7.1: Highland Ethiopia agricultural indicator Species

Soil Types	Land Use Patterns	
	short fallowed land (maasila and shook'a)	long fallowed land (ottse)
extremely fertile soil (daro aradda	kolebuchi Capsella bursa-pastoraris (Brassicaceae) jebbo Crambe hispanica (Brassicaceae) kafe ts'ungutts Cleome monophylla Cleome ramosissima (Capparaceae)	sorahe Bidens kilimandscharica (Asteraceae)
normally fertile soil (ch'ere aradda)	bella Bidens steppia (Asteraceae) zom'e Caylusea abyssinia (Resedaceae) k'ulk'unts' Hypericum peplidifolium (Hypericaceae)	adille Guizotia scabra ssp. schimperi (Asteraceae)
middle fertility soil (ints'o)	shonate Guizotia scabra ssp. scabra (Asteraceae) shol'o Paracynoglossum coeruleum (Boraginaceae) k'its'a *Salvia nilotica* (Lamiaceae)	zamma Bothriocline tomentosa (Asteraceae) maagano Helichysum formosissimum (Asteraceae)
poor fertility soil (goppo, ts'alda)	bets'ilta Pteridium aquilinum (Dennstaedtiaceae) gijje Carduus leptacanthus (Asteraceae)	oka Acanthus sennii (Acanthaceae) korde Kalanchoe petitiana (Crassulaceae)

Plants Associated with Soil Types and Land-Use Patterns

During the initial, structured survey of wild plant uses, none of the interviewees volunteered information about wild plants being used as agricultural indicators. However, during participant observation and unstructured interviews on their agricultural systems, especially how they identified individual soil types and conditions, they often referred to the wild plant species found in and around their fields. Table 1 lists the species mentioned in these contexts. Because information was elicited incidentally, it is undoubtedly incomplete. Significantly, the listed species are all annual or perennial herbs and grasses (i.e. *maata*). These species are very common in the area, and local farmers are familiar with them. Although trees and shrubs are understood in terms of their ecological settings as well, herbs and grasses are locally considered to reflect soil types and conditions more accurately.

Wild Plants Used as Indicators of Fertile Soils

Barley (*Hordeum vulgare*) is one of the most important cereals for the highland Malo, as well as other highland peoples of Ethiopia. Barley is chiefly classified as hulled (*banga*) and naked (*murk'a*) types. In Ethiopia, both have different levels of importance and different agronomic traits and uses (Zemede 1999). Among the Malo, the area of naked barley cultivation is small and decreasing because this type of barley is cultivated only in very fertile soils under a long-fallow system. On the other hand, hulled barley is sown largely in fields with soils of mid-range fertility (*ints'o*) under both short- and long-fallow systems.

In this context, *kolebuchi* (*Capsella bursa-pastoris*) and *jebbo* (*Crambe hispanica*), are thought to be good indicators of fields suitable for sowing naked barley. They are both well-known wild leafy vegetables used when cultivated Ethiopian kale (*Brassica carinata*), an edible green, is in short supply. They often grow spontaneously in highland homesteads and, when Ethiopian kale is available, are usually simply weeded and discarded. During my interviews on the uses of these plants, they were always identified as leafy vegetables. By asking specifically about agricultural practices, however, I learned that they are thought to appear only in 'very fertile soils' (*daro aradda*), which are suitable for naked barley cultivation.

In the lowlands, *bootsa wosho* (*Loudetia arundinacea*) and *woshlinge* (*Setaria megaphylla*) are regarded as indicators of high-fertility soils suitable for sowing tef and maize, respectively, although both cereals are also cultivated elsewhere. *L. arundinacea* is generally known for its good quality as thatch, though the area in which it grows is limited.

Wild Plants Used as Indicators of Degraded Fields

Other types of wild plant agricultural indicators occur in the highlands. Most highland outlying fields are successively cultivated by rotating crops such as wheat, hulled barley, sorghum, and peas. In such fields, farmers consider certain weed floras to indicate degraded soil conditions. Whereas weed floras include diverse herbaceous species, farmers pay much attention to grasses as distinctive indicators of agricultural conditions. Most weed grasses in the highlands are designated under the generic name of *sudda*, the most common species of which include *Eragrostis schweinfurthii*, *Eragrostis tenuifolia*, *Pennisetum stramineum*, *Sporobolus africanus*, and *Andropogon amethystinus*. Farmers take the presence of these grasses as an indication that the soil has not degraded significantly and that it remains sufficiently fertile for continued cultivation.

In contrast, farmers are sensitive to the occurrence of a weed called *p'ed'd'a* (*Digitaria abyssinica*), a notorious indicator of field degradation. They say that when the land is in good condition, this weed seldom occurs; however, when the soil becomes degraded (*laddiza*), *p'ed'd'a* appears and starts to spread. When farmers find this plant, they try to exterminate it, but these efforts usually fail. Once *p'ed'd'a* becomes rampant, the farmers have no choice but to abandon cultivation and leave the affected field fallow. In lowland fields, a grassy weed called *p'ar'o* (*Paspalum scrobiculatum*) is similarly regarded. Another grass called *holle kefe* (*Melinis repens*) is not so aggressively invasive, but is also an indicator of degraded soils.

Wild Plants as Indicators of Fertility Recovery

When determining when to resume cultivation following a fallow period, farmers do not depend upon the number of years or seasons that the field has been allowed to recover, but rather refer to particular wild plant species in and around the fields. Fallow fields are mostly dominated by *zamma* (*Bothriocline schimperi*) in the higher highlands of approximately 3,000 m in elevation, and by *adille* (*Guizotia scabra* ssp. *schimperi*) in the lower highlands of approximately 2,000 m; both are perennial herbs of the Asteraceae family. Farmers assess fertility recovery by examining the height and girth of these dominant plants. During the relatively slack period following harvest, farmers visit fallow fields and, taking into account other conditions, choose the optimal fields for sowing in the coming rainy season.

In the lowlands, long-fallow fields are more widespread. Indigenous tef millet is sown predominantly in outlying fields using four different tillage methods: plow cultivation, digging-stick cultivation, grassland-hoe cultivation, and woodland-hoe cultivation (Fujimoto 2002). The method by which a field is tilled is determined by the distance from the farmer's home and the site's vegetation. Hoe cultivation is widely practiced in the fields furthest from homes. There, dominant *Hyparrhenia* grasses (*H. diplandra* and *H. cymbaria*) are often used to assess whether the soil at a particular site is ready to resume cultivation and which method of hoe cultivation is most appropriate.

Wild Plants as Indicators of Seasonal Changes

Wild plants can be used to infer not only field conditions, but also seasonal transitions. As noted earlier, cereals are sown at the peak of the rainy season, from June to early September. Highland farmers consider the start of *bella* (*Bidens steppia*) flowering in September to indicate the end of the cereal sowing period. Farmers believe that cereals will not grow if they are sown after the yellow *bella* flowers emerge. Although I know only one example of a plant used as an indicator of seasonal transitions, similar uses may be widespread in Ethiopia (McCann 1995, Huffnagel 1961).

Discussion

Through examination of the Malo case, several general features of wild plant agricultural indicators can be revisited. Whereas most reports of agricultural indicators are studies of shifting cultivators, the Malo are clearly not so: rather, they are intensive, multi-crop farmers. While they may be an exception to the rule, it is noteworthy that all the indicator uses among the Malo occur in their outlying fields, and none in their homegardens, which are essentially sedentary agricultural systems. Indeed, most indicator uses were identified in the most remote fields where long-fallowed and hoe-cultivated shifting cultivation take place. Although the Malo depend more on root and tuber crops than on cereals as their staple food, all their indicator uses are related to cereal cultivation. Thus, although the literature review was not conclusive in attributing these patterns to agricultural systems rather than researcher bias, the variability within the Malo case suggests that cereal and shifting cultivation systems are, indeed, the most likely to make use of wild plants as indicator species.

While reports of seasonal indicators from around the world are generally those that signal the approach or arrival of the rainy season and the start of the sowing period, a seasonal indicator in Malo, the only case so far identified, signals the end of the cereal sowing period, suggesting that there are other types of seasonal indicators that have not been sufficiently investigated.

Hence, several significant features emerge from the Malo case that help to explain apparent patterns in the literature. I now turn to several additional features elicited from the Malo case which help to explain the apparent ommission of these uses from ethnobotanical surveys. In doing so, aspects of agricultural indicator used as central features of traditional ecological knowledge emerge.

Agricultural Indicator Plants Are Common Species

As already described, all the indicator plants are common species for the Malo, and some of them are even crop weeds. Farmers are familiar with the ecologies of these plants through daily observation. Thus the mere occurrence of an indicator plant is not always of much importance but rather its height, girth, and frequency (density), which suggest growth conditions, or its sprouting, leafing, flowering, and fruiting, suggesting cyclical and developmental stages, are of key significance. Plants used as agricultural indicators can be therefore distinguished and contrasted from those used as non-agricultural environmental indicators. The latter are noted for their rare but distinct occurrence under specific physical environments, such as the presence of metals, pollution, or underground waters (Cook 1995).

Knowledge of Indicator Uses Is Not Commonly Shared

The plants used as agricultural indicators are quite common, and farmers know their local names, as well as their direct uses, such as for leafy vegetables or thatching material. However, Malo farmers do not seem to share their knowledge of particular indicator uses. Women hardly know these uses because they seldom practise cereal cultivation in the outlying fields. However, even among male farmers, such knowledge is not commonly shared. While most farmers know direct uses of wild plants quite well, only some farmers know indirect uses as agricultural indicators, suggesting an unequal distribution of knowledge that is difficult to explain given the potential benefit of agricultural indicators.

One answer to this seeming contradiction is that one plant species often occurs across different agricultural landscapes. Although indicator plants are common species, they may not serve as indicators in every location. For example, *adille* (*Guizotia scabra schimperi*) is common throughout Malo territory. In the highlands, it does not appear in cropped or short-fallowed fields, only in long-fallowed fields, where it indicates the recovery of soil fertility. In contrast, in the lowlands, *adille* occurs in cropped and short-fallowed fields where it is considered a vexing weed. Hence, a particular species may be useful as an indicator only in particular parts of a species' distribution, unlike with direct plant uses. Even when a plant is known to have an indicator use, that use can differ from place to place, as exemplified by the uses of *Commelina benghalensis* among the Wolayta and Azande (Appendix). Therefore, knowledge of agricultural indicators is deeply embedded in local ecologies – a key characteristic of TEK (Hunn 1999).

Indicator Plant Uses as Integral to Traditional Ecological Knowledge

Through conversations with Malo farmers, I realised that, in their day-to-day life, most farmers do not think of agricultural indicator plants as such, but simply consider them to be no different from other weedy species (*maata*). However, some farmers pay scrupulous attention to these plants at critical points in the agricultural calendar when they need to make key decisions. They remember from past experiences which plant species are more reliable as indicators of certain conditions in their fields.

The ecological specificity of indicator uses has important implications for transmission of knowledge. One farmer's knowledge of indicator uses may be conveyed to other farmers through daily conversations. However, because each indicator use of a plant species is valid only in a small area and because ecological conditions often differ among fields even in the same village, this knowledge then must be minutely verified through experimentation by each new farmer in his own fields. On the other hand, identical or similar indicator uses are known for different plants across different environments, e.g. between the highlands and the lowlands. It may be the case that, although most farmers hear of some indicator uses, only some willing farmers validate these uses through experimentation in their own fields, thereby accumulating knowledge through experience. Knowledge of indicator uses is thus considered to rely more on development through experimentation by individual farmers than on mere transmission between farmers. All this may help to explain why knowledge of indicators may be implicit or even concealed. Knowledge of indicator uses is therefore embedded not only in local ecologies, but also in farmers' social contexts, another key characteristic of TEK, which helps us to understand why it has been largely overlooked, and why it might be missed through conventional ethnobotanical survey methods. In this case, as Heckler states in the introduction to this volume, TEK 'emerges as a(n)…interaction of movement through and engagement with a particular landscape and the socioeconomic context in which this knowledge is developed, evaluated, transmitted and applied'.

The complexity and pervasiveness of wild plant uses as agricultural indicators, despite the failure to acknowledge these uses during my initial wild plant survey, suggest that at least some of the failure to acknowledge agricultural indicators in most ethnobotanical surveys is related to a bias toward direct plant uses by researchers and farmers alike, rather than the actual lack of their uses. Thus, agricultural indicator uses, and more broadly, indirect plant uses may represent integral aspects of traditional ecological knowledge. If ethnobotany seeks to fully describe the diverse relationships between plants and people, such aspects of traditional ecological knowledge deserve consideration.

Conclusion

Ethnobotanical studies have traditionally focused on direct plant uses by local peoples; these uses are usually tangible and can be recorded along with the plant names. In contrast, indirect plant uses have been largely neglected because they are often invisible and, more importantly, are rarely mentioned in normal interviews about particular plant uses. However, if ethnobotany aims to study the comprehensive interrelationships between plants and peoples, aspects of TEK must be intentionally included in ethnobotanical methods. As outlined here, indirect plant uses can be found widely among agricultural societies, mostly among cereal-growing shifting cultivators in tropical regions. Reflecting localised ecologies, indirect uses are effective only in small areas. In addition, knowledge of such uses seems to be poorly shared among farmers. However, these do not immediately mean that indicator uses are negligible but rather suggest that such knowledge is so embedded in TEK that it is not fixed nor extractable, but instead is constantly adjusted and appended through farmers' ongoing experiences of particular climatic, edaphic and wider ecological conditions.

Moreover, indirect plant uses are not confined to indicator uses, which have been the focus of this paper. Indirect uses can include the use of plants as livestock fodder, honeybee pollen sources or ornamentals. Among the Malo, for example, spontaneous seedlings of some trees growing in homegardens and in outlying fields are not removed, but are tended or transplanted. These seedlings are tended not only for eventual practical applications, such as for construction materials or shade, but also for their crop compatibilities. Some tree species are considered to increase crop yields by fertilising the surrounding soils, whereas others are thought to decrease harvests by drying soils. Such knowledge of wild plants fertilising, restoring, maintaining, or sterilising agricultural soils (e.g. Amanor 1993, Richards 1986), may constitute the TEK of other indirect plant uses as well and is in need of proper attention. Other types of indirect plant uses will hopefully be explored in future research.

Acknowledgements

Field research was carried out as part of a research project directed by the late Professor K. Fukui and funded by a Grant-in-Aid from the Japanese Ministry of Education, Science, Sports and Culture.

Notes

1. Data for the neighbouring Gofa area to the east collected by the Ethiopian Meteorological Agency show that Sawla (altitude 1,300 m) and Bulki (2,400 m) have average annual rainfalls of 1,457 and 1,716 mm, respectively, of which more than 90 percent falls between March and November.

Bibliography

Allan, W. 1965. *The African Husbandman.* Edinburgh: Oliver and Boyd.

Amanor, K. 1993. 'Farmer Experimentation and Changing Fallow Ecology in the Krobo District of Ghana', in W. de Boef, K. Amanor and K. Wellard with A. Bebbington, eds., *Cultivating Knowledge: Genetic Diversity, Farmer Experimentation and Crop Research.* London: Intermediate Technology Publications, pp.35-43.

Asfaw, Z. 1999. 'The Barleys of Ethiopia', in *Genes in the Field: On-Farm Conservation of Crop Diversity,* ed., S.B. Brush. Boca Raton, FL: Lewis Publishers., pp. 77-107.

_____ 2004. 'The Enset-based Home Gardens of Ethiopia', in P.B. Eyzaguirre and O.F. Linares, eds.,*Home Gardens and Abrobiodiversity.* Washington, D.D.: Smithsonian Institute Press, pp. 123-197.

Balée, W. and A. Gély. 1989. 'Managed Forest Succession in Amazonia: The Ka'apor Case', (*Advances in Economic Botany* series, vol. 7) pp. 129-158.

Bayliss-Smith, T. 1985. 'Subsistence Agriculture and Nutrition in the Bimin Valley, Oksapmin Sub-district, Papua New Guinea', *Singapore Journal of Tropical Geography* vol. 6: 101-115.

Cook, F.E.M. 1995. *Economic Botany Data Collection Standard.* Kew: Royal Botanic Gardens Press.

Cotton, C. M. 1996. *Ethnobotany: Principles and Applications.* Chichester, UK: John Wiley and Sons.

Cunningham, A.B. and B.R. Gwala. 1986. 'Plant Species and Building Methods Used in Tembe Thonga Hut Construction', *Annals of the Natal Museum,* vol. 27, no. 2: 491-511.

de Schlippe, P. 1956. *Shifting Cultivation in Africa: The Zande System of Agriculture.* London: Routledge & Kegan Paul.

Donfack, P. et C. Seignobos. 1996. 'Des plantes indicatrices dans un agrosystème incluant la jachère: les exemples des Peuls et des Giziga du Nord-Cameroun', *Journal d'Agriculture Traditionnelle et de Botanique Appliquée* vol. 38, no. 1: 231-250.

Etkin, N.L., and P.J. Ross. 1994. 'Pharmacological Implications of "Wild" Plants in Hausa Diet', in N.L. Etkin, ed., *Eating on the Wild Side: The Pharmacologic, Ecologic, and Social Implications of Using Noncultigens.* Tucson: University of Arizona Press, pp. 85-101.

Elias, E. and I. Scoones. 1999. 'Perspectives on Soil Fertility Change: A Case Study from Southern Ethiopia' *Land Degradation and Development* vol. 10: 195-206.

Fairhead, J. and M. Leach 1996. *Misreading the African Landscape: Society and Ecology in a Forest-Savanna Mosaic.* Cambridge: University Press.

Friis, I. 1992. *Forests and Forest Trees of Northeast Tropical Africa.* London: HMSO.

Fujimoto, T. 2002. 'T'ef (*Eragrostis tef*(Zucc.) Trotter) Cultivation among the Malo, South-western Ethiopia', in B. Yimam, R. Pankhurst, D. Chapple, Y. Admassu, A. Pankhurst and B. Teferra, eds., *Ethiopian Studies at the End of the Second Millennium,* Addis Ababa: Addis Ababa University Press, pp. 767-784.

_____ 2003. 'Malo', in *Peripheral People: The Excluded Minorities of Ethiopia,* eds., D. Freeman and A. Pankhurst. London: C. Hurst and Company, pp. 137-148.

Howard, P.L. ed., 2003. *Women and Plants: Gender Relations in Biodiversity Management and Conservation.* London and New York: Zed Books.

Guijt, I. 1998. 'Valuing Wild Plants with Economics and Participatory Methods: An Overview of the Hidden Harvest Methodology'. in H.D.V. Prendergast, N.L. Etkin, D.R. Harris and P.J. Houghton, eds., *Plants for Food and Medicine.* Kew: Royal Botanic Gardens Press, pp. 223-235.

Hédin, L. 1932. 'La vocation des terres de la forêt tropicale africaine, d'après les indices fournis par la végétation spontanée: observations des indigènes sur la flore et les formations végétales', *Revue de Botanique Appliquée et d'Agriculture Tropicale* vol. 12: 111-121.

Huffnagel, H. P. 1961. *Agriculture in Ethiopia.* Rome: FAO.

Hunn, E. S. 1999 'The Value of Subsistence for the Future of the World', in V.D. Nazarea, ed., *Ethnoecology: Situated Knowledge/Located Lives.* Tucson: : University of Arizona Press, pp. 23-36.

Huss-Ashmore, R. and S.L. Johnston 1997. 'Wild Plants as Famine Foods: Food Choice under Conditions of Scarcity', in H. Macbeth, *ed., Food Preferences and Taste: Continuity and Change.* Oxford: Berghahn Books, pp. 83-100.

Joshi, P. 1985. 'Weather-Indicating Plants of Tribals in Southern Rajasthan', *Bulletin of the Botanical Survey of India* vol. 27: 100-104.

Kakeya, M. 1976. 'Subsistence Ecology of the Tongwe, Tanzania', *Kyoto University African Studies,* vol. 10: 143-212.

Knight, C. G. 1974. *Ecology and Change: Rural Modernization in an African Community.* New York: Academic Press.

Kuls, W. 1962 'Land, Wirtschaft und Siedlung der Gumuz in Westen von Godjam (Äthiopien)', *Paideuma,* vol. 8, no. 1: 45-61.

Levang, P. 1983. 'L'appréciation de la fertilité d'un sol par les Dayaks du Kalimantan Central', *Journal d'Agriculture Traditionelle et de Botanique Appliquée,* vol. 30, no. 2: 127-137.

Luxereau, A. 1997. 'Transformation du rapport au végétal et à la terre dans la région de Maradi (Niger)', in D. Barreteau, R. Dognin, et C. von Graffenried, eds., *L'homme et le milieu végétal dans le bassin du lac Tchad: Man and Vegetation in the Lake Chad Basin.* Paris: : Editions de l'ORSTOM, pp. 53-68.

Martin, G. J. 2004. *Ethnobotany: A Methods Manual.* London: Earthscan.

McCann, J. 1995. *People of the Plow: An Agricultural History of Ethiopia, 1800-1990.* Madison: University of Wisconsin Press.

Nietschmann, B. 1973. *Between Land and Water: The Subsistence Ecology of the Miskito Indians, Eastern Nicaragua.* New York: Seminar Press.

Oyama, S. 2003. 'Bujimi System in Miombo Woodland of Northwestern Zambia: Sorghum Cultivation under Multiple Soil Fertility System', *Ecosophia* vol. 12: 100-119 (in Japanese).

Padoch, C. 1986. 'Agricultural Site Selection among Permanent Field Farmers: An Example from East Kalimantan, Indonesia', *Journal of Ethnobiology,* vol. 6, no. 2: 279-288.

Richards, P. 1985. *Indigenous Agricultural Revolution: Ecology and Food Production in West Africa.* London: Unwin Hyman.

_____ 1986. *Coping with Hunter: Hazard and Experimentation in an African Rice-farming System.* London: Allen and Unwin.

Rival, L. ed., 1998. *The Social Life of Trees: Anthropological Perspectives on Tree Symbolism.* Oxford: Berg.

Sharland, R. W. 1994. 'Understanding Weeds in a Subsistence Society: Moru Perceptions of Herb Species in the Garden', in M.M.M. Ahmed, ed., *Indigenous Farming Systems, Knowledge and Practices in the Sudan.* .Khartoum: Institute of African and Asian Studies, University of Khartoum, pp. 191-211.

Sharma, N. K. 1990. 'Ethnobotany of Mukudras: Weather-Indicating Plants', *Journal of Phytological Research* vol. 3, no. 1/2: 65-70.

Smole, W. J. 1976. *The Yanoama Indians: A Cultural Geography.* Austin: University of Texas Press.

Turner, N.J. and A. Davis. 1993. 'When Everything Was Scarce': The Role of Plants as Famine Foods in Northwestern North America, *Journal of Ethnobiology* vol. 13, no. 2: 171-201.

Yamada, T. 1984. 'Nyindu Culture and the Plant World: The Dynamic Relationship between the Knowledge on Plant Use and the Change in House Form', *Senri Ethnological Studies* vol. 15: 69-107.

Appendix

Ethnic Group	Agricultural Type	Folk Name	Scientific Name	Indicator Use	Source
Malo, southwestern Ethiopia	Intensive mixed farming based on enset	kolebuchi	*Capsella bursa-pastoris*	Occurrence indicates that soils are so fertile that naked barley can be cultivated.	N/A
		jebbo	*Crambe hispanica*		
		bootsa wosho	*Loudetia arundinacea*	Occurrence indicates the soil fertility to be suitable for sowing tef.	
		woshlinge	*Setaria megaphylla*	Occurrence indicates soil fertility and humidity to be suitable for sowing maize	
		p'ed'd'a	*Digitaria abyssinica*	Dense occurrence indicates the soil to be so degraded that the field should be left for fallow.	
		p'ar'o	*Paspalum scrobiculatum*		
		holle kefe	*Melinis repens*	Occurrence indicates degraded soils.	
		zamma	*Bothriocline schimperi*	Density and height of this perennial indicate soil recovery.	
		adille	*Guizotia scabra schimperi*		
		k'ach'e	*Hyparrhenia diplandra*	Density and height indicate the site to be suitable for grassland hoe cultivation (kurche).	

Ethnic Group	Agricultural Type	Folk Name	Scientific Name	Indicator Use	Source
		k'aaliccho	*Hyparrhenia cymbaria*	Density and height indicate the site to be suitable for woodland hoe cultivation (*garpe*).	
		bella	*Bidens steppia*	Onset of flowering indicates the end of cereal sowing period.	
Wolayta, southern Ethiopia	Intensive mixed farming based on enset	maga mattas	*Urochloa panicoides*	Prevalence of the species indicates areas possessing higher fertility	Eyasu et al. 1999: 199
		dalasha	*Commelina benghalensis*		
		bisida	*Galinsoga parviflora*	Prevalence of the species indicates areas possessing lower fertility	
		girolia	*Eragrostis phalaris*		
		petta, lichea	*Digitaria spp.*		
Gumuz, western Ethiopia	Shifting cultivation of sorghum and millet		(Poaceae)	Particular grasses are referred to in choosing sites for shifting cultivation.	Kuls 1962: 50
Azande, southern Sudan	Shifting cultivation of sorghum and millet	anyakanari, abagambo	*Bidens pilosa*	The weeds are recognized as indicators of degradation.	de Schlippe 1956: 213
		rende	*Chloris sp.*		
		tita-moru	*Eleusine indica*		
		rekondo	*Commelina benghalensis*		
		ngamu	*Pennisetum pedicellatum*		
Moru, southern Sudan	Shifting cultivation of sorghum	kabalili	*Dolichos schweinfurthii*	Well recognized as fertility indicators	Sharland 1994: 208
		dodo	(Poaceae)		
		imba njere	*Boerhavia diffusa*	Indicate soils high in organic matter	
		awowa	*Commelina benghalensis*		
		teisezevo	*Chrysanthellum americanum*	A problematic weed indicating diminished fertility	

Ethnic group group	Agricultural Type	Folk Name	Scientific Name	Indicator Use	Source
Tongwe, western Tanzania	Shifting cultivation of maize and cassava	iswe	*Pennisetum purpureum*	Iswe grassland indicates that a site is suitable for dry season maize cultivation.	Kakeya 1976: 171
		lusali	*Hyparrhenia variabilis*	Lusali grassland indicates that a site is suitable for cassava cultivation.	
Nyiha, southwestern Tanzania	Shifting cultivation of finger millet, sorghum and maize	amabala	*Brachystegia utilis*	Specific trees are used as indicators of areas most suitable for woodland shifting cultivation.	Knight 1974: 98, 106
		ing'anzo	*Brachystegia boehmii*		
		ing'anzo	*Brachystegia longifolia*		
		ilaji	*Brachystegia spiciformis*		
		insani	*Brachystegia bussei*		
		ilenje	*Brachystegia sp.*		
		izimbwe	*Brachystegia sp.*		
		intonto	*Isoberlinia angolensis*		
		inchala	*Acasia macrothyrsa*		
		igonombila	*Hyparrhenia schimperi*	Specific grasses are used as indicators of areas most suitable for grassland shifting cultivation.	
		impilula	*Hyparrhenia variabilis*		
		ivunga	*Hyparrhenia colina*		
		impilula	*Trachypogon spicatus*	Indicator of the site having been recently abandoned.	
		usankwe	*Digitaria scalarum*		
		shisumbwe	*Dolichos sp.*	Indicator of the site having remained uncultivated for a long period.	
Kaonde, northwestern Zambia	Shifting cultivation of sorghum and maize	kibabe	*Hyparrhenia mutica, H. tamba, H. diplandra*	Indicates a site suitable for shifting cultivation.	Oyama 2003: 104, 108
		kalumba	*Striga asiatica*	Indicates soil fertility and sorghum yield decline.	
		kendankonganya	*Melinis repens*		
		sokotera	*Bidens pilosa*		

Ethnic group group	Agricultural Type	Folk Name	Scientific Name	Indicator Use	Source
Giziga and Fulbe, northern Cameroon	Shifting cultivation of sorghum and other cereals	mu bula kuli	*Centaurea senegalensis*	Indicate decline of ferreous soils.	Donfack et al. 1996: 238-241, 248
		teppere poola	*Chrysanthellum americanum*		
		gulejer	*Andropogon chinensis*	Indicate recovery of ferreous soils.	
		ngi ngel	*Cyperus pustulatus*		
		falaande	*Dactyloctenium aegyptium*		
		jeeliyaaho	*Digitaria ciliaris*		
		wuuluko	*Pennisetum pedicellatum*		
		mutsupatsupa	*Setaria verticillata*		
		jeeliyaaho karal	*Digitaria horizontalis*	Indicate recovery of vertisols.	
		pagguri ndewi	*Echinochloa colona*		
		wicco waandu	*Setaria pumila*		
		cakam'de	*Spermacoce stachydea*		
Maradi, southern Niger	Diverse farming of millet and other crops	gwadda	*Annona senegalensis*	Height of the tree marks the fallow periods	Luxereau 1997: 55, 57, 60
		gamba	*Andropogon gayanus*	Recolonization of this grass indicates soil recovery.	
		yambururu	*Merremia angustifolia*	Presence of these species indicates unsuitability of the soils for future cultivation.	
		yamanya	*Cucumis prophetarum*		
		kyasuwa	*Pennisetum pedicellatum*		
		fataka	*Pergularia nomentosa*		
Kuranko, southeastern Guinea	Diverse farming of rice and other crops	kaladu	*Andropogon gayanus*	Savanna land supporting the grass is preferred as suitable for transformation.	Fairhead et al. 1996: 142
		solon	*Imperata cylindrica*	Plains where the grass dominates are suitable for peanut cultivation.	

Ethnic group group	Agricultural Type	Folk Name	Scientific Name	Indicator Use	Source
		moloko	*Pennisetum purpureum*	Indicates sufficient fallow to suppress weeds.	
Bulu, Cameroon	Shifting cultivation of maize and other crops	essussuk	*Spathodea campanulata*	Height indicates soil fertility.	Hédin 1932: 113-115
		essombo	*Rauwolfia vomitoria*		
		edjom	*Aframomum sp.*	Dense population indicates soil fertility.	
		ndaoulo n'tangan	*Cassia alata*	Occurrence indicates fertile soil suitable for cultivation.	
			Panicum plicatum	Dense population indicates suitable field for maize cultivation.	
		okon	*Triumfetta sp.*	Occurrence indicates suitable field for peanut cultivation.	
		--	*Cassia occidentalis*	Occurrence indicates sandy and poor soil.	
		okas	*Dicrostachys nutans*	Occurrence indicates meagre or eroded land.	
Bassa, Liberia	--	zoe	*Macrolobium macrophyllum*	Dropping of the fruits indicates the close of rainy season and the time of clearance for plantation.	
Mende, Sierra Leone	Dry and wet rice farming	mbeli	*Harungana madagascariensis*	An abundance of the trees indicates that rice will do well there.	Richards 1986: 76
		tijo	*Phyllanthus discoideus*		
		ndewe	*Macaranga spp.*		
		koba	*Sterculia tragacantha*		
		bobo	*Irvingia gabonensis* or *Funtumia africana?*		
		gbota	*Antrocaryon micraster*	Flowering signs the approach of rainy season.	Richards 1985: 47

Ethnic group group	Agricultural Type	Folk Name	Scientific Name	Indicator Use	Source
Yoruba, southern Nigeria	Planting of yam, cassava, etc.	eki	*Lophira alata*	New leafing signs the approach of rainy season.	
Igboho, western Nigeria	Planting of yam, cassava, etc.	iroko	*Chlorophora excelsa*	Leafing signs the approach of rainy season and the beginning of planting season.	
		--	*Adansonia digitata*		
Jinga, Zimbabwe	Rain-fed cultivation of pearl millet, sorghum, etc.	mukamba	*Afzelia quanzensis*	seasonality indicator	Hot Springs Working Group 1995: 62
		muonde	*Ficus capensis*		
		matsamvu	*Ficus sp.*		
		mupfura	*Sclerocaya birres*		
Lun Dayeh, eastern Kalimantan, Indonesia	Paddy rice farming	serinit	*Rubus moluccensis*	Common plant species indicating good agricultural potential.	Padoch 1986: 286
		gugor	*Selaginella brevipes*		
		buyu' berek	*Piper caninum*		
		lapa'	*Curculigo bomeensis*		
		taneb luba'	*Cyrtandra trisepala*	Common plant species indicating average agricultural potential.	
		lio fade	*Lycopodium cemuum*	Common plant species indicating poor agricultural potential.	
		tamar	*Curculigo villosa*		
		anur sia'	*Timonius finlaysonianus*		
		anur ferian	*Clethra lonspicata*		
Dayak, central Kalimantan, Indonesia	Shifting cultivation of upland rice	bayur	*Pterospermum diversifolium*	Privileged indicators of good fertility.	Levang 1983: 134-135
		tawe	*Duabanga moluccana*		
		banuang	*Octomeles sumatrana*		
		bamban	*Phrynium macrocephalum*		
		itik	*Phrynium placentarium*		
		palingkau	*Gigantochloa sp.?*		
		uru dawak	*Selaginella willdenovi*		

Ethnic group group	Agricultural Type	Folk Name	Scientific Name	Indicator Use	Source
		akar tampilak	*Phanera semibifida*	Secondary indicators of good fertility.	
		betung	*Dendrocalamus asper*		
		biha	*Alocasia puber*		
		kayu batu	*Xanthophyllum sp.*		
		lentang mahambung	*Shorea parvifolia*		
		lunuk	*Ficus caulocarpa*		
		mahar	*Kleinhovia hospita*		
		mahawai	*Mezzetia parvifolia*		
		marsiung	*Phoebe sp.*		
		nangka aer	*Artocarpus kemando*		
		pantung	*Dyera costulata*		
		ramin	*Gonostylus bancanus*		
		ramin	*Gonostylus macrophyllus*		
		tabalien/ulin	*Eusideroxylon zwageri*		
		uei bungkuk	*Korthalsia scaphigera*		
		uei dahanen	*Korthalsia sp.*		
		banuas	*Shorea parvifolia*	Privileged indicators of bad fertility.	
		keruing	*Dipterocarpus grandiflorus*		
		bangkirai	*Hopea dryobalanops*		
		bangkirai	*Hopea mengarawan*		
		emang	*Dialium maingayo*		
		kempas	*Dialium sp.*		
		agathis	*Agathis dammara*	Secondary indicators of bad fertility.	
		belawan	*Tristania maingayi*		
		garunggang	*Cratoxylum arborescens*		
		kayu batu	*Xanthophyllum sp.*		
		keranji	*Dialium sp.*		
		mahaliau	*Strombosia rotundifolia*		
		pampaning	*Quercus subsericea*		
		rasak	*Vatica rassak*		

Ethnic group group	Agricultural Type	Folk Name	Scientific Name	Indicator Use	Source
		tamahas	*Memecylon myrsinoides*		
Bimin, New Guinea	shifting cultivation of taro	--	*Castanopsis sp.*	Indicate that a secondary forest stand is ready for a further phase of taro cultivation.	Bayliss-Smith 1985: 104
		--	*Lithocarpus sp.*		
Futuna, western Polynesia	shifting cultivation (and irrigated agriculture) of yams and taro	u	*Miscanthus floridulus*	Mark the degraded soils where poor yields may result.	Kirch 1994: 60, 106
		vao maselesele	*Scleria polycarpa*		
		sakato	*Dicranopteris linearis*	Associates with the degraded land, called toafa, unsuitable for cultivation.	
Bhil, western India	unspecified	nagdaman	*Arisaema tortuosum*	Sprouting of the tuber indicates the Monsoon arrival.	Sharma 1990: 67-68; Joshi 1985: 101-102
		chawlya kand	*Arum trilobatum*	Sprouting of the leaves indicates the onset of rains.	
		jatashankari	*Dioscorea bulbifera*	Sprouting of the branches indicates the Monsoon arrival.	
		ratalu	*Dioscorea globosa*	Sprouting of the leaves indicates the onset of rains.	
		kantaloo	*Dioscorea pentaphylla*		
		baramtoomari	*Kickxia ramosissima*	Rejuvination indicates the onset of rains	
		giloe	*Tinospora cordifolia*	Appearance of fresh leaves indicates rains within a few days	
		kachri, phoot	*Cucumis melo var. agrestis*	Abundant fruiting signals famine	
		jhadbor	*Ziziphus nummularia*	Abundant fruiting indicates sufficient rainfall	
		timru	*Diospyros melanoxylon*	Scanty fruiting signals good rains, while profuse one famine.	

Ethnic Group	Agricultural Type	Folk Name	Scientific Name	Indicator Use	Source
		mahuwa	*Madhuca longifolia*	Abundant fruiting indicates rich rains.	
		kadai	*Sterculia urens*	Simultaneous occurrence of inflorescences and leaves forecasts rich rains.	
		helpi, helapi	*Securinega virosa*	Onset of flowering tells following rains.	
Garasia, western India	unspecified	salar, halar	*Boswellia serrata*	Ample fruiting indicates appropriate weather for grain.	
		tendu	*Diospyros melanoxylon*	Profuse flowering signals good rains	
Kathodia, western India	unspecified	amli	*Tamarindus indica*	Fruiting indicates abundant rains and ripening of wheat and chickpea.	
Miskito, eastern Nicaragua	Shifting cultivation, fishing and hunting	--	*Aechmea magdalenae*	Indicates the "cool" land, suitable for clearance.	Nietschmann 1973: 134
		kira	*Guasuma ulmifolia*	Identify the "hot" land, thought to be bad for cultivation.	
		atak	*Geonoma?*		
Yanoama, Venezuela/Brazil	Shifting cultivation of plantains etc.	alemasijenaco	*Heliconia spp.*	Associated with ishabena good for plantains.	Smole 1976: 108
Ka'apor, eastern Amazonian Brazil	Swidden horticulture of manioc etc.	piki	*Caryocar villosum*	Believed to indicate good horticultural soils for new swidden and settlement sites	Balée & Gély 1989: 130
		tayi	*Tabebuia spp.*		

Chapter 8

How Does Migration Affect Ethnobotanical Knowledge and Social Organisation in a West Papuan Village?

Manuel Boissière

Introduction

Cultural hybridization has mainly been considered in the context of overlap between very different groups, such as 'western' societies and indigenous cultures (Gow 2001, Gupta 1998, Gupta and Ferguson 1992), for instance numerous comparisons between scientists and local farmers (Agrawal 1995, Sillitoe 1998a,b), or between indigenous and 'non-indigenous' knowledge (Dove 2000: 235), but very little work has been done on different ethnic groups that share the same cultural background and that have only minor power differentials. For instance, Thomas focuses on the relationship between colonial and colonised groups, and brings in the problem of hybridity as an individual or a collective construction (Thomas 1996). In so doing, he broaches questions relating to definitions of identity and ethnicity.[1]

Even though populations in New Guinea are isolated from one another, important trading and exchange channels have developed (Pétrequin and Pétrequin 1993), which are maintained during peace and war (Lemonnier 1990). It is therefore not a surprise to find two different ethnic groups sharing the same space, the same territory, as in the village of Holuwon, in the Heluk Valley, West Papua (Figure 8.1).[2] Local knowledge and practices are differently shared among the groups and may even be maintained by each group respectively. When hybridization is observed, which part of the collective knowledge and perception does it concern, and to what extent?

Figure 8.1: The village of Holuwon in the Heluk Valley

A key issue is the dynamics of knowledge sharing and the position of one group vis-à-vis the other. According to Ellen and Harris, local knowledge is not fixed or static, but is on the contrary 'constantly changing, being produced as well as reproduced, discovered as well as lost' (2000: 5). One means of transmission, oral, is one of the reasons for its frequent transformation and adaptation (see Vermonden, Chapter Nine, about the oral aspects of TEK's transmission and its imitation process). Therefore, local knowledge 'undergoes changes, which necessarily result from the specific orientations, strategies and agendas of those using it, as well as the transformations which inevitably occur through translation' (Ellen and Harris 2000: 19). Even if local knowledge is empirical, subject to transformations, and does not always depend on its origins, I show here that there is a historical component to the ethnic origin of this knowledge particularly evident in shamanism and cosmogony.

In the following discussion, I analyse the transformations of identities and the dynamics of knowledge sharing for two indigenous ethnic groups sharing the same village. Is there a predominance of one group over the other, in terms of language, social organisation, traditional ecological knowledge, or shamanism? To answer this, I compare different perceptions of the two groups of their history, myths and shamanism, which reveal pronounced cultural differences. I find that, although there is clear evidence that the Yali are more dominant than the Hupla, this dominance has not led to the obliteration of Hupla identity, or a uniquely Hupla ethnohistory, shamanism and ethnobiology. It is only with the introduction of Christianity that both Hupla and Yali shamanisms are threatened.

Methods

This work was a part of a PhD study during two field trips of respectively 3 and 6 months in Holuwon, West Papua, between 1996 and 1998. The study focussed mainly on the local perception of the forest landscape and on the traditional knowledge of natural resources (Boissière 1999a).

In Holuwon, two ethnic groups share the same territory: the Yali and the Hupla. During this study I worked with shamans, big men and other people of knowledge on the myths and traditions of the inhabitants of the Heluk Valley. Myths concerning the Hupla and Yali origins and migrations were collected during interviews with the elders who belonged to each ethnic group. Stories about the different features of the landscape were collected during these interviews and cross-checked during field activities in the forest, with different villagers. All interviews were carried out in Indonesian, with Yali translators when needed.

Shamans' knowledge was discussed separately with the two last shamans in Holuwon, representing the two main groups. I obtained the most complete data from the shaman belonging to the Yali group. The Hupla shaman was reluctant to discuss the old traditions, considering it useless to talk about practices that were abandoned after the Christianisation of the valley. To do this the shamans and I first made out a list of the plants and animals used during different rituals. Then, over a period of five months we went through the list, one item after the other, and studied the principal rituals from the perspective of the kind of plants used. More than one plant can play a role in the same or different phases of a ritual, and having the precise botanical information for all plants used can help to reconstitute each step of the ritual. Many details could be collected, clarified, and, ultimately, a reasonable overview of the main rituals was obtained. Herbarium samples from most of the plants used by the shamans, were collected, and processed and identified at the Herbarium Bogoriense (Bogor, Indonesia).

Yali and Hupla in the Heluk Valley

Although the Yali and Hupla languages both belong to the Great Dani linguistic family (Silzer and Clouse 1991), they each follow different though comparable rules and traditions and have different myths. These two groups have inhabited the same village, for generations[3].

The village of Holuwon numbers about 400 people, the majority belong to the Yali ethnic group, while the remainder (probably less than one hundred people) are of Hupla origin[4]. The names 'Yali' and 'Hupla' are not autodenominations, but rather relate to the original location of the two groups along the east-west trade route (Wilson 1988: 5). According to Wilson 'Yali means those to the east and is contrasted with Hupla, meaning those of the west' (1988: 5).

Holuwon is situated at about 1,000 m above sea level, at the meeting point of the Baliem and Heluk rivers, 70 km southeast of Wamena (Figure 8.2), the district capital (Boissière 1999a, Boissière 1999b). Holuwon is at the southern limit of Yali territory, and abuts Hupla territory which extends over a much smaller area (Figure 8.3). In 1988, within Yali territory, the Yali numbered 29,500, divided in three dialects: the Pass Valley dialect (Abenaho), spoken by 5,000 people; the Angguruk dialect, spoken by 15,000 people; and the Ninia dialect, spoken by 9,500 people (Wilson 1988: 5). On the other hand, in total, the Hupla numbered 3,000 (Silzer and Clouse 1991). Hence, the Hupla are a smaller group than the Yali, located in a smaller territory.

In Holuwon, both the Yali and the Hupla are subsistence farmers. Sweet potato (*Ipomoea batatas*) is the staple crop (Figure 8.4). But many other crops are planted in mixed gardens, such as groundnut (*Arachis hypogea*),yam (*Dioscorea alata*), sugarcane (*Saccharum officinarum*), banana (*Musa* spp.), cassava (*Manihot esculenta*), and many others (Boissière 1999c). One crop having seasonal and, previously, ritual importance, is the red pandanus (*Pandanus conoideus*), a commonly encountered species at this altitude (less than 1,000m ,).

Gardening activities do not require *slash-and-burn* techniques, as they do around Wamena (Purwanto 1997); however, shrubs and tree branches cleared in

Figure 8.2: Map of West Papua with the location of the Baliem Valley and Wamena

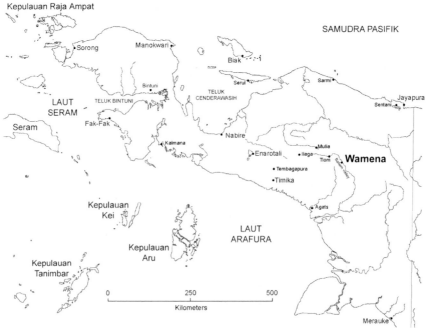

Figure 8.3: The Yali and
Hupla territories

Figure 8.4: A Yali woman digging
sweet potato in her garden

the first phase of garden preparation are burnt in piles, creating small areas of enhanced fertility (Boissière 2003). Agricultural practices are diverse: there are about six different types of gardens, named according to the techniques used to clear and prepare the soil.

Hunting and gathering often take place in or next to the cultivation zone (primarily in forest regrowth). These activities contribute to human modification, hence 'humanisation', of the territory. Each part of the territory, at each moment of its management, from the initial clearing of a garden, through the fallow period, until sufficient regrowth permits establishment of a new garden, provides food and other products for the villagers.

As means of communication increase, relations with Wamena, the largest neighbouring town in the Baliem Valley, have changed. This has also changed village livelihoods in that villagers often send vegetables, groundnuts, and pigs to town. They buy goods (machetes, axes, kitchen utensils *etcetera*) from the market and their children are often sent to Wamena for higher education (Holuwon has only a small primary school).

There is no leader or chief in Holuwon, a common situation in New Guinea, (village head, or *Kepala Desa*, is designated by the local government). Personalities of influence, or *Ab lohon* (lit. 'big men'), play an important role in the organisation of the society, along with the hornbill hunter (*hemangi),* and shamans (*hwalahun).* The hornbill hunter played a strategic role in previous times, as hornbills (*Rhyticeros plicatus)* were one of the key elements of shamanic rituals. The role and knowledge of the shamans will be considered in more detail later. Organisation of Holuwon society is similar to that described by Koch (1974) in Jalémo, near Angguruk: similar patterns of leadership and kinship based on moieties and organisation of the settlements are observed. Since the Christianisation of the valley, which occurred between 1967 and 1974, a Baptist church was established, called the GIDI (Gereja Injil Di Indonesia), under the Regions Beyond Missionary Union (RBMU) network.

This general description of the village does not highlight differences between the two ethnic groups: they follow the same general organisation, have similar livelihoods, and evince no major differences in land management. This is not surprising if we consider that local people's norms are not necessarily reflected in their behaviour and that some undifferentiated praxis may exist between the two groups (Kalland 2000). Agricultural practice is one of them, as it is largely a reflection of local ecological potentials and constraints, rather than the historical origins of the society. The literature on agriculture in West Papua shows similarities in certain agricultural systems between societies sharing the same ecological constraints, even far from one another. For example in the highlands (Pospisil 1963, Gardiner 1987, Cook 1995, Purwanto 1997, Boissière 1999a, Boissière and Purwanto 2007), among the Etoro, Amungme, Yali, Dani ethnic groups, the staple crops are sweet potatoes (*Ipomoea batatas*) and taro (*Colocasia esculenta)*, and the possible variations of agricultural practices linked to these crops are limited in number. They concern mainly the use of fires, mounds or fertilizer. It is therefore difficult to distinguish which agricultural practices originate from the Yali or the Hupla; they are both adapted to the topography, altitude, and crops. This said, in some cases, the villagers have borrowed specific techniques from their Dani neighbours in Wamena, such as mound building; nevertheless they have adapted them to local ecological conditions (Boissière 1999c). When myths, shamanism and narratives of history are examined, however, stark differences appear.

History and Mythology of Migrations

Bidou (1992) explains that time plays an important role in myths. According to Bidou (1992: 498), time legitimises the myths through their construction process. Myths represent the general 'history' of a society, where individual origins are merged into a common pot, but can be 'readjusted' as the society changes. For different reasons – importance of time, reflections of social perceptions, and fluidity of stories – myths are interesting indicators of the differences between the two ethnic groups in Holuwon. In this case, the Yali (Box 1) and Hupla (Box 2) each have their own myth related to the settling of Holuwon.

Figure 8.5: Yali and Hupla migration currents

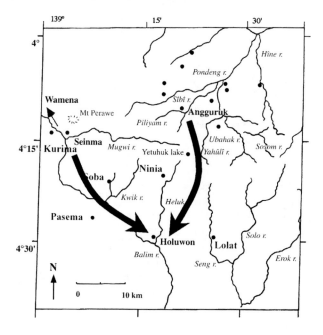

Box 1. *The Yali Myth*

A long time ago, the sky (*bohol*) and the earth (*kwenang*) were mixed together. The first human beings coming out of the ground at Walma, in Angguruk region, were a man, *Ahun Alpa* (man of the beginning) and a woman *Ohwe unuk Megen* (woman of the earth-quake). They separated the sky from the earth, an earthquake happened and *Dohlu* the pig arrived, together with *Dabe* the porcupine and *Siluwak* the snake. Megen and Alpa decided to kill Dabe and Dohlu and extracted from their stomach two long black stones named *Yeli asingip* (or 'remains of Yeli')[5]. Their son, *Dabe enggele,* gave pieces of these stones to a man, *Um Balim Balungwe* ('first Baliem man', in Hupla language), and asked him to go West to the Hupla lands. Um Balim Balungwe travelled underground, follow-ing the tail of the big snake Siluwak and arrived at the Ferawe Mountain, near Seinma (Figure 8.5).

Dabe Enggele planted one Yeli Asingip in the ground, tied to a stick, to prevent more humans from coming out of the ground, built a house and opened a garden (*yabuk*) with his wife *Yeli Milen* ('Thunder of Yeli'). But as the earth still shook because of the snake, they decided to move to a place named Asin, where the head of Siluwak came out in a red lake (*Mep Ahei*). On the next morning, after Megen and Alpa came back to Walma, to take care of the original hole in the ground, Siluwak's head came out of the lake and ordered Dabe Enggele to make a strap bag (*sum*) and to fill it in with leaves of several plants. Every night, Siluwak hid inside the strap bag and became *biggalem,* the moon. Every morning, he came out of the bag and became the sun, *mo.*

In Walma, Dohlu, the pig, and Dabe, the porcupine, were not yet dead. Dohlu ran away to Asin, where Dabe Enggele captured him, again opened his stomach and again got two Yeli Asingip, one for each moiety. He built a house, using the blood of the pig and leaves from the forest. Inside the house, four posts surrounded the central fire. The two posts (*fisingge*) situated far from the main entrance hosted the Yeli Asingip in their hole, and represented each moiety: one for the male part of the house and one for the female. Dabe Enggele implemented the first ritual to stabilise the earth around the village and by this act, he became the first shaman, or *hwalahun.* As Dohlu managed to escape, Dabe Enggele's children, two men and a woman, ran after him. They captured him before he escaped again. One night, in the mens' dream, Dohlu explained to them how to make a ritual house, or *ousayowa.* Each new generation of Yali settled in a new place, while pur-suing Dohlu, started a garden and planted seeds brought from their parents' village. They made a house and the next generation again pursued Dohlu. The places where the Yali settled, after Asin, were Seila and Wanim Alo. For each place, they extracted sacred stones from Dohlu, a pond appeared, and they started a garden. After many episodes, with Dohlu or Dabe to help and initiate them, they arrived in a place called Puplin, where no pond appeared, and they realised that they were at the end of the Yali territory, and at the beginning of a new territory, with different traditions. They couldn't find the Yeli Asingip in Puplin, but they found many nearby, under a tree named *Selem* (*Lithocarpus lauter-bachii*, Fagaceae). The traditions were different, so was the way to get the sacred stones. The new settlers mixed with the people from Hosahaikma, a village very close to Holu-won. In the meantime, Dohlu, who was in Walma, entered a pond, travelled under-ground and reappeared near the Prawe mountain, at Seinma.

Box 2. *The Hupla Myth*

In the beginning, when the sky (*bohol*) and the ground (*kwenang*) were already separated, two men opened a 'door' in a stone and came out of the ground, in a place called Seinma. They were *Hosiek* (litt. 'opening') and *Lariek* (litt. 'closing'). With them a boar named *Bemea* ('yellow hair') and a sow named *Luahe* ('cassowary bone') came out. The skin of the two men was still made from stone and their umbilical cord was still hanging. As many other persons with a stone skin were coming out of the hole, Lariek began to worry and closed the hole with a stone called Yeli Asingip. They began then to plant some crops (banana, sugarcane etcetera) after anointing the holes with pork fat, so that the crops grew fast. They then killed the boar and from its blood they produced 'stone' axes, cowrie decorations, and small Yeli Asingip.

With the other people who came out of the earth, they built a sacred house, *ousayowa*, and buried phalanger's hairs in the hole of one of the fire posts, and tied a Yeli Asingip to the post, to stop the earthquakes. Then they performed a ritual, named *wam akilit* ('pork fat'), by cooking the pork in an oven earth, and gave food to all the people near the sacred post of the ousayowa. Then, all the stone skins fell and the humans were free to go wherever they wanted. Hosiek and Lariek, after getting married, divided the people of Seinma in three groups, which went in three different directions:

One group went west and settled in the Baliem Valley; they belonged to the Dani ethnic group.

One group went to the North, to Kurulu, and learnt the Yali language.

The last group went south, to Pasema, they belonged to three different ethnic groups: the Kesing, the Hupla and the Yali.

The son of Hosiek, Balim Lembak, and the son of Lariek, Apmane, went to Heleyoma, near Soba, and built a new ousayowa and performed the ritual of Wam Akilit again. They asked some villagers belonging to the Kobak moiety to hunt phalangers and birds, and villagers belonging to the Bahabol moiety to look for red pandanus. As the Kobak refused to share the games with the Bahabol, a war began between the two moieties and the village was destroyed. The following day, Apmane with the Bahabol and some allied Kobak left the village and never came back. Every time they arrived in a place, a part of the group settled there and started a garden. When they left Soba behind, they began to change their language and to adopt the Yali language. They arrived in Hosahaikma and stayed there until an epidemic killed many of the villagers and forced the rest to move again to a village called Hewik ('where the wind comes'). Hewik is the old name of Ninia, the current subdistrict. Ninia was a name given by the missionaries later. The new settlers met the Yali and began to mix with them.

Different authors (Wilson 1988; Zöllner 1988) provide different versions of these myths. This is partly because the myths are orally transmitted, and the informants are geographically diverse in origin (Angguruk, Ninia or Holuwon): interpretation, elements and plots can be subject to modifications according to new experiences that informants integrate into their stories. It is just such 'audacious innovation' that Gow (2001: 9) refers to when describing the recent history and myths of the Piro Amazonian society. Citing Lévi-Strauss (1981), Gow explains that myths are not simply disturbed by history but rather exist because of history, to generate stability and coherence in a society facing historical disturbances (2000: 11).

In general, the Hupla myth is less detailed and fewer people in the village know the story of the Hupla migration from Seinma to Holuwon. The Hupla have some variations of the story indicating innovation in the face of the intrusion of Christianity in the valley: some stories involve the apparition of a white man from the hole used by Hosiek and Lariek in Seinma, who was forced to go back into the hole, but came again some time later. Another version mentions the presence of a sacred book, obviously referring to the Bible. This feature has been integrated into the general body of Hupla myths. The intrusion of Christianity appears also, if less clearly, in the Yali story of a mythical race between Siluwak, the snake, and Sibine, the hornbill: before death was known, the snake brought a message of rejuvenation and the bird a message of mourning to the humans. Wilson (1988) interprets the myth as the story of evangelisation, with the message of Jesus brought by the snake. Wilson's interpretation has been influenced by his being a former Holuwon missionary, and this myth more probably reflects the disturbance provoked by the recent history of the Yali from Angguruk and of their close neighbours, the Dugum Dani (Gardner and Heider 1968); whichever interpretation one chooses, this myth provides an example of adaptation.

These different myths are highly metaphorical stories and subject to individual re-appropriation and interpretation from each informant. This, in turn, may influence the information researchers collect, but some basic patterns remain, which can be cross-checked in the literature concerning the Yali (Wilson 1988; Zöllner 1988) and between the different villagers.

From these two stories, we can reconstruct that:

1. The Yali came from Angguruk to the west, after a long journey and after settling in several villages during the journey. One characteristic of this journey is that the travel was marked in the collective memory according to the location of each garden the migrants planted on their way.[6]

2. The Hupla came from Seinma to the east and followed the Baliem River to the Heluk Valley. After crossing the last Hupla language village, Soba, they began to speak the Yali language. In many respects (village organisation, presence of important personalities, agricultural practices and other productive activities), the Hupla and the Yali seem superficially quite similar; yet during discussions with villagers from both groups, I observed that people have a strong sense of belonging to separate ethnic groups and of following different moieties.

3. The overall distance for both migrations is short, less than 30 km (Figure 5), but according to these myths, seven or eight generations were required to reach the site of what is now called Holuwon. This is explained by people having settled temporarily many times before arriving at Holuwon.

In fact, encouraged by the missionaries, people moved to the location of Holuwon, in the lower part of the valley, when an airstrip was built in 1973. They migrated even though most preferred to stay in the upper valley (Ninia or Hosahaikma), where water was abundant and mosquitoes and sickness rare.

Both the Yali and the Hupla myth refer to the other group. In the Yali myth, this reference appears twice, when a man is sent to the Hupla territory to bring back sacred stones, and when the mythic pig went to Seinma. The Hupla myth refers directly to groups learning the Yali language and settling with Yali people. These myths imply that, for both groups, there is recognition of the identity of the other and acceptance of the cultural relationships between them. The myths also give explanations about how natural events happened (earthquakes, apparition of lakes, but also the alternation of the sun and the moon), and about the organisation of society (the moiety system, initiations and protection rituals).

Villagers often refer, in their stories and during their daily activities, to the legendary animals cited in the Yali myths (*Dabe*, *Dohlu* and *Siluwak*). The elements of the Yali myth are also present in some specific elements of the landscape, such as big stones, rivers, old villages, magic plants (*e.g.* charmed wild banana) and creatures of the forest. Generally, the villagers are more turned, in their attitude, towards the eastern part (Yali) of their territory than to the western (Hupla). Undoubtedly, there is bias in favour of the Yali customs and society, but this does not mean that the Hupla have been fully integrated into Yali society, and in some cases, Hupla traditions have been adopted by all villagers. All villagers, whatever their origin, often follow some of the Yali cultural aspects, such as stories linked to specific stones or forests in the shared territory, not far from the village, but in some circumstances, Hupla cultural aspects may also prevail. For example, one interesting motif of the Hupla myth is the reference to the fertility ritual carried out before planting crops in the gardens.

The Yali term '*yabuk anum*' translates as 'navel garden' or 'central garden'. Before the Evangelisation of the valley, these ritual plots were created when the villagers decided to establish a big collective garden, which included numerous small plots wherein cultivators from various group lineages worked together. From their name and their topographical position in the gardens, the 'navel gardens' represented the centre of the cultivated space. They were situated in the middle of the gardens, and all the other plots were started around this 'navel garden', which served to protect the villagers from diseases during the harvest, and to allow the crops to grow well. Even during the fallow period, navel gardens were maintained, protected by fences to prevent the incursion of pigs, until the forest grew again and all trace of human activity had disappeared. The navel garden is useful in many ways: as a symbolic starting place for working the soil, to grow food, to protect the cultivated area around it and the cultivators, and to accompany surrounding plots until they return to a state wherein the forest again dominates. It is noteworthy that, according to the informants, this ritual comes from the Hupla, hence, some activities and perceptions adopted in the village are of Hupla origin. These activities were religious and abandoned upon Evangelisation of the valley, but even so, villagers still remember them.

The main feature of the myths is the recognition of the different identities, and of the historical and cultural links between the two groups. Both myths are deeply connected and often refer to each other, through the main figures and aspects of the myths (legendary animals, ancestors and rituals). However, the relationship between identity and territoriality is clearly defined within the Hupla myth, as the migrants began to speak Yali language when they settled close to Holuwon. The Yali's and the Hupla's languages belong to the same family, villagers in Holuwon can speak both languages, but the main language is the Yali. When asked, all villagers admit that the Heluk Valley is located inside Yali territory.

Elements of myths are still present in the daily life of the villagers - with a bias in favour of the Yali ones – and they are often expressed in different representations of the surrounding landscape.

Representations of Landscape

In interviews and daily conversation, the Yali are able to give more names and explanations about the different sites around Holuwon than the Hupla. For example, Alukwanduk, the haunted forest, is a feature of Yali tradition (Boissière 1999a). The story goes that when the Yali were still in Bangga, during initiation rituals, women and non-initiated boys were not allowed to go outside their house: the village was 'closed' during the ceremony. At this time the second sacred house was built and named *Lit Bina*. Three sisters, old enough to be married, were staying together in the same house. Their names were *Punuahwe, Alukwanhwe* and *Nenggalehwe*[7]. Although the village was closed, Nenggalehwe took her sisters to the gardens. When the master of ceremonies went around the village to check if everybody had followed the rules, he found that the three sisters were missing. When they came back to the village, the sisters were put on trial and sentenced to banishment for life from the village. Left together and banished, the three sisters each denied responsibility for what had happened and they fought amongst themselves. When the fighting became so fierce that they drew blood, they decided to separate, after first crossing the

Solo River. Punuahwe stayed in a forest named Punua, near Weawen village. The two remaining sisters travelled together for a while, until they arrived in Wanim Alo village, where they were not allowed to stay because of their transgression. After crossing the Heluk river, they separated: Alukwanhwe staying in a forest close to the river (and near what is now the village of Holuwon), named Alukwanduk (or 'hill of Alukwan'), and Nenggalehwe decided to stay near Worua village, at the meeting point of the Heluk and Baliem rivers, in a forest called Nenggale.

The sisters' transgression of the ritual led to the loss of their social status; they became thereafter *mungguathwe,* or ghosts of women, bad spirits that kill men who get lost in their forests. They can give orders to animals (to phalangers, for example) to change into women to trick the lost men, eventually copulating with them, which results in the death of the men soon after.

This story, which originates from the Yali part of the village, is very important and still believed by all villagers. One night, when I was in Holuwon during the El Niño-Southern Oscillation in 1997 (Boissière 2002), we went near the Heluk River to check for forest fires, crossing the forest of Alukwanduk. The villagers asked me to keep the beam of my torch toward the ground so as not to attract the attention of Alukwanhwe to the forest fire, thereby making it worse.

A further example from my 1996 survey reveals the importance of these myths in Yali and Hupla society. After an epidemic killed many villagers (about twenty people died according to survivors), the entire population of Worua village abandoned the settlement and moved to Holuwon. When trying to understand why this disease had afflicted them, the villagers learned that before the move two young persons had gone into the forest not far from Nenggale, and made love near the river. The villagers concluded that Sigimhwe, a fish and an avatar of Nenggalehwe, had arrived after the young persons had left the riverbank and licked up that which remained from their lovemaking. Sigimhwe liked it so much that it followed them to the village and the villagers began to die. One night in December 1996, after the villagers had moved to Holuwon, some people observed a will-o'-the-wisp near the village. The following day, the priest of the village ordered everyone to stay in the village (just as the sacred man had done during initiation ceremonies) and the villagers spent the day in prayer. After that, Sigimhwe never came back.

These stories show that some traditional beliefs are still present and important in Holuwon, this despite the efforts of the missionaries and the mixing of the two cultures. All villagers, whatever their ethnic origin, and including the priest, were afraid to go outside the village when the will-o'-the-wisp was still present, openly dreading the Sigimhwe creature. Many other stories corroborate this. As a consequence, there are often debates between the villagers, the Hupla complaining that the Yali brought their traditions when they arrived in the valley. Even if the *mungguathwe* are of Yali origin, the Hupla villagers still recognise the strength of these bad spirits and therefore have adopted them. The different stories were explained to me by the men of knowledge of the village (*ab lohon*), and the shamans, who still strongly believe in the reality of these myths.

Village toponymy is based mostly on Yali names. Location names around Holuwon are generally linked to allegories (*e.g. Lahap neahun*, or 'don't look up', relates to a mother who told her son not to look at her from below while she worked in the gardens), myths, or, more simply, Yali plants names (e.g. *Binde-muhu* means 'place with a lot of Binde', a *Cyathea* sp. tree fern; *Sohondek*, is the place were the liana *Sohon*, [*Smilax odoratissima*] is abundant). Toponyms can be descriptive, too, as *Helepalma*, 'place of the stone (*helep*)', *Khwahe ambut*, 'at the end of the *Kwahe* river', or *Muliele*, 'the sound of the leech' etcetera. Finally, some places are named for activities that took place there: *Bisili*, (a traditional wood machete), so named because people used to go there to collect the wood for this tool; *Buakele*, for 'sound of the frog', a place where women often go to collect frogs at night. These are all Yali names.

Here again the traditions, language, and toponomy follow mostly Yali culture, even if the Hupla are recognised as an independent line with their own stories and traditions. These differences between the two poles making up Holuwon society are even more obvious when we study the role and knowledge of the shamans, the *Hwalahun*. In the society, these personalities control special knowledge relating to the forest and the uses of plants and animals.

Shamanism: A Reflection of Inequality

An analysis of shamanic (*hwalahun*) roles and functions in Holuwon society reveals, possibly more than any other factor, elements of distinction between the Yali and the Hupla, and can provide a better understanding of the relationship between the two ethnicities. According to Perrin (1998: 10), the shaman's role is to restore ecological, biological, and social equilibrium. He stands between two worlds: the human world, participating in daily village life, working in the gardens and acting as a medicine man; and the world of the dead, whose spirits might come back to disturb, even to kill, humans. Moreover, shamanism is diverse (Hamayon 1988: 13), differing in different societies, and changing as each society's relationship with other societies changes and its own economy changes. According to Hamayon (1988: 27), if the shaman fixes problems coming from different disorders and answers to different constraints, this represents his function, but not his *raison d'être*, which has its origins in the cosmology of any given society. This explains why the Yali and Hupla communities in Holu-won have shamans with similar functions, but with a *raison d'être* that takes its origin in different, but connected, cosmologies.

Descola and Lory (1988) compared the role of shamans in their social context between two societies, the Achuar from Amazonia and the Baruya from

Papua New Guinea. Many similarities are found between them, related to the medicinal curing power of the shamans but also to their capacity to fight using magic, this duality confers an ambiguity to their function: the possibility to both cure and to destroy a society. However, the second function, the ability to kill magically, is reserved for war, and in this way finds acceptance in the society (Descola and Lory 1988: 85). A similar situation exists in Holuwon. Regardless of their ethnicity, villagers are afraid to meet the *hwalahun* because of their powers, and in the men's house, no one dares to place himself before a shaman when he sits close to the fire. There are only a few remaining *hwalahun* in Holuwon, and some are in hiding, especially those of Hupla origin, because they are ashamed of their functions since the evangelisation of the village. Currently, there are no actively practising shamans.

During my fieldwork in Holuwon (Boissière 1999a), a total of 115 plants were recorded according to their uses by the *hwalahun* during different rituals. These plants are no longer used for their original functions, except some medicinal ones, but even in this case, villagers prefer to go to the small dispensary whenever possible. Even if not used anymore for rituals, some plants are still feared because of their potential destructive power. A wild banana called *don* in Yali provides a good example. During wars with the *Pasema* people, this banana was used to send spells to the enemy. The *hwalahun* uprooted a young shoot of *don*, opened the sheath of the petiole, put some pig fat in it and closed it again. He took the plant to the river, far from his village, and pointed the roots in the direction of the enemy's village. This wild banana was considered very dangerous, and even now, when a villager clears a new garden in a forest where this banana grows, he is very careful to avoid damaging any part of this banana. If a part of the banana is spoiled, the villager can become sick and even die.

There are many other examples that show the importance plants held and sometimes still hold in magical spells. However, by comparing the importance of different types of plants and birds for shamans from each group, some major differences in the purpose and manifestation of shamanism can be ascertained.

The Division of Botanical Knowledge in the Heluk Valley

Two classes of organisms were most often used by the *hwalahun* during the various rituals: plants (trees, shrubs and herbs) and birds. Soil, phalangers, stones, water and pigs parts are among a variety of other resources used in rituals. Notwithstanding, plants and birds were most frequently used by both Yali and Hupla shamans and, hence, are useful for comparison. All plants and birds used for shamanism have been analysed and classified according to specific use: shamans identified 26 categories of plant uses and 14 of bird uses.

The most common plant uses for both ethnic groups in Holuwon are curative (Table 8.1), suggesting that the most important shamanic function is curing illness. The most common plant use is for medicine[8] (21), followed by protection against epidemics (14). About 30 per cent of the identified plants are therefore used for curing, whereas only 5.7 per cent (7 species) are related to war activities. Even if the shaman is a frightening and powerful member of Yali and Hupla communities, his first and foremost function is to help villagers, to cure them and prevent the epidemics that can destroy the village.

There is a marked difference in the number of plants used by the respective shamans: the Yali shamans use more plants than the Hupla. Some Hupla shamans even admitted that the Yali *hwalahun* were more powerful than the Hupla, presumably by virtue of their greater knowledge of plant characteristics. Both the Yali and Hupla shamans used some plants for similar rituals, such as ritual against incest and protection against epidemics (Table 8.1). With the exception of one ritual category, medicinal plants, in which the Hupla named more plants than the Yali (11 versus 10), Yali shamans showed greater plant knowledge (67 plants are used exclusively by Yali shamans, whereas only 21 are used exclusively by Hupla).

Bird use showed a different pattern (Table 8.2). Among the 47 birds used by shamans, 20 were used exclusively by the Hupla and only 11 by the Yali. The Hupla shamans recognised more bird species than the Yali, particularly birds used for protection against magic attack by enemies. It seems that the use of birds and bird parts in their rituals is a pattern of the Hupla. The principal bird, common to Hupla and Yali, is *sibine,* the hornbill. Formerly, feathers from its wings and/or tails were used to make the *hwalasum,* the bag of the *hwalahun.* Hornbill guano was planted in the hole of the sacred house post and the bill was an important element in rituals and carried about everywhere in the *hwalasum.*

Plants and birds might have more than one use, in more than one ritual. For example, *salema* (*Evodia elleryana* Rutaceae), is an important tree, much used in rituals. It was carried everywhere by the shaman, worn as a bangle around his wrist to give him strength. This plant was also used for the initiation of young children; to cure arrow wounds; to prevent attack by spirits of the dead; to bind the spirit of the dead during cremation; and for the most important and power-ful curing ritual for villagers afflicted with malaria. During this ritual, the shaman built a small house called *salamak* in the forest, where the ill person stayed until the end of the ceremony.

Another plant, called *hobut aek* (*Decaspermum sp.* Myrtaceae), was used as a 'philosopher's stone'. Its leaves were eaten by the *hwalahun* in a specific way and, with the appropriate spells, the excrements of the shaman became, after some weeks, a valuable cowry[9].

Much more could be written about the various uses of the plants and birds recorded, but for the purposes of our discussion what is important is the com-parison of the general patterns of shamans' knowledge and how it relates to the effect of migration and hybridization on traditional knowledge. Shamanism is no longer practiced in Holuwon: Evangelisation has caused its disappearance.

Table 8.1: 115 plants used by shamans in Holuwon, according to use category and ethnic group.

Use	Yali	Hupla	Both	Total
Ritual				
All rituals	1	0	0	1
Ritual for end of red pandanus taboo	0	1	3	4
Incest ritual	3	0	5	8
Boy's initiation ritual	6	0	1	7
Hwalahun initiation ritual	6	0	0	6
Ritual for cannibalism	2	2	0	4
Ritual to begin house construction	0	0	2	2
Ritual to treat malaria	0	0	2	2
Ritual for war	3	0	4	7
Ritual to fight against spirits	0	0	3	3
Magic				
General Magic	9	4	0	13
Magic for dogs	1	0	0	1
Magic for a widower to remarry	6	0	0	6
Magic to kill enemies	1	1	0	2
General Medicinal	10	11	0	21
Medicine for pigs	0	0	1	1
Medicine for wounds	4	0	0	4
Protection				
General Protection	1	1	0	2
Protection against dead enemies	0	0	2	2
Protection against enemies	2	0	0	2
Protection against epidemics	5	1	8	14
Protection against mythic porcupine	4	0	0	4
Other				
Used as ritual rope	0	0	2	2
Used to make cord for ritual houses	0	0	1	1
Materials to build sacred house	1	0	0	1
Prohibited to young boys	2	0	0	2
Total	67	21	34	122*

* Some plants were used in more than one ritual.

Table 8.2: The 47 birds used by shamans in Holuwon, according to use category and ethnic group.

Use	Yali	Hupla	Both	Total
Ritual				
All rituals	0	0	2	2
Boy's Initiation ritual	4	1	2	7
Hwalahun initiation ritual	2	0	0	2
Ritual for war	0	2	0	2
Ritual to fight against spirits	2	0	0	2
Magic				
Magic for widower to remarry	0	0	4	4
Magic to kill enemies	1	3	0	4
Medicinal				
General medicinal	0	0	1	1
Protection				
General protection	0	6	0	6
Protection against dead enemies	0	1	0	1
Protection against epidemics	1	3	1	5
Other				
For widow to serve new husband	1	0	0	1
Materials to build sacred house	0	3	2	5
To calm bad behaviour	0	1	0	1
Total	11	20	12	43*

*Four birds are of unknown origin

However, as I explained, some plants are still known for their magical power and feared for it by all the villagers. On one hand, these practices contribute to the general history of the two groups (some rituals led by shamans are even described in the myths), on the other hand, shamanic power, rituals and spells were mostly kept secret from the other villagers. However, despite their secret nature, some rituals were shared between Hupla and Yali shamans.

Information on the origins of the knowledge on a particular plant or bird was principally provided by Yali shamans who knew which plant was exclusively used by the Hupla shamans and which one was shared by the two groups. This shows that hybridisation has taken place within the shamanic community itself, even long before Christianity created new relationships between the villagers. If the exact rituals were never communicated to non-shaman villagers, bridges were made to some extend between shamans from the two ethnic groups.

The differences of shamanic knowledge have been highlighted between the two groups, with the Yali shamans using more plants, and the Hupla more birds. The recognition by all the villagers, both Hupla and Yali, of the value and richness of the knowledge of the Yali shaman is clearly a sign of inequality between the two groups. All the villagers recognise the strength and predominance of the Yali shamans to fight enemies, diseases, to cure and to send bad spells.

Conclusion

The data presented here suggest that knowledge of forest landscapes and resources may be transformed by hybridization with another ethnic group. Rather than being dictated solely by the environment, strong cultural and historical elements determine the ecological knowledge of these groups. The integration of the two ethnic groups in the hybrid zone, the village of Holuwon, has led to changes affecting knowledge of myths, toponomy, plant uses and shamanic influence. I have shown, using different qualitative and quantitative approaches, the dynamics of knowledge sharing between two groups, which seem to have relatively minor power differences.

One of the main questions was if a predominance of one group over the other was observable, in terms of social organisation, language, ecological knowledge, and shamanism, all these cultural features being part of the collective knowledge within a shared landscape. From participant observation of the village and local livelihoods, I found that no particular distinction could be made between the two groups: the social organisation is identical, as are the subsistence activities. Mutual integration of the two ethnic groups has occurred progressively, through marriages, exchanges, trading, other connections and wars. Probably because they are still dependent upon small-scale agriculture and gathering for their subsistence, knowledge of plants useful for day-to-day life remains important to all villagers, regardless of ethnicity, and men and women alike recognise many forest plants. Of the seven hundred plant species inventoried from a study of twenty plots, villagers were able to name more than 80 percent (Boissière 1999a). The plants are used for fibre, dyeing, rope-making, food, various hunting functions, light and heavy construction, firewood and medicine. The greatest loss of knowledge concerns traditions and religion, especially that related to shamanism, rituals and the magic use of plants.

However, when another method is applied, that of migration myth analysis, a distinction between the two groups becomes evident. Myths represent a flexible knowledge, which is profoundly influenced by the recent history of both groups, as demonstrated by the fact that each myth refers to the other ethnic group. Each myth includes and accounts for the current cohabitation of the two groups, and refers to the point in time when they came together in one common landscape, the Heluk Valley. If we refer only to the myths, it is clear that both groups are represented and recognised by one another.

This said, the respective cultural backgrounds and cosmogony are ingrained in the myths, and through them the differences in the two cultures become apparent. An important aspect of the migration stories is the association of language with territoriality and identity. The Hupla myth acknowledges that Hupla migrants entered a new territory and, for that reason, they adopted the Yali language – even if they still speak the Hupla language sometimes – indicating Hupla cultural transformation in favour of Yali.

Further evidence of the predominance of one group over the other is confirmed by the analysis of landscape features and toponymy, where almost all elements of the landscape close to the village, including haunted forests, stones, and rivers, are named and explained from a Yali perspective. Interviews with Hupla residents show that they have accepted this situation and adopted it.

Through semi-structured and unstructured interviews about the role and value of shamanism, I have found that although the performance of shamanic rituals may be gone from Holuwon, their memory survives and all villagers still respect the shamans. The invisible features of the shamanic world are ever present in the daily life of the village: ghosts and bad spirits are still active, and whatever the villagers' ethnicity, be it Yali or Hupla, the spirits are still real. Interviews with shamans about their rituals, their use and knowledge of plants and animals, have shown that shamans from each group are specialised in different activities (e.g. more defensive or curative), and features (plants or birds). Nevertheless, they have certain practices in common, and some knowledge of the magic power of the other group. Moreover, knowledge sharing is more important between initiated shamans, regardless of ethnicity, than with non-initiated villagers.

The biggest inequalities in the relationships between the two communities are found in the production of shamanic knowledge. The greater power of the Yali shamans was recognised by a former Hupla shaman, during informal discussions, and by other Hupla villagers, who admitted that Yali shamans were more often requested – even by remote villagers of the valley – than the Hupla. This may be one of the reasons for the relative vulnerability of the Hupla to the negative effects of evangelisation.

The two groups have adapted differently to 'modernity' and to the new religion. The Hupla do not want to hear or to talk about the old stories and their shamans are ashamed of their ancient activities, which they now consider as mere tricks on their credulous brethren. In contrast, the Yali are still proud of their past. Although more research needs to be carried out to fully understand these dynamics, it is possible that the Hupla's already weakened sense of identity has made them more vulnerable to the influence of Christianity.

As the discussion above demonstrates, to fully understand the interaction between the Yali and Hupla, and its effects on traditional knowledge, it must be considered through multidisciplinary and dynamic (historical) approaches, centred on the valley landscape. Data collected from ethnobiological surveys of plants and social practices of West Papua can tell us much about the nature and origins of the hybridization of indigenous knowledge. Identification of scientific names, common names and plant uses are crucial not only to obtaining accurate information on shamanic rituals, knowledge of which is threatened, but also for understanding and interpreting the stories and myths of migration and how one group encountered another. Meanwhile, multi-method approaches are important for understanding the wider context in which plant and animal knowledge is transmitted and maintained. Hence studying environmental knowledge by using this approach gives a more nuanced and comprehensive perspective than any one of these methods on its own. It allows new and broader applications for ethnobiology, enabling the elucidation of the history of a given society, its migration, and an improved understanding of the complexity of the dynamics of shamanic knowledge.

Notes

1. For the purposes of my discussion, I define ethnicity to mean groups of individuals belonging to a shared linguistic, cultural and territorial group (Taylor 1992).
2. The term 'West Papua' refers to the western half of the island of New Guinea. While Papua New Guinea is an independent nation on the eastern half of the island, West Papua is part of Indonesia.
3. No precise data exists on the time the valley was first occupied. However, based on interviews, I estimate it to be a minimum of 6 generations ago.
4. As there are no official census data for the region, the exact number of villagers according to the ethnic group is not available.
5. Yeli Asingip are black ritual stones that are anointed with pig fat and were put inside the ritual houses, or *Ousayowa,* to stabilise the earth around the villages.
6. The garden is the centre of Yali identity (Boissière 1999a: 360). The Yali territory is organised around a large and permanent cluster of gardens, and only the settlements (villages and hamlets) can move around, along the time.
7. *Hwe* in Yali means 'woman'.
8. I consider medicinal plants as plants used to cure illness (malaria, flu, stomach aches, etcetera).
9. The cowry shell was used as money during pre-contact period.

Bibliography

Agrawal, A. 1995. 'Dismantling the divide between indigenous and scientific knowledge' *Development and Change* 26: 413-439.

Bidou, P. 1992 (1991). 'Mythe. Nature du mythe' in P. Bonte and M. Izard, eds., *Dictionnaire de l'ethnologie et de l'anthropologie.* Paris: PUF, pp.498-500.

Boissière, M. 1999a. *Ethnobiologie et rapports à l'environnement des Yali d'Irian Jaya (Indonésie),* thèse de sciences, Université Montpellier 2.

Boissière, M. 1999b. 'Gestion d'un terroir forestier par des cultivateurs Yali (Irian Jaya Indonésie)' in S. Bahuchet S., Bley D., Pagézy H., Vernazza-Licht N. eds, *L'homme et la forêt tropicale,* colloque de la Société d'écologie humaine. Marseille: Travaux de la Société d'Écologie Humaine, 327-346.

Boissière, M. 1999c. 'La patate douce et l'arachide, transformation d'une agriculture yali' *Journal d'Agriculture Traditionnelle et de Botanique Appliquée* 41(1): 131-156.

Boissière, M. 2002. 'The impact of drought and humanitarian aid on a Yali village in West Papua' *Asia Pacific Viewpoint,* 43 (3) décembre: 293-309.

Boissière M. 2003. 'La mémoire des jardins : pratiques agricoles et transformations sociales en Nouvelle-Guinée' *Annales de la Fondation Fyssen,* No.18, pp.111-128.

Boissière, M. and Y. Purwanto, 2007. 'The agricultural systems of Papua' in A.J. Marshall and
    B.M. Beehler, eds., *The Ecology of Papua* . Singapore: Periplus Editions, pp.1125-1148.

Cook, C.D.T. 1995. *The Amung Way: The Subsistence Strategies, the Knowledge and the Dilemna of
    the Tsinga People of Irian Jaya, Indonesia.* Ph.D. dissertation, Southern Illinois University at
    Carbondale, Illinois.

Descola P. and J.L. Lory. 1988. 'Les guerriers de l'invisible: sociologie comparative de l'agression
    chamanique en Papouasie Nouvelle-Guinée (Baruya) et en Haute-Amazonie (Achuar)'
    Voyages chamaniques 2, in *L'Ethnographie,* 87-88 (2-3): 85-111.

Dove, M.R. 2000. 'The Life-Cycle of Indigenous Knowledge, and the Case of Natural Rubber
    Production' in R. Ellen, P. Parkes, and A. Bicker, eds., *Indigenous Environmental Knowledge
    and Its Transformations. Critical Anthropological Perspectives.* Amsterdam: Harwood
    Academic Publishers, pp. 213-251.

Ellen, R., H. Harris. 2000. 'Introduction' in R. Ellen, P. Parkes, and A. Bicker, eds., *Indigenous
    Environmental Knowledge and Its Transformations. Critical Anthropological Perspectives.*
    Amsterdam: Harwood Academic Publishers, pp. 1-33.

Gardiner, S. 1987. 'Highland Horticultural Development, Irian Jaya. Jayapura' BPPD-
    UNDP/IBRD Project. Library of Congress microfiche.

Gardner, R. and K.G. Heider. 1968. *Gardens of War. Life and Death in the New Guinea Stone Age.*
    New York: Random House.

Gow, P. 2001. *An Amazonian Myth and its History.* New York: Oxford University Press.

Gupta, A. 1998. *Postcolonial Developments: Agriculture in the Making of Modern India.* Durham,
    NC: Duke University Press.

Gupta, A. and J. Ferguson. 1992. 'Beyond "Culture": Space, Identity, and the Politics of
    Difference' *Cultural Anthropology,* 7(1): 6-23.

Hamayon, R. 1988. 'Des chamanes au chamanisme' *Voyages chamaniques deux,* in *L'Ethnographie,*
    87-88 (2-3): 13-48.

Kalland, A. 2000. 'Indigenous Knowledge: Prospects and Limitations' in R. Ellen, P. Parkes, and
    A. Bicker, eds., *Indigenous Environmental Knowledge and Its Transformations. Critical
    Anthropological Perspectives.* Amsterdam: Harwood Academic Publishers, pp.319-335.

Koch, K.-F. 1974. *War and Peace in Jalémo. The Management of Conflict in Highland New
    Guinea.* Cambridge, MA.: Harvard University Press.

Lemonnier, P. 1990. *Guerres et Festins. Paix, échanges et compétition dans les Highlands de Nouvelle-
    Guinée.* Paris: Editions de la Maison des Sciences de l'Homme, Lévi-Strauss, C. 1981. *The
    Naked Man.* London: Jonathan Cape.

Pétrequin, P. and A.M. Pétrequin. 1993. *Ecologie d'un outil: la hache de pierre en Irian Jaya.* Paris:
    CNRS éditions.

Perrin, M., 1995 (1998). *Le chamanisme.* Que sais-je? coll. Presses Universitaires de France Paris.

Pospisil, L. 1963. *Kapauku Papuan Economy.* Yale University Publications in Anthropology
    No.67. New Haven, CT.: Department of Anthropology, Yale University.

Purwanto, Y. 1997. *Gestion de la biodiversité: relations aux plantes et dynamiques végétales chez les
    Dani de la vallée de la Baliem en Irian Jaya, Indonésie.* Thèse Univ. Paris 6. Sillitoe, P. 1998a.
    The Development of Indigenous Knowledge. *Current Anthropology.* 39 (2): 223-252.

Sillitoe, P. 1998b. What, Know Natives? Local Knowledge in Development. *Social Anthropology* 6
    (2): 203-220.

Silzer, J.P., H.H. Clouse, 1991. *Index of Irian Jaya languages.* A special publication of *IRIAN,
    Bulletin of Irian Jaya.* UNCEN and SIL.

Taylor, A.C. 1992 (1991). 'Ethnie' in P. Bonte and M. Izard, eds., *Dictionnaire de l'ethnologie et
    de l'anthropologie.* Paris: Presses Universitaires de France, pp. 242-244.

Thomas, N. 1996. 'Cold Fusion' *American Anthropologist,* 98 (1), pp. 9-16.

Wilson, J. D. 1988. (1999). *Scripture in an Oral Culture: The Yali of Irian Jaya.* Adapted from a
    dissertation, Faculty of Divinity, University of Edinburgh.

Zollner, S., 1988. *The Religion of the Yali in the Highlands of Irian Jaya.* Melanesian Institute for
    Pastoral and Socio-economic Service.

Chapter 9

Reproduction and Development of Expertise Within Communities of Practice

A Case Study of Fishing Activities in South Buton (Southeast Sulawesi, Indonesia)

Daniel Vermonden

Introduction

At the root of this chapter lies an apparent paradox noticed during my research with fishermen in South Buton (Sulawesi, Indonesia). The Convention on Biological Diversity states that: 'traditional (ecological) knowledge (TEK) is transmitted orally from generation to generation' (article 8 (j)). Yet, even though, by using structured interviews, I was able to elicit and record fishermen's extensive knowledge of fishes and, more generally, of the marine environment, during two years of participant observation, I rarely observed oral transmission of fishing knowledge or techniques. This contradiction gives rise to several questions about the nature of TEK in this context, including where fishermen's knowledge comes from, whether it results from some kind of transmission and, if so, what the process of this transmission might be.

Besides oral instruction, another process of social transmission is often suggested by TEK proponents: imitation (Ellen and Harris 2000: 4). However, promoting imitation as a process of TEK transmission in addition to oral instruction does not solve the question of TEK transmission. Rather, it raises questions about the nature of TEK and the relation between knowledge and practice. In considering that TEK is transmitted through oral instruction, these questions are implicitly answered as follows: (1) knowledge is lexically encoded and (2) practice consists in the application of this propositional knowledge. But if imitation is also a process of TEK transmission, the above assumptions are not self-evident anymore. Therefore, it is necessary to further explore the process of learning.

Richerson and Boyd (2005) propose an elaborate model of cultural transmission that takes into account both teaching and imitation. This model is based on the distinction between social learning (by imitation and teaching) and individual learning (by trial and error). Learning consists of the 'adoption' or 'acquisition' of 'traits' or 'elements' – beliefs, ideas, values, attitudes, programs – by individuals. For example, 'Making a living in the Arctic requires specialised knowledge: how to make weatherproof clothing, how to provide light and heat for cooking, how to build kayaks and umiak, how to hunt seals through holes in the sea ice' (Richerson and Boyd 2005: 128-9). These 'how to' are contents, information stored in the mind of individuals. Therefore, imitation and teaching in this model of transmission are different paths that lead to the same result: the acquisition of the information necessary for practice. In this framework, TEK may still be conceived as a corpus of information that is passed on from one generation to the other.

However, several studies and theoretical developments concerning knowledge, practice, perception and learning challenge the assumptions on which Richerson and Boyd's model is based (Bourdieu 1977, 1990; Merleau-Ponty 1962; Gibson 1979; Delbos and Jorion 1984; Ingold 2000, 2001; Lave and Wenger 1991; Wenger 1999; Rogoff et al. 2003; Lave 1988; Chevalier 1991; Martinelli 1996). More specifically, they challenge the assumptions that: (1) individuals and environment are discrete and pre-given entities; (2) knowledge is information about the environment; (3) knowledge is a content owned by individuals and stored in the mind, (4) practice is the application of knowledge and knowledge necessarily precedes practice.

Alternative models of the learning process have been developed. Ingold (Ingold 2000: 36-7, 157-71, 243-87, 373-91) relies mainly on Bourdieu's theory of practice (Bourdieu 1977, 1990) and on Merleau-Ponty's and Gibson's works on perception (Merleau-Ponty 1962; Gibson 1979)[1] to argue that learning does not consist of the acquisition of a content/information but in the development of skills, a process that involves the organism-in-the-environment as 'indivisible totality' (Ingold 2000: 19). Indeed, the world/environment is not an entity in front of us about which we hold information. The world is not in front of us but, rather, we are 'in the world': I form with the world a single and dynamic entity, a 'being-in-the-world' (in the sense of Merleau-Ponty 1962). The organism and the world emerge together progressively as we engage within it. Expertise is not an accumulation of information but the capacity to perceive and the 'ability to co-ordinate perception and action' (Ingold 2000: 356). In this perspective, transmission consists first of all of providing a context and guidance for the 'education of attention' (Gibson 1979: 254).

The ethnographically rooted, situated approach to learning also emphasises learning as participation in practice (e.g. Rogoff et al. 2003, Lave and Wenger 1991). Learning is not an explicit goal for participants and is not separated from practice, nor does knowledge need to precede practice. Rather learning is a by-product of participation. Participation provides motivation for learning and access to the resources for it simultaneously. The concept of legitimate peripheral participation (Lave and Wenger 1991) aims to call attention to the social dimension of learning. In this perspective, learning is inevitably a process of progressive incorporation within a community of practitioners, from periphery to centre. According to Lave and Wenger (1999), knowledge is not acquired and stored in individual minds but developed and reproduced within communities of practice (CoP). Wenger (1999) develops the concept of CoP further, leading him to place emphasis on the relationship between participation in practice, construction of identity and the formation of meaning.

These theoretical developments invite a redefinition of the question of TEK transmission. We cannot only consider the transmission of a corpus of knowledge/information because TEK only exists as a corpus as an artefact of the investigation method: elicitation leads necessarily to the recording of propositional knowledge. It is nonsensical to then ask how this corpus is transmitted, as the corpus is the product of the elicitation itself. However, elicited knowledge can serve as a gateway to the fisherman's world. In addition, from the above discussion, it appears that there is no simple relation between knowledge and expertise: we cannot reduce the development and reproduction of expertise to acquisition of knowledge by an individual. Rather, we need to investigate more broadly how expertise is developed and reproduced in a particular social and ecological setting. In order to understand the process of transmission, the above theoretical developments invite us to shift our attention from the content to the configurations of practice, the interactions and trajectories within communities of practice and the 'structural' transformation of the whole person-in-the-environment.

In this paper, I explore these issues through an analysis of a specific ethnographic case, that of fishing activities in South Buton. I consider three different kinds of fishing activities – trap fishing, angling and shark finning.

Methods

Buton is the twentieth biggest island of the Indonesian Archipelago. It is located in Southeast Sulawesi province, at the door of the Moluccas, also known as the Spice Islands. A single language, called cia-cia, is spoken in South Buton. (Figure 9.1). I conducted ethnographic fieldwork in Buton for twenty-

Figure 9.1: Map of South Buton with its location in Indonesia

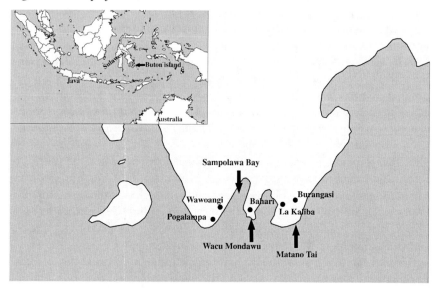

four months, between 1999 and 2002, mostly in Bahari village but I also made shorter visits (from a few hours to three weeks) to the other coastal villages of South Buton and two communities of Bahari migrants on other islands. I used a combination of participant observation and interviews (structured and unstructured). Investigation focused largely, but not exclusively, on sea-related activities (fishing, boat building and navigation).

I compiled a file for each fishing technique, including the following information: vernacular name, etymology, instruments (including origin of materials and process of fabrication), products exploited (with vernacular names), variants (if any), time (in relation to day, tide, lunar phase and season as well as possible specific weather conditions), places (and variations with time), team (minimum, mean and maximum number of participants, organisation of the team, sex and age range if relevant), duration (within both subsistence and commercial frameworks), history (historical depth and transformations), popularity (in the past and now) and sequence of implementation. I completed a total of almost one hundred files.[2] For gathering this information, I relied on structured and unstructured interviews with specialists (thirty-five persons, cross-checking the information between them), video recording and viewing with the participants, as well as observation of and participation in the techniques myself (both inshore and offshore[3]). I also collected twelve biographies of fishermen from different generations through structured and unstructured interviews spread over the fieldwork period.

Investigation of fishermen's knowledge about marine fauna started with a collection of local fish names and identifications (including sharks and rays), using illustrations. I showed a set of illustrations (from Allen 1997) to six fishermen from three different villages and a group of Bahari fishermen.[4] Using a discursive technique, I elicited not only the names provided but also the information related to the process itself, e.g. attention to specific elements of the illustration, additional information required by the fisherman and fishermen's remarks. Sometimes, when working with the group, the process of identification involved a discussion between fishermen present. In these cases, I recorded the arguments put forward by the different actors when defending their identification. Then I compared the lists and identified the differences between the fishermen's responses. I conducted additional interviews to investigate the nature of these differences (e.g. problems of identification, of synonymy, and of developmental stage). I also established a list of vernacular fish names that served as a basis for eliciting fishermen's knowledge about each fish: techniques used to catch the fish, place (and depth), time (of the day, lunar phase and season), behaviour, folk classification (and criteria on which this classification is based) and other remarks concerning the fish (e.g. taste, whether they are dangerous). In this way, I developed a detailed understanding of fishermen's knowledge of fish species and the techniques used to catch them.

Fishing activities in South Buton

Inhabitants of South Buton villages traditionally gain their subsistence from a combination of garden cultivation and fishing. Each household cultivates one or several gardens within the village territory. Maize and cassava are the two staple subsistence crops, complemented by cash crops, such as tomato, onions, bananas and cashew nuts. Garden productivity is limited by limestone soils (especially in the south eastern villages) and the long dry season associated with the southeast monsoon.

Fishing is the main source of proteins and also a source of household income. A diverse set of techniques are used to harvest fish. These techniques can be grouped into the following categories: angling, trapping (including fixed and portable traps as well as tidal weirs), collecting (including shell fishing), poisoning, netting, rod and line fishing, trolling, spearing and kite fishing. Among these techniques, some are widely distributed among South Buton coastal communities, (e.g. night and day collecting on the reef or angling with bait) while others have a more limited distribution. Environmental specificities partly explain fishing technique distribution. For example, fishing platforms[5] exploiting pelagic fishes (e.g. anchovies and sardines) are concentrated in Sampolawa Bay, where a river flows into the sea. However, fishing technique distribution cannot only be explained by the natural environment. Historical and social factors also influence the distribution. Kite fishing in South Buton is practised exclusively by Wawoangi fishermen. One of the best spots for the technique is the shore in front of Bahari village. However, despite the fact that Wawoangi fishermen kitefish in view of Bahari village, giving the villagers ample opportunity to observe the practice, they do not 'adopt' the technique. A Bahari villager acknowledged that he tried once this technique while he was in Maluku for a trap fishing expedition but 'that was just to give it a try'. Indeed, no Bahari villager has engaged seriously in the practice of kite fishing, as they consider themselves to lack legitimacy to practice and specialise in kite fishing: 'it is not one of our techniques'. By this, they mean that expertise for this technique is owned by Wawoangi fishermen. Gaining expertise in kite fishing would require access to this expertise. However, for Wawoangi fishermen, this expertise is an asset and helps to define their identity. They have no reason to let Bahari fishermen have access to it. In addition, for Bahari fishermen, requesting this access would also mean placing oneself in a position of inferiority, at the periphery of a CoP whose centre of expertise is located in Wawoangi. This would clearly be a challenge to their own identity. This example demonstrates that practice is not separated from social identity, a point made by Lave and Wenger (1991: 34-7). The opportunity to observe a technique does not automatically lead to its adoption; the legitimacy of the access also plays a role.

Men and women practise different techniques and women are less specialised than men. Women's fishing activities are limited to the exploitation of the reef flat. The total array of fishing techniques available to men is more diverse but each fisherman specialises in a limited number of techniques. His goal is to provide his family with a regular supply of fish and, for 'professional' fishermen, to earn money.

Although all types of fishing techniques require their own CoP, I focus on three case studies: portable trap fishing, angling, and shark finning. Each of these techniques offers important insights into how fishing knowledge is transmitted.

Portable Trap Fishing

Several kinds of traps are made and used in South Buton, corresponding to different fishing techniques. A small one, called *kukulu*, is baited and used on the reef flat by women for catching damselfish (Pomacentridae), small wrasses (Labridae) and small emperors (Lethrinidae). The bigger and semi-spherical *ngkalolobu* traps are also baited and used for catching triggerfishes (Balistidae) and spinefoots (Siganidae) on the reef bench. A conical trap called *kadhepe* is used for catching fishes hiding under the stones of the reef flat. Finally, there are quadrangular traps, on which I focus here.

There are different types and sizes of quadrangular traps (Figure 9.2). Baskets are distinguished by weaving technique, which may form rectangular (*kampi*) or polygonal (*salamata*) mesh. A second major distinction relates to the size of the traps. Small ones (*katambuni*) are set on the reef flat and are surrounded by stones. This fishing technique is for subsistence fishing. Larger traps (*kantano*) are set on the reef slope, to depth of maximum thirty five meters for commercial fishing .

Figure 9.2: Different types and sizes of quadrangular fishing traps

According to elder fishermen, collective trap fishing was a major commercial activity in South Buton. It continues to be practised, but has suffered a decline as new alternatives with better profit potential have become increasingly available throughout the second half of the twentieth century. During collective trap fishing, three or four fishermen form a team headed by a trap fishing specialist called a *parika*. Teams are composed of relatives usually living close to one another, preferably (if ego is the *parika*) ego, his sons and sons-in-law (who are also ego's relatives due to the practice of endogamy). The group constructs between twenty and thirty *kantano* traps, some of *kampi* type and others of *salamata* type. These traps are set on the reef bench and slope and checked every two or three days.

The *parika* is responsible for ensuring the success of the activity and his expertise is evaluated on this criterion. He decides when to begin the different stages of trap construction (cutting the bamboo trees, preparing the bamboo strips, weaving them and finally assembling the traps) and use. For each stage, he chooses a moment that augurs well. At sea, he also decides the place where the traps are lowered. After having collected fishes from the traps, he is the one who shares the catch on the beach between the different team members (if it is not sold to the market). In addition, he manages relations with the invisible *ompuno tai*, the 'guardian of the sea' who owns and controls the sea resources of the area. His relationship with the *ompuno tai* consists of an annual offering of some food on the beach and at sea and requesting that he help ensure a success-ful outcome to the fishing activities. Finally, the *parika* is in charge of the inter-pretation and resolution of any negative outcome. He must find the origin of the problem and a solution to it.

Being a *parika* for a given fishing activity is not only a position within a fish-ing team. It is also part of one's identity and social position within the local com-munity. Indeed, given that fishing involves a relationship with non-visible and non-human entities, the capacity to ensure fishing success simultaneously attests to one's knowledge of the world and its invisible entities and one's capacity to maintain good relationships with them. In addition, as it is only the more important fishing techniques that have *parikas*, it seems that there exists a cor-relation between the existence of a socially recognised expertise and the impor-tance of ensuring an activity's success. Besides trap fishing, there are also *parika* specialists for tidal weir fishing and 'tide-blocking' with nets. 'Tide-blocking' with nets may involve all the village inhabitants, especially during the biggest tides of the year. In this case, success is important because of the number of peo-ple involved and the limited opportunity to implement the technique. In the case of tidal weirs and portable trap fishing, it is the investment in time and effort for preparing the fishing instrument(s) that is significant. Therefore, for these fishing activities, failure may have critical consequences and relying on socially recognised experts may be considered a means to reduce that danger.

The prestige associated with a *parika*'s expertise depends on the importance of the activity within the local community. Hence, the status of the trap fishing *parika* was more prestigious when collective trap fishing was still the village major commercial fishing activity than it is now that new opportunities with better profit potential have become available (shark finning for example, see below). As a consequence, for young people, becoming a trap fishing *parika* is no longer an attractive endeavour in the framework of their career as fisherman. Moreover, as fewer people are involved in trap fishing and as the practice becomes less intensive, reproduction of *parika* expertise is a matter of concern.

When I asked how a person becomes a trap fishing *parika*, particularly how expertise was transmitted, the answer was that a *parika* only transmitted his knowledge when he was close to dying and usually only to just one of his rela-tives. I was not allowed to learn what information is transmitted at this occasion as it is kept secret. However, we need to take into account that the person cho-sen by the *parika* is also said to be the one who most often joins him in his fish-ing activities and displays a high interest in his expertise. Therefore, it is clear that the transmission of information at this crucial point only comes after a much longer process of enskilment, a process which I explore here.

Involvement in trap fishing does not start with learning to make traps and, thus, does not follow the same sequence of tasks as the technique itself, i.e. preparing the materials and assembling traps, installing them on the shore and then collecting the fishes. Indeed, from the age of six or seven, children begin accompanying their father or older brothers to collect the fishes trapped in *katambuni* traps on the reef flat. From the age of eight, they may carry out this task autonomously. By doing so, they provide their own contribution to the trap fishing harvest. Simultaneously, they learn how to interact with the trap. They engage in a process of appropriation of the trap as a fishing instrument and learn of the world of the shore and the world of fishes. In other words, participation in the activity leads to an 'education of attention' (Gibson 1979: 254) of newcomers. For example, it is strictly forbidden to pass one's hand or one's arm through the trap entrance or the trap opening. If one does not respect this precaution, no fish will come into the trap anymore 'because of the smell'. Moreover, observing which fishes are caught with each type of trap, *kampi* and *salamata*, they learn, on their own, the difference between the two types of traps.

The next step in a novice's participation in trap fishing is learning to make traps. Children do not learn to make traps before adolescence. By this time, no explanation of the process is needed as the novice has already observed the trap-making process many times. Traps are built outside, beside the house or on the beach for the bigger traps and children are free to observe the process. The scene of trap making can be considered as an externalisation of the expert's knowledge. However, the observation of trap making does not lead simply to the internalisation of a program that the novice would then simply implement. Indeed, when engaging in trap making, the novice usually encounters difficulties that he had not expected. For example, I observed a novice attaching the last mesh of the *pani*, the 'wing' of the trap, when assembling it (Figure 9.3).

Figure 9.3: Assembling a fishing trap with a close-up of the wing attachment

This was corrected by a more experienced fisherman. The experienced fisherman thus serves as a resource to help the novice if needed and to prevent him from making mistakes that would pose problem later in the fabrication. Therefore, engagement in trap making is more adequately conceived as a 'guided discovery' (Ingold 2000: 356) in which the novice's attention is attracted to specific elements that he had not noticed by himself. Among these elements are the appropriate means of determining the length of bamboo strips and their orientation during assemblage. The novice's perception of the trap is transformed during this process.

The novice may ask explanations about specific elements of trap making. If we return to the example above, why the novice should not attach the last mesh, we might suppose that it is motivated by the risk of a structural weakness of the trap. However, the explanation provided by the experienced fisherman was different: 'If you attach the last mesh, the trap will no longer be able to hear the fish call. Indeed, when he is in front of the trap entrance, the fish asks, 'May I come in?' and the trap answers: 'Yes, come in.'

Should we classify this as a belief and therefore conclude that experienced trap makers are not aware of the strength issue? The concept of belief presents at least two problems: (1) it requires a clear distinction between what is technical and what is not and (2) it tends to reify and isolate ideas from the context of practice. Rather, I argue that we do not need to choose between technical and non-technical. Indeed, the above conception is simultaneously a means to call the attention to the importance of not attaching the last mesh and a contribution to the 'poetics of dwelling' (Ingold 2000: 26): the fish calls to the trap before coming in, just as humans ask permission to enter a house. However, the novice is not required to 'believe' in this, but simply to avoid attaching the last mesh.

When making traps, the maker's objective is not just to transform a material, namely bamboo, into a technical object but to fabricate a 'quasi-object' (Latour 1997), that is a trap that will be able to attract fishes. Attention to laths, measurements and orientation as well as the use of spells are strategies to optimise fishing success. Engaging in trap making, the novice is introduced to these strategies and, as a consequence, obtains access to, and becomes an actor in a world of relations between humans and non-humans. For example, the basic length for bamboo strips is taken from one's own body or, better, from a wife's body. Indeed, women are conceived of as recipients of the household good fortune, an idea based on the local conception of the procreation process. Men's semen already contains all the constituents of the future baby. Woman's role is to nurture this semen in order to transform it into a baby. From this idea stems the association of women's bodies with good fortune. Using measurements taken on a woman's body is a means to transfer the good fortune associated with women into the object.

Finally, an engagement in trap making also leads to another kind of transformation: the shaping of the fisherman's physicality. The meshes of a novice's first traps are generally not uniform. The novice still lacks the capacity to feel the correct thickness of the bamboo strips with his fingers, for twisting them around one another during assembly and for homogenising the mesh using the pointed hammer (*kacikia*). He develops and incorporates these skills progressively through repeated practice throughout his career as trap fisherman.

In the same way that, at the scene of trap making, the expert's knowledge is externalised for the benefit of the observers, the *parika*'s expertise is displayed to team members as they participate in the fishing activity. At sea, each member of the team can observe where the traps are set at different times of the year and the quantity of fish caught as a result. From this perspective, fisherman's knowledge is the result of an accumulation of experiences. Knowledge is not a pre-requisite to participation but a product of this participation, development of that expertise relying on the attentive observation of the practice while participating in it.

Participation in practice contributes to shaping a fisherman's knowledge of fishes. This appears clearly in the responses provided by fishermen while eliciting fish names and characteristics. First, the fishing techniques practised delimit the repertoire of the fishes the fisherman is concerned with and interested in. Traps capture only some of the fish species present in South Buton waters. When presented with a plate of illustrations of herrings and relatives (Allen 1997: 51), not captured by traps, La Mala,[6] a trap fishing specialist, simply said 'I do not know these fishes' without trying to examine further the fishes of the plate. However, he had certainly seen some of them from his visits to the local market, at the very least. His answer reflects a lack of interest in this kind of fish. When presented with plates of cardinalfishes (Allen 1997: 100-1), another group that are not caught in quadrangular traps used by men, he only provided the name: '*isa pikadhepea*', that is 'fishes caught when fishing with the trap *kadhepe*'. Fishing with a *kadhepe* trap is a women's activity. Hence, he does not try to further distinguish the fish involved, despite the fact that more specific names are available in the local language. Providing a very general name for cardinalfishes is another mean for pointing out his disinterest in this category of fishes. Therefore, it appears that expertise does not consist in trying to master the largest repertoire of fishes but, rather, focusing on the fishes the fisherman interacts with, as if the delimitation of the repertoire was an element for constructing one's identity.

Fishing practice not only shapes which species a fisherman is interested in, but information provided for each fish also differs depending on a fisherman's specialisation. For each fish, trap fishermen can provide the following information: whether or not it is caught in traps, type of traps (*katambuni* or *kantano*, *kampi* or *salamata*), and place on the reef where it is caught (including association with coral heads). But, in contrast to anglers, trap fishermen cannot provide any information about feeding behaviour. Furthermore, the manner in which information is provided for a specific domain also differs. Trap fishermen express information about the place where the fish is found by using the vernacular terms of reef subdivisions that express both place and depth: *nambo* (reef flat), *mpanga-mpanga* (reef edge), *rumara* (upper reef slope and reef bench), *kito* (lower reef slope and beyond). For the fishes living beyond the reef, and therefore not caught using traps, the general term *kondalo* is provided, referring to the area beyond the reef slope (*kito*), regardless of depth. Information provided by anglers differs in two ways. First, information concerning fish location is not limited to an area on the reef. Anglers also point to specific environments, (cliff, Sampolawa Bay) or artificial (Fish Aggregating Device[7]), or to a geographical area of the coast (Wacu Mondawu 'The Fallen Stone', Matano Tai 'The Eye of the Sea'). In addition, they provide the depth range where the fish is caught, expressed in fathoms. Table 9.1 illustrates the difference between information from trap fishermen and anglers for four species of fish, demonstrating that fisherman's knowledge is mediated by their fishing instruments. But we can also formulate this in a different way. Merleau-Ponty (1999: 20-33, 318-20, 343-4) argues that the entire history of interaction with an object is present when one perceives this object at any given moment. From this perspective, the same fish exists differently for specialists of different techniques and, more broadly, these specialists live in different environments.

Table 9.1: Fish location as provided by trap fishermen and anglers.

Kind of Fish	Location as Provided by Trap Fishermen	Location as Provided by Anglers
Sogo lala (*Sargocentron* spp.)	Reef edge (*mpanga–mpanga*) – upper reef slope and reef bench (*rumara*)	3 to 5 fathoms
Pogo bulanci (*Rhinecanthus rectangulus*)	Reef edge (*mpanga–mpanga*) – lower reef slope and beyond (*kito*)	20 to 30 fathoms
Mbungawao (*Lutjanus* spp.)	Reef flat (*nambo*) – lower reef slope and beyond (*kito*)	Reef flat (*nambo*) to 40 fathoms
La Ngoa (*Caranx* sp.)	Beyond the reef (*kondalo*)	3 to 30 fathoms

In addition to enabling the reproduction of knowledge about fishes, participation in the activity also leads team members to learn more about how to behave and to discover further characteristics of their world. For instance, each team member builds at least one trap on his own. This enables the identification of the source of any bad luck. If one of the traps remains abnormally empty, the one who made it must investigate the origin of the problem. *Parika* can guide him by suggesting different possibilities, often the lack of harmony between the fisherman and his wife.

If we return to the moment near death, when the *parika* is said to transmit his knowledge, we can now see that, at this moment, most, if not all, of the *parika's* expertise has already been developed. Decades of collective implementation of fishing techniques have enabled team members to develop their own expertise through attentive observation of practice. While the *parika* might transmit something significant to his heir at this occasion, no oral transmission could replace these years of collective engagement.

To this point, I have focused on interactions within a single fishing team. However, observing the practice of other teams carrying out the same activity within the same area also offers a resource for improving fishing skills. This resource is especially useful for a trap fishing variant called '*bhamohora*', in which the fishermen must arrange the 'seating' of the trap by adding or moving stones. It targets shoals of fusiliers (*andou*, Caesionidae spp.). The goal is to spot the big coral head at depths of four to seven fathoms where shoals of fusiliers gather for the night. Fishermen dive around coral heads in the morning or in the evening to spot a shoal. When they find one, they put a trap close to the coral head and arrange its 'seating'. Depending on the trap's exact position, the fusiliers may or may not enter the trap. It might be necessary to adjust the position several times before finding the right one. When the trap is set correctly, it can catch up to four hundreds fishes. The teams exploiting the same area on the shore are in competition with each other and so wish to keep such valuable information secret. But it is not necessary that the information be shared voluntarily. It is accessible directly through observation and others teams come to place their own trap besides that of the first team.

Finally, participation in trap fishing does not lead only, at each new generation, to the reproduction of predecessors' knowledge and expertise, but may be developed and improved upon. A major development occurred in the 1960s with the combination of traps and the newly available fish aggregating devices (FAD), called *rompo* in the vernacular language. FADs are probably imported from the Moluccas but the combination of FADs with traps is said to be a local innovation. This new technique consists of suspending a *kantano* trap to a floater anchored to the sea bottom. Actors explain the process as follows: 'Palm leaves are attached close to the trap and attract small fishes; bigger fishes come to eat them but the small fishes take refuge in the trap; the bigger ones come into the trap to chase them but cannot escape.' This important development in trap fishing enables the exploitation of the area beyond the reef slope, the traditional limit of trap fishing. However, because of the ownership of certain techniques by certain communities, the use of FADs with traps is limited to the community of La Kaliba. This new technique is a new way to explore the environment. Its implementation leads to the development of new knowledge and expertise, or, in other words, of a new community of practice (see e.g. Ellen et al. 2000 for other examples of knowledge development as a result of implementation of new activities).

Angling

The learning process for angling is slightly different from trap fishing. Angling is a general category that includes about thirty different techniques. Engagement in angling consists of two simultaneous processes: practice of angling techniques with other children of similar age and peripheral participation in adult practice. Among the array of angling techniques implemented in South Buton, are some that are only practised by children. These techniques focus on the exploitation of the reef flat area, with or without canoes. Children start by practising techniques that exploit the area very close to shore, such as *hohokolo*. *Hohokolo* consists in trolling a line equipped with a small hook along the beach at high tides, within twenty centimetres of water. As the child grows, he implements angling techniques further on the reef flat. While each child manipulates his own fishing line, the practice of other children in the same area offers a resource for improving ones' own practice by (1) copying elements from others' practice (e.g. time, location, gesture, bait, size of hook) and (2) evaluating one's expertise by comparing one's fish catch with that of others.

Children have also the opportunity to participate in adults' angling activities beyond the reef before being old enough to implement these techniques on their own. La Sidu, an angling specialist, accompanied his older brother from the age of six. Now La Sidu is accompanied by his youngest son. At the time of fieldwork, he was eight years old and would join his father for angling or trolling activities beyond the reef. He not only observed the practice but also participated in it, being offered the opportunity to manipulate fishing lines. As is the case with trap fishing, learning does not follow the same sequential pattern as the technique itself: children manipulate the lines at sea before being able to prepare these lines by themselves. Peripheral participation enables the child to discover and participate in different fishing techniques without the need for him to learn anything beforehand, e.g. preparation of the fishing lines, choice of time and place. The context of practice enables the novice to learn many of these other details and techniques. By the time he starts preparing his own lines, there is no need for oral instruction on the size of hooks, the bait to be used, *etcetera*. These elements were already incorporated during his peripheral participation.

As the above example demonstrates, learning occurs as a by-product of engagement in practice. There is no framework where the goal is exclusively to learn. When the child practises angling on the reef flat, he is catching fish that are consumed by household members and this serves, at least in part, as his motivation. When he accompanies his father out to sea, this activity is not framed as his father being the teacher and he the student, because the explicit goal of the interaction is to catch fish. In this way, the child contributes to the household economy.[8]

The practice of fishing activities on the reef with other children combines with peripheral participation in adult activities. Through practice, newcomers progressively discover a world, enacting what they discover, hence, shape their own 'being-in-the world'. The practice of angling shapes his interaction with fish, particularly fish eating habits and fish behaviour when hooked. La Sidu, an angler, provided the following information concerning fishes that he would catch using different angling techniques: how it is caught (using which techniques and which bait if any), where (place and depth range), and when (in reference to the day, the lunar phase and the season). This information recorded through formal interviews can be stored in a database, but this does not mean that a fisherman's knowledge is organised in a similar structure. Rather, as argued above and based on Merleau-Ponty's approach to perception (Merleau-Ponty 1999: 20-33, 318-20, 343-4), all this information is present in an angler's perception of the different fishes. Angling practice is an exploration of the world of the sea through the means of hooks; for the fisherman, fish existence is the result of this exploration. Angling practice leads to the emergence of a specific entity: the angler-in-the-world. This process also includes the development of skills such as the feel of the fish's first touch on the line. And this feeling becomes an aspect of the way the fish exists for the angler.

Anglers usually specialise in a limited number of techniques that they particularly enjoy. They call these techniques their *hobi* (from English 'hobby', via Indonesian 'hobi') and practise them intensively. Specialisation enables the fisherman to focus the accumulation of experience and, as a result, is a major element of expertise development. La Sidu's *hobi* is tuna trolling with lure (*hokolo*). *Hokolo* (literally 'to follow') consists of spotting a shoal of tunas and passing over them trolling a line equipped with a big hook hidden by a lure made of a mix of colour threads. After the shoal of tunas has been spotted, the fisherman must rely on his ability to mix the lure's colours so that it corresponds to the tuna's preferred food at that moment. Until recently, La Sidu was the recognised expert in this technique in Bahari village as he used to come back with the most fish.

During the 1980s, tuna price increased significantly and *hokolo* became a more attractive activity to local fishermen. As a consequence, they became interested in La Sidu's expertise, but he restricted access to it. Fishing expertise is a fisherman's asset and he is not prepared to share it widely. Being recognised as an expert in a fishing technique is a significant component of one's social identity within the village community. La Sidu is proud to assert that, as the foremost expert in tuna trolling, 'people used to ask me to provide them with tunas when there was a marriage in the village'.

Given these concerns, La Sidu offered to share his expertise with only two persons. The nature of this access was different for each. His brother-in-law (who is also a neighbour) used to come to visit him in the evening after a day of tuna trolling to discuss the fishing events of the day and, more specifically, to find out what kind of lure La Sidu had used that day. La Sidu agreed to share his experience with him because 'He is my brother-in-law, I could not lie to him'. Given the kinship ties, this access was considered legitimate, but it was limited to discussions and sharing of information outside of the angling context. One of La Sidu's young cousins benefited from a better access to expertise as he had the opportunity to accompany La Sidu regularly for several years. This cousin has now become Bahari's foremost *hokolo* specialist. This is surely no accident and attests to the efficiency of shared practice for the development of expertise. The key element here is the access offered to expert practice. La Sidu's cousin had no official status of apprentice but the access La Sidu offered to his practice was a kind of tacit recognition of this status. In contrast, the limit of the access offered to his brother-in-law was a deliberate strategy to restrict the possibility of this brother-in-law becoming an expert himself. Finally, practice of the same technique within the same area offers, like with trap fishing, a resource for different fishermen even if they do not interact directly with each other. In the case of *hokolo* fishing, when a fisherman has found a shoal of tunas, the others follow him.

Angling and trap fishing are longstanding activities in South Buton. In contrast, shark finning is a recent introduction to the area and, as such, demonstrates how expertise is built-up, rather than passed down from a previous generation and how pre-existing expertise can be adapted to take on new techniques.

Shark Finning

In 1991, a new fishing technique was introduced to Bahari: shark finning using floating longlines. This activity has progressively replaced almost all other commercial fishing activities in Bahari. Shark finning using longlines developed in the 1980s in Gamumu, a Bahari expatriate community in the Moluccas,[9] stimulated by a demand for shark fins from middlemen. Longlines were set in the evening not far from Gamumu Island and pulled in the morning, using local sailboats. Because the device was floating on the surface and there was a danger of damage if a boat passed through it, longlines were kept relatively short, composed of around thirty hooks. The catch was limited to two or three sharks per night maximum. Then, from 1991, another type of longline was adopted for shark finning, modelled on the one used by foreign boats (called by locals 'Taiwanese boats') operating in the Moluccas. This type of longline can be much longer because vessels can pass through without damage as the longline is maintained at a depth of about twenty-five metres.

The appropriation of shark longlining by Bahari fishermen has relied on the same process as the one used for learning other fishing techniques: participation. Some Bahari fishermen went to Gamumu and joined local crews. The legitimacy of their access relied on their family ties with boat owners and crew members. Back in Bahari, they implemented this new activity using their own boats, formerly used for maritime transport and trade. The activity has developed quickly. Crew members accumulated enough capital to start operating their own boat and formed their own crews. Crews are composed of five to eight people. Priority is given to close kin (children, sons-in-law, brothers) but today crews also include people from neighbouring villages since more than one hundred boats are involved in shark finning in Bahari (total population is only about 2,000 people).

While shark finning is a new activity, pre-existing elements continue to be enacted within this new context to enhance fishing success. For example, when making the longline, special attention is paid to measurements for houses, boats, traps and fish lines, enacting a relationship between the object and its maker (or its maker's wife) to enhance the object's capacity to attract good fortune. Another technique employed to improve a device's good fortune is the use of spells. For instance, during a shark finning expedition in the Moluccas —after fifteen days at sea, the captain was preoccupied by the small quantity of sharks caught. In order to renew the longline's good fortune, he poured a bottle of water on the longline before setting it. Before leaving on the expedition, an elder from the village had cast a spell over the bottle, transferring the spell's power into the water. A third technique ensures the beneficial mediation of the guardian of the sea (*ompuno tai*). Before fishing near a new island, the boat captain goes ashore, places some food and cigarettes on the ground in front of him and addresses the *ompuno tai*, asking permission to exploit the area around the island.

The development of shark longlining in Bahari has also benefited from pre-existing knowledge and skills concerning navigation and tuna trolling (for collecting bait). It is also possible that a pre-existing stock of knowledge of shark behaviour already existed. Indeed, the most successful shark finning boat in Bahari belongs to a former angling specialist renowned for his expertise in *pitambo*, an angling technique that targets big fishes and sharks. *Pitambo* consists of angling with a line equipped with one big hook baited with a large chunk of fish. *Pitambo* was not very popular because success rates were low and, when sharks where caught, the price offered for fins at the local market was low.

Within the framework of the new activity, experimentation also enables an exploration of shark behaviour and, as a result, a development of local knowledge about sharks. A fisherman said that he used to throw tuna blood into the sea to attract sharks. Another one said he used bombs for the same purpose. Fishermen also experiment with the choice of bait. Just as with the other techniques, the fisherman continues to learn during practice by observing the relationship between environmental conditions and quantity of sharks caught. During the shark finning expedition in which I participated, I recorded the following remarks from La Sini, the boat captain: 'The sea is too calm here. In such conditions, the shark does not eat, he is continually satisfied' and 'In the Nusa Tenggara area, sharks eat close to shore when the moon is bright in the sky. Here, they also eat by full moon but not necessarily close to shore'. It is important to note that I obtained this information during participation in the activity and not in the context of an interview.

Productive locations are also important pieces of information for successful shark finning. No pre-existing knowledge was available to local fishermen. *Pita-*

mbo fishing was only implemented close to shore within the South Buton area and shark fishing in Gamumu did not extend far from the island. In contrast, Bahari fishermen venture much farther. Fishing grounds extend from East Kalimantan[10] to east of the Moluccas and to the Australian border in the south. Knowledge of the best spots for catching sharks is a product of the implementation of the activity and of the evaluation of catch quantity. New fishing grounds are constantly explored, motivated by the hope to be the first to discover a new good place and, therefore, to get plenty of sharks. For example, La Rawali circumnavigated Sulawesi Island armed with nothing more than a map from a school book. General information about quantity of sharks taken and fishing grounds exploited is widely available within the village but information concerning the location is deliberately imprecise. Nevertheless, this information can enable a boat captain to choose his next destination. However, if he wants more precise information, he needs to have legitimate access to it.

During fieldwork, La Dami came back from a two-months expedition with a quantity of shark fins worth seventy million Indonesian rupiah. La Dami's father and La Sidu were co-owners of La Dami's boat. They also co-owned another boat, whose captain was La Sidu's first son-in-law, La Nali. Therefore, they decided that La Nali would follow La Dami for the next expedition in the area. Similarly, La Baru, an experienced and successful shark fisher who owns four boats, organises expeditions with the four boats together. By doing this, he shares his expertise but also benefits from it, as he gets more revenue from his share of the profits.

An investigation of shark names and identifications reveals two additional changes in fishermen's relationship with sharks. These changes are (1) the development of the shark taxonomy and (2) the focus on fins in the identification process. The development of the nomenclature is an element of a larger process of reification characteristic of the development of communities of practice (Wenger 1999: 57-62).[11] If we compare the shark taxonomy of Pogalampa village where no shark finning is implemented with the one of Bahari, the difference is striking. Six lexical distinctions were recorded in Pogalampa and twenty in Bahari (Table 9.2).[12]

Among the fifteen additional lexical distinctions made in Bahari, some refer to species which, according the local fishermen, are not observed locally (*mongiwa mina, mongiwa antuga, mongiwa ntongori and mongiwa tombi*). But some other specific names highlight distinctions among shark species that were observed previously. Pogalampa fishermen acknowledge having observed at least some *Carcharhinus* spp. but they do not make any lexical distinction between them, naming them *mongiwa* or *mongiwa mosega* (literally 'fierce shark'). In Bahari, however, six specific names were recorded for *Carcharhinus* spp.

Shark finning activity stimulates the development of the shark nomenclature in two ways. First, shark finning offers a new opportunity for observing sharks,

Table 9.2: Vernacular names for sharks in Pogalampa and Bahari villages

	Vernacular Name and Translation	Scientific and English Name(s)	Remarks
Names from Pogalampa (also present in Bahari)	*Mongiwa bhocika* 'Spotted shark'	*Rhincodon typus* (Whale shark)	World's largest fish, maximum total length at least 12 m.
	Mongiwa ntoke 'Gecko shark'	? Scyliorinidae sp. (Catshark)	Named from the sound emitted when holding its throat.
	Mongiwa bhingku 'Adze shark'	Sphyrnidae spp. (Hammerhead sharks)	Characterised by flat and elongated head.
	Mongiwa karakaji 'Saw shark'	Pristidae spp. (Sawfish)	Characterised by saw-like snout.
	Mongiwa lontara	*Rhinobatos typus* (Giant shovelnose ray)	
	Mongiwa curinga 'Skipjack tuna shark'	*Isurus oxyrinchus* (Shortfin mako)	Like skipjack tuna (*Katsuwonis pelamis*), it can leap out of the water.
Additional specific names in Bahari.	*Mongiwa kabuci* 'Scorpionfish shark'	*Heterodontus zebra* (Zebra bullhead shark)	Name from stout spine on dorsal fins, evocating scorpionfishes spiny dorsal fin.
	Mongiwa mina 'Oil shark'	*Hexanchus griseus* (Bluntnose sixgill shark)	Exploited for its oil in Gamumu community, using bottom longlines.
	Mongiwa tombi 'Standard shark'	*Alopias* spp. (Thresher sharks)	
	Mongiwa koicu	*Stegostoma fasciatum* (Zebra shark)	
	Mongiwa buncici 'Satisfied shark'	? *Rhina ancylostoma* (Shark ray)	
Carcharinidge spp.	*Mongiwa ntongori* 'Mackerel shark'	*Galeocerdo cuvier* (Tiger shark)	Large dark spots similar to *tongori* (*Scomberomorus* spp., mackerel).
	Mongiwa kabhea 'Stupid shark'	*Negaprion acutidens* (Lemon shark)	
	Mongiwa La Karanda 'The Blue shark'	*Prionace glauca* (Blue shark)	Distinctive blue colour (in comparison with other Carcharhinidae spp.).
Carcharhinus spp.	*Mongiwa ekor hangus* 'Burnt fin shark'	*Carcharhinus brevipinna* (Long-nosed grey shark) and *C. melanopterus* (Blacktip reef shark)	Black tips on fins.
	Mongiwa bulamba 'Depigmented shark'	*Carcharhinus albimar-ginatus* (Silvertip shark)	White tips on fins.
	Mongiwa ngkawalea 'Quickly tired shark'	*Carcharhinus longimanus* (Oceanic whitetip shark)	'Quickly dies after hooked'
	Mongiwa hone 'Sand shark'	*Carcharhinus* sp. (possibly C. leucas)	
	Mongiwa antuga	*Carcharhinus* sp./spp.	'With large and thick fins'
	Mongiwa konduru	*Carcharhinus* sp.	

increasing both the frequency and the quality of the observation. Before, when sharks were rarely caught, observation consisted of nothing more than spotting shark dorsal and caudal fins at the sea surface. In addition, shark finning activity prompts fishermen to talk about sharks while relating their experiences of the expedition with other fishermen. Sharks have become a common subject of conversation and shark names are tools for relating experiences. For newcomers, these names are tools for shaping their perception, as they highlight distinctions between different types of sharks. The use of different names for a family of sharks is an invitation to discriminate more specific entities (see also Waxman 1999). A detailed lexicon is an asset to the CoP and serves as an instrument for reproducing a perception. Approaches that assume a universally perceived structure of nature necessarily overlook this dimension of the naming process. This is the case, for example, of Berlin's theory of folk taxonomy (1992). Naming, for Berlin, is just a process of labelling elements that already exist as distinct entities because perception is presupposed rather than being considered as an outcome of a process in which an actor and the world are both active (e.g. Merleau-Ponty 1962).

The focus on fins is another result of the increased importance of and contact with sharks. At fish identification sessions, shark fishers defended and justified their identification by referring to characteristics of the fins. Remarks made about the different species also relate to fins. *Mongiwa antuga* (*Carcharhinus* sp.) individuals are characterised by their 'large and thick fins', and are therefore of 'high value'. Fins of *mongiwa hone* (*Carcharhinus* sp.) are 'large but thin', whereas *mongiwa kabhea* (*Prionace glauca*) is characterised by his 'four fins'. When the shark taken has no specific name, it is designated using the classification based on fin size employed by fin buyers: 'super' for the big ones, 'korea', 'class two', *etcetera*. The longer the fins the higher the price per kilogram.

Therefore, the development of shark finning activity in Bahari has led to a collective enhancement of knowledge about sharks. It has also stimulated the shaping and fine-tuning of fishermen's perception of sharks. The enrichment of shark related nomenclature can be seen simultaneously as a reification of this finer perception and as an asset of the Bahari community of practice as it facilitates the development of this perception among newcomers in the activity.

Discussion

The analysis of the three different kinds of fishing activities in South Buton enables a distinction of two kinds of CoP: those in which members work together in a common enterprise, and practitioners of a particular fishing technique from the same community. In those CoPs where members share a common enterprise, the process at work is legitimate peripheral participation (LPP) (Lave and Wenger 1991). The practice is configured so that newcomers are offered the opportunity to progressively discover it while simultaneously partic- ipating in it. Knowing is not a prerequisite for doing but a product of partic- ipation in practice. In trap fishing, the child first participates by collecting the fish in the traps set on the reef flat, then he engages in trap making, as an adult he joins a team of trap fishers, then finally attains full expertise when holding the position of *parika*. In angling, I presented two examples of LPP: La Sidu's child joining him for fishing outside of the reef; and La Sidu authorising his cousin to join him for tuna trolling. With the presence of an expert, the novice does not need to master all the dimensions of the activity beforehand but can develop his expertise progressively. The example of shark finning highlights two kinds of LPP: (1) the novice joining a team and discovering the practice at this occasion and (2) several boats of the same owner implementing shark finning in the same place.

In all of these situations, participants share the same motivation: the success of the activity. The experts pay attention to the novice's activities as his mistakes would be detrimental to the entire team. Conversely, development of a novice's mastery is profitable for the team as a whole. In addition, the novice's participa- tion in practice is simultaneously a process of social integration, self-transforma- tion and disclosure of a world (including the invisible entities), or, in other words, a process of emergence of a new entity: fisherman-in-the-world (Mer- leau-Ponty 1962, Ingold 2000).

The second kind of CoP is composed of practitioners of a given fishing tech- nique from the same community, for example: trap fishing teams – especially those implementing the *bhamohora* technique focusing on shoals of fusiliers around a coral head; children angling on the reef flat; adults tuna trolling within the same area; La Sidu relating his experiences with his brother-in-law at the end of the day; and Bahari villagers developing their own shark finning prac- tice. In all these situations, a comparison of catches can serve as a reference for assessing one's own expertise. On the basis of this information, others' practice can serve as a resource for improving one's own technique. However, in this case, access to others' expertise is restricted for at least two reasons. The first is that different people or teams do not share in the profits of the activity, nor will they suffer from a failure. Second, because expertise in a particular activity delimits a social status within the community, fishermen are in competition with one another. Nevertheless, people can gain information via observation of others' practice and voluntary or involuntary sharing of experience. This enables the development of a repertoire for each specific activity that leads to the development of the community's expertise and, hence, to the specialisation of local communities in fishing.

Conclusion

This paper began with a brief critical review of theories of TEK transmission and, more precisely, with the discrepancy between the transmission process put forward in the Convention of Biological Diversity, namely oral instruction, and my data on fishing activities in South Buton. Another process by which TEK transmission is often seen to occur, imitation, matched the South Buton experience more closely, thereby enabling a closer examination of the nature of TEK, of the relations between knowledge and practice and of the learning process itself. Several theoretical developments seek to avoid restricting the process to a transmission of content – as conceived in Richerson and Boyd's model (2005) – and encourage us to consider the trajectories of newcomers, the configuration of the practice, the resources offered to newcomers and the 'structural' transformations occurring in the process.

Following these theoretical developments, I have engaged in an exploration of the process of expertise reproduction and development for three fishing activities in South Buton: trap fishing, angling and shark finning. In this context, learning is mainly a by-product of newcomers' participation in practice and that learning does not follow the same sequential pattern as the technique itself. Activities are configured to enable different kinds of participation according to one's level of expertise and access to practice. Different kinds of access enable the development of different levels of expertise. I have proposed a distinction between two types of CoP, each offering different types of access and different types of resources.

The process of learning relies first on 'imitation' understood as the exploitation of the living context accessible as a result of participation. It also includes 'oral instruction' or 'teaching' but only as a complement of the participation in practice and not prior to it. In addition, according to Richerson and Boyd's model, imitation and teaching are categorised as social learning and contrasted with 'trial and error', which is classified as individual learning. However, it appears from the present analysis that 'trial and error' does not occur out of context; rather, it occurs within the context of communities of practice and, hence, should not be considered as 'individual learning'. Moreover, participation in practice within a CoP does not lead to an accumulation of information about the environment, which is systematically stored in the mind, but rather to forging a specific being-in-the-world. This being-in-the-world includes a particular perception of fish shaped by interaction with them according to the technique, a particular physicality and an attention to invisible entities, such as spirits. Finally, I have shown here that expertise is not only owned by individuals. Expertise develops and is owned collectively within the CoP.

This analysis contributes to the emerging direction of TEK studies as promoted and outlined by Heckler (Introduction this volume), in several ways, namely with the concepts of process and landscape. TEK research needs to consider change as a primary element of TEK and focus on the analysis of the dynamic aspects of TEK. The exploration and analysis of the complex process of reproduction and development of TEK is precisely the object of this chapter. In addition, Heckler proposes landscape as an integrating analytical concept for this new phase. Following this direction, I have approached TEK within the framework of fishing activities and analysed fishermen's enskilment process as a result of their engagement within the environment (including its social dimension, with the concept of community of practice). This enskilment process includes the progressive structuring of an environment/landscape.

The emerging direction of TEK studies advocated in the introduction also highlights the incorporation of more qualitative 'in-depth' methods and a phenomenological approach. The present analysis of fishermen's knowledge dynamics puts this call into practice. Unsurprisingly, it leads to a challenge of the conception of TEK as a mere content to be recorded. Heckler has pointed out that focusing on change necessarily leads us to question the nature of TEK itself. Rather than relying on a preconceived definition of TEK, exploring the dynamics of TEK is therefore also an opportunity to explore the nature of TEK. The present analysis of the South Buton case demonstrates that TEK cannot be transmitted through oral instruction because TEK does not exist as a clearly delimited corpus of information specific to a local community. Rather, TEK is specific to particular communities of practice and includes the living context that serves as a resource to its members.

Acknowledgements

Fieldwork in Buton was sponsored by Lembaga Ilmu Pengetahuan Indonesia (LIPI) supported by grants from the Communauté Française de Belgique and the Fondation Belge de la Vocation. Participation in the International Congress of Ethnobiology in 2004 was supported by a grant from the Royal Anthropological Institute (U.K.).

Notes

1. In addition to Ingold (2000), see Varela et al. (1993) for a discussion of Gibson and Merleau-Ponty's approaches to perception.
2. The exact number is variable because the distinction between a variant and a technique is not easy to establish.
3. I joined a team of Bahari fishermen for a three-week shark finning expedition in the Moluccas.
4. The fishermen I worked with for the collection of fish names and identifications were among the ones I worked with for investigating the fishing techniques and recording of fishing curriculum.
5. There are two types of fishing platforms: *ngkuru-ngkuru* and *baga*. The fishing technique is similar for both, consisting of attracting fishes under the platform using pressure lamps and capturing these fishes with a square net lowered below the platform. *Ngkuru-ngkuru* platforms are composed of two canoes connected together. The bigger *baga* platforms are composed of a big central hull with an outrigger on each side.
6. I modified personal names to protect privacy.
7. Fish Aggregating Devices are artificial floating objects placed on the sea surface and anchored to the bottom to attract schooling fish species.
8. This has significance for methodology, because the question 'who teaches you' and similar ones, might not be considered meaningful in this context.
9. From the end of the 1930s, an activity of maritime transport and trade developed in South Buton. This activity facilitated a process of migration of Bahari villagers to the Moluccas. During trade and transport voyages in the Moluccas, crew stopped at different places and discovered opportunities to start their own gardens for cultivating cash crops like copra and cloves. Relationships with family members who stayed in Bahari were sustained by the frequent stops of Bahari boats in expatriate communities.
10. Kalimantan is the Indonesian part of Borneo island.
11. Wenger defines reification as 'the process of giving form to our experience by producing objects that congeal this experience into "thingness" (Wenger 1999: 58).
12. The vernacular category for shark, *mongiwa*, includes elongated batoid fishes.

Bibliography

Allen, G. 1997. *Marine Fishes of South-East Asia*. Singapore: Periplus Editions.

Berlin, B. 1992. *Ethnobiological Classifications : Principles of Categorization of Plants and Animals In Traditional Societies*. Princeton : Princeton University Press.

Bourdieu, P. 1977. *Outline of a Theory of Practice*. Cambridge: Cambridge University Press.

_____ 1990. *The Logic of Practice*. Oxford: Polity Press.

Chevalier, D. ed., 1991. *Savoir faire et pouvoir transmettre: Transmission et apprentissage des savoir-faire et des techniques*. Paris: Editions de la Maison des Sciences de l'Homme.

Convention on Biological Diversity. 1992. Retrieved 30 October 2005 from http://www.biodiv.org/doc/publications/guide.asp

Delbos, G. and P. Jorion. 1984. *La Transmission des Savoirs*. Paris: Editions de la Maison des Sciences de l'Homme.

Ellen, R. and H. Harris. 2000. 'Introduction', in *Indigenous Environmental Knowledge and Iits Ttransformations*. Amsterdam: Harwood, pp. 1-34.

Gibson J.J. 1979. *The Ecological Approach to Visual Perception*. Boston: Houghton Mifflin.

Ingold, T. 2000. *The Perception of the Environment: Essays in Livelihood, Dwelling and Skill*. London and New York: Routledge.

_____ 2001. 'From the transmission of representations to the education of attention' in H Whitehouse, ed., *The debated Mind: Evolutionary Psychology versus Ethnography*. Oxford: Berg, pp. 113-53.

Latour, B. 1997. *Nous n'avons jamais été Modernes. Essai d'Anthropologie Symétrique*. Paris: La Découverte.

Lave, J. 1988. *Cognition in Practice*. Cambridge: Cambridge University Press.

Lave, J and E. Wenger. 1991. *Situated Learning: Legitimate Peripheral Participation*. Cambridge: Cambridge University Press.

Martinelli, B. 1996. Sous le regard de l'apprenti. Paliers de savoir et d'insertion chez les forgerons Moose du Yatenga (Burkina Faso). *Techniques et Culture*. 26: 9-40.

Merleau-Ponty, M. 1962. *Phenomenology of perception*. London: Routledge and Kegan Paul.

_____ 1999 [1945]. *Phénoménologie de la perception*. Paris. Gallimard.

Richerson, P. and R. Boyd. 2005. *Not by Genes Alone: How Culture Transformed Human Evolution*. Chicago: University of Chicago Press.

Rogoff, B., R. Paradise, R. Mejia Arauz, M. Correa-Chavez and C. Angelillo. 2003. 'Firsthand Learning through Intent Participation' *Annual Review of Psychology*. 54: 175-203.

Varela, F, E. Rosch and E. Thompson. 1993. *L'inscription corporelle de l'esprit*. Paris: Seuil.

Waxman, S. R. 1999. 'The dubbing ceremony revisited: Object naming and categorization in infancy and early childhood' in D.L. Medin and S. Atran, eds., *Folkbiology*. Cambridge, MA: MIT Press, pp. 233-284.

Wenger, E. 1999. *Communities of Practice: Learning, Meaning, and Iidentity*. Cambridge: Cambridge University Press.

Chapter 10

Review of an Attempt to Apply the Carrying Capacity Concept in the New Guinea Highlands

Cultural Practice Disconcerts Ecological Expectation

Paul Sillitoe

The relation of population to land is fundamental and long standing. Ever since Malthus formally stated the issue in the early nineteenth century, pointing to the spectre of human numbers exceeding the resources needed to support them, it has been subject to debate, albeit with varying urgency. The two assumptions that underpin the argument seem indisputable, namely that planet Earth has finite land resources and human populations have a propensity to grow. Consequently, the idea of carrying capacity is perennial, and we see repeated attempts to calculate and refine it for different regions, even the entire globe (Cohen 1995). It is popular in archaeology (Zubrow 1971; Hayden 1975; Glassow 1978; Chapman 1988). In a recent publication, for instance, Read and LeBlanc (2003) ask how it is that some human populations, notably hunter-gatherers in the past, have apparently kept their numbers in check in a density-independent way, infrequently experiencing carrying capacity stress. They propose a 'multi-trajectory model' to understand interaction between the factors influencing population growth for 'potential growth is always under some degree of control, with the control ultimately linked to carrying capacity' (2003: 75), as illustrated by the observation that a hunter-gatherer population of one thousand reproductive individuals would grow, with a doubling rate of thirty-five years, to exceed the world's current six billion population in eight hundred years (2003: 61).

Another area where the idea of carrying capacity has featured is in assessing the relation of shifting cultivators to their land, as evident, for instance, in New Guinea (Brookfield and Brown 1963; Clarke 1971; Waddell 1972). Regardless of thorough-going criticism of the concept some time ago (Hayden 1975; Brush 1975; Dewar 1984; Street 1969), it continues to recur either in work that explicitly uses carrying capacity to assess subsistence farmers' relations with their land (Kinoshita 1995; Ohtsuka 1994, 1995; Henley 1997; Wohlt 2004) , or implicitly draws on it and assumes that it can be calculated, as in arguments about intensification of land use (Allen et al. 2001), which relate to longstanding land survey approaches that seek to assess the productivity of resources (Dent and Young 1981; Davidson 1992; Young 1998). Even after noting some of the criticisms of the idea writers still accept it; for example, Ohtsuka (1995: 318) concludes that 'the concept of carrying capacity is useful in working toward sustainable agricultural development'. A probable reason for its popularity is that the assumed problems of human-land relations remain much the same, namely that there has to be some limit to the population that any given land area can sustain with a given technology without degradation and loss of productivity long term, and no viable alternative has been developed to assess the relationship between finite land resources and expanding human populations.

If one mentions carrying capacity to agricultural scientists, they are most likely to think in terms of land areas to support herds of animals. We might anticipate that problems will attend an approach that parallels the conventional assessment of the grazing capacity of an area of land with human capacity for land management. For whereas animals will graze an area of pasture in a predictable way, humans continually intervene in their relations with their land resources, largely through technology, making similar calculations far harder. The conundrum facing attempts to relate human population numbers to land resources is that complex cultural practices repeatedly undermine the assumption of reductionist science that carrying capacity can be calculated using a few key variables. An alternative is to discuss land and population issues with local people to find out what they think of them, an approach that finds favour with social scientists, and anthropologists in particular. But it likewise runs into problems as many people are apparently reluctant to discuss these matters. While I advocate that those who seek to intervene should listen to what locals have to say (Sillitoe 1998, 2002), this does not get us far when their knowledge is largely experiential, as with land use. It is not something they are used to talking about, it is knowledge encompassed in performance. They get on with farming without talking about it. The problem of human land relations remains and we find ourselves again drawn back to the idea of carrying capacity with all its shortcomings.

It would be difficult for local people in some regions, such as the Highlands of Papua New Guinea, to discuss the issues that feature in carrying capacity calculations, even if they conceived a need to do so, for they (like scientists) cannot escape the constraints of their cultural practices, as outlined here. The issue of human-land relations is of particular interest in the Highlands region. Since the penetration of the outside world in the mid-twentieth century, some have argued that the population is on the verge of exceeding land resources and threatens their degradation, or in some places may even have done so, and we need some way to assess these dire predictions. While scientists talk of land as scarce in the region, people living in the Was valley of the Southern Highlands, about whom this chapter is written, do not express such concerns. It is possible that, while they may not perceive any voiced scarcity, they experience some restriction in the supply of cultivable land available without acknowledging it. In an attempt to assess if their views match geographical 'reality', and the extent to which they challenge the prevailing scientific opinion of land shortage in the Highlands region, I tried to calculate the carrying capacity of their region under the current farming regime. But, as Ohtsuka (1995: 311) notes 'there are many problems in applying carrying capacity', which as I recount here, appear insurmountable currently. This paper discusses problems that I encountered in trying to assess the ecological status of local perceptions of land use and availability, and population trends in the western Wola-speaking region.

Land under Cultivation and Population

The areas required under cultivation in the Was valley to support a given population suggest that there is an abundance of land to meet needs. Data from surveys of all gardens under cultivation on the territories of two neighbouring *semonda* called Aenda and Ebay, together with demographic data from a series of censuses conducted in the region, support the proposition that these communities have abundant land resources. (A *semonda* [literally large family] is a kin grouping somewhat equivalent to what others call a 'clan' elsewhere, and comprises a number of smaller kin groups called *semgenk* [literally small family] equivalent to 'sub-clans'.) The simplest measure is the amount of land under cultivation compared to the total land available for agricultural purposes.

According to these data, the two neighbouring *semonda* communities had a total of 21.18 and 33.24 hectares under cultivation on two occasions (Table 1).[1] There are comparative data on the geography of garden distribution for the Chimbu (Brookfield and Brown 1963, Brookfield 1973), several Eastern Highlands groups (Pataki-Schweizer 1980), and the nearby Nembi Plateau (Allen 1984). An assessment of the total land available to these two groups is difficult to calculate with similar accuracy, which intimates problems with carrying capacity calculations. A calculated estimate of the combined areas of their territories suggests that they have 32.8 km^2 under montane forest and 6.0 km^2 under regrowth, largely cane grassland (Sillitoe 1996: 181). The area under cultivation at any time is less than one percent of their territories (0.6% and 0.9% respectively), which suggests that cultivable land is not scarce. While they shift swiddens periodically and some of the land will be unsuitable for cultivation, these figures reveal that there are considerable areas of potential cultivable land, sufficient to the comfortable operation of the farming regime. The various site selection factors indicate how some locations will be judged unsuitable for gardening (Sillitoe 1999a), reducing the potentially arable area from the entire territory of a *semonda* to parts of it. Even if 50 percent of the land is unsuitable for subsistence cultivation because too steep, wrong aspect and so on, a large area of potentially cultivable land remains. In short, these data appear to justify agreeing with the Wola view that there is more than enough potentially arable land to meet their needs and that there is no pressure on such resources.

Table 10.1: *Number of Was gardens and areas under cultivation*

		1st Survey		2nd Survey	
		No. Gdns	Area. (m²)	No. Gdns	Area (m²)
Aenda *semonda* residents†:	Aenda *sem* land	166	129,399	270	189,700
	Other *sem* land	67	47,893	85	52,503
Resident elsewhere:	Aenda *sem* land	15	8,682	31	18,123
Ebay *semonda* residents†:	Ebay *sem* land	72	70,782	130	121,361
	Other *sem* land	29	23,812	40	26,996
Resident elsewhere:	Ebay *sem* land	4	2,909	6	3,249

†Includes those families maintaining houses and gardens on two *sem* territories, one of which is Aenda or Ebay.

The relation between population and territory, namely the numbers of people fed from the surveyed area, further confirms this conclusion. We can use such figures to calculate a statistic to show the area households need to cultivate to support a given number of persons. Relating the garden survey data to demographic information not only allows for an assessment of the extent of current resource exploitation but also possible future trend, that is, we might estimate when we can expect cultivable land to start to become scarce. In short, we can crudely estimate the carrying capacity of the land under the current farming regime. Censuses conducted at the time of the garden surveys show that the total population supported with the foregoing areas of land under cultivation was 307 and 323 persons (Table 10.2).[2]

Table 10.2: Population at time of garden surveys

| | Aenda *semonda* | | | | Ebay *semonda* | | | |
| | Adults | | Children (<18 yrs.) | | Adults | | Children (<18 yrs.) | |
	Male	Female	Male	Female	Male	Female	Male	Female
1st Survey	49	56	50	46	32	30	14	30
2nd Survey	48	53	56	47	27	34	26	32

While the population shows relatively little change over this period, the area under gardens varies considerably. According to these data, the areas under cultivation varied from 690m^2 to 1029 m^2 per person. The extent of the difference between the areas under cultivation expressed as a function of demography intimates further possible problems with carrying capacity assumptions. The porcine population varies somewhat more between the two surveys, although not greatly (Table 10.3).[3] It approximates the human one in numbers, which is the usual pattern between large exchange-festival-slaughters of animals (Sillitoe 2003: 282). In respect of carrying capacity, we can put the pig population to one side on the grounds that these animals are fed largely on waste tubers and other vegetable refuse that are the by-product of supplying human food demands, which makes calculations more straightforward (compare the complex calculations attempted by Rappaport 1968: 288-98).

Table 10.3: Pig populations at time of garden survey

| | Aenda *semonda* | | Ebay *semonda* | |
	Pig population†	No. men with title to pigs	Pig population	No. men with title to pigs
1st Survey	155	90	90	22
2nd Survey	184	93	93	25

† We should expect about one third of the population to be piglets (according to pig census data in Sillitoe 2003:289)

The Was Perspective

The views of the Was valley inhabitants and supporting demographic-ecological evidence appear to challenge accepted wisdom about the relation of population to land resources in the New Guinea highlands. Since some of the pioneer ethnographies, the widespread view has been that highlanders experience land resource pressures and that some are suffering overpopulation and land shortages

(Brookfield and Brown 1963; Kelly 1968; Meggitt 1965; Sillitoe 1977; Wohlt 2004). More recently, and closer to the Was valley, researchers have argued for similar pressure on land in areas of the Southern Highlands Province, both in the Tari Basin to the northwest (Wood 1984; Umezaki et al. 2000) and on the Nembi Plateau to the southwest (Crittenden 1982; Allen 1984). These commentators on land use and population elsewhere in the Southern Highlands follow Brookfield (1996; 2001), who has extended Boserup's (1965) argument to New Guinea that technological innovation and agricultural intensification create space for population growth, effectively reversing the Malthusian argument that population growth exerts pressure to innovate technologically to avoid shortages.[4] They adopt Brookfield's idea of 'social production' to account for output beyond subsistence requirements, where inputs may be energetically unprofitable but tolerable for the social returns.

Ethnographic data from the Was valley question the suggestion that production dramatically exceeds what a population needs biologically to support itself, particularly to support pig herds (Sillitoe 2003). Over the years Brookfield (2001) has distanced himself from earlier intensification arguments, speaking of them as 'reductionist' for focussing on too few parameters, and arguing for attention to farmers' management skills, which correlates with my experiences. Others remain wedded to the intensification argument, such as Allen (2001) who maintains that data from a Papua New Guinea wide Mapping of Agricultural Systems project (see Bourke et al. 1995 for Southern Highlands) demonstrate, with some admitted anomalies, significant associations between population density and farming intensity, farmers intensifying as population increases and causing environmental degradation, worsening their predicament without adequate innovations. (See also Ohtsuka 1994, 1995, and Kinoshita 1995, for arguments covering some of the same issues.)

Calculating Carrying Capacity

It is arguable that the above statistics of areas under cultivation and population misrepresent the position, only grossly signifying land use under a nominally shifting farming regime. In an attempt to demonstrate how distant the Was valley population is from the Malthusian precipice, I resolved to refine these gross calculations and to work out in detail the carrying capacity of the region. Such computations calculate 'the point beyond which population cannot grow, *ceteris paribus*, without causing some damage to the basic resource of the system, land' (Brush 1975: 800). Problems arise, as we shall see, with the *ceteris paribus* 'other things being equal' assumption, as they are rarely, if ever, equal. This chapter is an account of the difficulties encountered. It critiques the carrying capacity concept in a particular ethnographic context to specify in detail where its assumptions fall down, particularly the cultural barriers to its application. These vitiate the attempt and question efforts to quantify human-land relationships in the New Guinea highlands and the declarations of some observers that they reckon there is an impending resource crisis.

All carrying capacity equations do the same thing (see Ohtsuka 1995: 312 for various equations): they assume that the ratio of land farmed to total farmable land relates to that between contemporary population and carrying capacity (Feacham 1973).[5] They also assume that we can accurately measure these variables. While some authorities have used these formulae to calculate carrying capacity in the New Guinea highlands (see Brookfield and Brown 1963: 108-124; Rappaport 1968: 92-96, 285-298; Clarke 1971: 187-191; Waddell 1972: 168-176: Ohtsuka 1994; Kinoshita 1995;Wohlt 2004: 151-155), applying them in the Was valley presents considerable problems. We have already touched on one of these, namely the variation in the areas under cultivation at different times when expressed as land farmed per head of population – which area should we take, or should we calculate another value, according to average garden yields and individual nutritional needs (Sillitoe 1983: 217-246)? The calculation of carrying capacity demands data on three parameters: the length of the cultivation cycle (divided into time under cultivation and time under fallow); the area needed under cultivation to feed a specified population (e.g. expressed as an average area per head annually); and the total area of available arable land. There are difficulties with all three in the Was valley.

Cultivation Cycle

Assessing the duration of the cultivation cycle is not straightforward given the nature of what I have called the 'semi-permanent shifting cultivation' system (Sillitoe 1996). Time under cultivation and fallow varies widely for Wola gardens such that it is difficult to specify how long any area might be cropped or fallowed. Households farm some gardens only once, for a year or so, and others they cultivate many times, for decades. They say that they do not know beforehand how long a garden may remain in production but act according to how their crops fare following cultivation, and other considerations such as convenience to homestead and ease of keeping pigs out. Likewise there is no standard time for which they leave land under fallow; it may be months or many years. Rappaport (1968: 91) points out similar problems estimating lengths of fallow periods in the Jimi valley (see also Ellen 1982: 42; Ohtsuka 1994, 1995). Hardesty (1977: 201) observes that differences in intensity of land use have implications for carrying capacity calculations, and both Brush (1975: 807-808) and Dewar (1984: 605) note that wide variations may occur in fallow periods, something compounded by 'multiple use of fields, the effects of not starting new swiddens each year, and the constraints of field-to-village distance' (Dewar 1984: 605). It is difficult to calculate the degree of rotation; indeed it challenges definitions of shifting cultivation (Sillitoe 1996: 36-39), even those that seek to employ a metric such as Ruthenberg's R value (1976: 15). A way around this problem of calculating the rotational factor might be to compute an average time under cultivation and fallow, but these would be artificial values given the wide spread of time that garden plots are under cultivation and fallow, and they would demand an extensive body of data to be anything like representative, collected over decades for fallow areas.

There is also the boundary problem of deciding when an area is under cultivation and when under fallow. The Wola divide the life of a garden into several different stages, including a tilling and planting stage (*way bway*); new crops stage (*waeniy*) which they divide into an early not eating phase (*waeniy ora*) and a subsequent harvesting and eating one (*waeniy nokmay*); a mature crops stage (*puw*) following the first harvest of tubers; and a senescent stage (*mokombai*) when only a few long term crops remain. The productivity of gardens varies between stages, declining from the *waeniy* 'new' one onwards. The areas involved vary considerably in the Was valley (Table 10.4). It is necessary to decide at what point we should judge an area to be under cultivation and at what it ceases to be so. It may be appropriate to include only gardens currently yielding food, omitting those currently being planted and those with new crops not yet harvestable. At the other end of the cultivation cycle we have to determine when a garden area is abandoned to fallow, which the Wola often say is the *mokombai* 'senescent' stage, although such plots may still support a few long-standing crops (such as bananas, sugar cane and pandans). It often happens that gardeners recultivate and replant such areas before harvesting some of these long term crops, returning them to the tilling and planting, and subsequent new stages. It is common to see gardens comprising patches in different states of cultivation (such as an area currently being tilled and planted among adjacent grassy senescent and established cropped areas), which further complicates efforts to distinguish cultivated from fallow land.

In seeking to specify the maximum density of population that a farming system can sustain without environmental degradation, carrying capacity calculations assume a static arrangement. They overlook human ingenuity. It is feasible that increased land pressure might trigger changes in the farming system and increase intensity of land use, altering the cultivation cycle. These need not feature large changes, as intimated by the Wola farming regime where families often abandon gardens not because the fertility of the land falls (the classic reason given for moving on), but because they are difficult to keep enclosed and pigs out. It is conceivable that as population increases, communities will find that they have sufficient labour to keep larger areas enclosed for long periods of time and allow households to keep more land under cultivation for longer periods. Another possible innovation that could likewise make larger areas available for longer term cultivation might feature a change in the way families herd pigs,

Table 10.4: Number of Gardens and Areas under Cultivation According to Garden Type and Cultivation Status.

Garden Type	Cultivation Status	1st Survey						2nd Survey					
		Aenda & Ebay Residents				Resident Elsewhere		Aenda & Ebay Residents				Resident Elsewhere	
		Aenda & Ebay Land		Other *Sem* Land		Aenda & Ebay Land		Aenda & Ebay Land		Other *Sem* Land		Aenda & Ebay Land	
		no.	m²	no.	m²	no.	m²	no.	m²	no.	m²	no.	m²
Sweet Potato	Planting	20	13162	5	2432	1	439	33	24037	15	7872	6	2489
	New	83	94611	40	32649	7	3397	136	110632	34	20317	17	9933
	Mature	90	82920	46	35614	8	7448	175	159328	61	45605	13	8866
	Sub-total	193	190693	91	70695	16	11284	344	293997	110	73794	36	21288
Taro	Planting	0	0	0	0	0	0	0	0	0	0	0	0
	New	4	1230	0	0	1	129	22	10024	11	4472	0	0
	Mature	2	1495	0	0	0	0	2	1954	2	836	0	0
	Sub-total	6	2725	0	0	1	129	24	11978	13	5308	0	0
Mixed Vegetable	Planting	1	36	0	0	0	0	2	533	0	0	0	0
	New	29	3998	5	1010	2	178	17	2872	1	272	0	0
	Mature	9	2729	0	0	0	0	13	1681	1	125	1	84
	Sub-total	39	6763	5	1010	2	178	32	5086	2	397	1	84
Totals		238	200181	96	71705	19	11591	400	311061	125	79499	37	21372

reducing the need to enclose gardens by keeping animals penned up, as currently practised in other highland regions such as Chimbu (Hide 1981); although there would be a knock-on effect with the animals demanding increased fodder, no longer rooting around and supplying so much of their own food needs, increasing the volume of garden produce fed to them. Other changes could have more far reaching consequences for the farming system and have to be allowed for in any carrying capacity discussions, as Street (1969) points out (see also Hardesty 1977: 199-200; Ellen 1982: 44). Clarke 1971: 189 gives the example of the arrival of steel tools in the highlands, which he thinks have increased land degradation with more trees felled than previously. Such technological innovations are difficult to predict but they can have a dramatic effect on land use, throwing carrying capacity calculations completely out.

Area under Cultivation

The second parameter, specifying the area needed under cultivation to feed a population, presents further problems. As Hardesty (1977: 199) notes, 'assumptions in estimating per person land need are particularly numerous and difficult to justify, thus introducing many sources of error into the calculation of carrying capacity'. The calculation of the area under cultivation per head of population (including pigs or not), from total area farmed and demographic data gives only a rough measure. It again includes all categories of cultivation without any distinction, such as *waeniy* 'new' and *puw* 'mature', and also different types of garden, which vary considerably between households (some not having some types, such as taro gardens), and certainly varying widely in the crops available at any time (Sillitoe 1983: 234). While it is possible to calculate areas under cultivation per head of the population (Table 10.4) according to cropping sequence and garden type, it is necessary to decide which of these to include in any carrying capacity estimates. I decided to omit the *mokombai* 'senescent' stage, not knowing at the time of survey whether such areas might soon be recultivated or were entering a fallow period of unspecified duration. The inclusion of *way bway* 'planting' areas is perhaps questionable too, and possibly the *waeniy ora* 'very new' areas not yet yielding sweet potato tubers (although such areas may be yielding other, faster maturing crops – Sillitoe 1983: 194). Nonetheless by the end of the months-long garden surveys, many of these areas had passed onto the next cropping stage. This relates to the problem that carrying capacity calculations assume a single snapshot in time of dynamic farming regimes, whereas data collection may extend over a considerable period and cropping patterns documented at the beginning may have changed by the end.

Another issue is the considerable difference between the areas under cultivation at the time of the two surveys, which occurred without a commensurate increase in population[6] nor any major climatic perturbation (such as an El Niño oscillation-caused food shortage). It suggests that the area that can support a population may vary considerably as new areas are cleared and come into harvest, while others pass into fallow. Considerable variation can occur between households. A review of the data according to households shows (Table 10.5) a range of 504m^2 to 3679 m^2 under cultivation per household member. Crittenden (1984: 137) reports a similar variation at the household level on the Nembi Plateau for area cultivated per adult. The implication is not that some households are going without sufficient food to eat, but that there is a wide variation in swidden yields and daily sharing of food (Sillitoe 1983: 217-228). This variation further calls into question attempts to come up with a precise figure for area under cultivation per head. It parallels the position with respect to the foddering of pigs where rations can vary widely (Sillitoe 2003: 323-25). These are not finely gauged issues. They illustrate the implications of tacit knowledge prominent in such farming systems.

We should anticipate that some variation will occur where experiential knowledge informs decision-making, various households judging their needs differently. A possible response to this variation might be to use a range of values representing households with the largest and smallest areas under cultivation per head – in this event we need to ensure that we survey a sufficiently large sample of households to represent the spread. And if the intention of the carrying capacity calculation is to compute the largest possible population a region can support under its current farming regime without land degradation, we might legitimately take the smallest area as the minimum a family requires to survive. Regarding the tacit nature of much farming knowledge, this further questions any implication that farmers are aware of the limits that feature in carrying capacity formulae and act to keep within them or know what might happen if they fail to do so (Brush 1975: 808). Any assumption, as Glassow states, that a 'population has perfect and total information about the resources in its environment and is able to use this information with complete effectiveness in calculating and comparing costs of exploiting different resources' (1978: 44) is untenable.

Table 10.5: Area under cultivation per head by household.

	Area per adult head equivalent (m^2)†				
	<999	1000-1499	1500-1999	2000-2499	>2500
No. households	25	31	25	10	7

†In these calculations, children <14 years old counted as ½ an adult consumer, and those with gardens elsewhere not surveyed also counted as ½ an adult consumer (long term visitors and suw pa kab families).

Another possible response to such variation is to use data on crop yields and food consumption to compute the area needed under cultivation per head.[7] If we know people's food requirements and the yields of their gardens, we can calculate the area they need under cultivation to supply them. While such data are available for the Was valley (Sillitoe 1983: 217-246), their use poses other problems. If we go down the yields and consumption route, we shall have to define minimal nutritional requirements, which is a notoriously difficult. (See Hardesty 1977: 200 for further criticisms of consumption measurements and sources of error.) We shall also have to determine what children eat at different ages compared to adults and adjust consumption statistics accordingly; furthermore Rappaport (1968: 91) points out that food requirements of individuals of the same age and gender may vary such that any mean is a misrepresentation. And we shall have to decide what to do about the produce fed to pigs, whether to set it aside as waste or include it. The problem here is that what are waste tubers at one time, may in hard times be eaten by humans. On the yield side we need an extensive sample of measurements collected over a fair period of time to accommodate variations such as occur between different points in the cropping cycle, for example *waeniy* 'new' and *puw* 'mature' stages, differences in fertility between swiddens, and fluctuations due to changes in the weather (see Bourke 1988: 45-83 for detailed discussion of variation in food supply). Again, we have to decide,

faced with such variation, what data we should use in carrying capacity calculations. An average yield will hide a wide range of variation and advocates of such
calculations might argue for the use of the highest and lowest figures in any
computation, to represent the spread of possible values, which presupposes not
a single carrying capacity figure but a range.

Furthermore, given climatic variations, what is a typical period of time to
which we might apply a carrying capacity equation? We have considerable differences in garden output due to climate, such that in a severe condition there
may be insufficient food for all (Sillitoe 1996: 73-101). Again, on the grounds
that the aim of a carrying capacity calculation is to work out the largest possible
population a region can support sustainably, we might opt to peg data values to
the leanest times, as these represent the real resource ceiling, for while people
may be able to support a larger population in the good times, they will see their
families culled in the worst times back to the numbers they can feed during a
famine. Hayden (1975), pointing out that resources fluctuate over time (sometimes cyclically over decades or centuries), asks how carrying capacity estimations might accommodate to such cycles, and enquires if it is necessary to say
that people 'experiencing frequent, intermediate or rare famine and mortality are
really over their carrying capacity' (1975: 14). He suggests measuring morbidity
in stress periods, arguing that populations well adjusted to resource availability
will suffer lower death rates.

The focus of carrying capacity calculations on swiddens also omits non-
farmed food sources (Brush 1975: 806), which in normal times may not be significant but in hard ones may substitute for cultivated crops, ensuring people's
survival and skewing upper resource use estimations; however in the Was valley
wild resources such as game and forest products are relatively insignificant (Sillitoe 1996; 2003). But there is something awry with the assumption that there
is a famine related ceiling to a population, for there is a danger that a percent-
age of people will perish whatever its size. Even if the population of the Was valley was only one family it would still likely not have cleared more gardens than
an average household today, which would be just as drought and possibly frost
prone as much larger areas under cultivation. It would consequently find that it
had insufficient food to feed itself – with the forest yielding relatively little wild
food (Sillitoe 2003: 223-24). The implications for carrying capacity are to imagine all available arable land incorporated in the farming system and calculate the
oscillation between good and bad times, on the assumption that following a devastating famine the population will increase again to carrying capacity, or
beyond if it passes the calculated threshold of environmental degradation.

The spectre of starvation is mercifully only of theoretical interest today with
the possibility of outside famine relief intervention, as has occurred in previous
droughts (Bourke 1988), which throws a question mark over attempts to calculate carrying capacity at all, as food supply now has a potential global dimen-

sion. This relates to criticisms of carrying capacity calculations for assuming sub-sistence regimes disconnected from wider regional and national economies and markets (Hardesty 1977: 205), although with the breakdown of state machin-ery in the Southern Highlands this is largely so in the Was valley currently. Dewar (1984: 610) points out that migration can render carrying capacity cal-culations for small populations suspect with people changing residence as resource availabilities change. Unfavourable trade relations, as Ellen (1982: 45) points out, could further depress populations by extracting a surplus of resources from the immediate area.

Arable Land Availability

The third parameter, specifying the total area of available arable land, presents yet further problems (Ohtsuka 1994, 1995), as intimated previously. We encounter the issue of boundary definition again. It is difficult to specify *semonda* 'large family' territories geographically with accuracy as they are not clearly delimited. Different people put boundaries in different places, depend-ing on their various *sem* 'family' affiliations, what relatives had told them, what they remember of previous land disputes and the interpretation they put on out-comes, and so on. While individuals have mental maps of the extent of their ter-ritories, and these overlap somewhat, they do not necessarily agree. And in a stateless context there is no authority to legislate on where boundaries are (Silli-toe 2003: 102). Nor are boundaries an issue unless someone claims land some-where that others consider belongs to their *sem* 'family'. It is during ensuing disputes that people seek to resolve the position of boundaries, otherwise they adopt a 'let sleeping dogs lie' attitude. The idea that one should be able to agree the delineation of the boundaries of entire territories is an alien one, which would provoke an endless dispute. While we can make do with an estimate for carrying capacity purposes, as nothing else is possible, we need to realise that it compromises the accuracy suggested in the use of a mathematical equation. Again, faced with such variation, we might decide to use the highest and lowest estimates in any calculation to represent the spread, which will give a range of carrying capacity estimates and require the use of more complex simultaneous equations. This would not surprise swidden farmers as they routinely 'deal with ranges of variables rather than with fixed variables' (Brush 1975: 807), as evident in site selection (Sillitoe 1999a).

There is also the issue of drawing boundaries around the communities that use the land of *sem* 'families', of determining membership by tying people to ter-ritories. There are some families that maintain gardens and houses on two terri-tories, called 'two place' people (*suw pa kab*) and we have to decide how to account for such families. The total arable land they access is twice that of oth-ers. But then all families have rights to claim land on several territories (see Sillitoe 1999b), although they may be farming on only one or two. The spread of gardens across several *sem* 'family' territories also occurs through men granting 'women's boundaries' (*tenon tomb*) to female kin – sisters, daughters etcetera – who live elsewhere. Families not only consume from the areas they establish but also those of other households where their female members are allocated patches, both on the territory of their *sem* 'family' of residence and others elsewhere. There is a strong social component to this distribution; it features an element of exchange. The survey data, documenting which relatives' gardens women have *tomb* 'areas' in, indicates the extent of this sociality; wives occupy the overwhelming majority (64 percent of area), followed by mothers (13 percent), sisters (5 percent) and daughters (4 percent), the remainder (14 percent) occupied by a wide range of kin (Table 10.6).[8] The practice of granting 'women's boundaries' also serves to some limited extent to distribute the variety of crops that come from a new garden around several households, a practice that benefits all in the long run, assuming that allocations tend to even out over time.

Table 10.6: Relationship of women to male pioneers of gardens in which they have areas to cultivate

Female Cultivators' Relationship to Tenant	Total No. Gardens	Total Area Cultivated (m²)	% Area	Female Cultivators' Relationship to Tenant	Total No. Gardens	Total Area Cultivated (m²)	% Area	Female Cultivators' Relationship to Tenant	Total No. Gardens	Total Area Cultivated (m²)	% Area
½BBD	1	523	0.09	FFF½BSSSW	1	272	0.05	MFBSSW	1	314	0.05
½BD	7	1840	0.31	FFFBSSD	1	105	0.02	MFFF?BSSD	1	230	0.04
½BMBW	1	670	0.11	FFFBSSSSSW	1	2007	0.34	MFFF½BSSSSW	1	167	0.03
½BSW	1	31	0.01	FFFFB?DSSSW	1	397	0.07	MFFF½BSSSW	1	209	0.04
½BW	2	1401	0.24	FFFFF?DSSSW	1	439	0.07	MFFFFBSDSD	1	146	0.02
½Z	13	4982	0.85	FFFFFBSDSSW	1	209	0.04	MFFFFDSSD	1	272	0.05
½ZD	2	276	0.05	FFFFM?BDSSSW	1	42	0.01	MFZD	1	355	0.06
BD	3	867	0.15	FFFFM?SSSSSSW	1	167	0.03	MFZSD	2	795	0.13
BW	19	9713	1.65	FFFFZSSSD	1	251	0.04	MFZSDD	1	585	0.10
BW½Z	1	314	0.05	FFFMBSSSSW	1	377	0.06	MZ	5	1808	0.31
D	39	21141	3.59	FFFMBSSW	1	125	0.02	MZD	1	251	0.04
Dist F relative W	1	418	0.07	FFM?ß?SSSSSSW	2	334	0.06	Step FF?BSSD	1	84	0.01
F½BDSW	1	564	0.10	FFZSDD	1	146	0.02	Step FFBSSW	1	52	0.01
F½BSSW	1	251	0.04	FFZSSSW	1	251	0.04	SW	6	3596	0.61
F½BSW	1	188	0.03	fiancée	1	125	0.02	W	587	378011	64.12
F½BWMFF½BSSDSW	1	272	0.05	FM relative	1	1025	0.17	W relative	2	198	0.03
F½ZSD	1	481	0.08	FM?ß?BSSSSD	1	167	0.03	W½Z	2	564	0.10
F½ZSSW	1	188	0.03	FM?ß?BSSSSSW	1	84	0.01	WBD	4	5415	0.92
FBD	3	780	0.13	FMBSD	1	293	0.05	WBW	4	1588	0.27
FBSD	3	1150	0.20	F relative	1	418	0.07	WD	1	502	0.09
FBSSW	3	898	0.15	FZD	2	711	0.12	WFFFFF½BSSSD	1	293	0.05
FBSW	2	522	0.09	FZDSW	2	650	0.11	WFFFFF½BSSSSW	1	125	0.02
FBW	1	334	0.06	FZSW	1	146	0.02	WFZD	1	212	0.04
FF rel	1	397	0.07	M	138	75294	12.77	WM	24	10192	1.73
FF½BSSD	2	418	0.07	MBD	1	334	0.06	W step FF½BSW	2	585	0.10

The wide geographical spread of gardens that results is evident from the location of the cultivations of Aenda and Ebay *semonda*, which extend well beyond the Was valley. In seeking to quantify the total arable area available, where are we going to draw our boundaries, as territories flow one into another from the perspective of farmers' land use, extending ultimately over large regions of the highlands in an interdigitated fashion? We can see that the idea of bounded areas is an increasingly contrived one, albeit necessary for carrying capacity calculations. In order to proceed, we might assume as a rough rule that those living elsewhere with areas on the home territory of interest – Aenda and Ebay *semonda* here – balance the areas that its *sem* residents have elsewhere – although in the surveys reported here this would under represent the area so farmed by the home groups by four to six times (Table 10.1).

Even if the delineation of territories was straightforward, there is the problem of defining what area comprises arable land. It is a challenge to decide where to draw the line between land that is farmable and that not, given the Wola ability to cultivate markedly unpromising steep slopes and broken terrain. They defy conventional land use criteria, as an agronomist colleague once exclaimed 'how do these people farm such land?' Asking locals would likely further confuse issues, as different persons would have different ideas as to what is farmable land. Whose judgement should we take? This assumes they offer one. Many would decline to do so, saying that it takes clearance of a garden to establish the position, some unpromising sites proving productive – one cannot know until one farms them (Sillitoe 1996: 315). Even a close physical survey of a territory would find it difficult to delineate tracts of land as arable with changes in topography occurring over short distances. On top of this is the issue of projection; in using topographic maps, aerial photos or satellite images to assess usable land, it is necessary to correct for precipitous terrain (that is 'flatten it') or seriously underestimate available land area. While there are parametric procedures and software that can do the necessary transformations, they demand technical know-how, and are difficult to apply accurately, no matter how skilful one is,[9] in very broken-up terrain such as the Was valley region with its markedly irregular slopes.

Furthermore, not all arable land is the same as the carrying capacity equations assume. Brookfield and Brown (1963: 108) propose a modification featuring simultaneous equations to accommodate different land types (Wohlt 2004: 152-153 attempts something similar in calculating his 'occupational density index'). This demands the assessment of land types, a skilled job that needs a soil surveyor (McRae and Burnham 1981; Nortcliff 1988; Landon 1991). Even such a person would find the Was valley challenging because of the way land varies over small distances; as mentioned above. The use of topographic classes (Sillitoe 1996:115-120) to distinguish arable land types is too gross; the region of interest here all comprises steep-sided mountains and karst. Some writers try to accommodate different kinds of garden by attributing them to different topographically defined classes of land (Brookfield and Brown (1963: 105-116; Rappaport 1968: 286-87) but such a strategy fails to distinguish between different garden types or one-off swiddens and semi-permanent plots in the Was valley. The entire spectrum of land use is to be seen in small areas, such as on the same slope, reflecting the physical variability that occurs over short distances. It parallels the fragmentation of land holdings that makes boundary definition so problematic. Besides physical factors we also have cultural ones, as Ellen (1982: 41-46) points out, that inform the idea of land type and decisions about garden location, such as ease with which sites can be enclosed and convenience to homestead.

Over the decades, authors have come up with many other problems with carrying capacity including determining when degradation occurs (Fosberg 1963: 5; Street 1969; Clarke 1971: 188; Brush 1975: 807; Dewar 1984: 605-6); the failure to recognise that crops and farming regimes often change (Street 1969; Rappaport 1968: 91; Ohtsuka 1995: 315), that the assumption of homeostasis is no longer accepted by ecologists (Thomas, Chapter Six), let alone being applicable to people (Brush 1975; Glassow 1978: 32); and that many other factors not captured by these equations, including disease and political factors, determine human population distributions (Dewar 1984).

Knowing Human-Land Relations

The conundrum in assessing human-land relations is that local practices undermine etic attempts to use a universal equation to calculate carrying capacity because of difficulties measuring some of the parameters. In short, the system is too complex for such simple modelling. Yet we cannot turn to the local people for an alternative emic assessment because even though these relations are manifest in their behaviour they are not familiar with discussing them. But there are other indirect ways to gauge local views. While estimation of areas under cultivation and discussion of demographic data are alien to the Was view, people are aware, for example, that their population is expanding over time and their territory finite. It is evident that *sem* 'family' groups are growing in size. Some persons speak of the possibility of certain larger *semgenk* 'small families' dividing in two in the future as their numbers increase.

When asked about the implications of an expanding population, people do not talk about land becoming scarce. They are more likely to refer to problems finding other resources. Men may talk about the shortage of suitable hardwood timber for fencing, such as beech and oak, near where they cultivate gardens. Such shortage of available timber may prompt them not to cultivate some grassland areas, judging the labour needed to transport stakes cut elsewhere to be too demanding; it is not necessarily that the land is agriculturally poor (Allen 1984:

75 for a similar impact on the Nembi Plateau). Another concern that people might mention is the availability of firewood, which can be an issue where settlement is dense, men having to carry heavy timber considerable distances. Further, some resources are uncommon in forest adjacent to settled areas as a result of heavy local demand; such as rattan that is widely used in making a range of things (Sillitoe 1988). Given these examples, a more appropriate way to gauge pressure on resources, certainly more pertinent from a Wola perspective, would be to assess the supply of key forest products.

Those living in the Was valley are aware that they, and their ancestors, have deforested parts the region; for instance, when cultivating grassland, people sometimes dig up pieces of *pel* beech root (*Nothofagus* spp.), a dominant forest tree. But this has occurred piecemeal over many generations and they do not seem to think it is anything they should worry about unduly. If they thought that it represented serious deforestation, I should expect people to express more marked concerns about diminishing forest resources and need for action to conserve them. Nonetheless, while the Wola have no explicit cultural code of conservation, it is possible to detect a certain regard for the forest. These are evident in their beliefs of malicious forest demons called *iybtit* and *saem* (Sillitoe 1996: 201-217), which reflect an ambivalent attitude towards the forest, of esteem mixed with circumspection; they value it apprehensively. But even with the conservation message conveyed by outside western-informed education over twenty years, of which some younger persons are aware, there is little evident concern about protecting the land. It is not the Wola experience that they dominate their environment and that they are beating it up with unsustainable subsistence practices that are leading them to the edge of some Malthusian precipice. Rather the dominant party in the relationship is the environment that on occasion beats them up with climatic perturbations that make their subsistence practices ineffective, with famine occasionally taking them over the edge. (Sillitoe 2006)

Regardless of their apparently casual attitudes, the Wola have shown themselves sound custodians of their land and forest. It is not the amount of forest destruction that is surprising but that it is not more extensive, given the time humans have inhabited the region. It is probable that human activity (collecting raw materials and plant food, hunting and clearing for cultivation) has influenced and impacted upon the forest for millennia – archaeological evidence from elsewhere in the highlands suggests human presence for thousands of years (Denham 2006). This activity has contributed in some measure to the forest we see today. The current pace at which they are clearing primary forest is slow when compared with the total area cleared for cultivation. The survey data indicate that families establish some 24 percent of their new swiddens from forest (8 percent from mature rainforest), clearing the remainder from grassland (overwhelmingly *Miscanthus* cane grass) with some associated trees. This suggests that the rate of forest destruction is not as high as perhaps expected for a system featuring 'shifting cultivation' under an expanding population; only 2 percent to 3 percent of the area under cultivation at any time will have been cleared from montane rainforest. The time land lays fallow is significant concerning the rate of forest clearance. Many families bring abandoned areas back into cultivation within a few years. The shifting system evidences considerable inertia, as noted some areas remaining under cultivation for decades with occasional brief periods under grass (Sillitoe 1996). It allows the intensive cultivation of land with brief fallow interludes, something that makes it problematic to call the system shifting at all (Brookfield and Brown 1963: 162-67). The result is large areas under a virtual monocrop regime, featuring a degree of permanence that allows relatively small areas to support high densities of population compared to other shifting farming regimes.

Conclusion

The idea of carrying capacity is an engagingly simple one but when confronted with the complexity of such farming systems as those of the New Guinea highlands we encounter considerable problems with it. While we can overcome some of these technically, so long as one or more parameters remain guesstimates this will invalidate any calculation. The suggestion by Clarke (1971: 190) that we take carrying capacity to be a gradient rather than a critical limit (which suggests a range of calculations as noted using different values), does not solve the data issues. While some authorities consider it helpful to calculate carrying capacity, regardless of the problems that attend some of the data (Brookfield and Brown 1963; Rappaport 1968; Clarke 1971; Ohtsuka 1994,1995; Kinoshita 1995; Wohlt 2004), I am not convinced there is any point for the Was valley. Others signal scepticism by putting scare quotes around 'carrying capacity' (Hviding and Bayliss-Smith 2000: 139).

The declaration by some, using such calculations, that there is land shortage and degradation in parts of the highlands illustrates their shortcomings, for no Malthusian crisis has materialised decades later. It is nearly fifty years since it was suggested that highlanders are experiencing land resource problems, yet with continuing expansion of population, no ecological calamity has apparently occurred, beyond periodic food shortages resulting from El Niño fluctuations. The farming system has continued adequately to feed the increased numbers of people, where we might expect evidence of serious malnutrition or worse. Reflecting with hindsight on his earlier work, and after witnessing Chimbu gardens under cultivation for several decades, Brookfield has subsequently pointed to the robustness of local arrangements, concluding 'I can say with some confidence that I do not believe that my field area is heading for an early ecological collapse' (Brookfield 1996: 82). Recent findings in Amazonia are an object lesson here. Until a decade or so ago, there were various arguments relating land scarcity to issues such as warfare and kinship (Meggers 1996), including attempts to measure carrying capacity (Carneiro 1960). But a review of the archaeological evidence has demonstrated that Amazonia previously supported as many as ten times the number of people as currently, complying with the early explorers' reports of dense populations (Roosevelt 1989). It has also led to the reappraisal of *terra preta* anthrosols, black earths of considerable fertility that could support substantial population densities (German 2003; Prance 2004). Furthermore, the Amazon's mosaic of ecotypes and soil fertility makes region wide generalisations about land use and arability untenable (Moran 1993).

Regarding the Was valley, I am not denying Malthus's or Boserup's logic. It is indisputable that those living there have finite land resources. The argument is not about whether the Malthusian precipice exists but how close people are to it. I do not think that the Wola are yet staring over it. While the Was valley population is growing and is cutting into the surrounding forest, the gross calculations made here show that it currently has adequate land resources to cope with expansion. People are aware of this expansion too and that land resources are finite, although for them not yet scarce. They have yet to face the spectre of not enough land, currently difficult for them to imagine – although it is conceivable that their watchful guarding of their territorial rights (Sillitoe 1999b) stems in some measure from such deep-rooted albeit unrealised fears.

While forest clearance is substantially less than we might anticipate for an expanding population, which relates to the land use efficiency of the present agricultural system, clearance is nonetheless happening piecemeal. Looked at over the long term, the Wola and their predecessors unquestionably have cleared substantial areas of original forest, and look set to do so increasingly in the future with their growing numbers. There may be a crisis looming in the future as people reach the limits of their land resources and their capacity to live off their ancestors' innovativeness and capital investments (such as crop cultivar selection, composting techniques, land improvement, regrowth management, and so on), even though we cannot specify when this might occur with the accuracy suggested by carrying capacity equations. This assumes no changes in land use, the system eventually running as currently constituted over the land shortage edge. But change is probable under pressure from the outside capitalist world now impinging upon the Wola valleys with a possible oil and gas boom in the offing.

The possibility that human ingenuity will kick in and technological innovations occur before scarcity becomes a critical issue (after Boserup 1965) further questions the point of such problematic calculations. When we realise that population growth and technical change are continuous processes – whether or not related in any causal way – we have 'no discernible plateaus of stability' and consequently we have the potential of a population 'always at carrying capacity under these conditions' or below it (Glassow 1978: 41). It is arguable that economic change and opportunities for waged labour with the arrival of the capitalist market have dramatically changed the position in the highlands (Ohtsuka

1995: 316-18). Migration out of densely populated regions may have prevented a population-resource crunch; for example, participating in resettlement schemes such as the Cape Hoskins oil palm plantation programme, or seeking work at mines such as Ok Tedi with its booming town of Tabubil, or finding employment in urban centres such as Port Moresby and Lae (Keig 2001). But this again begs the point of carrying capacity calculations for limited locales, such as a single valley, when migration involves larger regions, even the entire country of Papua New Guinea or beyond.

In her introduction, Serena Heckler talks of a new TEK synthesis, advocating an approach that incorporates various aspects of peoples' lived experience and understanding of their environments, to encompass political-economic, structural or cognitive, phenomenological and applied perspectives. She suggests that we might do so by elaborating further on the trendy topic of landscape. But in discussing it, many social scientists appear to discount the physical side of landscape in their current debates (Hirsch and O'Hanlon 1995; Ingold 2000; Stewart and Strathern 2003), to the consternation of natural scientists. They discuss landscape as human-made and interpreted, as people indubitably modify the places where they live through socially informed activities (as the Wola do with their gardens) and represent place to one another in various culturally coded ways (as the Wola do with toponyms). But while the landscape may exist in the mind, it is equally out there, and subject to both natural processes and human interference. Any 'new synthesis' will need to draw on both physical and cultural aspects, as long customary in TEK studies. This chapter continues in this tradition. By focussing largely on land use, it seeks to deepen our understanding of the landscape as subject both to natural processes and human activities.

An aspect of this catholic natural and social perspective is the combination of qualitative with quantitative research. This chapter supports our editor's contention that we can enrich our understanding of people's environmental relations and knowledge by drawing on both sorts of data; something that my work takes as self-evident. The rigorous collection of data relates to another recurring issue, namely the problems we face in drawing on the sort of tacit knowledge that informs much of what people know about their environment, discussed in this chapter and elsewhere in this book. We have to rely on close observation and participation to tap into this knowledge, but we need to take care in framing any resulting understanding that we think we achieve, which inevitably draws on our worldview, as the postmodern critique affirms. While there are certain features of life that we might postulate are universal, such as people having finite resources at their disposal and their populations changing in size, the socio-cultural context in which we research these issues may varyingly influence outcomes, human-beings interpreting and intervening in their environments in many different ways. In this respect it is necessary to allow the ethnography to guide enquiries; an approach that I have tongue-in-cheek labelled 'ethnographic determinism' (Sillitoe 2003: 336-39). It should, I think, continue to be central to any 'new TEK synthesis'. It allows for cultural twists, not imposing a preconceived theoretical straightjacket, be it eco-systems, Marxist-feminism or whatever. It avoids the Z- logic chopper of European thought, so far as this is feasible, and allows us to glimpse, in tried and tested fashion, the ᚶᚶ, ᚱ· or ᛗ choppers of other understandings.

Notes

1. The figure given in Sillitoe 1996: 181 differs from these because it includes some cultivations recently under fallow; these figures include only areas currently under cultivation.
2. These population figures differ from those reported later under the discussion of demography because they include only those persons for whom I have data on all the gardens from which their homesteads consumed food; they omit some those with residences and gardens in two places, where I have incomplete data on the areas they have under cultivation elsewhere.
3. These pig population data were collected during the surveys of gardens. They were not included in the herd analysis published in *Managing Animals in New Guinea*, as they do not represent one point in time censuses, conducted between the mid and late 1973 pig census points and before the early 1977 one.
4. See for instance the contributions to the special 2001 autumn issue of *Asia Pacific Viewpoint* (volume 42, parts 2/3) that focuses on Brookfield's ideas on agricultural intensification and transformation.
5. Brush (1975: 800-801) discusses the common features of these various formulae, equating Allan's and Carneiro's without changing the mathematical relationship between the variables.
6. Unlike the Maring data reported by Rappaport (1968), who attributes a change in area under cultivation to a decline in size of a pig herd following a ritual slaughter.
7. Furthermore, as Rappaport (1968: 91) points out, calculations based on areas under cultivation do not tell us if peoples' nutritional requirements are adequately met, assuming that we can define adequate nutritional requirements.
8. There is a certain, perhaps expectable, correlation here with the relationship of women to the men who claim title to the pigs they herd, wives herding over three-quarters followed by mothers, daughters and sisters, with a range of relatives responsible for the remainder (Sillitoe 2003: 308).
9. Rappaport 1968: 285-86 refers to the difference between orthographic and surface areas and uses a factor of 16.15:15 (assuming constant 20° degree slope) to calculate increase of surface over planimetric area.

Bibliography

Allen, B. J. and Crittenden, R. 1987. 'Degradation and a Pre-Capitalist Political Economy: The Case of the New Guinea Highland'. in P. Blaikie and H. Brookfield, eds., *Land Degradation and Society* London: Methuen, pp. 143-156.

Allen, B. J. ed., 1984. *Agricultural and Nutritional Studies on the Nembi Plateau, Southern Highlands.* UPNG Geography Department. Occasional Papers (New Series) No. 4.

Allen, B.J., C. Ballard, and E. Lowes, eds.,. 2001. Special Issue of *Asia Pacific Viewpoint* 42 (2/3) on Intensification in the Asia Pacific Region.

Allen, B. J. 2001. 'Boserup and Brookfield and the Association between Population Density and Agricultural Intensity in Papua New Guinea' *Asia Pacific Viewpoint* 42 (2/3): 237-254

Bayliss-Smith, T. 1978. 'Maximum Populations and Standard Populations: The Carrying Capacity Question' in D. Green, C. Haselgrove and M. Spriggs, eds., *Social Organisation and Settlement* British Archaeological Reports International Series (Supplementary) No. 47, pp. 131-133 .

Boserup, E. 1965. *The Conditions of Agricultural Growth: The Economics of Agrarian Change Under Population Pressure.* London: Allen and Unwin

Bourke, R.M. 1988. *'Taim Hungre': Variation in Subsistence Food Supply in the Papua New Guinea Highlands.* Ph.D. dissertation, Australian National University.

Bourke, R.M., Allen B.J., Hide, R.L., Fritsch, D., Gran, R., Hobsbawn, P., Kanabe, B., Levett, M. P., Lyon, S., and Varvaliu, A. 1995. *Southern Highlands Province: Text, Summaries, Maps, Code Lists and Village Identification.* Agricultural Systems of Papua New Guinea Working Paper No. 11. Canberra: Human Geography Department, A.N.U.

Brookfield, H.C. and Brown, P. 1963. *Struggle for Land : Agriculture and Group Territories among the Chimbu of the New Guinea Highlands.* Melbourne : Oxford University Press.

Brookfield, H. C. 1973. 'Full Circle in Chimbu: A Study of Trends and Cycles' in H. Brookfield, ed., *The Pacific in Transition.* London: Edward Arnold, pp. 127-160.

Brookfield, H.C. 1996. Untying the Chimbu Circle: An Essay in and on Hindsight. in H. Levine and A. Ploeg, eds., *Work in Progress: Essays in New Guinea Highlands Ethnography in Honour of Paula Brown Glick.* Frankfurt: Peter Lang, pp. 63-84.

Brookfield. H.C. 2001. 'Intensification and Alternative Approaches to Agricultural Change' *Asia Pacific Viewpoint* 42 (2/3): 181-192.

Brush, S.B. 1975. 'The Concept of Carrying Capacity for Systems of Shifting Cultivation' *American Anthropologist* 77: 799-811.

Carneiro, R. 1960. 'Slash-and-burn Agriculture: A Closer Look at Its Implications for Settlement Patterns' in A.F.C. Wallace, ed., *Men and Cultures.* Philadelphia: University of Pennsylvania Press, pp. 229-234.

Chapman, J. 1988. 'Putting Pressures on Population: Social Alternatives to Malthus and Boserup' in J.L. Bintliff, D.A. Davidson and E.G. Grant, eds., *Conceptual Issues in Environmental Archaeology.* Edinburgh: Edinburgh University Press, pp. 291-310.

Clarke, W. C. 1971. *Place and People : An Ecology of a New Guinea Community.* Berkeley and Los Angeles : University of California Press.

Cohen, J. 1995 'Population Growth and Earth's Human Carrying Capacity' *Science* 269: 341-46.

Crittenden, R. 1982. *Sustenance, Seasonality and Social Cycles on the Nembi Plateau, Papua New Guinea.* Unpublished Ph.D. thesis, Australian National University, Canberra.

Crittenden, R. 1984. 'Pigs and Women, Colonialism and Climate' in B.J. Allen ed., *Agricultural and Nutritional Studies on the Nembi Plateau, Southern Highlands.* UPNG Geography Department. Occasional Papers (New Series) No. 4, pp. 121-172.

Davidson, D. A. 1992. *The Evaluation of Land Resources.* Harlow: Longman.

Denham, T. 2006. Envisaging Early Agriculture in the Highlands of New Guinea. in I. Lilley, ed., *Archaeology of Oceania: Australia and the Pacific Islands* Oxford: Blackwell, pp.160-188.

Dent, D. and Young, A. 1981. *Soil Survey and Land Evaluation.* London: Allen and Unwin.

Dewar, R.E. 1984. 'Environmental Productivity, Population Regulation, and Carrying Capacity' *American Anthropologist* 86 (3): 601-614.

Ellen, R.F. 1982. *Environment, Subsistence and System: The Ecology of Small-Scale Social Formations.* Cambridge: Cambridge University Press.

Feacham, R.G.A. 1973. 'A Clarification of Carrying Capacity Formulae' *Australian Geographical Studies* 11: 234-36.

Fosberg, F.R. 1963. 'The Island Ecosystem' in F.R. Fosberg, ed., *Man's Place in the Island Ecosystem.* 10th Pacific Science Congress, Honolulu: Bishop Museum Press, pp. 1-6.

German, L. A. 2003. 'Historical Contingencies in the Coevolution of Environment and Livelihood: Contributions to the Debate on Amazonian Black Earth' *Geoderma* 111: 307-331.

Glassow, M.A. 1978. 'The Concept of Carrying Capacity in the Study of Culture Process' in M.B. Schiffer, ed., *Advances in Archaeological Method and Theory* Vol. 1:. 31-48. New York: Academic Press.

Hardesty, D. L. 1977. *Ecological Anthropology.* New York: John Wiley and Sons.

Hayden, B. 1975. 'The Carrying Capacity Dilemma: An Alternative Approach' in A.C. Swedlund, ed., *Population Studies in Archaeology and Biological Anthropology.* Society for American Archaeology Memoir No. 30, pp. 11-21.

Henley, D. 1997. 'Carrying Capacity, Climatic Variation, and the Problem of Low Population Growth among Indonesian Swidden Farmers: Evidence from North Sulawesi' in P. Boomgaard, F. Colombijn and D. Henley,eds., *Paper Landscapes: Explorations in the Environmental History of Indonesia* Leiden: Koninklijk Instituut voor Taal-, Land- en Volkenkunde Press, pp. 91-120.

Hide, R.L. 1981. *Aspects of Pig Production and Use in Colonial Sinasina, Papua New Guinea.* Ph.D. dissertation, University of Columbia.

Hviding, E. and Bayliss-Smith, T. 2000. *Islands of Rainforest: Agroforestry, Logging and Eco-Tourism in Solomon Islands.* Aldershot: Ashgate

Keig, G. 2001. 'Rural Population Growth in Papua New Guinea between 1980 and 1990' *Asia Pacific Viewpoint* 42 (2/3): 255-268.

Kelly, R. C. 1968. 'Demographic Pressure and Descent Group Structure in the New Guinea Highlands' *Oceania* 30: 36-63

Kinoshita, F. 1995. 'Which Model Shall We Use? Carrying Capacity, Optimum Population, the Boserup Model and Their Application to New Guinea Highland Society' *Japanese Journal of Ethnology* 59(4): 428-41 [in Japanese].

Landon, J.R., ed., 1991. *Booker Tropical Soil Manual.* Harlow: Longman Scientific and Technical.

McRae, S.G. and C.P. Burnham. 1981. *Land Evaluation.* Oxford: Clarendon Press

Meggers, B. J. 1996. *Amazonia: Man and Culture in a Counterfeit Paradise.* Washington: Smithsonian Institution Press.

Meggitt, M. 1965. *The Lineage System of the Mae Enga of New Guinea* Edinburgh : Oliver and Boyd.

Moran, E. 1993. *Through Amazonian Eyes: The Human Ecology of Amazonian Populations.* Iowa City: University of Iowa Press.

Nortcliff, S. 1988. 'Soil Survey, Soil Classification and Land Evaluatio'. In A. Wild, ed., *Russell's Soil Conditions and Plant Growth* 11th Edition. Harlow: Longman Scientific and Technical, pp. 815-843.

Ohtsuka, R. 1994. Subsistence Ecology and Carrying Capacity in Two Papua New Guinea Populations. *Journal of Biosocial Science* 26: 395-407.

Ohtsuka, R. 1995. Carrying Capacity and Sustainable Food Production: The Facts and Prospects from Papua New Guinea. *Anthropological Science* 103 (4): 311-320.

Pataki-Schweizer, K.J. 1980. *A New Guinea Landscape: Community, Space, and Time in the Eastern Highlands.* Vol IV Anthropological Studies in the Eastern Highlands of New Guinea. Seattle: University of Washington Press

Prance, G. T. 2004. 'Indian Black Earth – *terra preta do Índio*' *Tropical Agriculture Association Newsletter* 24 (1): 32-33.

Rappaport, R.A. 1968. *Pigs for the Ancestors: Ritual in the Ecology of a New Guinea People.* New Haven: Yale University Press.

Read D.W. and LeBlanc, S. A. 2003. 'Population Growth, Carrying Capacity, and Conflict' *Current Anthropology* 44 (1): 59-85.

Roosevelt, A. 1989. 'Resource Management in Amazonia Before the Conquest: Beyond Ethnographic Projection in Resource Management in Amazonia: Indigenous and Folk Strategies'. In D. A. Posey and W. Balée (eds.) *Advances in Economic Botany* vol. 7 New York: The New York Botanical Garden, pp. 30-62.: Clarendon Press.

Sillitoe, P. 1977. 'Land Shortage and War in New Guinea' *Ethnology* 16 (no. 1): 71-81.

Sillitoe, P. 1979. *Give and Take : Exchange in Wola Society.* New York: St. Martins.

Sillitoe, P. 1983. *Roots of the Earth: The Cultivation and Classification of Crops in the Papua New Guinea Highlands.* Manchester: Manchester University Press.

Sillitoe, P. 1988. *Made in Niugini : Technology in the Highlands of Papua New Guinea.* London: British Museum Publications.

Sillitoe, P. 1996. *A Place Against Time : Land and Environment in the Papua New Guinea Highlands.* Amsterdam: Harwood Academic.

Sillitoe, P. 1998. 'The Development of Indigenous Knowledge: A New Applied Anthropology' *Current Anthropology* 39 (2): 223-252.

Sillitoe, P. 1999a. 'Where to Next?: Garden Site Selection in the Papua New Guinea Highlands' *Oceania* 69 (3): 184-208.

Sillitoe, P. 1999b. 'Beating the Boundaries: Land Tenure and Identity in the Papua New Guinea Highlands' *Journal of Anthropological Research* 55 (3): 331-360

Sillitoe, P. 2002. 'Participant Observation to Participatory Development: Making Anthropology Work' in Paul Sillitoe, Alan Bicker, and Johan Pottier, eds., *'Participating in Development': Approaches to Indigenous Knowledge.* London Routledge, pp. 1-23.

Sillitoe, P. 2003. *Managing Animals in New Guinea: Preying the Game in the Highlands.* London: Routledge

Sillitoe, P. in press 'The Demography of a New Guinea Highlands Valley' *Asian Population Studies.*

Street, J. 1969. 'An Evaluation of the Concept of Carrying Capacity' *Professional Geographer* 21: 104-107.

Umezaki, M., Kuchikura, Y., Yamauchi, T. and Ohtsuka, R. 2000. 'Impact of Population Pressure on Food Production: An Analysis of Land Use Change and Subsistence Pattern in the Tari Basin in Papua New Guinea Highlands' *Human Ecology* 28: 359-381.

Waddell, E. 1972. *The Mound Builders: Agricultural Practices, Environment, and Society in the Central Highlands of New Guinea.* American Ethnological Society Monograph No. 53. Seattle: University of Washington Press.

Wohlt, P. B. 2004. 'Descent Group Composition and Population Pressure in a Fringe Enga Clan, Papua New Guinea' *Human Ecology* 32 (2): 137-162.

Wood, A. W. 1984. *Land For Tomorrow: Subsistence Agriculture, Soil Fertility and Ecosystem Stability in the New Guinea Highlands.* Ph.D. thesis, University of Papua New Guinea.

Young, A. 1998. *Land Resources: Now and for the Future.* Cambridge: Cambridge University Press.

Zubrow, E.B.W. 1971. 'Carrying Capacity and Dynamic Equilibrium in the Prehistoric Southwest' *American Antiquity* 36: 127-138.

Chapter 11

Managing the Gabra Oromo Commons of Kenya, Past and Present

Aneesa Kassam and
Francis Chachu Ganya

Introduction

In this chapter, based on an ethnographic case study, we dispute the 'mainstream view held by many colonial and postcolonial administrators in East Africa, that claims that nomadic pastoralists mismanage their environment (Sandford 1983: 11-19). This belief was given scholarly credence by the 'tragedy of the commons' thesis propounded by the biologist Garrett Hardin (1968), based on the notions of 'carrying capacity' (for a discussion of this concept see essays in Behnke et al. 1993, and Sillitoe, Chapter Ten) and of population growth. The thesis was also used to support the argument of rangeland ecologists, such as Lamprey (1983), that pastoralists were responsible for causing desertification, or severe land degradation. These views influenced the formulation of misguided development policies, which resulted in the irreversible break down of numerous traditional systems of pastoral management in East Africa and contributed to the tragic loss of nomadic livelihoods.

As research undertaken in Africa by ecologists in the last two decades indicates, these hypotheses are based on 'equilibrium' approaches to the environment (Ellis and Swift 1988; Behnke et al. 1993; Thomas, Chapter Six). The term equilibrium 'connotes an ecosystem or community where populations are more or less in balance with resources, other populations or external forces like climate', such as in wetlands (Ellis 1995: 37). 'Non-equilibrium' ecosystems, on the other hand, 'are those where populations or other components are not in long-term balance with other elements of the system, thus are unpredictable and sometimes undergo complex dynamic behaviour' (Ellis 1995: 38). Tropical drylands are characterised primarily by non-equilibrium systems. This revisionist view, inspired by the work of Holling (1973), recognises that communities living in the arid and semi-arid lands developed complex strategies for coping with environmental stress. These findings have new implications for development policy and planning in pastoral societies (Scoones 1995).

Similarly, Hardin's thesis came under scrutiny by common property theorists who demonstrated that most collectively owned lands are managed according to a set of rules and regulations that prevent the overexploitation of resources. As part of their analysis of common property regimes (henceforth CPR), contributors to the volume *Making the Commons Work* (Bromley 1992) applied a conceptual framework developed by Ronald Oakerson. However, none of these case studies deal specifically with traditional ecological knowledge (henceforth TEK). Berkes (1999: 8) defines TEK as 'a cumulative body of knowledge, practice and belief, evolving by adaptive processes and handed down through generations by cultural transmission, about the relationships of living beings (including humans) with one another and with their environment.' He considers indigenous ecological knowledge to be a subset of TEK.

In this chapter, we apply a modified version of this framework to examine the case of the Gabra Oromo camel nomads of northern Kenya.[1] We describe how they managed their rangelands based on their indigenous ecological knowledge and show how this system of natural resource management (henceforth NRM) has survived to the present day, albeit with some changes. In other words, we show that this knowledge is 'traditional', but not static, in that it can dynamically incorporate change, whilst continuing to draw on the practical and experiential lessons of the past.

We begin with a discussion of the theoretical and methodological issues pertaining to the commons and explain why it was necessary to modify the Oakerson framework. We then provide ethnographic and historical background to the Gabra community and to the formation of their territory in Kenya. The sections that follow outline the physical features of Gabra territory and describe their property rights, strategies of herd management and land-use, units of resource management and decision-making processes. Finally, we evaluate the Gabra system of NRM based on the empirical evidence and conclude that it is a sustainable and resilient one.

The Commons Problematic

The term the 'commons' derives from Anglo-Saxon common law and refers to communal lands or resources that are governed by formal or informal institutional arrangements, generally consisting of rules or practices vested in custom, tradition, kinship and social mores, which regulate use (Ciriacy-Wantrup and Bishop 1975: 715). The concept became the subject of theoretical focus following the controversy raised by Hardin (1968), in which he claimed that individuals have a tendency to overexploit common resources for their own benefit, bringing about a 'Tragedy of the Commons' for all the users. He took the overstocking of communal grazing land as symptomatic of such behaviour.

In the debate that ensued, scholars argued that it was important to distinguish between common land in which access is open to all (*res nullius*, 'unowned property') and common land in which a community of users restricts access (*res communes*, 'communal property') (Ciriacy-Wantrup and Bishop 1975: 715). As Hardin (1991) himself later clarified, the kind of tragedy that he had described only occurred when access to land was *unregulated*. In fact, as researchers demonstrated (see Bromley 1992), most forms of communal land are held under what is known as a 'common property regime' or set of rules that regulates access and collective use.

The anthropological engagement with the commons debate (see McCay and Acheson 1987) followed an earlier tradition in the study of property rights and land-tenure in pre-capitalist societies by emphasising the social embeddedness of such regimes (Hann 1998: 1-47). As Peters (1987: 172) explains, 'The commons system is by its very nature a socio-cultural system embedded in historical specific time and space.' She adds: 'The definition of rights, of relative claims, of appropriate uses and users are not only embedded in specific historical sets of political and economic structures, but also in cultural systems of meanings, symbols and values' (Peters 1987: 178). This work intersects with the anthropological interest in TEK and in the management of natural resources in non-western societies.

Analytical Frameworks for Studying Common Property Regimes

In our analysis, we apply the following conceptual framework outlined by Oakerson (1992: 41-59) but also extend and modify it. The framework identifies four levels of analysis, which are dynamically interrelated:

1) physical and technical attributes of the resource: 'limiting conditions' of joint production, technology used; boundaries, excludability and divisibility of resource;

2) decision-making arrangements: social institutions, operational rules regulating use; arrangements with external bodies (government, market forces); sanctions imposed; problems of equity (through corruption and abuse of authority);

3) patterns of interaction between users: cooperation and non-cooperation; individual strategies in relation to collective ones, the 'free-rider' problem;[2]
4) outcomes: criteria for evaluating efficiency and equity and consequences for users.

As Oakerson (1992: 42) notes, this framework can be adapted to fit specific case materials. There are, however, three problems associated with its application to the study of a traditional system of NRM, such as that of the Gabra: (1) it is ahistorical – it does not take into account how such CPRs develop and only partially how they change over time; (2) it is not culturally grounded – it does not take into account the particular knowledge system through which the resources are managed; (3) its criteria for evaluating the efficacy of a CPR are rather limited.

In our application of this model, we therefore follow Berkes (1999: 13-14) in adding an historical dimension and in treating the Gabra NRM system as part of what he terms a 'knowledge-practice-belief complex'. Berkes sees this complex as being made up of four interrelated levels (1) local knowledge of land and animals; (2) land and resource management systems; (3) social institutions; (4) worldview. These levels of analysis cannot be applied as systematically as those of Oakerson, but can serve to complement his framework. In addition, on the basis of empirical studies, we assess whether the Gabra NRM system has indeed managed to avert a tragedy of the commons, and use the alternative criteria of sustainability and resilience to discuss its long-term performance (on the problem of criteria, see Berkes 1996: 101-102). Sustainability refers to the ability of a system to survive and persist over time (Constanza and Folke 1996: 19), whereas resilience refers to the ability of both human and natural populations to absorb and recover from the perturbations that are intrinsic features of non-equilibrium systems (Holling 1973; Holling and Sanderson 1996). This modified framework has enabled us to reinterpret and to elaborate on other studies of the Gabra and to show how the different components of their pastoral system still function as parts of an integral whole. In addition to our own fieldwork and professional experiences, this analysis draws extensively on the cultural ecological and historical studies of Torry (1973), Robinson (1985; 1989) and Sobania (1980; 1988; 1990).[3]

The Gabra

The Gabra pastoral nomads live on both sides of the Kenya-Ethiopia border and currently number some 50,000 persons (Tablino 1999: 19) (Figure 11.1). They are divided into two sub-groups. The highland Gabra Miigo (about 15,000) live mainly on the Ethiopian side, whilst the lowland Gabra Malbe (about 35,000) are found predominantly on the Kenyan side. The Gabra probably emerged historically as a distinct ethnic group as a result of a shift from cattle pastoralism to camel pastoralism over the past three centuries, due to increasing environmental desiccation (Robinson 1985; Sobania 1980; 1988). This specialisation eventually led to the adoption of a new identity. The Gabra clans are made up of an amalgamation of groups and individuals that trace their origins to a number of other ethnic groups in the region (Goto 1972; Kassam 2006). This composite structure, which is common in the area (see Hjort 1981; Spencer 1973; Sobania 1980), is a reflection of some of the environmental upheavals that the Gabra have undergone in the past and of the types of social accommodation that they have reached in order to survive ecological catastrophe.[4] Gabra culture reflects these diverse origins, but has, nevertheless, managed to achieve a remarkable degree of coherence (see Tablino 1999). The Gabra share cultural elements, such as language, religion, social organisation and system of NRM, with the territorially adjacent cattle-keeping Borana pastoralists, whilst their ritual and calendrical systems, material culture and techniques of camel production are common to other camel peoples. Like the Borana, the Gabra belong to the larger nation of Oromo peoples of the Horn of Africa. Little is known about the Ethiopian Gabra Miigo. In this study, we focus on the Gabra Malbe of Kenya.

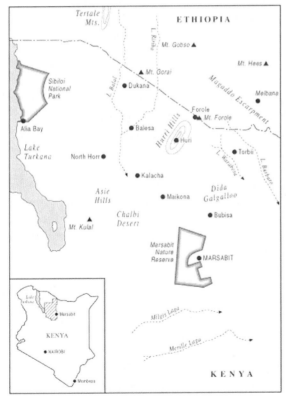

Figure 11.1: Map of Gabra territory on the Kenya-Ethiopia border

Formation of Gabra Malbe Territory

The Gabra Malbe are divided into five territorial sections (*gosa*), or phratries: the Algaana, Gaara, Galboo, Sharbaana and Odoola. These phratries currently occupy a territory (*laftii Gabraa*) of between 35,000-40,000 square kilometres in the Marsabit District of northern Kenya. This territory is demarcated by Alia Bay on Lake Turkana to the west, the Magaddo escarpment to the north, the Dida Galgalloo plains to the east, and a line, which runs from Marsabit mountain in the southeast, across the expanse of the Chalbi desert (Robinson 1985: 26-27). These boundaries are designated by the term *seera* (literally, 'law'). In effect, Gabra and Borana traditionally conceptualised their relationship with their environment as one based on custom and law (*aadaa seera*) (Kassam and Megerssa 1994).[5]

   This territory corresponds approximately to the 'tribal grazing area' that was delimited in the 1920s by the British colonial authorities as part of the policy of separating the different pastoralist groups in the area (Sobania 1980: 273-287). These new boundaries overlaid the more fluid ones that had previously existed between the groups (Sobania 1990). Until the closing decade of the nineteenth century, the rangelands of the Gabra constituted one of the components of the Borana territorial system, which exploited different ecological niches (Kassam 2006). These rangelands formed part of the lowland climatic zone (*deeda golbituu*), which was suited to camel production (Oba 1998: 10). The Gabra had full user-rights to this territory, which included access to dry season wells and pastures. Other camel-keeping groups, like the Adjuran, Garre and Sakuye, were also accorded user-rights to water and pasture. All these groups were expected to adhere to the traditional body of customs and laws that governed resource use, regulated mutual relations, and provided mechanisms for conflict resolution. These laws were reviewed every eight years at a pan-Borana assembly (*gummii Gaayoo*), which is still held today, as part of their traditional system of governance (see Shongollo 1994). These communities also formed part of the military alliance (*goolii*), through which the Borana defended their territory from incursion by the Somali. Until the introduction of modern firearms at the end of the nineteenth century, the Borana, who had a mounted cavalry, were largely successful in defending this territory.

   In 1897, the traditional lands of the Borana and Gabra were divided into two separate territories by an international border, which demarcated the limits of what were to become the Ethiopian and British colonies. Due to the Ethiopian tactic of terrorising the local population and extracting tribute (*gibr*) in the form of livestock and labour, large numbers of Borana and more than half of the Gabra sought refuge on the Kenyan side (Sobania 1980: 234; 267). The Ethiopians retaliated by launching armed attacks against these fugitives, whom they considered to be their tribute-paying subjects, and demanded their repatriation. In 1914, these continued acts of reprisal led British administrators to allow the Gabra refugees to stay in the colony and to offer them official protection (Robinson 1985: 398).[6]

This decision raised the problem of where the Gabra should be allowed to graze and water their animals. Whilst this allocation was being made, the Gabra had begun to reoccupy their former dry season grazing tracts in the Hurri Hills and to use watering points in the surrounding areas. In 1919, when the tribal grazing areas of each group were officially delimited, this part of the district was attributed solely to the Gabra, at the expense of the Rendille and Samburu pastoralists, who had also previously used it. In 1938, the boundary between the Gabra and Rendille, known as the Stigand Line, was officially drawn (O'Leary 1990: 58). In the same year, British authorities enlarged the territory of the Gabra, by opening up an area in the northwest corner of Marsabit District, which had been a kind of 'no man's land', due to the problems of insecurity. Despite the border restrictions, the Gabra continued to return to southern Ethiopia in times of drought and to make pilgrimages to their sacred sites every eight years.

Through the delimitation of these tribal grazing reserves, the British authorities created exclusion zones around each of the pastoral groups in the area, which they enforced through armed patrols. Any trespass of these zones resulted in the forcible relocation, fines and confiscation of the livestock of the pastoralists, which were only partially lifted during drought periods (see O'Leary 1990: 60). These new boundaries radically changed the ways that groups had previously negotiated access to each other's territories, and led to shifts in their traditional grazing and watering patterns.[7] The loss of rangeland by the Rendille to Gabra and Borana in the Chalbi basin and on Marsabit mountain also had a detrimental effect on the ethnic relations between these groups, aggravating conflicts over resources.

Natural Resources and Property Rights

The major limiting condition for pastoral production in the arid and semi-arid lands of northern Kenya is that of low annual rainfall. At lower altitudes, such as in the Chalbi basin, rainfall varies from 150-200 mm, whilst at higher altitudes, such as on Marsabit mountain, it can measure up to 1,000mm (Bake 1983). As in the rest of East Africa, the rains are bimodal, and precipitation is influenced by the monsoon system. However, this pattern of rainfall varies considerably from year to year and is unevenly distributed. Rain is produced through localised storms that occur within a very short radius, sometimes as little as five kilometres wide, which leave inter-storm areas completely dry (Wallen and Gwynne 1978: 27). As a result, forage production, which is dependent on rainfall, is also highly variable (McPeak 2003: 517). The Gabra distinguish four seasons: the long rains (*ganna*) that occur between April and June, with the onset of the southeast monsoon; a long, cool dry season (*adolessa*) which extends from June to early October; short rains (*hagaya*) that begin in late October and last until December, brought by the northeast monsoon; followed by a hot, dry, windy season (*bon hagaya*) (Robinson 1985: 40).

Among the Gabra, as for the Borana (see Bassi 2005), the communal natural resources of pasture and water are governed by customary laws (*seera marra bisaan*), which are implemented through the units of resource management described below. Grazing land is theoretically open to all members of the community, but in practice pasturage is dependent on access to water. Cattle must be watered every three to four days in all seasons, sheep and goats must be taken to water every three to five days, and camels watered every eleven to fourteen days in the dry season. Water resources are thus subject to a strict set of regulations. This water code is common to both the Gabra and Borana (see Helland 1984).

Wells (*eela*), both shallow (*adadi*) and deep (*tulla*), and springs (*maddo*) are the only sources of permanent water. These wells constitute, therefore, a critical and strategic resource and are subject to a high degree of communal control. A form of property right is applied, known symbolically as *konffi* (after the wooden digging stick that was used in excavating wells in the past). The person who originally invested stock and labour in digging a well is said to be the 'father of the well' (*abba eelaa*), in the sense of being its 'custodian'.[8] The well is named after its excavator. This is an inalienable right, held in perpetuity by the male heirs of the individual. It gives the custodian's family priority to, but not exclusive use, of the well. The living custodian usually forms part of the local well council (*jarsaa eelaa* 'elders of the wells') that is constituted to manage the wells in a particular area. This council appoints an official (*abba hareegaa*) to oversee the watering schedule through which equitable use rights are allocated to all the herd owners encamped in the area. The well council is also responsible for allocating and supervising all the tasks required for maintaining the well.

The custodianship to a well extends to its immediate vicinity. The zone (*itisa*) outside the well, where the animals are held as they await their turn to be watered, and any shade trees in this holding area are said to 'belong' to the father of the well. Similarly, the watering troughs (*nanniga*) and the perimeter (*dargula*) immediately outside the well where livestock rest after drinking are also under his care, and no one may enter or use these areas without prior permission. Any infringement of the laws (*seera lafaa eelaa*) governing the temporary and permanent water resources is deemed to have damaged the pans and wells of the community (*hara-eela boranaa baleesa*) and is sanctioned by a fine imposed by the council of elders (*jaarsa gosaa*) of the phratry.[9] The ultimate sanction is exclusion.

Livestock, on the other hand, is 'owned' by the head of the family unit (*abba warraa*), who acts as the principal manager and custodian of the animals on behalf of his dependents. Individuals, including women, have specific property rights in the collective herd, which are acquired through generation-set, marriage and other rituals (O'Leary 1985: 206-209; Torry 1973; Dahl 1979).

Strategies of Herd Management and Land Use

As part of their system of managing these resources, Gabra have developed a number of herd management strategies, which include (a) herd division, (b) mobility, (c) species diversification, (d) territorial dispersion and (e) risk minimisation (see Dahl 1979: 40). Such interlinked strategies function as a form of land use (see Swift 1975: 443-454).

Gabra employ a rotational system of range use, which follows a highland/lowland axis (Torry 1973: 219-220). The seasonal migrations in this transhumant orbit are known as *qayath* and *kunn* (Ganya et al. 2004: 64). As part of their strategy of herd division, Gabra divide the different categories of livestock spatially into base camp or home herds (*warra*) consisting of young and lactating animals whose milk can be used to provide food for women, children and elderly, and into satellite camp (*foora*) herds, made up of dry and non-productive animals. This division of the herds enables Gabra to use pastures (*allo*) at the furthest limits of their territory for dry stock so that they are not competing for grazing from milk-herds. In the dry season, home herds are generally located within a day's walk of permanent water, whilst satellite herds, depending on the category of livestock, may use rangeland as far as 70 kms away (see Robinson 1985: 232). Satellite camps thus have the maximum amount of mobility. At the beginning of the wet season, the base camps move up (*qayath*) to the Hurri Hills, where the animals can browse on fresh vegetation growth and use groundwater pools and water in rock catchments, and more recently, man-made dams. When these sources of pasture and water begin to dry out, base camps gradually move down (*kunn*) back to the dry season pastures in the lowland. Base camps may also make shorter moves (*gargalfachitii*) to prevent tick infestation and dung accumulation in enclosures. Base and satellite camps generally come together for a short period for communal sacrifices (*sorio*), which are normally held in the two wet seasons, when milk is plentiful, and for the celebration of the New Year (*almado*). In the past, this pattern of mobility allowed the dry season pastures in the proximity of permanent wells in the lowlands to lie fallow for a season and to have time to regenerate. However, this pattern of use is changing, due to the greater sedentism of base camps.

Following their strategy of herd diversification, Gabra keep four different categories of livestock: camels, cattle, sheep and goats, all of which are adapted to the harsh ecological conditions (Alberro 1986; Dahl 1979: 40).[10] Since these different species of livestock have different watering and pasture needs, they are dispersed in different parts of the territory. This herd dispersal stretches the labour capacity of the family, but in the event of a disaster, it is a way of minimising risk.

In the past, as part of this strategy of risk minimisation, Gabra, like other pastoralists in the region, established wide-ranging networks of exchange for coping with total or quasi-total herd loss when the rains failed completely, when
disease struck or when people became victims of inter-ethnic raids (Dahl 1979;
Sobania 1980; 1988; 1990; Torry 1973). This system of exchange functioned at
both the intra- and inter-ethnic levels. At the intra-ethnic level, herders were
linked by a wide circle of stock friendships (*jaala*) through which they made
loans (*dabarree*) of lactating or breeding stock to men belonging to the same age-
grade. These 'animals of friendship' created a bond between the two individuals
and their families and extended their primary kinship and affinal networks. This
form of loan still exits between men who have viable herds.

At the inter-ethnic level, a system of institutionalised exchange (*tirrissoo*)
linked Gabra and Borana, which enabled them to keep camels or cattle herds in
each other's territories and to assist one another in times of need (Torry 1973:
52-54; Oba personal communication to Kassam 2004). A symbiotic relationship also linked them to Waata hunter-gatherers. In addition, Gabra had trading relations with the Konso and Arbore agro-pastoralists of southern Ethiopia,
with whom they exchanged small stock for grain. These forms of exchange
served as a means of redistributing stock to poorer families through which the
participants gained status and prestige in the community. They also had practical functions, buffering herd owners from sudden losses and providing a way of
solving problems of labour shortage. In good ('boom') years, herd owners, especially those who have access to a larger work force, still tend, therefore, to accu-
mulate stock and maximise their herds as an insurance against bad ('bust') years.

Units of Resource Management

Gabra units of resource management (Figure 11.2), like the Borana ones, are
embedded in the social structure. They are made up of a number of concentri-
cally nested social units, which carry out economic and other activities. These
interlocking socio-economic units provide the institutional arrangements
through which the pasture and water resources are managed and were defended
in the recent past. The arrangements operate on a set of rules encoded in custom and law, which inform resource use and protect culturally and economically
important trees and certain wildlife species.[11] Any infringements are dealt with
at the different levels and livestock fines are imposed on the offender(s) by phratry officials. The following units of resource management can be identified
(adapted from Torry 1973: 170-210 and updated):

(1) *Warra*, the 'family homestead', is the basic unit of social and economic
    organisation. It represents the primary stock-owning unit, comprising of
    a number of spatially dispersed sub-units of animals of different species,

under the management of the male head of the family. The family homestead is usually made up of one or more consanguinely related households (*ibidda*, literally 'hearth'), each of which is represented by a tent
(*mana*). Together, these households constitute 'the smallest group of people which can take independent decisions over the allocation of its members' domestic and herding labour and over the use, allocation and
location of their livestock capital' (Dahl 1979: 70). This family homestead is the minimal herding unit and pens its stock together. It forms a
unit of consumption, sharing any non-food resources and performing
rituals together.

(2) *Solola* are 'clusters of homesteads', which may sometimes decide to band
together for the sake of mutual convenience. The members of these clusters are generally 'linked by first-order affinal ties or close patrilateral
bonds' (Torry 1973: 202), with a strong tendency towards the former.
The most senior man in the cluster will act as the head of the unit in all
decision-making meetings in respect to the use of water and pasture
resources. These homesteads pen stock together, but each has its own
gate (*karra*) within the enclosures of the different categories of livestock.
The members of the cluster cooperate in a number of economic tasks,
taking their animals out to graze and watering them together, and send-
ing their dry herds to the same satellite camps, supplementing each
other's food resources and celebrating all rituals together.

(3) *Olla* 'base camps' are made up of homesteads from the same or different
Gabra phratries that merge temporarily for one or more seasons. This is
the most common form of socio-economic grouping, which is normally
made up of about ten or more homesteads. The camp has a headman
(*abba ollaa*) who is generally from the most senior clan and/or phratry
and is responsible for all affairs pertaining to the camp, including the resolution of conflict. He confers with the other heads of households in
making decisions about the use of resources in the vicinity of the camp,
representing the camp in meetings (*kora*) at the neighbourhood level to
negotiate use of wells for the camp and prepares the watering schedule.
He receives and caters for all visitors and any new families wishing to
join an established camp must first seek his permission. When the camp
decides to move, he arranges for scouts to be sent out to assess the new
sites. Camps are close-knit communities, which assist each another and
participate in all activities that take place. They are also a unit of ritual
organisation and the heads of household plan and perform their rites
together. Anyone who fails to cooperate in these tasks is socially
ostracised (*albakkuu*).

(4) *Reera* is a 'neighbourhood cluster' made up of three or more camps that
live within a short distance of each other and form a larger unit of coop-

eration. Such camp clusters generally share a common shade tree for meetings. At these meetings, the household heads of neighbouring camps meet to adjudicate and settle disputes, formulate watering policies and regulate use of pastures. They also perform rituals together.

(5) *Arda*, meaning 'locality', is a unit made up of several neighbourhood camp clusters. In the past, it was responsible for managing a complex of wells or springs associated with it. Today, such localities have become the sites of permanent settlements, such those of Maikona, Kalacha, North Horr, Bubissa, and Dukana, and are a blend of the traditional and the modern. They consist of large semi-sedentary populations, some living in nomadic tents, others in permanent mud houses with metal roof sheeting, which are grouped around a police post, school, church, dispensary and small shops. These settlements also serve as centres for the distribution of famine relief in times of drought. In the colonial period, such districts had government appointed local chiefs or headmen. Until the recent past, high ranking phratry or clan officials presided at meetings held at this level to oversee the use of the pasture and water in the area, to resolve conflict and to collect livestock contributions (*hirba*) that would assist families who had suffered stock losses due to a raid or some other disaster. Today, both Gabra and non-Gabra officials may participate in discussions relating to the welfare of the community. Gabra leaders continue to regulate and monitor the use of water and pasture in and around the settlements, but not as effectively as in the past. In some of the larger settlements, therefore, environmental management committees made up of phratry officials, the local chief and councillor, and women and youth representatives, have been formed to perform these and other functions.

(6) Localities form part of the 'phratry rangeland' (*deeda*) customarily associated with each of the five sections, within which they follow ritually circumscribed circuits. Each phratry has a council (*yaa*) that serves as an administrative and political organ to oversee the affairs of the section. The council is made up of the leader of the set in power, custodians of the phratry's sacred objects, legal dignitaries (*hayyuu*) and their assistants (*jallabaa*) and retired religious elders (*jaarsa loota*). Council officials represent the phratry for a period of seven years. The functions of the assembly include the adjudication of disputes that have not been resolved at the other levels, the settlement of issues relating to collective resource-use, the imposition of fines, the performance of major rituals for the well being of the phratry as a whole, and the hand over of power to the next set. Today, the councils also participate in development issues pertaining to the section (see Linquist and Adolpf 1996).[12]

(7) The inter-phratry council (*kora dibbee shanaan*) is the highest decision-making body and judicial authority governing the Gabra and their resources. It meets at infrequent intervals to resolve conflicts and problems that may be causing disunity within the Gabra people as a whole. It met in 1884 to review judicial matters, and in 1887 to make livestock distributions to the impoverished (Robinson 1985: 108-109). The most recent meeting was held in 1997 to discuss internal divisiveness caused by the national election (Soga 2005; Tablino 1999: 242-3). The council also called, amongst other things, for greater environmental protection around the settlements.

Figure 11.2: Gabra units of resource management

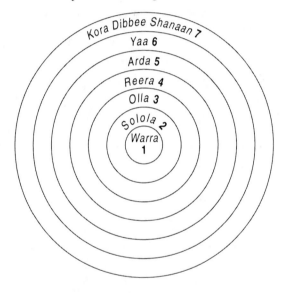

1 Family homestead
2 Cluster of affinally related homesteads
3 Base camp
4 Neighbourhood cluster
5 Locality
6 Phratry council
7 Inter-phratry council

Decision-Making Processes

As we have seen, the harsh conditions of the environment in which the Gabra live require that they have a high degree of mobility. In order to deal with the variable conditions and seasonal changes in water and pasture, herd owners need to track forage opportunistically whilst taking into account the watering needs of the different categories of livestock.[13] The decision (*mari*) that a herd-owner makes in respect to when and where to move is critical to the survival of people and animals. As O'Leary (1985: 175) notes, 'the factors which influence decisions regarding movement are multiple, complex and interrelated.' These factors include the availability of labour and problems of security. This decision-making process forms part of a highly developed system of information sharing between male heads of households through which a cumulative oral data base on the climatic and environmental history of the area has been built up over time. Oral historians (*jaarsa argaa dhageettii*) specialise in recording this information, which forms part of an elaborate system of time reckoning (Tablino 1999; Robinson 1985). Based on this historical and climatic knowledge system, these elders are able to predict drought and to advise those who consult them to plan accordingly (Robinson 1985; 1989).

The male head of the household normally takes decisions relating to the movement of the home and satellite herds in consultation with his eldest son. In the case of the home herd, this decision is usually taken when pastures begin to be exhausted, an indication of which is the lower milk yield from stock. Before a decision is reached, herd owners gather information about the water and pasture availability at the new site during stock watering or at community meetings. Generally, the decision to move is made when rain can be seen to be falling in the distance, which heralds fresh vegetation growth. Stock camps thus 'follow the rain' (Robinson 1985: 227-231). In this case, the camp may decide to send out scouts (*aburruu*) to assess the amount of rainfall, the quantity and quality of vegetation growth generated, and the numbers of people moving towards the new site. The scouts also report on security in the area. As Oba (1998: 466) has shown, these scouts evaluate a site both in terms of its grazing suitability and potential capacity. Their assessment is based on a number of criteria, which include the proximity of salt licks, soil and vegetation types and their suitability for different species of livestock, as well as historical knowledge of an area. Among Gabra, this knowledge is embodied in two concepts, those of *finna* and *koshee*, which relate to the 'fertility' of an area in a broad sense, through which animals prosper or not, in spite of good grazing.[14] As Oba (1998: 466) explains, '*Finna* is a product of climate, ecology and socio-political events that influence the lives of people and livestock.' When this element is missing, livestock do not gain weight, do not produce milk, do not mate, and their general body condition is not good. This is not a permanent condition of the range; it fluctuates. *Koshee* relates more specifically to the nourishing power of the grass and vegetation due to the quality of the soil, which makes the animals grow fat and keeps them healthy (Leus 1995: 517). Gabra identify at least one hundred and fifty plant species and know where and when particular species can be found in their territory, and the type of soils with which these plants are associated (Stiles and Kassam 1991; Kassam fieldnotes 1985-1989; O'Leary 1985: 210-213).

Gabra have an elaborate method for recording this environmental information as part of their historical chronology (Robinson 1985). Like the Borana, they have a cyclical view of history and see events as repeating themselves. They use an eight-year cycle (*bara*) as the basic unit of historical computation, which is linked to the initiation of their religious elders (*dabeelaa*) and to the promotion of a new generation-set. Due to Islamic influence, Gabra name each of the years in this cycle according to the days of the week (see Tablino 1999: 36-44). Each of these days is also associated with an animal or has some other connotation, which gives the day its special 'character' or 'nature' (*ayyaana*). These week-day names form a cycle of eight when the same day returns (i.e. Monday to Monday). Thus, 2008 is a Saturday Year, and 2009 will be a Sunday Year and so forth. Friday years, when religious elders are normally initiated, mark the beginning of the cycle.

Gabra name each of these years in the cycle according to the most significant events that marked them. For example, 1896 to 1897 is named the 'Saturday Year the Ethiopians Came' (*Sabdi Siddam Dufe*) from the north and the 'Saturday Year the British Came' (*Sabdi Ferenjii Dufe*) from the south (Robinson 1985: 114; 364). They also record the climatic conditions that prevailed in that particular year. Using this week-year cycle as a mnemonic device, most herd owners are able to remember where they and their herds were in most years, the amount of seasonal rainfall or its failure, and any out-of-season rainfall. Gabra also have precise terms for the different types of rain, which enables them to record whether rain was light, medium or heavy. These oral rainfall data correlate extremely well with scientific records (Robinson 1985; 1989). They also remember any livestock and animal diseases that occurred, invasion of pests (like locusts), astronomical events (such as an eclipse), as well as any raids from neighbouring groups that took place.

Most of the elders interviewed by Robinson (1985) could recount the years back to the beginning of the last century, whilst the oral historians could do so as far back to about 1870. Through these records, historians are able to discern cyclical weather patterns of different lengths, which enable them to predict drought and to advise others in making strategic decisions of where to move their stock in order to minimise herd losses. These oral traditions contradict scientific studies, which were unable to identify cyclical trends (see Bake 1983). This 'cyclical' conception of time and change, which is based on the idea of fertility and takes into account unpredictable factors, is a central aspect of the worldview of the Gabra and Borana.

Sustainability and Resilience of the Gabra System of Natural Resource Management

Scientific studies of the Gabra system of management would indicate that their CPR is effective. Between 1976 and 1984, the Integrated Project for Arid Lands

(IPAL) established by UNESCO as part of its Man and Biosphere Programme, carried out research on livestock, vegetation, soil and geomorphology, hydrology, climate, and human ecology of the pastoral groups of Marsabit District. A number of reports pertaining to these topics were published. Contrary to the assumption that pastoralists were responsible for causing desertification, these findings revealed that range degradation was not widespread, but was limited to the areas immediately surrounding the permanent settlements that had arisen since the 1960s. As Lusigi (1986: 340) observes, 'the deterioration of the range observed in northern Kenya cannot be attributed to the proper strategies for range utilisation, but rather to modern developments like population growth, reduced home range of the pastoralists, lack of herding labour due to schools, decreased movement of camps due to development of permanent water boreholes and missionary and marketing centres.'

In effect, a report by Schwartz et al. (1991) characterised 80 percent of the rangelands in the district as being in good condition, 18 percent as fair, and only 2 percent as being poor or very poor. This localised degradation was attributed to the reduction of the territories of the groups in the colonial and post-colonial eras and to problems of insecurity in the area, which meant that 40 percent of the rangeland in the district was being under-utilised (Lusigi 1986: 342). Lusigi suggested that if this problem were addressed, exclusion zones could be enforced to reverse the process of degradation. The studies also showed that whilst there was over-stocking at the micro-level, at the macro-level the problem was one of livestock distribution on the range, rather than of excessive holdings. In fact, they indicated that the district could support twice its livestock densities (Lusigi 1986: 342). The major problem identified by IPAL was rather one of population growth in the settlements, where a large number of famine-relief dependent pastoralists, rendered quasi-destitute by the droughts of the 1960s and 1970s, had become sedentarised, putting pressure on the surrounding rangelands.[15] Researchers reported that this trend was particularly marked among the Rendille, but noted that Gabra base camps were also confining their migratory orbits to within easy reach of water resources in the lowland areas. However, they added that satellite camps were still highly mobile in both groups. The project recommended, therefore, that these constraints be addressed and that the indigenous systems of management be strengthened and supported (Lusigi 1986: 344).

Subsequent studies on the Gabra by McPeak (2003, 2005) supported IPAL's findings on localised degradation, under-stocking of the range and distribution of livestock due to problems of insecurity. In particular, McPeak's (2005) analysis of herd accumulation shows that far from being an irrational strategy, it has an economic logic, the benefits of which outweigh the investment in a savings account. He found that this practice did not result in a significant stocking externality outside of the main settlements (see note 2).

Between 1990 and 2004, the German Agency for Technical Cooperation (GTZ), initiated the Marsabit Integrated Development Programme to continue the work of IPAL in the district. The programme held intra- and inter-community workshops to address some of the problems that had been identified. Led by these discussions, environmental management committees that built on the traditional units were established to manage resources at the locality level. Later, these management units were grouped into larger grazing area units that encompassed several localities. Finally, peace committees were formed to deal with the problem of insecurity and ethnic tension between groups at the intra-territorial level. Despite the problems of instituting these parallel management structures, some of the environmental problems were fairly effectively tackled and areas unused in the past due to inter-ethnic conflict were opened up (McPeak et al. 2005). However, a number of problems highlighted by IPAL, such as that of land-tenure, still remain to be resolved.

The contemporary Gabra system of natural resource management can, therefore, be largely described as a sustainable and well functioning one. This success can be attributed to the resilience of the Gabra and to their ability to recover from the multiple social, economic, political and ecological crises that have occurred in their system of production and way of life over the last century or more and to their capacity to rebuild their herds. According to oral historians, the conjunction of such disasters, which represent critical 'breaking points' (*cinna*), have occurred nine times in the past, the most recent being the rinderpest pandemic of the 1880s. The Gabra coped with these crises by reorganising themselves, deploying a number of time-tested strategies of survival (see Robinson 1985: 322-426), and finding solutions to new problems. The 2005 drought (a 'Wednesday' Year, prone to drought) also severely tested those capabilities. Whilst it is true that the Gabra, like other pastoralists in the region, have become more dependent on food aid and other forms of external assistance, in the 1984 drought (also a 'Wednesday' Year), they were amongst the last groups to receive help and amongst the first to become self-reliant (Robinson 1988: 3, 35). This recovery is a testimony to their system of management. The Gabra have also been fortunate in that, unlike in many other pastoral groups in Kenya and unlike among the Borana in Ethiopia, there has been minimal external intervention in their system of production, which has enabled them to pursue their way of life free from undue outside interference.

Conclusion

In this chapter, we have combined two frameworks, one drawn from common property theory (Oakerson 1992: 41-59) and the other from NRM studies (Berkes 1999: 13-14) to challenge the thesis that nomadic groups, like the Gabra, cause environmental degradation through the 'irrational' tendency of their members to over-stock the range beyond its carrying capacity. As Oakerson (1992: 43) notes, a framework is a heuristic tool, rather than a prescriptive and predictive model. He observes that: 'As scholars use and apply a framework, and share ideas, the framework too, becomes a subject of change-elaboration or modification-in view of experience' (1992: 57). We would add that the application of a framework is not an end in itself, but must further goals of social justice, by analysing and critiquing scholarly models that have led to the implementation of inappropriate policies.

Oakerson's framework identifies four 'bundles' of variables pertaining to the commons: 1) physical attributes and technology; 2) decision-making arrangements; 3) patterns of interaction; 4) outcomes. However, it has a number of problems. First, although Oakerson states that this framework can be applied recursively at different points in time to study change in a CPR, it does not enable us to trace the origins of such a set of rules, nor to understand the reasons for such changes. Second, the framework does not take into account the knowledge system that informs the management of a particular commons, which has evolved to deal with its physical attributes and has contributed to the development of its technology. Third, it does not account for the ideologies that underpin institutionalised decision-making arrangements. As Feeny (1988: 170) explains, 'Ideology is seen both as a normative system and a comprehensive worldview that orders, interprets, and legitimizes beliefs'. It orientates social practices. Fourth, whilst Oakerson (1992: 51) states that 'the analyst is required to stipulate the use of evaluative criteria', for him outcomes appear to be negative, rather than positive, in that they are linked to identifying 'problematic conditions' (1992: 55). Nevertheless, despite these shortcomings, Oakerson's framework 'allows a systematic approach to the study of a phenomenon that has great variation' (1992: 42).

Whilst the framework developed by Berkes (1996, 1999) includes both local ecological knowledge and worldview, and his work recommends taking a historical perspective and suggests alternative criteria, it is less systematic in nature. We have, therefore, built these two attributes into the Oakerson framework and added two different criteria, those of sustainability and resilience, to evaluate the Gabra system of NRM and the effectiveness of its CPR. The latter criterion reflects new thinking in ecology, which holds that in unpredictable environments, such as those inhabited by many pastoral groups, land, animals and people are able to recover from the crises that they periodically undergo based on resilience.

By applying these sets of variables from the two frameworks, we have shown that the Gabra CPR derives from the Borana one. According to oral tradition, the latter may date back some three thousand years. In the pre-colonial period, it was used to manage a system of NRM that exploited different ecological niches, through hunter-gathering, and cattle and camel pastoralism. These forms of subsistence represented alternate economic choices in times of crisis.

They were based on institutionalised forms of exchange, which included links to agro-pastoralists in the region. Strategic to this pre-colonial system was a complex of deep wells (*tulla saglaan*), developed by the ancestors of the Borana, using rudimentary technology.

At the end of the nineteenth century, with the advent of Ethiopian and British colonialism, the Gabra were forced to reorganise their system of production and to develop their own separate CPR, by using their former dry season pastures beneath the Ethiopian escarpment as their principal rangeland. They were able to do so because they had lost the majority of their cattle holdings in the crises of the 1880s and had become more reliant on camels. Gabra lands were held in trust by the British Crown. By allocating this territory *de jure* to the Gabra and by instituting exclusion zones between the nomadic groups in the area, the British reified the present 'ethnic' groups and destroyed the fluid boundaries across which these communities had previously interacted and supported one another in times of crisis (see Sobania 1990: 3-10). As a result of the ensuing resource conflicts, which have continued to the present day, large tracts of rangeland became unusable due to the problem of insecurity, leading to a reduction of the available pastureland and to 'over-stocking' and soil degradation. These problems were blamed on the pastoralists. Between the 1930s and 1950s, measures were taken to reverse these trends, but only succeeded in aggravating them (see Sobania 1990: 11-14).

We have also shown that the Gabra CPR operates on a set of 'institutional arrangements' through which decisions affecting pasture and water are taken. The common property literature does not really provide a satisfactory definition of this expression for our purposes. In his study of local institutions, Uphoff (1986: 8-9) differentiates between institutions and organisations. For him, an institution is a complex of norms and behaviours that persist over time by serving some socially valued purpose, while an organisation is a structure of recognised and accepted roles (Uphoff 1986: 8-9). Among both Gabra and Borana, these normative arrangements are based on customs and laws, which are implemented by the nested units of resource management that comprise their social organisation. The elders who represent these units hold regular meetings at different levels to ensure equitable use and to discuss and solve through consensus any problems arising, as well as to impose sanctions on those who do not comply with the rules. These meetings are highly democratic and participatory in nature. At all these levels, there exist informal and formal redistribution mechanisms, based on the communitarian ethos, for assisting those who are unable to meet their subsistence needs. Rituals performed at these different levels reinforce these social relations.

We have also described how the Gabra have developed a number of livestock production strategies by diversifying their holdings and splitting their herds in order to avoid putting pressure on the range. In good years, they also maximise their livestock holdings, or deliberately over-stock the range. As ecologists now recognise, such strategies, far from being 'irrational' as previously thought, are 'logical' in environments that are prone to periodic drought and do not have a long-term detrimental effect. As this new school of ecology also concedes, 'movement is central to the survival strategies of transhumant pastoral systems' (Scoones 1995: 9). This mobility enables the opportunistic management of resources, based on tracking fodder spatially, and allowing previously used rangeland to recover. We have shown that these strategies and system of land-use by the Gabra derive from a knowledge base of their animals and of the environment that has been developed through practical experience over a long period of time. Interestingly, Gabra perceive their environment in terms of its fertility (*finna*), rather than of its aridity. This is a complex notion, which relates to their conceptions of time and of events, both of which are believed to leave an invisible imprint on the land and affect its productivity. Contrary to the 'scientific' belief that there are no discernible cyclical weather trends (Bake 1983), the Gabra have evolved a sophisticated calendar for recording climatic and social changes that has predictive value, particularly for critical decision-making during times of drought. In this sense, their knowledge system is 'indigenous', in that it is based on the historical continuity that they have with this region, to which they trace their origins.

After Kenya's independence in 1963, the Gabra lands were held in trust by the Marsabit District Council. The government imposed a state of emergency in the district, due to Somali irredentism. Later, in the mid-1980s, it authorised oil exploration in the area. Despite these and other disruptions, the Gabra were able to continue to manage their territory more or less unhindered according to their customary rules and to benefit from the charitable assistance of Catholic missionaries. Fortunately, due to their remoteness, the Gabra were also not directly affected by the policies advocated by the World Bank in the 1970s to transform subsistence pastoralists into commercial ranchers. These policies had devastating effects on the livelihoods of some of the groups in the region and led to the collapse of their CPRs. Subsequent development interventions, informed by the new thinking, such as that of GTZ from the early 1990s, have attempted to build on their traditional institutional arrangements rather than destroying them.

Finally, by expanding the criteria of equity and efficiency of the Oakerson model to evaluate the efficacy of the Gabra system of NRM, we have demonstrated that the system is sustainable and effective. We have also discussed the resiliency of the Gabra. Like the land in which they live, they have managed to recover from the adversities that they have periodically undergone. They have survived the droughts and disasters that have beset them with great fortitude and by adopting a flexible attitude to external change. They have adapted to new ways, whilst maintaining their cultural heritage (Tablino 1999: 242). The Gabra themselves attribute this resilience to their steadfast observance of traditions and laws.

It is hoped that our modified version of the Oakerson-Berkes models, which enables the researcher to include both the emic (indigenous knowledge) and etic (scientific knowledge) perspectives, to take into account synchronic (the current situation) and diachronic (history; change; resilience) processes, as well as to deal critically with development interventions, can be used by other scholars to study traditional systems of resource management elsewhere in the world.

Notes

1. We follow Tablino (1999) in the spelling of Gabra. Other authors spell it as Gabbra.
2. The 'free-rider' problem is one in which the individual shirks his responsibility to the community (Runge 1986: 625) and imposes negative externalities, or costs, to other users by his actions.
3. We did not consult Wario and Witsenburg (2008), whose study was not available to us at the time of writing.
4. Sobania (1980: 52) indicates that most of the ethnic groups in the region derive from a common parent stock.
5. On the problem of defining 'boundaries' in pastoral societies, see Schlee (1990). Sperling and Galaty (1990: 78-79) suggest that 'domain', in the sense of sphere of influence of a particular group, may be more appropriate. For the Borana and Gabra, resource boundaries are defined by the customary law. All those who live within them must adhere to the customs and laws of the land.
6. The British were less tolerant of the Borana, whom they regarded as Ethiopian subjects, and attempted periodically to forcefully repatriate them (Legesse in preparation).
7. Before the colonial period, the Gabra negotiated access to the territories of their neighbours through a process known as *balalfachitii*. More research needs to be done of this external arrangement.
8. As Baxter (1966: 121; 126) indicates, the term *abba* 'father', implies custodianship rather than ownership. A man acts as a 'warden' or 'trustee' of the well or herd for which he is responsible.
9. Under customary law, the rights exercised by the custodian over a well are equated to those of a man over his wife, and any violation is punishable by the same sanctions.
10. Gabra goats belong to the short-eared, short-haired white variety, which is intermediate in size between the Oromo and East African types. Sheep are a sub-type of the black-headed, fat rumped Somali breed. Cattle are of the Borana drought-resistant *zebu* type (Mason and Maule 1960). Gabra dromedary camels are similar to Rendille ones, but smaller and hardier than Somali ones.
11. Prior to the ban on hunting in 1977, Gabra only killed ungulates for food and for the manufacture of material culture items.
12. This new function has led to a certain amount of corruption of the leaders of the phratry.
13. An 'opportunistic' strategy is one in which 'the number of livestock grazing is continuously adjusted according to the current availability of forage'. It is contrasted to a conservative one,

in which a 'constant number of livestock graze through good and bad years alike' (Sandford 1983: 38).

14. *Finna* is a semantically complex term, which literally means 'that which is handed down', or transmitted from the past. It is linked to Oromo 'cyclical' concepts of time, to development, and to social and cultural production and reproduction, hence in a broad sense to 'fertility'.

15. Lusigi (1981: 22) identifies population growth as a problem in the district by comparing it to the colonial census of 1949. In fact, growth rate in Marsabit District as a whole was only 2.64 percent in the period 1979-1989, with a population density of less than three people per square km (Fratkin 1994: 58). The problem is rather of growth around major settlements on Marsabit mountain.

Bibliography

Alberro, M. 1986. 'The Borana Cattle and Their Tribal Owners' *World Animal Review* 57: 30-39.

Bake, G. 1983. 'An Analysis of Climatological Data from the Marsabit District of Northern Kenya' IPAL Technical Report B-3. Nairobi: UNESCO.

Bassi, M. 2005. *Decisions in the Shade. Political and Juridical Processes among the Oromo-Borana*. Trenton, NJ: Red Sea Press.

Baxter, P.T.W. 1966. 'Stock Management and the Diffusion of Property Rights among the Boran' in *Proceedings of the Third International Conference of Ethiopian Studies*. Addis Ababa: Haile Selassie International University, pp. 116-127.

Behnke, R.H., I. Scoones and C. Kerven, eds., 1993. *Range Ecology at Disequilibrium. New Models of Natural Variability and Pastoral Adaptation in African Savannas*. London: Overseas Development Institute.

Berkes, F. 1996. 'Social Systems, Ecological Systems and Property Rights' in S. Hanna, C. Folke and K-G Mäler, eds.,, *Rights to Nature. Ecological, Economic, Cultural and Political Principles of Institutions for the Environment*. Washington, DC: Island Press, pp. 87-107.

_____, 1999. *Sacred Ecology. Traditional Ecological Knowledge and Resource Management*. London: Taylor and Francis.

Bromley, D.W., ed., 1992. *Making the Commons Work: Theory, Practice and Policy*. San Francisco: Institute for Contemporary Studies.

Ciriacy-Wantrup, S.V. and R.C. Bishop. 1975. 'Common Property as a Concept in Natural Resource Policy' *Natural Resources Journal* 15: 713-727.

Constanza, R. and C. Folke. 1996. 'The Structure and Function of Ecological Systems in Relation to Property Rights', in S. Hanna, C. Folke and K.-G. Mäler, eds., *Rights to Nature. Ecological, Economic, Cultural and Political Principles of Institutions for the Environment*. Washington, DC: Island Press, pp. 13-34.

Dahl, G. 1979. *Suffering Grass: Subsistence and Society of Waso Borana*. Stockholm: Stockholm Studies in Social Anthropology, 8.

Ellis, J.E. and D.M. Swift. 1988. 'Stability of African Pastoral Ecosystems: Alternative Paradigms and Implications for Development' *Journal of Range Management* 41: 450-459.

Ellis, J.E. 1995. 'Climate Variability and Complex Ecosystem Dynamics: Implications for Pastoral Development' in I. Scoones, ed., *Living with Uncertainty: New Directions in Pastoral Development in Africa.* London: Intermediate Technology Publications.

Feeny, D. 1988. 'The Demand for and Supply of Institutional Arrangements' in Ostrom, V., D. Feeny and H. Picht, eds., *Rethinking Institutional Analysis and Development. Issues, Alternatives and Choices.* San Francisco: International Center for Economic Growth.

Fratkin, E. 1994. 'Pastoral Land Tenure in Kenya: Maasai, Samburu, Borana and Rendille Experiences, 1950-1990' *Nomadic Peoples* 34-35: 55-68.

Ganya, C., H. Guyo and G. Borrini-Feyerabend. 2004. 'Conservation of Dryland Biodiversity of Mobile Indigenous People – The Case of the Gabbra of Northern Kenya' *Policy Matters* 13: 61-71, Special Issue on History, Culture and Conservation.

Goto, P.S.G. 1972. *The Boran of Northern Kenya: Origins, Migration and Settlement in the Nineteenth Century.* B.A. dissertation. Nairobi: University of Nairobi, Department of History.

Hann, C.M., ed.,. 1998. *Property Relations. Renewing the Anthropological Tradition.* Cambridge: Cambridge University Press.

Hardin, G. 1968. 'The Tragedy of the Commons' *Science* 162: 1243-1248.

_____, 1991. 'The Tragedy of the Unmanaged Commons: Population and Disguises of Providence' in R.V. Andelson, ed., *Commons without Tragedy.* Savage, MD: Barnes and Noble, pp. 162-185.

Helland, J. 1984. *Pastoralists and the Development of Pastoralism,* 2nd ed. Bergen Occasional Papers in Social Anthropology, 20. Bergen: University of Bergen, Department of Social Anthropology.

Hjort, A. 1981. 'Ethnic Transformation, Dependency and Change: The Illigira Samburu of Northern Kenya' in J.G. Galaty and P.C. Salzman, eds., *Change and Development in Nomadic and Pastoral Societies.* Leiden: E.J. Brill.

Holling, C.S. 1973. 'Resilience and Stability of Ecological Systems', *Annual Review of Ecology and Systematics* 4: 1-23.

Holling, C.S. and S. Sanderson. 1996. 'Dynamics of (Dis)harmony in Ecological and Social Systems' in S. Hanna, C. Folke and K-G Mäler, eds., *Rights to Nature. Ecological, Economic, Cultural and Political Principles of Institutions for the Environment.* Washington, DC: Island Press, pp. 57-85.

Kassam, A. and G. Megerssa. 1994. ' "Aloof Alollaa": The Inside and the Outside. Boran Oromo Environmental Law and Methods of Conservation' in D. Brokensha, ed., *A River of Blessings. Essays in Honor of Paul Baxter.* New York: Maxwell School of Citizenship and Public Affairs, Syracuse University, pp. 85-98.

Kassam, A. 2006. 'The People of the Five "Drums": Gabra Ethnohistorical Origins' *Ethnohistory* 53(1): 173-194, Special Issue on the Lake Turkana Basin, guest edited by M. Mirzeler.

Lamprey, H. F. 1983. Pastoralism Yesterday and Today: The Overgrazing Problem, in
    F. Bourlière, ed., *Tropical Savannas*. (*Ecosystems of the World*, vol. 13.) Amsterdam:
    Elsevier Press, pp. 643-666.

Legesse, A. In preparation. *The Oromo Republic: Decline under Imperial Rule*. Trenton,
    NJ: Red Sea Press.

Leus, T. 1995. *Borana Dictionary. A Borana Book for the Study of Language and Culture*.
    Yavello: Catholic Church, Dadim.

Linquist, B.J. and D. Adolph. 1996. 'The Drum Speaks – Are We Listening?
    Experiences in Development with a Traditional Gabra Institution – The Yaa
    Galbo' in P. Blunt and D.M. Warren, eds., *Indigenous Organisations and
    Development*. London: Intermediate Technology Publications, pp. 1-6.

Lusigi, W.J. 1981. 'Combating Desertification and Rehabilitating Degraded
    Production Systems in Northern Kenya' IPAL Technical Report A-4. Nairobi:
    UNESCO.

_____, 1986. 'The Integrated Project on Arid Lands (IPAL) Kenya' in P.J. Joss, P.W.
    Lynch and O.B. Williams, eds., *Rangelands under Siege. Proceedings of the Second
    International Rangeland Congress*. Cambridge: Cambridge University Press, pp.
    338-349.

Mason, I.L. and J.P. Maule. 1960. *Indigenous Livestock of Eastern and Southern Africa*.
    Farnham: Royal Commonwealth Agriculture Bureaux.

McCay, B.J. and J.M.Acheson, eds.,. 1987. *The Question of the Commons. The Culture
    and Ecology of Communal Resources*. Tucson: University of Arizona Press.

McPeak, J. 2003. 'Analyzing and Assessing Localized Degradation in the Commons'
    Land Economics 78(4): 515-536.

_____, 2005. 'Individual and Collective Rationality in Pastoral Production: Evidence
    from Northern Kenya' *Human Ecology* 33(2): 171-197.

McPeak, J., G. Haro and G. Doyo. 2005. 'Linkages between Community,
    Environment, and Conflict Management' *World Development* 33(2): 285-299.

Oba, G. 1998. 'Assessment of Indigenous Range Management Knowledge of the
    Boorana Pastoralists of Southern Ethiopia: Part I, Report on the Boorana
    Lowlands Pastoral Development Program' Negeelle Borana: BLPDP/GTZ.

Oakerson, R.J. 1992. 'Analyzing the Commons: A Framework' in D.W.Bromley, ed.,
    Making the Commons Work. Theory, Practice and Policy. San Francisco: Institute for
    Contemporary Studies, pp. 41-59.

O'Leary, M. 1985. 'The Economics of Pastoralism in Northern Kenya: The Rendille
    and Gabra', IPAL Technical Report F-3. Nairobi: UNESCO.

_____, 1990.' Changing Responses to Drought in Northern Kenya: The Rendille and
    Gabra Livestock Producers' in P.T.W. Baxter and R. Hogg, eds.,,, *Property, Poverty
    and People. Changing Rights in Property and Problems of Pastoral Development*.
    Manchester: International Development Centre, University of Manchester,
    pp. 55-79.

Peters, P.E. 1987. 'Embedded Systems and Rooted Models: The Grazing Lands of
    Botswana and the Commons Debate', in B.J. McCay and J. M. Acheson, eds.,
    The Question of the Commons. The Culture and Ecology of Communal Resources.
    Tucson: The University of Arizona Press, pp. 171-194.

Robinson, P.W. 1985. *Gabra Nomadic Pastoralism in Nineteenth and Twentieth Century Northern Kenya: Strategies for Survival in a Marginal Environment.* Ph.D. dissertation, Northwestern University. Ann Arbor: ProQuest.

_____. 1988. 'An Assessment of the Hurri Hills Grazing Ecosystem Project. Final Report' Nairobi: Lutheran World Relief.

_____. 1989. 'Reconstructing Gabbra History and Chronology: Time Reckoning, the Gabbra Calendar and Cyclical View of Life' in T.E.Downing, K.W. Kangethe, and C.M. Kamau, eds.,, *Drought in Kenya: Lessons from 1984.* London: Lynne Rienner Publications, pp. 151-168.

Runge, C.F. 1986. 'Common Property and Collective Action in Economic Development' *World Development* 14(5): 623-635.

Sandford, S. 1983. *Management of Pastoral Development in the Third World.* Chichester: John Wiley.

Schlee, G. 1990. 'Policies and Boundaries: Perceptions of Space and Control of Markets in a Mobile Livestock Economy' Working Paper 133, Faculty of Sociology, University Bielefeld.

Schwartz, J., S. Shaabani and D. Walther. 1991. *Range Management Handbook of Kenya, Vol. 11-1, Marsabit District.* Nairobi: Republic of Kenya, Ministry of Livestock Development.

Scoones, I., ed., 1995. *Living with Uncertainty. New Directions in Pastoral Development in Africa.* London: Intermediate Technology Publications.

Shongollo, A. 1994. 'The Gumi Gaayo Assembly of the Boran: A Traditional Legislative Organ and Its Relationship to the Ethiopian State and a Modernizing World' *Zeitschrift für Ethnologie* 119: 27-58.

Sobania, N.W. 1980. *The Historical Tradition of the Peoples of the Eastern Lake Turkana Basin, c. 1840-1925.* Ph.D. dissertation. London: School of Oriental and African Studies, University of London.

_____, 1988. 'Pastoralist Migration and Colonial Policy: A Case Study from Northern Kenya' in D.H. Johnson and D.M. Anderson, eds.,, *The Ecology of Survival: Case Studies from Northeast African History.* London: Lester Crook Academic Publishing, pp. 219-239.

_____. 1990. Social Relationships as an Aspect of Property Rights: Northern Kenya in the Pre-Colonial and Colonial Periods' in P.T.W. Baxter and R. Hogg, eds., *Property, Poverty and People. Changing Rights in Property and Problems of Pastoral Development.* Manchester: International Development Centre, University of Manchester, pp.1-19.

Soga, T. 2005. 'Five Drums: How the Gabra Pastoralists in Northern Kenya React to the 1997 Election' *Journal of the Faculty of Humanities* (Hirosaki University) 13: 167-195.

Spencer, P. 1973. *Nomads in Alliance: Symbiosis and Growth among the Rendille and Samburu of Kenya.* London and Oxford: Oxford University Press.

Sperling, L. and J.G. Galaty. 1990. 'Cattle, Culture and Economy: Dynamics in East African Pastoralism' in J.G. Galaty and D.L. Johnson, eds., *The World of Pastoralism. Herding Systems in Comparative Perspective.* London: Guildford Press, pp. 69-98.

Stiles, D. and A. Kassam. 1991. 'An EthnoBotanical Study of Gabra Plant Use in Marsabit District, Kenya' *Journal of the East Africa Natural History Society and National Museum* 81 (198): 15-37.

Swift, J. 1975. 'Pastoral Nomadism as a Form of Land-Use: The Twareg of the Adrar n Iforas' in T. Monod, ed., *Pastoralism in Tropical Africa*. London: Oxford University Press, pp. 443-454.

Tablino, P. 1999. *The Gabra. Camel Nomads of Northern Kenya*. Nairobi: Paulines Publications.

Torry, W.I. 1973. *Subsistence Ecology among the Gabbra: Nomads of the Kenya/Ethiopia Frontier*. Ph.D. dissertation, Columbia University. Ann Arbor: University Microfilms International.

Uphoff, N. 1986. *Local Institutional Development. An Analytical Sourcebook with Cases*. Hartford: Kumarian Press.

Wallen, C.C. and M.D. Gwynne. 1978. 'Drought: A Challenge to Range Management' in D.H. Hyder, ed., *Proceedings of the First International Rangeland Congress*. Denver, Co: Society for Range Management, pp. 21-31.

Wario, R.A. and K. Witsenburg. 2008. *Surviving Pastoral Decline. Pastoral Sedentarisation. Natural Resource Management and Livelihood Diversification in Marsabit District, Northern Kenya*. 2 vols. New York: Edwin Mellen Press.

Index